Keeping Holy Time

Keeping Holy Time

STUDYING THE REVISED COMMON LECTIONARY
Year B

EDITED BY

DOUGLAS E. WINGEIER

Contributors: David A. deSilva, John O. Gooch,
M. Bass Mitchell, Denise Nutt-Beers,
Mary Jo Osterman, Sondra B. Willobee

ABINGDON PRESS / Nashville

KEEPING HOLY TIME
Studying the Revised Common Lectionary Year B

Library of Congress Cataloging-in-Publication Data
Keeping holy time : studying the revised common lectionary, year B / edited by Douglas
E. Wingeier ; contributors, David A. deSilva ... [et al.].
   p. cm.
ISBN 0-687-05234-3
1. Bible—Study and teaching. 2. Lectionaries. 3. Christian education of adults.
I. Wingeier, Douglas E. II. DeSilva, David Arthur.

BS603 .K45 2002
264'.34—dc21

2002006180

This book is printed on acid-free paper.

MANUFACTURED IN THE UNITED STATES OF AMERICA.

02 03 04 05 06 07 08 09 10 11—1 2 3 4 5 6 7 8 9 10

Contents

Introduction

Y OU are about to embark on a study of the Scripture passages selected for use in the Revised Common Lectionary, Year B. Your primary resource for this study will be the Bible itself. Scripture passages quoted in this book are from either the New Revised Standard Version (NRSV) or the New International Version (NIV), but reference to other authorized versions and translations is also encouraged. In addition to this book, you will want to make use of other resources—commentaries, Bible dictionaries, Bible word books, concordances, study guides—a short list of which appears on page 9.

This book draws on many such resources, combining their background and insights into a concise commentary on the four lections designated for each Sunday and most special days. It highlights common themes and points of continuity, offers questions for thought and reflection, and provides a format for weekly study by lay groups designed to correlate with worship and preaching based on the lectionary.

It is important in any kind of Bible study to know and make intentional use of the principles of responsible biblical interpretation, on which this study guide is based. In summary fashion, these are the following:

1. *Examine the life-world* out of which the passage comes. This involves study of the historical background and cultural setting of both the times in which the events occurred and the time when the passage was written.

2. *Relate parts to the whole.* Although the Bible is made up of sixty-six books, many of which are composite strands of oral or written tradition put together by an editor, it is also *one* book with a coordinated message, related cast of characters, and continuity of development in the story of a people. Hence, any passage we read must be correlated with the story and message of the Bible as a whole.

This involves several processes: understanding verses in relation to their immediate context (passages before and after), interpreting passages in light of the overall message and purpose of the book where they appear, viewing words and passages in terms of their meaning at the time they were written, considering the type of literature in which the passage is found, and weighing the import of a particular passage in relation to the overarching message and central themes of Scripture.

3. *Look for unifying themes.* The biblical message is like a tapestry composed of major and minor threads. It contains significant theological pluralism, clashes of opposing views and emphases, and stories and beliefs in direct contradiction to the life and teachings of Jesus. Hence, all passages must be tested against the central themes of Scripture, like covenant faithfulness, love and redemption, the cross and discipleship, and justice and righteousness under the reign of God.

4. *Identify the intentionality of the text.* Ask: What is the writer trying to say? What does God want us to hear? Put the main point in a single sentence that reflects the intention of the writer and God's purpose behind this.

5. *Consider our contemporary life/world.* Keep in mind the cultural situation, prevailing worldview, value system, lifestyles, needs, issues, and dreams of society today, and look for differences and similarities between these and the culture of the biblical world.

6. *Be aware of the persistent life concerns of today's readers.* Hold in view the key questions people in our time and place are asking—questions of identity, survival, relationship, meaning, security, affection, esteem, and fulfillment. Relate these to the major themes of Scripture.

7. *Study communally.* "No prophecy of scripture is a matter of one's own interpretation" (2 Peter 1:20). Bible study is a group process. We are mutually supported and held accountable within the covenant community. We need to rely on and listen to the insights, knowledge, and experience of other Christians, in order to enrich and evaluate our individual interpretations.

8. *Consider our current life situation.* What is going on in our lives right now? What decisions, disappointments, wounds, victories, projects, relationships, issues, and concerns are we dealing with? How do the Scriptures we are studying speak to these?

9. *Expect God to speak and act.* The inspiration of the Bible is as available to the reader as it was the writer. When we come in an attitude of prayer and seeking, God is with us as we study. When the intentionality of the text encounters our life situation, sparks fly, insights flow, new directions are pointed out. A biblical theme speaks to a persistent life concern. We find ourselves in the experience of a character in Scripture. A Bible story becomes our story.

10. *Be ready to respond.* We also can expect God to ask us to do something in response to our encounter with Scripture. We must be open to change. Since Scripture is a record of God's mighty acts with and through God's people, we can anticipate that God will want to move history through us as well. Our interpretation of Scripture must be concrete in terms of our

action and response in the here and now. The key question to ask is, How must my life become different when I take this passage seriously? Then act on the answer!

As you and your group explore this year's lections with the aid of this book, keep these overarching guidelines in mind.

May your lectionary study during this church year be as stimulating and challenging to you as the editing and writing of this resource has been to me!

Douglas E. Wingeier, editor

Resources

Harper's Bible Commentary. James L. Mays, general editor. Harper and Row, 1988.

Harper's Bible Dictionary. Paul J. Achtemeier, general editor. Harper and Row, 1985.

The Interpreter's Dictionary of the Bible, Volumes I–IV. George A. Buttrick, general editor. Abingdon Press, 1962. Supplementary Volume, edited by Keith Crim. Abingdon Press, 1976.

The Interpreter's One-Volume Commentary on the Bible. Charles M. Laymon, editor. Abingdon Press, 1971.

The New Interpreter's Bible, Volumes I–XII. Leander E. Keck, convener and senior New Testament editor. Abingdon Press, 1994–2002.

ADVENT

Lections for First Sunday of Advent

*M*ANY Old Testament: Isaiah 64:1-9

scholars believe that three authors are responsible for canonical Isaiah, the first 39 chapters deriving from Isaiah of Jerusalem (740–700 B.C.), Chapters 40–55 coming from the period of the Exile (after 597 B.C.), and Chapters 56–66 written after the return from Exile (at the end of the sixth century B.C.). Strong cases are still advanced, however, for attributing the whole work to Isaiah. His prophetic ministry would then be viewed as somewhat different from the typical prophet's work in that he sees farther into Israel's future and addresses future generations more directly than other prophets. Either way, today's lesson carries the same import.

Leaning on God's Fidelity

Isaiah 63:7–64:12 looks back to God's earlier dealings with Israel from the Exodus to settlement in Canaan. The people's ongoing provocation of God through sinning has made the destruction of the independent state and exile for the inhabitants inevitable, but Isaiah still calls upon God to act. Prior to the opening of today's lection, Isaiah calls upon God to remember God's zeal and compassion for the people brought out of Egypt.

God's "name," that is God's honor and reputation in the world, is also bound up inseparably with the fate of this people and their land. Isaiah in particular knows that it is God who both hardens the heart and inspires repentance (see 6:8-13). He therefore begs God to soften the hearts of Israel, rather than allow their sin to continue to drive them to disobedience and resulting misery.

Only God Can Set Things Right

Lamenting the condition of the people, Isaiah cries out to God for another theophany (God's self-revelation or appearing "in person") such as the one

12

at Sinai, when the mountains first shook. God's manifestations of self and the power to save were unexpected and awe-inspiring. The prophet longs for another unexpected in-breaking of God to work wonders in Judah's situation. Like so many people in distress and confusion, he longs for the "one who is real" to break silence, to break through the veil and set the world in order once again.

According to Isaiah, God does not need to wait for human beings to "do the right thing" before intervening. True, the people are swept away in their sins. True, the voices calling upon God are few and far between. But as 64:8 will go on to say, human beings are but clay, while God is the potter. It is the potter who shapes, who acts upon the clay, who decides when it is time to work the lump again. We are best advised to yield our hearts and lives to the Potter's loving hands.

What gives Isaiah hope is the character of God. Pleading for God not to "be exceedingly angry" (64:9), he asks God to show compassion and mercy toward the people. Isaiah knows God will vindicate God's honor in the sight of the nations. God will restore the people and revive their sense of justice and righteousness.

Think About It: Isaiah recognized that God's visitation was the people's only hope. Have you ever cried out for God to break in and set things straight? What were the circumstances? Was your concern for yourself, friends or loved ones, or an issue in society? What sustained you through that trial? How did God speak or act in response to your cries? What changes took place? How did you learn or grow through the experience?

Psalter: Psalm 80:1-7, 17-19

This psalm is a communal lament deriving from the same sort of desperate situation envisioned by Isaiah. The psalm may refer to the conquest of Israel by Assyria in 721 B.C., given the prominence of Ephraim and Manasseh. The psalmist cries out to God, "enthroned upon the cherubim." This is a reference to the belief that the invisible God could be found directly above the ark of the covenant, the top of which was decorated with two cherubim and was called the mercy seat.

Isaiah looked back to the Exodus and wilderness experiences as the manifestation of God's care and devotion. Here the psalmist also speaks of that period, using the metaphor of the vine (80:8-9; see Isaiah 5:1-7) that God brought from Egypt and spread throughout the whole land (that is, at the height of the reigns of David and Solomon).

That vine has now been hacked into pieces and burned, and the people cry out to God for their restoration (Psalm 80:3, 17, 19). Ultimately, it is God's past devotion to this vine that commits God to it now. The faithful God, the psalmist knows, will never leave the people. God will not withhold a favorable response to their prayers in anger (80:4) but will again extend help.

Epistle: 1 Corinthians 1:3-9

The church founded by Paul at Corinth caused him considerable anguish. At various times he addressed their strange tolerance for immorality, their competition for status based on spiritual gifts, their factionalism expressed in arguments over the best qualified apostle, their accusations about Paul's dipping into the collection, and their tendency to value one another and their leaders in terms of appearances. Nevertheless, Paul's thanksgiving at the outset of this letter is sincere. He is glad they have received many spiritual endowments from God. Now he needs to teach them how to use those gifts wisely—not as claims for esteem and recognition, but as tools for strengthening the whole community.

Waiting for the Day

Isaiah's longing for a day in which God would "break into" everyday reality and establish God's justice was also foundational for the worldview and passion of the early church. This comes to the fore in 1 Corinthians 1:7-9. The spiritual gifts (prophetic utterances, wisdom, knowledge, ecstatic speech, and interpretation) are all provided by God to be put into service for sustaining the believing community through the period of waiting for Christ's appearing.

Think About It: "You are not lacking in any spiritual gift while you wait for the revealing of the Lord." Are you aware of your gifts? How are you using them for the glory of God?

The emphasis on the last day is not ornamental. Time after time Paul returns to the Day of Judgment as the time when every person's work will be known for its true value (3:10-15). It is the day when each person's heart and motives will be exposed so that praise and censure can be rightly dealt out (4:3-5) and when each will receive just reward for "what has been done in the body, whether good or evil" (2 Corinthians 5:10).

In addition, pointing believers ahead to "that day" reminds them that what they have received is merely fuel for the journey. Their real prize and full inheritance lies ahead. The present time is for waiting, an active waiting that seeks out the life that will please God (2 Corinthians 5:9) so one will be found blameless (1 Corinthians 1:8, 10). There is no leisure for rivalry, competition or boasting within the church—only for leaning on the strength of the faithful God and for helping one another on toward the goal.

Gospel: Mark 13:24-37

This week's Gospel lection closes Mark's version of Jesus' apocalyptic discourse. Mark 13 opens with the disciples acting as tour guides, pointing out to Jesus the sights in Jerusalem, particularly the massive Temple compound constructed from huge stones, which gave the impression of permanence. Jesus told them not to be impressed with edifices, for the Temple will be utterly destroyed.

Warning Signs of Christ's Coming

The disciples asked about the signs that will precede the destruction of the Temple, leading into Jesus' predictions concerning wars, famine, natural disasters, and persecution. The climax concerns the "desolating sacrilege" (13:14): when it appears, people should flee the city to escape the worst horrors.

That Jesus had in mind the destruction of the Temple, which occurred at the hands of the Romans in A.D. 70, is clear for a number of reasons. First, the disciples' question was specifically about this event. Second, Jesus himself declared that the generation present to hear his words would live to see their fulfillment (and, indeed, many alive in A.D. 30 were still around in 70). Finally, Luke (21:20-33) confirms this reading of Mark 13:14-31 by making the connections between Jesus' words and the events of that siege more explicit. In Luke's Gospel, Jesus specifically mentions the destruction of Jerusalem.

Jesus draws a connection between the blossoming of the fig tree as a sign of the imminence of summer and the destruction of Jerusalem as a sign of the imminence of the end. This was meant, no doubt, to strengthen and encourage the Christian community (especially the Jewish Christian community) as it faced the heart-wrenching devastation and pitiable tragedies surrounding the fall of Jerusalem. Its meaning for modern readers is rather shocking—the end can come at any moment! Those who develop charts of events that must still happen before the end miss the point of Mark 13 entirely. It is not the foretelling of future events that is important but rather the assurance that the direction and outcome of history are sure. Our destiny, and that of the world, are in the loving care of Almighty God, whose messenger will in the fullness of time gather together God's scattered flock (Ezekiel 34:11-16).

Watch

The closing parable poses a special urgency. Jesus declares that no one has knowledge of the end except God. All who claim to know in what year the end will come are mistaken. Every day "he is near, at the very gates" (Mark 13:29). Obviously there has been some delay, but here Mark considers how abruptly that delay will end when God breaks into history.

The parable's meaning is clear. We are the servants, entrusted with continuing in our work while the master is away. The task of the doorkeeper, specifically commanded to keep watch for the master's return, receives special emphasis. The danger is that we will be unprepared to receive the master and will be found sleeping instead of remaining watchful and diligent.

Think About It: A common joke in the workplace is: "The boss is coming; look busy!" That the end can come at any moment requires continuous readiness. What things do you do that you would not want to be found doing at the end? How can focusing on the Master's return reinforce consistency in discipleship?

This parable encourages watchfulness as the night wears on—as indeed it has for two millennia. We do not know where we are in the night. Perhaps the first ray of dawn is about to break; perhaps it is not even midnight. All we need to know of the time, however, is that "salvation is nearer to us now than when we became believers" (Romans 13:11) and to continue faithfully to carry out the work Christ has given us to do.

Study Suggestions

A. Highlight Advent

Note at the outset that this is the first Sunday in Advent, a time for preparing our hearts and lives for the coming of the Christ. All four lections address this theme from different perspectives and time periods.

B. Open With Song

Begin your Advent study by singing all stanzas of "O Come, O Come, Emmanuel." Ask the group to consider that they sing not just to the Baby but to the coming Christ who can grant the prayers gathered in this ancient hymn.

C. Open Your Hearts

Read aloud Isaiah 64:1-9 and review the commentary on pages 12–13. Ask: What things grieve Isaiah as he considers his people? Where does he find hope for facing these circumstances?

D. Gather Your Sorrows

Just as Isaiah looked deep into the sin and sorrow of his nation, invite group members to gather up their sorrows that weigh heavily and seem beyond their power to resolve. To stimulate discussion, use the hymn and the complaints of Isaiah as touch points. Ask: How do you relate to these petitions and laments? Do not get caught in a gripe session. Seek rather to provide a space for expressing pain, due to either a personal, national, global, or ecclesiastical crisis. Try to broaden members' awareness of how much pain and need exist beyond their own, building solidarity with the plight of other people and nations. Ask members to write their laments to God in a few words.

16

E. Write a Psalm

Now read Psalm 80 together and review the commentary on pages 13–14. Drawing on the causes for grief and heartbreak for the nation, church, and world, compose a new psalm to offer God. Begin with Psalm 80:1-3; then ask members to add their causes for lament. After each new lament, have the group respond with the refrain in verse 3; then finish the psalm.

F. On the Road to "Blameless"

Read aloud 1 Corinthians 13:1-9, setting the context using the commentary on page 14. Ask: What is Paul's setting? What did the Corinthian congregation face that seems similar to our circumstances today? How does Paul advise them?

On this first Sunday in Advent, this lection from First Corinthians invites us to self-examination. In small groups ask each person to finish the sentence, "If Christ were to return today, he would find me blameless except for _____. Confess these shortcomings to God, and exchange assurances of God's pardon.

G. Waiting for the Lord

Read Mark 13:24-37. Before reading the commentary, ask group members to discuss the impact this passage makes on them. What emotions does it arouse? What suggestions does it implant?

Now read the commentary on pages 15–16. Ask participants to consider their role in the Master's household. Most denominations emphasize the ministry of all believers. Lay and ordained persons have different areas of ministry, but all are called to use their gifts as they are able. Each has her or his work for the Master. Ask: What is your service to the household of God? In what aspects of service is God prompting you to grow?

H. Draw the Lections Together

Isaiah 64, Psalm 80, and Mark 13 all present situations of great distress that only God can remedy. But they also offer the assurance that God will intervene. All four lections speak to the issue of how we can wait (actively) for God's intervention. Ask the group to identify the models for waiting given in these texts. Ask: Which of these models have characterized your waiting? In which areas can you grow? How might that begin this week as part of your Advent preparation?

I. Close With Prayer

End the session with an extemporaneous prayer, asking God to help to ready our hearts and lives to receive Christ during this Advent season.

Lections for Second Sunday of Advent

A Old Testament: Isaiah 40:1-11

*A*S mentioned last week, even though Isaiah is presented as one book, scholars have identified two or three writers who lived at different times and who addressed different historical experiences. Today's passage begins "Second Isaiah." This unknown prophet lived in Babylon during the Exile of the Judeans, nearly two hundred years after "First Isaiah."

Isaiah's Listeners

Second Isaiah's listeners were middle- and upper-class members of Judahite society—royalty, military leaders, craftsmen. They had been stripped of power and removed from their land by their Babylonian conquerors in 597–587 B.C. After years in exile, living among people who worshiped other gods, they had been influenced by pagan religious practices and had doubts about the extent of God's power and their status as God's people.

Second Isaiah answered their doubts: God (YHWH*) still had compassion for them. God was guiding history and would soon demonstrate divine power and grace by leading them on a journey even more glorious and promising than their ancestors' exodus from Egypt—the journey home.

God's Compassion and Power

In Second Isaiah's first words, YHWH commanded the lesser divine beings in the heavenly court to comfort the people. More than words were involved,

---

*The four letters of the divine name are used to render the name unpronounceable. This use is followed to reflect sensitivity to the Jewish prohibition against pronouncing the name of God.

18

however. A highway for YHWH was to be built through the desert wilderness from Babylon to Judah (today's Syria and the Golan Heights). Second Isaiah's language reminded his listeners both of their ancestors' exodus from Egypt and of the Babylonian custom of preparing special roads for the festive processionals of their gods. YHWH's greater power and glory would be seen in this magnificent journey through the wilderness.

In verses 6-8, a voice from the heavenly court reassures the people that God is eternally reliable compared to the transient nature of human existence. In verse 9, YHWH calls on Zion (Jerusalem) to serve as a herald, announcing to all Israel the good news of God's presence among them.

> **Think About It:** The return from exile was seen as evidence that God was at work in history. What events in our time demonstrate God's activity and power?

God is then portrayed as a mighty conqueror (verse 10) and a shepherd with his flock (verse 11), reminding the exiled listeners once again of God's power and compassion.

God's Justice

You might ask: If God cared for the descendants of Jacob enough to promise comfort and restoration to their land, why would God allow them to suffer in exile in the first place? Second Isaiah suggests that God's compassion was never absent, but that God's sense of justice required that the nation's idolatry and unjust treatment of the poor be punished by an enemy invasion, the destruction of their Temple and

> **Think About It:** Isaiah called for the exiled Judahites to prepare a highway through the desert wilderness so God could lead them home. Have there been times in your life when you needed God's deliverance? What deliverance do you seek at this time in your life?

homeland, and exile to Babylon. In fact, Judah had to pay "double for all her sins" because her suffering was to be both purifying for Judah and redemptive for all the nations. This notion of redemptive suffering is later applied to Jesus who would redeem the world through his agony on the cross.

Psalter: Psalm 85:1-2, 8-13

Psalm 85 may have been a community prayer written after the Judahites returned from exile. Isaiah's glorious vision of restoration had not happened. The Temple was in ruins; famine was rampant; many religious traditions were being blended together. The people needed a further restoration by God.

Biblical scholar Walter Brueggemann suggests in *The Message of the Psalms* (Augsburg, 1984) that "the predominant patterns of thought and speech in the psalms also correspond to the characteristic flow of human life, from 'satisfied seasons of well-being,' through 'anguished seasons of hurt, alienation, suffering and death,' to 'turns of surprise when we are overwhelmed with the new gifts of God.' "

Some of this pattern exists in Psalm 85. Verses 1-2 recall God's forgiveness and favor in the past (satisfaction). Verses 4-7 indicate that those who rejoiced earlier have met hard times again and need God to restore them yet again (anguish). Verses 8-13 affirm that God will offer salvation, peace, and well-being (new gifts). Psalm 85 is an appropriate prayer for any situation. God will set things right; God is present with the faithful.

Epistle: 2 Peter 3:8-15a

The writer of Second Peter claimed to be "Simeon Peter, a servant and apostle of Jesus Christ." Scholarly consensus holds that he was a close associate of Peter's in Rome who wrote after Peter's death. Ancient texts were frequently written to honor the memory of the person named as author. The practice also lent greater credibility to the work.

Scoffers' Arguments
The first generation of Christians believed that Christ would return to judge the world during their lifetime. But by the time Second Peter was written, that first generation had died. This led scoffers to claim that the apostolic teaching about Jesus' return was a misguided interpretation. Scoffers claimed that the world operated by chance (not divine plan) and that since God had not judged human behavior in the past, this would not happen in the future either; therefore, people could live as they pleased.

These alternative, nonapostolic teachings held a certain appeal for late first-century Christians. The Christian life prescribed by early leaders in effect excluded Christians from many aspects of daily business and social life because of pagan rituals and meeting places. Thus, if Christ were not returning, if God's final judgment were not real, then these Christians could get on with daily life among the pagan majority without fear.

Apostolic Teachings
Second Peter wrote to counteract these messages. He reminded his listeners that God has judged the wicked in the past (2:4-16). Then, in our lection, he explains the delay of the end in two ways. First, God's time is different from ours. What seems to us to be a holdup is not so for God. Second, the deferral of God's judgment is a sign of divine patience and kindness, not weakness. The delay allows sinners time to repent, but the time is limited. Christ will return unexpectedly; then all will be judged, and the ungodly destroyed (3:8-10).

20

Finally, Peter asks: What sort of person ought you to be while you wait for Christ's return and God's judgment? (The writer believed this would occur during the lifetime of his audience of second-generation Christians.) His answer: You are to live a holy and godly life. You are to be "found by him at peace, without spot or blemish" (verse 14), when God's judgment finally comes.

> **Think About It:** The scoffers in Second Peter lived in the last years of the first century. We are now in the twenty-first century—and still no final judgment. What meaning does a final judgment hold for you? Are you at peace with facing the end?

Gospel: Mark 1:1-8

Notice how abruptly Mark begins his Gospel: "The beginning of the good news of Jesus Christ, the Son of God." The word *gospel* originally meant "proclamation" or "good news" rather than one of the four books (Matthew, Mark, Luke, and John) we now know as the Gospels. Our Christian heritage thus began, not with a new book, but with a new message. Most of Mark's original audience would hear his Gospel rather than read it. He had "good news" for them.

New Gospel, Old Roots

Mark's beginning is radical. But the titles *Christ* and *Son of God* in verse 1 are so familiar today that it is hard for us to imagine what Mark's listeners would have heard and felt. To them *Christ* meant "messiah" or "anointed one." It signified that Jesus was the one Israel longed for, that Jesus was a specially anointed agent of God.

The title *Son of God* originated in the Jerusalem royal cult and referred to the relationship between God and the Davidic king. A newly anointed king was declared to be God's adopted son. To Mark's first listeners then, *Son of God* would have suggested royalty. But until they heard the good news about Jesus' resurrection it would not have suggested the incarnate divinity, which Christians have come to associate with Jesus. As we read Mark's Gospel, we know that Jesus is the Son of God. However, the people who interacted with Jesus generally did not recognize this fact until after the Resurrection. Perhaps this is Mark's way of reminding us to focus on Jesus' humanity.

For Mark, Jesus exhibited a full range of human emotions and experiences. The title *Jesus Christ, the Son of God* should bring to our minds the human faithfulness and human suffering that Jesus experienced as well as the claim he is God's divine Son.

In verses 2-3, Mark immediately ties his good news of Jesus Christ, Son of God to Old Testament prophecies of salvation from Malachi (3:1) and Isaiah

21

(40:3). By linking his good news with the Old Testament, Mark underscores his claim: Jesus, the Christ, the Messiah, is the promised one who fulfills the prophecies of the Hebrew Scriptures. Through Jesus, God has come to bring salvation to all people.

Preparing the Way

Finally, having given his listeners a concise preview of his good news, in verse 4 Mark plunges into the story of John the Baptist who prepares the way for God's anointed one. John the Baptist's ministry was one of prophetic leadership that encouraged people's hopes for renewal and liberation and had a double meaning. On one level it reminded Mark's listeners of the next part of the story. Jesus came to preach good news, and he was obedient even to the point of being crucified. On another level Mark's story, likewise, calls us to prepare for God's coming among us.

> **Think About It:** The voice in the wilderness cries out, "Prepare the way of the Lord." Preparing involves personal action. How will you practice repentance and seek reconciliation during Advent?

For some of us, "preparing the way of the Lord" may mean getting ready for the actual, concrete return of Jesus and God's final judgment. For others, it may mean preparing for times throughout our lives when God will unexpectedly enter into our midst. In any case, to "prepare the way for God's return" involves actions like repentance and baptismal renewal (as in John the Baptist's ministry). Preparing the way for God's return also involves acts of forgiveness, reconciliation, and walking in the way of Christ in our daily lives.

Study Suggestions

A. Sing Along

Sing along with "Prepare Ye" from the soundtrack of *Godspell* (Bell Records, 1973). Report on feelings in response to this celebrative piece.

B. Read Isaiah Aloud

Ask four volunteers to read dramatically Isaiah 40:1-11 while the others receive it with all their senses. (Voice 1 reads verses 1-2; voice 2 reads verses 3-5; voice 3 reads verses 6-8; voice 4 reads verses 9-11.) Discuss: What did you hear, see, or seem to smell? What images of God and our experience do you find?

C. Imagine Ourselves as Exiles

The glorious vision of Isaiah 40 did not exactly happen as Second Isaiah had promised. Ask participants to imagine that they are disillusioned ethnic

Albanian refugees returned to their ruined homes in Kosovo or Mayan Indians back in their overgrown mountain villages in Chiapas, Mexico. Pray Psalm 85 aloud together. Ask: How do you feel as exiles sitting in your ruined lands? What are your anxieties and fears? What doubts do you have about God? What do you hope and pray for?

D. Explore the Scoffer in Us

Read 2 Peter 3:8-15a and the interpretation below. One commentator says: "The scoffers are indicative of our tendency to despair of the promises of God when God does not respond to our pleas within the time span we have set as reasonable or convenient. . . . We may not scoff verbally, but our prayer life, church attendance, and overall lifestyle may begin to suffer as we despair of God's promises" (*New Interpreter's Bible,* Volume XII, page 358). Does this describe you or your church? What promise of God is most helpful to you when you feel disheartened?

E. Prepare the Way

Read Mark 1:1-8 and the explanation on pages 21–22. What is the double meaning of Mark's story of John the Baptist? What actions do we as individuals or as a church need to take to "prepare the way for God's return"? (Consider such things as examining our hearts and habits, seeking forgiveness and reconciliation, living uprightly, working for peace and justice, leading others to Christ.) Which of these actions might we or our church be inclined to emphasize? Which might we omit or neglect? What does this suggest about our Advent preparation?

F. Tie It Together

Our lections today progress from the exiles' return to John the Baptist to second-generation Christians in Second Peter. In each case the people were waiting for God's deliverance. In what way do we know present salvation even as we wait for the fulfillment of all things?

G. Preparing for Christ's Coming

Sing "Hymn of Promise," which offers a modern interpretation of God's ancient promise of salvation and of the coming day of a new heaven and earth. Close by inviting the group to offer brief prayers asking God to help them use this Advent season to prepare their hearts and lives to be receptive to the coming of Christ.

Lections for Third Sunday of Advent

Old Testament: Isaiah 61:1-4, 8-11

*O*UR lection from Isaiah is part of a larger passage written after the Persian emperor Cyrus II conquered Babylon and declared in 538 B.C. that the exiles could return to Jerusalem. Scholars identify Isaiah 55–66 as Third Isaiah. The situation here is different from earlier chapters. Second Isaiah had addressed the Judahites while they were in exile in Babylon; Third Isaiah speaks to those once again living in Judah.

Judah's "second exodus" had not been as grand and glorious as Second Isaiah had predicted. Life was hard for the returned exiles. Those remaining in the land while their compatriots were in Babylon had adopted pagan religious practices; crops were failing; famine and poverty were prevalent; the Temple and the cities were in ruins. In the midst of their despair, Third Isaiah announced God's judgment on Judah's oppressors and promised deliverance, prosperity, and blessing.

God's 'Anawim Redeemed

Isaiah 61 is a poem with one central theme: the righteous afflicted (God's *'anawim*) are to be recompensed. They will be glorious among the nations as a people whom God has blessed. All five terms in verses 1-2 (*oppressed, brokenhearted, captives, prisoners, mourners*) are synonyms for the righteous victims who have been unjustly kept from their reward. Third Isaiah announces a year of the Lord's favor (jubilee) when God will right wrongs. Jubilee is an ancient Hebrew tradition specifying that every fiftieth year (among other things) land was to be returned to its original owners, slaves freed, and debts forgiven. (There is no historical evidence that this vision of God's justice was ever carried out, but it became an ideal that has guided and held out hope to God's people from that time to this.)

Third Isaiah proclaims that once God's righteous ones are liberated, they will be festally attired and called "oaks of righteousness." Oaks, long-lived trees with spreading branches, reflect God's victory and power. Oil, turbans ("garland"), and splendid garments imply priestly attire, suggesting that God's redeemed people will be dressed like Israel's priests, a specially blessed group. After God redeems the afflicted, all nations will see that they are specially graced. Once they are vindicated by God and given an everlasting covenant, they will build a just society.

Jesus, according to Luke (4:18-19), began his ministry by quoting Isaiah 61:1-2. He preached God's deliverance for the righteous poor. God would reverse their situation because the just Creator was insulted by human injustice.

> **Think About It:** Isaiah announces good news of God's deliverance to all God's righteous people who have been unjustly treated. What people in the world today are being unjustly treated? (Possibilities are persons of minority races, immigrants, refugees, inmates on death row, sweatshop workers.) How can you and your church be a means of sharing God's good news with such persons?

Give Thanks to God

Finally, in verses 10-11, Third Isaiah anticipates celebrating God's restoration of Israel. He sings a song of thanksgiving. "I will greatly rejoice in the Lord, / my whole being shall exult in my God." God will dress Israel like a bride and bridegroom with garlands and jewels. Salvation and praise will spring up like shoots in a garden.

Psalter: Psalm 126

Psalm 126, like Psalm 85, reflects the patterns of our common human experience. First, the community remembers God's past deliverance (verses 1-3). Then they pray for God's help for more current difficulties (verses 4-6). God's people alternate between "satisfied seasons of well-being" and "anguished seasons of hurt, alienation, suffering and death" (Brueggemann). This tension makes this psalm relevant for every generation.

The phrase "restored the fortunes" in verse 1 may refer to the return of the people from Babylon to Jerusalem. God's past deliverance evoked joy and laughter, even though the return was plagued with difficulties and setbacks. Yet, the returned exiles were not without hope. In verse 4, the phrase "streams in the Negev" (NIV) expresses both the people's new needs and their trust in God's ability to deliver them again. Even today the streams in the Negev (a desert in southern Israel) are often dry, but they can suddenly become rushing torrents during seasonal rains.

In verses 5-6, the imagery shifts to sowing and reaping, also signs of anticipation and hope. The psalmist is emphatic; there will be a joyful harvest. God will come through. We will receive surprising new gifts. Psalm 126 helps us remember that every divine act of deliverance is an event for joy and praise, and every setback a time for renewed prayer and trust that God will help.

Epistle: 1 Thessalonians 5:16-24

First Thessalonians, the earliest writing in the New Testament, was written by Paul about A.D. 51. After a bad experience in Philippi, Paul and his companions had traveled to Thessalonica where they established a church. Intense opposition from the Jewish community forced them to leave. Paul later sent Timothy to check on the new church. First Thessalonians is Paul's response written after Timothy reported they were doing well (though under continuing persecution) but were anxious for Paul to return to them.

Paul's Message

Paul praised the Thessalonians for enduring tribulation, which is part of a cosmic struggle between the gospel and Satan, and encouraged and consoled them over the death of some their members (perhaps victims of persecution). He urged them to persevere and to live ethical Christian lives while awaiting the return of Christ.

Think About It: Paul identifies a number of religious acts of a faithful Christian's life. What signs of the religious life would you put on such a list today? As you examine yourself in Advent preparation, how would you rate your faithfulness in regard to both Paul's criteria and your own?

In today's lection, Paul turns from ethical to religious concerns. Anxious about their community life, he urges them to respect their community leaders and to support one another. He encourages them to rejoice, pray, give thanks, and not quench the Spirit or despise prophesying. They are to test everything, hold fast to what is good, and abstain from every form of evil. These are the acts of a Christian life.

Benediction

Paul's letter concludes with a blessing or benediction (5:23-24). The "God of peace" offers shalom to both individuals and the world. Paul's blessing assumes that Christ is coming again soon, a theme he had addressed earlier in the letter. The blessing stresses the faithfulness of God.

Gospel: John 1:6-8, 19-28

The writer of the Gospel of John is often called the Fourth Evangelist to distinguish him from John the Baptist, who appears in Chapter 1.

Incarnation: God in Jesus

The ultimate concern of the Fourth Evangelist is with God. His good news is the revelation of God in Jesus. We miss this Gospel's central claim if we focus exclusively on Jesus' earthly life: Jesus is God Incarnate—the Word, the light, the one who existed with God before creation, who was in the world when it came into being (verses 1-5).

First Witness

Immediately, however, the Fourth Evangelist ties his announcement of God's incarnation in Jesus to a concrete historical event, the witness of John the Baptist. He proclaims that John has been sent by God to testify that Jesus, the "true light," is coming into the world soon (verses 6-9). After further theological interpretation (verses 10-18), the Evangelist describes John's direct testimony (verses 19-28), which comes in the form of a trial. His interrogators are part of the religious establishment (the source of most of the opposition to Jesus' ministry according to this Gospel).

The interrogation of John centers on the question "Who are you?" John confesses he is not the Christ, even though he was not asked that. His strong denial may imply that some of his followers were claiming that he was the Messiah. There may have been rivalry between the Baptist's followers and the early Christian community for whom the Gospel of John was written.

His interrogators then asked John if he is Elijah, who was transported to heaven without dying and was expected to return in the last days. John said no. Then they asked, "Are you the prophet?" *Prophet* refers to a messianic forerunner (Deuteronomy 18:15), so John was now asked about his relationship to the Messiah. He denied any ties. After many questions, he finally quoted Isaiah 40:3: "I am the voice of one crying out in the wilderness, 'Make straight the way of the Lord' " (1:23).

The interrogation shifts in verses 24-28. The questioners are now identified as Pharisees. During Jesus' lifetime, the Pharisees were only one of many groups of Jewish religious leaders; but by the time of John's Gospel, their successors, the rabbis,

> **Think About It:** John witnesses that Jesus is the Light and the Lamb. The disciples identify him by other titles. Whom do you say Jesus is? What does he mean to you?

had become dominant. The Evangelist is making a link between the authorities who opposed Jesus and those who opposed the Johannine community in the late first century.

The representatives from the Pharisees want to know: If you are not Elijah or Moses or the Messiah, why are you baptizing people? John shifts the focus away from his own activities and witnesses about Jesus: "I baptize with water. Among you stands one whom you do not know, the one who is coming after me; I am not worthy to untie the thong of his sandal" (1:26-27).

27

Other Witnesses

In the rest of Chapter 1, several other titles are used for Jesus, including *Lamb of God*. As the disciples witness about Jesus, they identify him variously *as rabbi, messiah, king of Israel, son of Joseph from Nazareth,* and *the one of whom Moses and the prophets spoke.* The disciples each see Jesus through their own unique experiences, expectations, and needs. This variety of titles cautions us not to limit our image of Jesus to preconceived categories and expectations, but to stay open to surprising new revelations of God.

Study Suggestions

A. Identify God's *'Anawim* Today

Discuss: How is life today like that of the Judahites' when they returned home after the Exile? Who are God's *'anawim* in our world today?

Read Isaiah 61:1-4, 8-11, and the commentary on pages 24–25. If you are one of God's *'anawim* today, what message can you take from this Scripture? If you are one of the "oppressors" of God's *'anawim,* what is its message to you? What signs of "jubilee" do we see today? (forgiveness of poor nations' debts? asylum for refugees fleeing persecution? land reform providing farms to landless peasants?)

B. Explore Deliverance

Refer to Psalm 126. "Restore our fortunes" can refer to a historical change or an entirely new state of affairs. Ask: How has God restored our fortunes in the past as a church? as a community? as a nation? What disillusions us today? What would it look like for God to restore our fortunes today? What new state of affairs do we long for?

C. Keep an Open Mind

Mark identifies Jesus as "Christ, the Son of God" (1:1). John says he is the "Light" and "Lamb of God." What qualities of Jesus mean most to you? List other names or phrases we use to describe Jesus. Ask: Does using only a few titles or ascriptions for Jesus miss the fullness of his identity? How might new images help us as disciples?

Review John 1:6-8, 19-28, and the commentary on pages 26–28. What is John's role? Who are the luminaries that the people thought the Baptizer might be? How do John's answers about himself point to Jesus, and what do they anticipate about Jesus' ministry? How do we point to Jesus in our lives?

D. Examine Paul's Advice

Paul advises the Thessalonians about living a Christian life while awaiting God's return and judgment. Review 1 Thessalonians 5:16-24 and the interpretation on page 26. Ask: What do you think Paul meant by "do not quench the Spirit"? by "do not despise prophesying"? How might we put these two guidelines into action today when our church is so divided on major social issues?

E. Test Our Criteria

Another piece of Paul's advice was to "test everything; hold fast to what is good." Paul's criterion for testing things was "what is good?" Ask: How would Paul have defined good? How might we apply this criterion in our personal lives? to church controversies? (Two dangers: We identify "good" as what we are most comfortable with. Or we apply a rigid standard without considering peoples' circumstances or needs.) How can we overcome these dangers? (One idea: test things in the larger Christian community, not on our own.)

F. Tie It Together

Today's four writers (Third Isaiah, the psalmist, the Fourth Evangelist, and Paul) all witnessed about God. Individuals and churches witness in different ways. How are you and your church witnessing to God's promise of deliverance? How are you helping to liberate God's 'anawim?

G. Respond With Faith and Praise

Consider what these Scriptures call us to do or to be. How might your life be different (or better) if you were to take seriously their message? Sing the Advent hymn, "Come, Thou Long Expected Jesus"; then read Psalm 126 responsively.

Lections for Fourth Sunday of Advent

T Old Testament: 2 Samuel 7:1-11, 16

OGETHER First and Second Samuel describe the reigns of Israel's first two kings, Saul and David. These accounts mark Israel's transition from judgeship to kingship. They are part of the Deuteronomic history, which begins with the Israelites' conquest of Canaan and ends with Israel's destruction by Assyria and Judah's exile to Babylon. This history tells of God's continual efforts to maintain a relationship with the chosen people. This passage is arguably the most important theological text of this whole story, and verse 16 is its key.

God's Traveling House
After Saul's death, David defeated the Philistines in a series of battles and slowly acquired the thrones of both Judah and Israel. He then set up his capital in Jerusalem in Judah and moved the ark of the covenant there to help unite all the tribes of Israel under his rule. The ark, a chest that Israel believed held God's presence, was kept in a tent and traveled with the people.

A Different House
David was grateful to God for a peaceful and united Israel. He was comfortable in his house (a palace) and planned to build God a permanent house (a temple). But God turned the tables on David and said, No, I will build you a house (a dynasty). Your dynasty and your throne will be established forever (verses 14-16).

The idea of a hereditary monarchy did not exist before this. Further, the covenant with the house of David seems less conditional than the Sinai covenant. Now God's covenant becomes unconditional: My love will be steadfast and your dynasty will endure, even though I will judge you when you disobey.

God and the Temple

For Israel this passage explained why Solomon, not David, built the Temple. It clarified that God's presence was not dependent on a tabernacle or a temple. It legitimized a dynastic succession of kings by making it God's will. It emphasized that God's promise to David would endure, even when strong divine judgment was called for.

God's promise to David was very important to the exiled Judahites who received the Deuteronomic-edited version of this story about five hundred years after David's reign. It gave them hope that even though no descendant of David was on the throne, a king/messiah would eventually arise to restore the dynasty God had promised.

For Christians, verse 16 is key because Joseph was a descendant of David. Jesus thus could lay claim to the Davidic throne, a hope that his followers held in a time when Judea was ruled by Rome. In Advent, we remember that God's promise was fully realized through Jesus, who established the dynasty or reign of God forever—though much differently than David imagined!

> **Think About It:** God's will changed, reflecting the change in the people's lives. God approved the change from tabernacle to temple; from judges to kings; from conditional to unconditional covenant; and, in Jesus, from earthly dynasty and political rule to a reign of God based on reconciliation and just, ethical relationships. How does God's will continue to unfold in our lives?

> **Think About It:** What does the promise to David mean for the modern state of Israel? What promises did God make to the Palestinians who are also descendants of Abraham?

A New Testament Psalm: Luke 1:46-55

Mary's song, traditionally called "The Magnificat," opens by praising God, who has made her the mother of the Savior, Jesus. She sings of God's redeeming work as if it had already occurred: The proud are scattered and the powerful brought down. The lowly are exalted, the hungry fed, and the rich dispossessed. This reversal of events has come about, not through a rebellious uprising of the afflicted, but through God's arrival in human history as a tiny baby.

Luke almost makes Mary a prophet. She has a proclamation to make, but no further commission to witness. Jane Schaberg (*The Women's Bible Commentary*, Westminster/John Knox Press, 1992, page 284) calls the Magnificat "the great New Testament song of liberation—personal and social, moral and economic." Mary is God's witness for the poor and marginalized, a major theme that emerges in Jesus' ministry.

In verse 47, Mary praises God as Savior. For Luke, Jesus brings about God's salvation by calling people to repent, forgiving sinners, healing the sick, defending the marginalized, casting out demons, eating with outcasts, and dying a redemptive death. First and last, God is Savior.

Epistle: Romans 16:25-27

The last chapter of Paul's Letter to the Romans has generated much speculation since scholars are unclear where Paul actually ended his letter. Some think he wrote Chapter 16, at least up to verse 20, which is also a benediction. The last few verses are liturgical; some think the Romans added them for use in worship. Others argue that Paul wrote them himself for the same purpose, knowing that the letter would be read publicly in worship settings.

An Early Doxology

Today's lection is a doxology, a hymn of praise. The word *strengthen* in verse 25 implies that the Romans needed help in overcoming the opposition of dissenters (mentioned in 16:17-20). The phrase "revelation of the mystery that was kept secret for long ages but is now disclosed" (verses 25-26) implies that God's full message and salvation were only just then (in Jesus' time) being fully revealed. God's promise was made through Jesus in order to bring all persons to faith. The doxology ends in verse 27 with a word of praise, returning to God what is most due: glory. Some ancient manuscripts lack the words "to whom" in verse 27, without which it reads: "to the only wise God be the glory through Jesus Christ forever. Amen." Either way the emphasis is on praising God for what has happened in our lives.

Early Christian Worship

Early Christian worship evolved into something radically different from Jewish worship. The word *worship* still meant "bow down" but had also gained a Greek emphasis on service or piety. No sacrifices were performed in Christian worship, since Christ's death was believed to constitute the perfect sacrifice. Only three early Christian liturgical observances are known: baptism, the Lord's Supper, and the laying on of hands. Of these, only the Lord's Supper was celebrated regularly, in memory of Jesus' death, in celebration of his resurrection, and in anticipation of the coming of the kingdom of God.

> **Think About It:** Early Christian worship was full of praise to God. What are you praising God for in your life and church today?

Early Christians generally gathered on the first day of the week, although some may have met daily. At these gatherings, they would sing, pray, teach, exhort, prophesy, read letters (such as Paul's), and break bread. Above all, early Christian worship was filled with joy and praise of God. Thus, as a hymn of praise, these closing verses of Romans hint at early liturgical practices. Even today it gives us a biblical basis for benedictions we use in worship.

Gospel: Luke 1:26-38

No more waiting, people of God! God is beginning to do a wonderful new thing. God's Child is coming into the world to bring salvation to all.

God's Announcement

Our lection from Luke is part of what is called the "infancy narrative," which, in embryonic form, proclaims the gospel and calls us to receive it. In previous verses the miracle of the coming birth of John the Baptist to the barren Elizabeth has been announced. Today's passage relates an even greater miracle: the imminent birth of one greater than John—Jesus. In these two births we see God's redemptive action beginning.

First-century biographies often began with accounts of astonishing omens and events accompanying a person's birth. Such omens foretold the person's future greatness and offered clues about the role that person would play in history. Luke uses this literary approach when he defines the roles of John and Jesus through the prophecies given about their births. He shows that while John will prepare the way, Jesus will be the Messiah.

While the visible characters in our story are Gabriel and Mary, the central figure is really God, who has graciously designed a plan for the salvation of all humanity. The angel Gabriel, sent by God, told Mary that the child she will bear is to be named Jesus. He will be called the Son of the Most High. God will give him "the throne of his ancestor David. He will reign over the house of Jacob forever" (1:33). He will be called "Son of God" (1:35). These words echo the promise made to David by the prophet Nathan that God would establish the dynasty forever with the house of Jacob (2 Samuel 7:9, 13-14).

> **Think About It:** Gabriel reassures Mary that "nothing is impossible with God." What seems impossible for you today, but is possible for God?

Scandalous Blessings

When the angel Gabriel appeared to Mary, he said, "Greetings, favored one! The Lord is with you" (Luke 1:28). But how was Mary favored? Not the way we might expect; not with things we value, like a good life, social standing, wealth, good health. No, Mary was favored in a strange way by

God. She was "blessed" with the announcement that she would become pregnant out of wedlock. For this "blessing" she faced possible scandal and loss of social standing.

Even the angel's advent is a strange "blessing." The appearance of an angel probably reminded Mary of a folk tale popular in her time. A jealous angel appears on a bride's wedding night and kills the bridegroom. A strange blessing, indeed.

Later, Mary would again be strangely blessed by God when her child was executed as a criminal. Yes, Jesus would be named Savior and Mary would be greatly revered. Yet the story of the announcement of Jesus' birth is so familiar that its scandal is often masked. God's blessings seldom focus on things we value: acceptability, prosperity, comfort. God entered human history, not in a grand way, not to a rich, prominent family, but to an ordinary poor woman, betrothed but not yet married. God entered human history, not as a powerful leader, but as a helpless baby.

Here Am I

When the angel's job was done and Mary's questions answered (or not), Mary responded, "Here am I, the servant of the Lord; let it be with me according to your word" (Luke 1:38). She responded obediently, trustfully, and faithfully. What if she had not? Would God have forced Mary to have the child against her will? No; Mary is an important example of one who is faithful to God even at risk to herself.

Study Suggestions

A. Sing a Hymn of Praise

Sing "My Soul Gives Glory to My God" or another hymn that celebrates Mary as mother. This hymn is based on Mary's hymn of praise to God.

B. Reflect on Mary's Witness

Mary witnesses in Luke 1:47 that God is her Savior. (Review Luke 1:46-55.) What things do we sometimes look to today to save us? (Things like technology, educational innovations or "back to basics" reforms, laws allowing the Ten Commandments in schools, or gun control might be mentioned.) Although these fall short, how might they play a role in God's work of salvation?

Mary also witnesses to God's redeeming acts in verses 51-55. God always has a bias for the poor, the powerless, the oppressed. Ask: What other situations might God be trying to reverse in our modern world? When and how might we or our church be the proud, the powerful, the rich? As we respond to God as Savior, what would it mean to put ourselves and our church on God's side?

C. Examine the Scandal

Read Luke 1:26-38 and the commentary on pages 33–34. Ask: What "scandal" is revealed? What does this "scandal of Christmas" say to us about how God relates to us?

D. Explore God's Grace

Among other things, in 2 Samuel 7:1-11, 16, God promises David unconditional grace. Discuss in pairs: How did this promise unfold for David? What were the long-term implications for him? What does "unconditional grace" mean to you? Were there times in your life when you thought God's grace was conditional on your believing or acting in a certain way? What does "unconditional grace" mean in the life of your church? your denomination? Now re-form the total group and ask the pairs to tell some insights they gained about unconditional grace.

E. Explore God's Demand

Ask: Where do we see God's demand of obedience in the Samuel passage? Review 2 Samuel 7:1-11, 16, and the commentary on pages 30–31.

Reflect silently: What is God demanding of you that conflicts with your wishes? After a brief silence, invite people to share as they feel comfortable doing so. Ask: What does this story of David and Nathan say to us today about discipleship? How does your faith move you to stand and speak boldly in tense situations involving social and political issues?

F. Tie Things Together

The Samuel passage tells of God's promise of a dynasty for David. The Luke passage announces the birth of Jesus. Ask: Why are these passages linked together in Advent? (Suggest that this may be to show the continuity between David, father of the messianic line, and Joseph, a descendant of David. God's incarnation in Jesus is linked with God's promise to David, implying that we do not know God's promises apart from human history.)

G. Pray Paul's Doxology

Form two groups. Have them stand and face each other. Invite Group One to start reading Romans 16:25-27 aloud. (Be sure everyone is reading from the same translation.) When they come to a comma, Group Two reads. At every comma, change sides. Practice it once; then use it as your benediction.

CHRISTMAS

Lections for Christmas Day

Old Testament: Isaiah 52:7-10

*T*HE long days of waiting and preparation are over at last. In the world of nature, the winter solstice in the northern hemisphere marks the beginning of the slow transition from long nights and short days to less darkness and more daylight. It is a sign of hope. In the church year, the twelve days of Christmastide is a time of joyous celebration, marking the end of Advent and moving toward Epiphany, the manifestation of God in our midst—Emmanuel, God with us!

Arrival, Expectation, Hope

This theme of arrival, expectation, and hope is expressed in this lection from Second Isaiah, which describes the coming of YHWH to Zion. This is the Day of YHWH, when God will ascend the throne, save his people, pronounce judgment, and establish peace.

The historical event in the prophet's purview is the impending defeat of Babylon by Cyrus and the Persians, allowing the people of Judah to go free and return to their homeland. But there is a cosmic aspect to the vision as well—God's sovereignty will be asserted over all the nations, and all people will recognize the divine authority and be blessed by God's redemption and justice.

The vision commences with the sight of a messenger approaching to announce the new era (verse 7). What a beautiful spectacle it is to witness the first signs of a transition to better days—like the ice breaking up at the end of winter, the first pains of labor heralding the end of a difficult pregnancy, or the return of the first robin. The messenger brings good news of peace, salvation, and of a coming new reign—the reign of God!

It is not only sights but sounds that herald the new day (verse 8). Now it is not just one messenger running but a whole contingent of sentinels that shout and sing the good news. God reigns! Let the whole earth be glad! The desolation that was Zion is soon to be restored to its former glory. The sovereign that was absent—or so they thought—was now returning to take charge once again. Pay heed! It is a time for singing!

Joining in the Festivities

But it is not enough just to watch and listen. We must join in the festivities and "burst into songs of joy together" (verse 9, NIV). God's loving redemption is cause for rejoicing. No longer do fear and despair dominate their lives. A new era is breaking in. Their destiny is about to change.

The good news comes first to persons of faith who have eyes to see, ears to hear and voices to proclaim the good news. But these glad tidings cannot be contained in that small company. It will soon become apparent to all that YHWH is sovereign over the entire earth. All people will benefit from God's universal redeeming love (verse 10).

Isaiah's vision of the coming of God's rule and redemption proclaimed in the sixth century B.C. was fulfilled in one sense several decades later in the return from exile. But its ultimate realization came on Christmas Day in a stable near Bethlehem when the kings saw a star, the shepherds heard singing, and an angel announced, "good news of great joy for all the people: to you is born this day . . . a Savior, who is the Messiah, the Lord" (Luke 2:10-11). God has come in human form, and "we have seen his glory!" (John 1:14).

> **Think About It:** How beautiful it is to see the signs of a transition to better days. What signs have you seen of such transitions? Were the signs obvious at first, or could you see them only with the "eyes of faith"? In what ways is Christmas such a sign for you? How can we distinguish between a Pollyanna attitude that sees only the brighter side and refuses to recognize grim realities and a genuine awareness that God is at work bringing about change for the better? How can we work with God to help foster such transitions?

Psalter: Psalm 98

Today's psalm is one of a number of "enthronement psalms" that celebrate the inauguration of a new era. The old order of injustice and faithlessness is being replaced by the coming reign of YHWH, which will be characterized by blessing on the righteous, judgment on the oppressor, and a time of rejoicing by all the earth. Enthronement psalms were likely sung at the enthronement of a new king. For the church, the enthronement psalms signal on ongoing hope that the messianic age is just around the corner.

The "new song" (verse 1) is sung not about an earthly ruler but in praise of the mighty works of YHWH. The "marvelous things" and "victory" refer to events in Israel's history, the credit for which is ascribed to their loving, faithful God (verse 3a). Not only is Israel convinced of this, but God's vindication is evident to "the nations" unto "all the ends of the earth" (verses 2, 3b).

Because the reign of God is at hand, all are called to bring out their instruments and make joyous melody before the Lord (verses 4-6). Both sea and land are to join in the mighty chorus announcing and celebrating that YHWH is coming to bring justice to all the earth (verses 7-9).

On Christmas, we bring out the trumpets, hold parties and pageants, fill our homes and churches with bright lights and poinsettias, and sing the "Hallelujah Chorus"—all to proclaim the good news that the Messiah has come to inaugurate a new era, the Reign of God on earth.

Epistle: Hebrews 1:1-4 (5-12)

Hebrews 1:1-4 constitutes a single long sentence in Greek that introduces the themes of the entire letter, connects these with Jewish tradition, and highlights the central place of Jesus Christ in fulfilling God's purposes for the world. The author (who is unknown) begins by reminding his Hebrew readers of the messages God had given them in the past through their prophets (verse 1)—messages their forebears had too often ignored.

Message From a Higher Source

But now, the message has come from a higher source—the Son of God himself, who is creator and ruler of all things (verse 2). He is identified directly and intimately with God—in status (glory), nature (very being), function (sustains all things), and authority (powerful word) (verse 3a). He has forgiven sin, been elevated to the heavenly realm, and been given an identity and position (name) greater than the angels (verses 3b-4).

These central themes are stated in concise prose in verses 1-4, then amplified in more poetic language in verses 5-12. The angels are not called sons (verse 5), but instead must fall down and worship him (6). They are God's servants and messengers (7), but the Son reigns with God, over both them and all creation (8). He is thus rewarded because he stood for the right (9). He was with God at creation (10), will outlast all created beings (11), and will remain the same eternally, while all else will change (12).

> **Think About It:** Which appeals to you more: the Baby Jesus in the manger, the earthly Jesus as teacher and healer, or the divine Christ who reigns eternally at God's right hand? Why? What does each aspect contribute to the church's teaching about Jesus Christ and his impact on personal lives and human history?

The second- or third-generation Christians who wrote and read this work near the end of the first century A.D. had become convinced that the Babe born in Bethlehem, who died on Calvary and rose on Easter, was not only a human prophet but the divine Son of God who both pre-existed with God and would reign eternally on a heavenly throne. It is both the earthly Jesus and the eternal Christ whom we worship and praise on Christmas.

Gospel: John 1:1-14

John 1:1-18 is called the Prologue to the Gospel because it lays out the perspective from which the entire book is written. It gives a short synopsis of the Old Testament, from the Creation through the prophets to the last prophet, John the Baptist. The author's purpose is to present Jesus, not as a babe born in a manger or a Galilean teacher and healer and the promised Messiah, but as the human manifestation of God's creative, saving love.

So the Prologue deliberately begins with a reference to the first verse in Genesis and the Creation story it introduces. It uses the term *Logos* (Word), which refers to more than the phrase in the Genesis story, "And God said . . . ," followed by a series of acts of creation. Rather, it speaks of God's creative energy, which has a meaning similar to wisdom and refers to the intelligent, loving power that brings all that is into being and is the foundation for all of life. This is a reference to the Old Testament idea of the wisdom of God radiating from the very being of God that is responsible for the creation of the universe (Proverbs 8:22-31) and to the Word of God that brought into being all that is (Psalm 33:6-9).

The Word in Human Form

This divine energy is not just an abstract creative principle; rather it is a living being who illuminates all of creation and strives to bring all into saving relationship with himself. This creative, redemptive Word, who seeks to sustain, love, and be in relationship with the entire universe, has, at this point in history—wonder of wonders—taken on human form in the man Jesus. The Almighty God, through becoming incarnate in Jesus Christ, has shined the divine light of truth into all the dark corners of the world. But sadly, the very people who might be expected to rejoice and receive God's Son have, in fact, rejected him. Happily, though, others who have recognized and accepted him as Lord and Savior through baptism have become the adopted children of God. They have recognized the glory of God in the man Jesus who walked among them, and through him have been ushered into the very presence of God.

Source of Grace and Truth

Moses gave the law that paved the way. John the Baptizer, following a series of prophets, was the messenger and forerunner. But Christ alone is the source of God's grace and truth. God is too high and holy to be seen and approached directly; but through his Son Jesus, the loving, redemptive nature and purpose of God have been revealed to us, and we are invited into his blessed presence.

This is the Christmas story according to John. It is rooted in the Old Testament references to the Creation, the prophets, and the wisdom of God. At the same time it uses categories from Stoic philosophy, which taught that the world was made and sustained by a divine Reason (Logos, Word). Thus, the Evangelist's message was calculated to appeal to and to convince both Jews and Greeks. But the uniqueness of John's message, unlike that of either the Jewish prophets and rabbis or the Greek philosophers and mystics, was that this divine creative and redemptive Word actually became incarnate in a human life who demonstrated through suffering love what God is really like.

> ***Think About It:*** John's message of the creative love of God embodied in a human life addressed both Jews and Greeks. What does it communicate to us in twenty-first-century America? How do you express what Jesus means to you in ways that appeal to those you know? How does the Christmas story of the shepherds, angels, and kings enhance and obscure the message of the Incarnation?

Study Suggestions

A. Love Came Down at Christmas

Open by singing the carol, "Love Came Down at Christmas." Note that this hymn combines elements of the manger story with the emphasis in John's Gospel on Christ as the embodiment and revelation of God's redemptive love. Discuss the questions from the "Think About It" box above.

B. A Time of Transition

Note that the winter solstice has just passed and the days are slowly getting longer, a sign of hope that the spring sunshine and flowers are on the way. Since the actual birth date of Jesus was unknown, the early church assigned it to this solstice season, when the Roman festival of Saturnalia was being celebrated with much revelry and debauchery. The coming of Christ marks a similar but much more significant transition—from darkness to light, from a world in sin to the promise of salvation.

Read aloud Isaiah 52:7-10 and offer the explanation on pages 38–39 of its meaning and relevance to the Christmas theme of transition. Ask: What transitions have you experienced in your life recently? What were the signs that change was coming? How did you become aware of what God was doing? Who have been the messengers who announced and the sentinels who heard and rejoiced at the coming transition? What are the signs of hope that speak to you on this Christmas Day?

C. The Centrality of Christ

Divide into twelve groups (even if there is only one person per group). Ask each group to paraphrase one verse of Hebrews 1:1-12. Write all paraphrases on chalkboard or large sheet of paper in sequence. Compare and contrast these with the explanation of the verses' meaning given in the commentary on pages 40–41.

Now discuss the "Think About It" questions regarding which aspect of Jesus has most meaning and what each contributes to the church's belief about Jesus. Ask members how they (would) present what Jesus means to them to their friends and neighbors and how they would decide what to share and emphasize.

D. The Word Made Flesh

Read aloud one or more contemporary paraphrases of John 1:1-14, such as those of *The Living Bible; The New Testament in Modern English,* by J. B. Phillips; or Clarence Jordan's *Cotton Patch Version.* Have members follow along in either the NRSV or NIV, and compare and contrast the translations. Review the interpretation given in the commentary on pages 41–42. Discuss: What insights do you get about the meaning of Christ's coming from comparing these various renderings? If you had to boil it down into one sentence, what is the real significance of Christmas? How could Jesus have been both human and divine?

E. Praise and Celebration

In celebration of the glorious coming of the Son of God to save all people from their sins, invite members to share brief thoughts about what this Christmas means to them. Close by standing in a circle to read Psalm 98 in unison; then sing "O Come, All Ye Faithful."

Lections for First Sunday After Christmas Day

F Old Testament: Isaiah 61:10–62:3

IRST Isaiah (written before the Exile) described Jerusalem as a prostitute. He condemned the city for its pagan practices and warned that if it did not reform, it would be destroyed. A century later this prophecy was fulfilled when Babylon plundered Jerusalem in 598 B.C. and then leveled it in 587 B.C.

Salvation Is Sure

Our passage today is from Third Isaiah, written after the Judahites returned from exile to find Jerusalem in ruins. As we learned previously, the returning exiles did not experience the glorious restoration that Second Isaiah had promised them. Yet, after promising that God would restore Judah to its former greatness, Third Isaiah offered a song of thanksgiving as if God had already rescued and restored Jerusalem and given it a new name.

A New Name and Image

Isaiah declares he will not rest until Jerusalem's triumph is so visible that all the nations will see her victory and call her by a new name. In the Bible, a name reveals one's essence. Remember how Abram and Sarai became Abraham and Sarah and how Jacob became Israel? A new name implies a new direction. Here, Jerusalem will forsake the sinful, destructive ways of her past. The new name for Jerusalem, Zion, is given by the prophet; but it is really YHWH's to give.

> **Think About It:** Isaiah said that God would give Jerusalem a new name: Zion. We know that in the Bible new names indicate a new direction. Have you ever changed your nickname to reflect that you had changed? If you were to choose a new name to reflect a new direction in your life, what might that be and what new name would represent it?

Speaking as if he were the new Zion, Isaiah describes himself as a bride-groom dressed in a priestly turban (garland), implying that it will be a new priestly Zion that will reveal God's glory to the nations. In verse 11, he reassures his postexilic listeners that Zion's salvation and praise by the nations is as sure as the green shoots that come up in the spring. The image of a crown of beauty and a royal diadem in 62:3 refers to the encircling walls of Jerusalem, which are held by God as a sign of the nation's glory.

No Longer a "Scorned Woman"

Before the Exile, First Isaiah portrayed Jerusalem as a scorned woman, a harlot. Second and Third Isaiah, however, used positive female images. Bible scholars speculate on why this positive female imagery emerged in sixth-century B.C. Judah. Leah Bronner argues that with the Temple and the monarchy gone, sixth-century writers turned to the one social unit that still functioned, the family. Writers drew images from marriage, child-birth, and motherhood.

Jo Ann Hackett, on the other hand, contends that in an era of social upheaval, women were able to exercise more power in the public arena. Therefore, the prophet's use of female imagery may reflect a temporary increase in women's status.

Think About It: Women's image, status, and power were enhanced in times of social disruption. Comparing Israel in exile with our contemporary experience, do you agree with Bronner that women's greater recognition is associated with their domestic role, or with Hackett that women are a source of strength and stability?

Psalter: Psalm 148

This psalm calls for universal praise of God. Verses 1-6 invite the heavens—both angelic inhabitants and the sun, moon, and stars—to praise God as their creator. Verses 7-13 call for everything on earth—the inanimate (hail, snow, fire, and wind) and the animate (animals and human beings)—to praise God.

In the last verse the psalm makes a particular claim: this cosmic God who deserves universal praise has called out a particular people through whom to fulfill the divine purpose. The horn is a symbol of God's power to be raised on behalf of this faithful people to strengthen or protect them. The people of Israel show their ultimate praise by being who they are, God's redeemed people.

Psalm 148 pushes the limits of universality. Every being and every inanimate thing are called to praise God. The psalm links servanthood (theology) with stewardship (ecology). We humans are charged to exercise our power as

God does: as suffering servants. Rather than having dominion (power) over the earth and the heavens, we are to be in partnership with everything on earth and in the heavens. With Francis of Assisi we call the sun, wind, and fire our brother, and the moon, waters, and earth our sister.

Epistle: Galatians 4:4-7

In Galatians, Paul attempted to convince his newly founded churches that they should not shift their allegiance away from him to his opponents. The identity of these opponents has long been debated. Some scholars identify them as Jewish Christians; others as Gentiles attracted to the Jewish faith. Some see them as resident Galatians; others as missionary outsiders. In any case, they were trying to persuade the Galatian Christians that they needed to be circumcised and follow the law to be saved. Paul wrote to prevent this shift.

Saved by Faith, Not Law

To understand this passage, we must grasp Paul's larger argument. In 3:1-29, he reassured the Galatians that, having heard the gospel, they had received the Holy Spirit. Justified by faith, they could look forward confidently to their eternal inheritance. If they belonged to Christ, they were Abraham's seed, heirs of God's promise.

Think About It: Paul's point is that those who believe are Abraham's true descendants and God's heirs. How do you put yourself under a biblical "law" or other rules in order to please God?

In 4:1-11, afraid that the Galatians might still believe they needed to become observant Jews to be faithful to Christ, Paul explains how the law belongs to a time of spiritual childhood. He compares the situation of a minor heir (who has restricted freedom under the authority of a guardian) with that of those under the law.

All God's Heirs

Having laid out his example, Paul first applies it to Jews like himself (verses 4-5). As Jewish Christians they could claim to be direct heirs of God. They came into their spiritual majority when God sent the Son to redeem those under the law.

Then in verse 6, Paul applies his example to the Gentiles too. When God sent the Son to redeem those under the law, God also adopted the Gentiles as children. Because of their faith (not any legal or moral works) the Galatians likewise could call God "Abba." They had come into their spiritual majority and were heirs of God's promise. In 4:8-11, Paul concludes that before they knew Christ the Galatians were enslaved like minor heirs. Placing themselves under the law now would not perfect their faith as Paul's opponents claimed. It would only make them spiritual minors again.

Gospel: Luke 2:22-40

This closing story of Jesus' birth has at least three themes: (1) the law is fulfilled; (2) God's promise of salvation is realized; and (3) God's saving acts through Jesus' ministry will be opposed. In his infancy narrative, Luke previews the gospel story.

Law Is Fulfilled
Luke notes several times in the birth story that the Jewish law was fulfilled. Jesus was circumcised at eight days old as required. Mary observes the purification law; Joseph fulfills the law of the redemption of the firstborn male (1:21-24).

According to Jewish law, a mother was considered ritually unclean for forty days after the birth of a male child (eighty days for a female). She had to observe a ritual of purification, offering a lamb and a turtledove as sacrifices in the Temple. If she was poor, a pair of pigeons sufficed (Leviticus 12:2-8). The fact that Luke 2:24 mentions only doves or pigeons may have been Luke's way of noting that Jesus was born poor.

Also according to law, the firstborn male child belonged to God and was presented to God by the father at the Temple. The child could be redeemed (taken home) by means of an offering (Exodus 13:2, 12-13). Luke blends both of these traditions. Luke 2:22-23 refers to Joseph's redemption act. Verse 24 mentions Mary's purification sacrifice.

God's Promise Is Fulfilled
In 2:25-33, we meet Simeon, a devout man, who had been promised by the Holy Spirit that before he died he would see the Messiah. The Spirit guided him to go to the Temple at the time that Mary and Joseph brought Jesus. When Simeon saw Jesus, he praised God for allowing him to see God's "salvation" before he died. In his praise he shows an expanded understanding that Jesus (God's salvation) is not only for Israel but also for the Gentiles.

Conflict and Pain Ahead
In verses 34-35, Simeon tells Mary that Jesus will face the conflict between God's saving purpose and people's opposition. Many will resist God's saving actions. Jesus will be rejected and pierced with a sword, and Mary will share in his pain.

Women's Roles
The prophet Anna also praised God and spoke about Jesus (verses 36-38). Luke often paired a man and woman in his stories of Jesus. A man said or

did something, and then a woman said or did something similar. However, we note here that Anna's specific message is only alluded to.

The Importance of Ritual

The appropriate religious rituals and blessings are experienced in Jesus' presentation at the Temple. There is always a danger that religious observances can become empty ceremonies, deprived of deep meaning. In this passage we see the power and significance of worship and devotion to God through the divinely appointed sacrifices and liturgical observances. In our busy modern lives we are apt to ignore the crucial place of rituals that recognize the sacredness of life and the presence of God in our daily lives.

Think About It: The Gospel stories abound with rituals. What makes the worship of the church sacred and meaningful in your life?

Study Suggestions

A. Sing "Joy to the World"

Sing stanza 1. Substitute "our God" for "the Lord." How does this change your understanding of who is savior?

B. Imagine What Anna Said

Read Simeon's specific words of praise and prediction from Luke 2:29-32. Look at Anna's role in 2:36-38. Note that verse 38 only summarizes what Anna said. Have members pair off and write out what Anna might have said, then compare what they have written. Ask: How does the message you imagined Anna giving compare with Simeon's? How might their perspectives have differed?

C. Interpret Psalm 148

Read the psalm aloud together. Then read Genesis 1:26, 28. Ask: What does "dominion over the earth" mean in relation to the psalm? Does it mean "power over"—ability to control everything? Or "partnership with"—ability to work with God's plan? How do we praise God differently if we are exercising dominion over or are in partnership with?

Give members paper and colored markers. Ask them to divide the paper in half. On the left draw a symbol of "dominion over the earth"; on the right draw a symbol of "partnership with all the earth." Have them explain their drawings.

D. Compare Vision and Reality

Our vision of God's salvation (like Isaiah's expectations in 61:10–62:3) is often more than human reality allows, even after the birth of Jesus. Ask: Why is the vision and promise of God's salvation more than has yet been realized? What does this say about how we live as faithful Christians?

E. Examine Your Certainties

Paul was certain he had preached the "right gospel" to the Galatians. Ask: Can we as humans ever have a sure enough grasp of God's plan to assume that our interpretation or beliefs are the only true way? How can we share Jesus without assuming superiority over other religions?

F. What Saves Us?

Read Galatians 4:4-7 and the commentary on pages 46–47. Recall the words of Simeon and Anna. What are these persons of faith telling us about salvation? How do the law and ritual defeat our hope for salvation? How do they free us for salvation?

G. Tie It Together With "What If"

Before the session, create a timeline on a long length of paper. Show David at 1000 B.C., Third Isaiah and the returned exiles at 500 B.C., Jesus at 0, Paul and the Galatians at A.D. 50, and your local church at A.D. 2000. Assign each of five groups one spot on the timeline. Ask them to write on the timeline a one-line summary of the human need for God's salvation in that time. Then ask: How is our situation like the others? How different? If God decided to enter incarnate in human history in the third millennium, would we recognize the one sent from God?

H. Close With Hymn and Prayer

Sing either "Good Christian Friends, Rejoice" or "Go, Tell It on the Mountain." Thank God for the gift of salvation and equality of all in Christ.

EPIPHANY

Lections for the Epiphany
of the Lord

Old Testament: Isaiah 60:1-6

*W*HAT would it be like to have "the glory of the Lord . . . risen upon you"? The prophet says it would be light, like the sun suddenly breaking through clouds after a heavy rain, or walking from the dark confinement of a prison cell out into the bright light of freedom. It would be hope when we had only despair, new life when death seemed almost welcome. Isaiah of Jerusalem had written, "The people who walked in darkness have seen a great light" (Isaiah 9:2). Here, at the end of the Exile, the prophet sings that the darkness of banishment is over, that light has come, that God's glory has been revealed.

What did the world see when it saw God's glory? It saw a small band of exiles, returning home to Jerusalem from Babylon. True, they brought with them at least some of the holy vessels from the Temple and money from King Cyrus to help rebuild the house of YHWH, so there were gifts from the kings of the nations. But how pitifully small even Cyrus's generosity seemed compared to the ruin of Jerusalem! What kind of new age was this? Where was the source of hope?

The New Age Is Dawning

The prophet says God's new age is about to dawn. This has nothing to do with all the language and confusion about "new age" in our time. This is the new age of God's reign breaking forth upon the world—and, by the way, Christians ought to be bold to reclaim the language of the new age from those who have diverted it to something eclectic, individual, and psychological.

The new age begins when God's *kha-bodh* or "glory," appears over Jerusalem. This is the same glory that Moses could not bear to look upon (Exodus 33:18-23); only now it is revealed for all to see. The glory is public, so that the nations (or at least their kings) will come to see it for themselves and thereby become convinced of the universal sovereignty of YHWH.

Check It Out

"Look," the prophet says (60:4-5), "this is how you come back from exile. Your sons walk; your daughters are carried." The implication is that the sons are old enough and strong enough to walk; the

> ***Think About It:*** Christians often give up on language because some other group has taken it over. What has "new age" come to mean in our culture? Do you have friends or family members who are into new age spirituality? What can we learn and share from dialoguing with them? What would it mean for the church to reclaim that language and talk about the new age that God is beginning in our time?

daughters are evidently toddlers unable to make the long journey across the desert on foot. They need and will receive help.

The prophet says the people of Judah will be radiant with joy. Then they will look to the west and see great fleets of ships coming, bearing gifts for the new Temple. They will look to the east and south (60:6-7) and see camel caravans coming of their own accord, flocks of sheep and goats coming on their own, eager to be sacrificed on the altar in Jerusalem. The camels come from Midian, a tribe of Bedouins associated with Moses, and from Sheba, carrying gold and frankincense. These two items were considered the epitome of wealth in the ancient world and were the economic reason why Solomon courted the Queen of Sheba. God's greatness is shown in the gifts the nations bring to Jerusalem to welcome the new age and to honor the majesty of YHWH. This promised manifestation of God's glory in the return from exile is precursor to the epiphany (appearance) of God in the human form of Christ Jesus associated with the coming of the Magi (Gentiles) to Bethlehem.

Psalter: Psalm 72:1-7, 10-14

We are reminded (verses 1-7) that "government" is NOT a four-letter word. The purpose of government is to care for those who cannot care for themselves, to bring justice to the poor and marginalized of society. The only responsibility of the king is to "deliver" or to "defend" the needy.

All that is said about the king depends on God's justice and righteousness. These characteristics of God's rule were also to be practiced by the king as God's agent. Only when God's will (justice) is done, is there shalom, wholeness, for the people.

Verses 10-14 are about how God's rule (and the function of the king) are extended into a wider realm. A universal political dominion does not depend on military might or economic power but on the care for the poor and oppressed.

Think About It: What would life be like if ultimate power in our world rested in those who cared for the poor, the hungry, and those left behind in the race for "the good life"? How does our constitutional concept of limited government translate into limited justice for the poor and the weak?

There is always a discrepancy between the will of God and our attempts to embody it. This does not excuse us from trying to live it out, however. Christians see the intent of this psalm being fulfilled in Jesus, who came to "preach good news to the poor." But God also wants to see it fulfilled in the people who claim Jesus as Lord—in you and me in our political and economic lives.

Epistle: Ephesians 3:1-12

The writer of Ephesians talks about the mystery of Christ. In this case, the mystery is not "Whodunit?" but "What did he do?" Christ has triumphed over the principalities and powers and given the church the task of proclaiming God's will to them. The principalities and powers were the earthly domination system with its spiritual aura and heavenly counterparts who were under God's authority but were not always obedient to God. But the mystery of Christ is still greater than this. (Now, here is a clue. How do we read Scripture? We do not read for occasional solutions to moral problems but for insight into the mystery of Christ. That's the real clue to the question, "What did he do?")

The "commission of God's grace" (verse 2) is about communication—telling others about the mystery of Christ. What is the mystery? It is that the Gentiles are fellow heirs of the gospel. No one is excluded from the welcome of the gospel, from the good news of God's love and salvation. Under God's rule, there is no "we" and "they." There is only "we," because Christ has broken down all the barriers that once kept us separate.

Think About It: Who are today's "Gentiles" (outsiders)? (Consider immigrants, refugees, people of color, poor children, the mentally ill.) In what ways do we want them to become "like us" before we welcome them into the church?

We see this unity in the apostles and prophets; both offices in the early church involved preaching. The revelation to them is not for their exaltation, but for the purpose of communicating God's good news to others.

54

We Are in It Together

Historically, the Gentiles were "them"—all those who were not Jews. Some in the early church said that for Gentiles to come into the church they first had to become Jews, that is, they had to become "like us" to be welcome. Nonsense, the writer says. All those outsiders are now insiders, members of the same body, who share in the promise in Christ—not because they have become like us, but because God has called them in their very difference.

This hidden mystery, that all of us are one in Christ, was inherent in the Creation. Unity was a part of God's plan from the beginning (3:11-12); that's the way God intended it.

Gospel: Matthew 2:1-12

This text contains two emphases. The first is the contrast between the baby and King Herod. This is reminiscent of the contrast between Moses and Pharaoh, right down to the killing of all the boy babies. In both stories, one baby miraculously escapes and becomes a savior for his people. The second is the homage offered by the wise men and their interactions with Herod and the baby.

King and King of Kings

Herod was the ruler in Jerusalem, but he was incredibly vulnerable. His family had been Jewish for only three generations—and had been forcibly converted. Yet here he was, king of the Jews. He is called "the Great" because of his major building projects, including the Temple in Jerusalem. But he was a tyrant who ruthlessly eliminated anyone he saw as a threat. The hint of an unknown king was a major threat to him. The wise men came asking about the "child who has been born king" of the Jews. That did not just mean a new baby but one with royal blood who was king by right of birth.

"Wise Men" From the East

Actually, these were not kings but astrologers, persons who sought to read the future from the stars. They had seen a new star, which seemed to promise the birth of a king, and had come to "worship" him. They came from the East, which was probably the area around Babylon, the traditional home of astrologers. It was also the seat of a strong Diaspora (dispersion) Jewish community, so they could have possessed both astrological and biblical understandings. The idea that the magi were kings probably comes from Matthew's reading of Psalm 72:10, 15, and Isaiah 60:3, 6, and 10.

There are some puzzling things about the story. Why did they ask Herod for directions when they were following a star? Would not that have been enough direction? Why did Herod trust them to come back and "tell on" the baby? Why did not somebody as sneaky as Herod send spies after them, instead of trusting these strangers?

The astrologers also brought gifts—gold, frankincense, and myrrh. Psalm 72 shows that these are gifts appropriate for royalty. Christian tradition has interpreted each of these gifts as having a significance for Jesus' life and death (see the hymn, "We Three Kings"), but these ideas find no support in the Old Testament roots of this story.

What's Going on Here?

The magi began their search in unbiblical ways, following messages hidden in an alien faith and wisdom. But their search led them to the God of the Bible. There is a lesson here for us. These Gentiles followed the star, building on their own notions of what it meant. They may have been following their own wisdom, but it was God who put the star in the sky to attract them. Note carefully: they were Gentiles and were among the first to recognize the birth of the Messiah. Already, in the birth of Jesus, Matthew sees the dividing walls between "us" and "them" breaking down.

> **Think About It:** In the birth of Jesus Matthew sees the dividing walls between "us" and "them" breaking down. How is our world divided today? How does the gospel overcome our divisions?

What about that star? Was it a supernova? a comet? We do not know. But identifying the star would not change the faith about which Matthew is writing. The star is important, he says, because it is God's gracious gift.

The dream is also about God's grace. "Going home by another way" has been represented as language of conversion and changed lives, and it could mean that. It could also mean simply "to take a different road when you go home." God is revealed not only in the special revelation of Scripture but in our natural world as well.

Study Suggestions

A. Reflect on an Epiphany Hymn

Sing "We Three Kings." Invite sharing of memories involving the "three kings" story. Tell group members that today's session will show that this story is both simpler and more profound than we may think.

B. Define *Epiphany*

Note that this word comes from the Greek *epiphaneia*, meaning "appearance" or "manifestation." In the church year, the Festival of Epiphany is observed on or near January 6 to celebrate the revelation of God to humanity in the person of God's Son Jesus and the recognition of this by the wise men from the East, who were Gentiles.

C. Talk About the New Age

Ask for reactions to the term *new age*. What images come to mind? In some cases, reactions may be negative, for we may think of "new age" as somehow non-Christian. Other participants may have friends or family members who are alienated from the church and attracted to new-age spirituality and are trying to understand its appeal. Point out that Isaiah, John the Baptist, and Jesus all talked about the coming of a "new age."

Read aloud Isaiah 60:1-6, then ask the group to call out words and phrases describing what Isaiah thinks the new age will be like. Review the commentary on pages 52–53. Ask: How does the prophet describe God's glory? What are some contemporary manifestations of glory?

D. Examine a Sign of God's Rule

Read Psalm 72:1-7, 10-14 and point out that this was a coronation psalm. Ask: What does the psalm call on the king to do? (In Israel, the king was the government.) How would the world be different if governments put major focus on caring for the poor and oppressed?

Push a bit further by asking: What is a main topic of debate in Congress? If we took this Scripture seriously, what would we want Congress and the President to be working on? using tax money for?

E. Look Again at the New Age

Read Ephesians 3:1-12. Ask: What is Paul talking about? Note that "principalities and powers" refer to both earthly and spiritual forces that dominate people's lives. Focus on the mystery of Christ by asking: What did the writer understand this mystery to be? Refer to the explanation on pages 54–55 and to other commentaries in discussing these questions.

Ask: What does God call the church to do about the mystery of oneness in Christ? Who are today's "Gentiles" (rejected ones)? How does the gospel help us recognize that all persons are very much alike as far as the kingdom of God is concerned? How does the writer say God wants us to welcome them?

F. Unravel Another Mystery

Read Matthew 2:1-12. Ask: What is happening in this story? List responses on chalkboard or a large sheet of paper. Ask: What in this story reminds you of Moses? Give some background on who the magi were. Discuss: What might God be saying to us through this story?

G. Put It All Together

Each of these lections speaks about outsiders. Ask: How are the outsiders alike and different in each of the lections? What, in each passage, is the connection between insiders/outsiders and God's new age?

H. Reach Out

Offer a prayer thanking God that when the outsiders were included it was possible for us to become members of the household of God.

Lections for Baptism of the Lord
(First Sunday After the Epiphany)

"I Old Testament: Genesis 1:1-5

*I*N the beginning," that is, at the beginning of ordered creation, time actually began with God's ordering. The creative work began to shape something that was already there (the "formless void"). In that inchoate abyss, darkness covered the face of the deep, which probably refers to the waters that covered the earth. In Hebrew thought, the "deep," the ocean, is the epitome of chaos. So it is that God began creative work by bringing order out of chaos, form out of confusion.

Think About It: What if the conversation between science and religion concentrated more on praising God for the wonders of the universe than on worrying about how both the Bible and quantum physics can be true? What might that do for our faith? What are the problems science has with religion? religion with science? How do you reconcile the two approaches to investigating the meaning of the cosmos?

In modern accounts of creation, we hear about the "Big Bang," the theory of an awesome explosion at the beginning of time, from which the order and wonder of the galaxies around us all sprang. What we have learned from our remote spacecraft—about the rings of Saturn, the ice volcanoes on one moon, the possibility of an ocean on another—would have set the Hebrew psalmists dancing for sheer joy at these displays of God's creative power.

The Spirit of God

A wind (*ruach*) from God was moving over the water. The Hebrew word *ruach* can mean "wind," or "breath," or "spirit." The verb can be translated "move," "sweep," or "hover over." Each verb suggests another possibility of meaning. *Hovering,* for example, can also mean "brooding," which reminds us of a mother bird sitting on her eggs. *Sweeping* suggests a fresh wind blowing out stale air and bringing in fresh. *Movement* has purpose, direction, meaning. God was present; the activity was creative.

God Said . . . and It Was So

Speaking (verses 3-5) is another metaphor for God's creative activity. Hebrew thought emphasizes the power of words. They are not just sounds but have the capacity to bring about what is spoken. When God speaks, things really happen. And the metaphor of speech reminds us that creation is not an accident—it is an expression of God's will and purpose, God's word.

Speech also suggests that God is separate from the created order. God spoke and the Creation came into being. Creation did not emanate from God and continue to hold some of the reality of God within itself. God does not create by sending some of God's substance out into the world. God utters a creative word and calls something new into being.

Light

There was, at this point in the account, no sun or moon—just light. Light was called into being and separated from the darkness. In the Bible, light is a symbol of life and salvation. It is also fundamental to the Creation. Indeed, many believe that Creation was the first of God's acts of salvation. There is a sense in which each morning is a kind of new creation. The darkness (chaos) of the night is dispelled by the first rays of the morning sun creeping over the horizon, and brightness and warmth soon follow. Finally, God evaluates God's own work and calls it good.

> **Think About It:** Many believe that Creation was the first of God's acts of salvation. What might this mean? How does the natural order express God's gracious presentation of creation?

Psalter: Psalm 29

This may be the oldest psalm in our Bible. It reminds us of Canaanite hymns to Baal, the fertility god of rain. The psalmist says that the power over storms rightly belongs to YHWH alone.

God's glory consists of the strength that is mentioned in verse 1, described in verses 3-9, and exercised on behalf of God's people in verse 11. In verses 3-9, we read "the voice of the Lord," seven times—a number symbolizing perfection. God's strength is all-powerful. The effects of the storm are a sign of God's power over all creation.

On another level, the psalmist reminds us that the religion of Baal (and its modern, secular equivalents) gives the illusion that we are in control and that our efforts are enough to make us secure. Psalm 29 says it is God who is in control. *Shalom* begins with our openness to God's claim upon us.

Epistle: Acts 19:1-7

Although Paul and Apollos were not coworkers, they were partners in ministry. Because of their differences, they appealed to different people. Paul was a former Pharisee, who had been converted to radical Christianity. Everything he had been before became insignificant to him. One result was his constant struggle against other leaders and disciples who were convinced that one could not be a Christian without observing Jewish traditions.

Apollos was, apparently, a Jewish Christian, who had a background in a Jewish tradition that was Hellenistic. He probably came out of the church in Alexandria, Egypt, which was founded within a few years of the first Pentecost. Apollos and Paul had basic disagreements but were able to work together in mutual purpose and love.

Ephesus—What a Place!

Ephesus was one of the leading cities in the Roman province of Asia (modern Turkey). The Roman proconsul had his headquarters there as did the provincial high priest of the imperial cult. The imperial cult was much more active in Asia than elsewhere in the Empire. This, in turn, meant that Christians in Ephesus who did not participate in the cult were in more danger than in other cities.

Ephesus was also a major commercial city, a seaport linked to the caravan routes that ran inland across provinces all the way to the Indus River (modern India). The great architectural glory of Ephesus was the temple of Artemis, the Phrygian mother goddess, which was one of the Seven Wonders of the World.

Paul and Baptism

In Ephesus Paul met some Christians who knew only the baptism of John the Baptizer. In fact, Apollos himself may have known only John's baptism. These disciples may have been John's followers, who then turned to following Jesus. Somehow, their faith and experience seemed incomplete to Paul. They had not received the Holy Spirit, indeed had not even heard of the Holy Spirit. So Paul taught them in the new way, and then he baptized them.

Remember, there was a major difference between John's baptism and Christian baptism. John's baptism was for repentance, to prepare the way for the coming of the Messiah. Christian baptism is a rite of initiation into the life and kingdom of that Messiah. Paul then laid hands on them and they received the Holy Spirit.

It is interesting that, in the oldest baptismal rite we have, the Church Order of Hippolytus, which probably reflects practices in Rome about A.D. 100, there is both water baptism and laying on of hands by which one receives the Holy Spirit. Some of our practices have very deep roots!

> *Think About It:* When there is a service of baptism in your church, is it made clear that the laying on of hands is a giving of the Holy Spirit? Why is this essential for Christian baptism?

Gospel: Mark 1:4-11

This Sunday's liturgy celebrates the baptism of Jesus. Since baptism is a more important issue in our common life today than it has been for some time, it is important for us to look at Jesus' baptism and what it can mean for us.

Repentance for Forgiveness of Sin

John the Baptist came preaching a baptism of repentance—but not just repentance in general. John wanted people to repent because the Messiah was coming, and he wanted people to be ready.

The description of John sounds like the description of Elijah in 2 Kings 1:8. The locusts and wild honey that John ate are also signs that he is a prophet. These are "natural foods," which hermits and other religious ascetics ate. The official word in Israel was that prophecy had ceased at the time of Ezra (around 400 B.C.). So John's appearance meant a revival of the prophetic movement. The ties with Elijah are also important because the Book of Malachi, the last of the literary prophets, had said that God would send Elijah before "the great and terrible day of the Lord" (Malachi 4:5).

> *Think About It:* How was Jesus' status as the Son of God made manifest in baptism? How does baptism announce to us we are children of God?

John's baptism was not a repeatable purification rite, something people could go back to when they felt the need for forgiveness. It was a one-time event. Nor was it a forgiveness that could never be lost. Persons could receive John's baptism and then sin again. John's baptism was the reorientation of a person's life, *in that moment.* It marked the baptized person as one of God's chosen, who was leaving behind the sins of the past and making a fresh start, who was committed to welcoming the coming Messiah. John was building a community that was ready for reign of God.

So Why Was Jesus Baptized?

If Jesus were sinless, why was he baptized for repentance and forgiveness? (Of course that begs the unanswerable question of what Jesus might have believed.) Surely if he were God's Messiah, he did not need to make a commitment to be ready for the Messiah. So why was he baptized?

Remember that Jesus took the initiative to be baptized; it was not forced on him. That gives us some important clues. Can we say that Jesus wanted to associate himself with John's mission—with the gathering of God's chosen to prepare the way for the Lord's coming? The most basic reality of the Christian faith is the Incarnation—the faith that in Jesus God entered the world as a human being and identified with all humanity. So the Incarnation means that Jesus associated himself with our sinfulness and need for repentance.

The Voice and the Dove

The tearing apart of the heavens, the voice, and the Spirit descending like a dove are all affirmations of who Jesus is—God's beloved Son. In Mark's account, Jesus is the only one who saw the dove and hears the voice. In Matthew and Luke, the descent is more public.

One of Mark's literary devices is something called "the Messianic secret," in which only other spiritual beings, such as the demons, recognize Jesus for who he is—until the end when the Roman officer names him Son of God. We are not clear why this was important to Mark; we simply note it is part of his Gospel. The words Jesus heard come from Psalm 2:7, which is an enthronement psalm, and from Isaiah 42:1. In the enthronement, it was believed, God adopted the king as a son.

Study Suggestions

A. Reflect on a Hymn of Creation

Sing "Morning Has Broken." Ask: What feelings do you have when you walk outdoors on a clear morning? What about other new beginnings? (A birth, a move, a new job, a marriage could be mentioned.) Do they feel anything like the beginnings in the song?

B. Check Out the "First Morning"

Read Genesis 1:1-5. Ask: What was that "first morning" like? Refer to the discussion about the "Big Bang" theory in the commentary on page 58. Reflect on the "first morning" from the perspective of both the Genesis writer and the more modern "Big Bang" account. Encourage participants to look at what the Bible actually says, not what they think it says.

Refer to the wind or spirit moving or hovering over the waters as mentioned on pages 58–59. Ask: How are you affected by the image of the Spirit brooding over the waters? What meaning do you find in the alternative image of the wind sweeping over the deep?

C. New Beginnings at Ephesus

Read Acts 19:1-7 and the commentary on pages 60–61. Ask: What do you think this story is about? Why was/is the baptism question so important?

Note the contrast between the baptism of John and Christian baptism. Ask: What is the relationship between baptism and the Holy Spirit? What concepts present in John's baptism are also present in Christian baptism?

Distribute copies of your hymnal or book of worship and locate the baptism liturgy. Are there instructions for the pastor (and others) to lay hands on the newly baptized person(s)? What does the pastor say? Generally this will correspond to the baptismal rite found in the Church Order of Hippolytus and with the action of Paul.

D. Reflect on Power and Creation

Invite stories from participants about what it is like to be caught in a powerful thunderstorm.

Read Psalm 29 aloud. Ask: What are some elements in the psalm that remind you of thunderstorms? What kind of power is possible in a strong wind or rainstorm? When big storms hit, how much control over the forces of nature do we have? What are some signs of God's control over all this power?

E. Check Out Baptism

Read Mark 1:4-11, a key text for the celebration of the baptism of the Lord. Ask: What happens in this event? (Jot down an outline of the story.) What is the theological plot? What was God doing here? (Do not try to force a common understanding.) Who sees and hears what God is doing?

Now review the commentary (on pages 61–62), and talk about Jesus' baptism. Ask: What is God saying to us in Jesus' baptism? Many persons are confused and uncertain about this. You may not be able to reach unanimous agreement on this question.

F. Put It All Together

Look for some common threads in today's lections linking Creation, the Holy Spirit, and baptism. What other connections, or common threads, were there? If baptism is about "new creation," what is the message here of Creation and new creation?

G. Close With Prayer

Close with a prayer of thanksgiving for God's work in Creation, for our baptism, and for the new creation in Christ.

Lections for Second Sunday After the Epiphany

T Old Testament: 1 Samuel 3:1-10

HIS story is both fascinating and frightening, for it conjures up thoughts of God speaking to us in the middle of the night. What would we do? What would we say? It also contains a memorable response to God's call: "Speak, for your servant is listening." What better words for voicing one's commitment to faithful discipleship?

While we tend to think of this story as Samuel's "call," it is more accurately a theophany (a report about God appearing in the world). The story identifies Samuel as the only source of God's word in a time of upheaval: "The word of the LORD was rare in those days" (3:1).

Where Is the Word?

Eli was old and unable to control his sons, who were extorting money and other gifts from the people, instead of serving YHWH faithfully. God's word was rare, not only for these irresponsible sons but for the whole population. Now this rare word was about to come to Samuel.

It was night. Everyone was settled in. The "lamp of God had not yet gone out" (3:3). This might mean it was not yet dawn, since the supply of oil had not run out. It could also mean that Eli's lamp had not gone out. He might be old and blind, but he could still see what God was doing.

> **Think About It:** "There was no way he could have known it was God speaking to him." How would we know if God were speaking to us? How can we discern the voice of God from among the clamor of voices demanding our attention?

When God Calls

The last thing Samuel was expecting was that God would speak to him. He was sure Eli had called him, so he went running to see what he wanted. At this point Samuel knew something about the Lord, but he did not yet know the Lord. There was no way he could have known for sure that it was God who was speaking to him.

After this happened for the third time, old, blind Eli saw what was going on and told Samuel how to respond. This reminds us how important it is that older persons share with younger ones ways they can recognize God. This is an important part of the nurture and vitality of a congregation. The young do not always recognize what God is saying to them and need someone to help them understand. At times we all benefit from a spiritual mentor or guide.

Samuel was called by God in a time of spiritual desolation, religious corruption, personal immorality, political danger, and social upheaval. Sound familiar? The word of God was rare. Eli was old and sick, and he no longer held the influence and respect he once had. His sons were corrupt, and people had no respect for them. Who would take Eli's place as spiritual leader in Israel?

On the political front, the Philistines were threatening Israel, and there was no one with the charisma or ability to organize resistance to them. On the spiritual level, the people had fallen away from faithful observance of the law, just treatment of their neighbors, and vital worship of YHWH. At stake was nothing less than the survival of God's people.

Think About It: How does the experience of the boy Samuel parallel some early religious experiences in your life?

In a time of crisis, God raised up Samuel, who himself was a sign that God was still present with the people. God does not give in to evil, whether in institutional religion, personal life, social corruption, or foreign threats.

Psalter: Psalm 139:1-6, 13-18

The key to verses 1-6 is that "you" (YHWH) know "me." This is good news and bad news. It is good that God knows us, because we are understood by the Power behind the universe. The bad news, if we can call it that, is that to be known is to be fully open and vulnerable, and that is scary. But the psalmist celebrates even the vulnerability.

Verses 13-18 remind us that human life is the result of God's creative will. They affirm God's loving care for every person. Note the metaphor of God as a weaver, one who "fearfully and wonderfully" weaves us together. Let us be clear: This is a statement of faith about our relationship to God rather than a statement of our conception or origins. It does, indeed, have ethical implications because of the insistence that God knows and cares for each person individually.

Epistle: 1 Corinthians 6:12-20

Today's Epistle lection responds to the question: How does the church deal with sexual immorality? Paul devoted most of Chapter 5 to this question. Now he observes that the matter of immorality raises the larger issue of Christian freedom. This makes it much more relevant to the whole church than the narrower question of immorality.

The Question of Freedom

Apparently the saying "All things are lawful for me" was often used by the Corinthians. Behind the saying was a pagan world-view. That world-view assumed that physical acts do not affect the inner person. What we do with our bodies has no effect on who we really are. We read that statement with a sense of disbelief, since we know that our actions do, in fact, help define who we are.

Think About It: When we want to claim Christ as our Redeemer, we also have to obey him as Lord and Master. What ethical standards does Christ require that make us uncomfortable?

This world-view was called neo-Platonism. Some neo-Platonists held that the real person was spiritual and was confined in a body only for a time. What happened to the body did not really affect the spirit. Paul had to deal with this philosophy. Another issue was elitism. Elitists said, "Yes, we need all those rules for the common people; but for anyone as intelligent and self-directed as I am, the rules do not apply."

Getting to the Point

In response to pagan ideas, Paul raises two questions. First, "Is it helpful?" Second, "Will it make me a slave to passion and destroy the freedom I thought I had?"

The first question forces us to consider how our actions affect others. Will my freedom be helpful to other Christians? Paul returns to this in more detail later. The second question requires us to think about how our actions affect ourselves. It is like asking, "Whom are we kidding?"

Here's REAL Freedom

For Paul, the only real freedom lies in whom we choose as our master. What is the ultimate goal of our bodies? We are meant for the Lord—body, mind, and spirit.

A human being is an organic whole, and each part is related to every other part.

In baptism, we have become part of Christ. This union is an exclusive one—anything that is incompatible with being part of Christ's body is illicit. We have to choose between one union or the other. Self-indulgence does affect our relationship with Christ. Since some prostitution in Corinth may have been sacred prostitution, the question of idolatry was also involved.

We belong to Christ—we were bought with a price. This refers to buying the freedom of a slave. The slave is free but is obligated to the one who purchased his freedom. We are not really proud, self-sufficient individuals. We belong to Christ.

Gospel: John 1:43-51

Philip, whom Jesus called to be a disciple, must have been the second disciple (with Andrew) who heard John the Baptizer identify Jesus as the Lamb of God. These two disciples spent the night talking with Jesus and came to believe that he was, in fact, God's Son. Andrew brought his brother Simon to meet Jesus (John 1:35-42). Now Philip found his friend Nathanael; they began talking about the Messiah.

Here He Is
Philip opened the conversation by saying, "We have found him. The one for whom we have been looking is the fulfillment of all Scripture." We often think of fulfillment in terms of "proof" (that is, "Here is a verse that proves the prophet six hundred years ago was thinking about Jesus").

What the Gospel means by *fulfillment* is more complex and wonderful than this. Fulfillment means that all our hopes and dreams and longings for God have come true in Jesus. A specific verse may be an expression of those hopes and dreams, so we quote it as an example; but the real fulfillment is in the person. This is God's act in our midst. Philip continued the witness to Jesus as Son of God. He also witnessed to Jesus as a human being—the son of Joseph from Nazareth.

Nathanael's response reflected conventional wisdom: "Can anything good come out of Nazareth?" (1:46). This is like saying, "What can you expect from those people!" Nazareth was off the beaten path, obviously insignificant to Nathanael. Philip took a different tack. He simply said, "Come and see for yourself." This may be the best response to those who dismiss our faith claims and who doubt Jesus can mean anything for their lives.

> **Think About It:** "Come and see." "Check it out." How are these statements among the most effective of evangelism? Who among your friends might you approach this way?

Under the Fig Tree

Jesus immediately hailed Nathanael as an Israelite in whom there was no deceit (1:47). This conversation between Jesus and Nathanael is full of references to the story of Jacob/Israel. Jacob was certainly full of deceit—lying to his father, cheating his brother, cheating his uncle. But here was one of Jacob's descendants who was an honest man! Nathanael asked, "How do you know me?"

Jesus' answer would not be convincing to most of us, so there must be something behind the story that we do not see. Certainly it persuaded Nathanael to confess that Jesus is Son of God. This is a true statement about who Jesus is and where he comes from (in addition to Nazareth). "King of Israel" is a positive term in John's Gospel. It witnesses to Jesus' significance for his people.

Jesus promised Nathanael he would see "greater things than these" (1:50). The saying about the open heavens and the angels ascending and descending is another reference to Jacob, who dreamed that there was a ladder set up between him and heaven with angels ascending and descending on it. But what does the reference to Jacob's dream mean here? The Son of Man (Jesus' term for himself) is, indeed, the bridge over the gulf that exists between heaven and earth; and that opens up the relationship between God and humanity.

Back to Nathanael

Nathanael's response changed from skepticism to confession. What marked him as a disciple? He saw the Son of God in the man from Nazareth. For the writer of this Gospel, this is enough. One's identity as a disciple is grounded in the identity of Jesus. When we confess that identity, that Jesus, the man from Nazareth, is also the Son of God, we have become disciples.

Study Suggestions

A. Reflect on the Week

Invite members to relax, close their eyes, and silently give thanks for an experience in the past week through which they became aware of God.

B. Explore Voices in the Night

Ask participants to tell briefly about a dream so real that they awakened sure that something had happened. Ask: Have you ever thought you heard a voice calling you when there was no one around? This happened to Samuel.

Explain that Samuel was only about twelve years old, and Israel was living in desperate times. Samuel lived with Eli, an old, blind priest, and was learning about God from him. Then read aloud 1 Samuel 3:1-10, and review the commentary on pages 64–65. Ask: What is the difference between knowing about

God and knowing God? Samuel did not expect to hear God; do you? If we have no expectation, is this why "the word of God is rare"? How could Samuel have known it was God speaking? How would you recognize God speaking to you?

C. How Do We Know What Is Right?

Read 1 Corinthians 6:12-20 and the commentary on pages 66–67, particularly about the issues of sexual immorality and Christian freedom. Point out the two questions Paul asked about ethical decision-making ("Getting to the Point"). Ask: Do these still sound like helpful guidelines for Christian action today? How do we feel about "keeping the rules"?

Ask: What did Paul consider to be REAL freedom? What do you think he meant when he said that we are meant for the Lord? What is the meaning of the biblical idea "to have Christ as our Master"?

D. Face Reality: God Knows Us

Read Psalm 139:1-6, 13-18. Ask: How might God's knowledge of us lead to discomfort? Can we find comfort in believing God knows us altogether?

Since knitting was considered woman's work in Israel, what does the image of God knitting us suggest? How does God's concern for us define the love God invites us to have for others?

Distribute paper and markers, and ask members to create a picture or symbol of what it feels like to be fearfully and wonderfully made by God. Have these shared one-by-one, and then displayed on the classroom walls.

E. Know the Messiah

Introduce John 1:43-51 with the comments in the first paragraph of the commentary on page 67; then read the Scripture. Ask: What is the plot here? Reconstruct the conversation on the chalkboard or on a large sheet of paper. What was the perspective of each person in the conversation?

Focus on Nathanael's question, "Can anything good come out of Nazareth?" What if his preconceptions had caused him to miss Jesus? What biases of ours might cause us to miss Jesus?

Talk about Jesus' promise to Nathanael ("Under the Fig Tree" on page 68). Be sure group members catch the Old Testament imagery. Ask: Why did Nathanael respond by calling Jesus the Son of God? How is Jesus the bridge between heaven and earth? How do you invite others, as Philip did, to "come and see"?

F. Tie It All Together

Summarize the common thread in these texts: being known by a God who speaks directly to us. How do we know when God is speaking to us? If you were to take these lections seriously, how do you hear God claiming your life?

Close with the hymn, "Lord, Speak to Me," and a prayer to hear and heed God's word.

Lections for Third Sunday After the Epiphany

"G" Old Testament: Jonah 3:1-5, 10

"*G*ET up and go to Nineveh, Jonah," God commanded for the second time. But Jonah hated Nineveh; and he was afraid if he went there, the people would repent. God would forgive them, and how he would hate that! So, Jonah took a ship—in the opposite direction—to Tarshish (Spain) in order to get away from God. God sent a storm, and Jonah saw another way to escape. He persuaded the sailors to throw him overboard, and the ship would be saved. Perhaps he might drown, then how could he go to Nineveh? God sent the fish, and Jonah found himself back on dry ground. Jonah again was confronted by God.

OK, OK, I Will Go!

Jonah still did not want to go to Nineveh. But he had one hope. Maybe they would not repent, and God would destroy them after all. Jonah was not excited about what he was doing—he went only part of the way into the city, and then gave the shortest sermon on record: "Forty days more, and Nineveh shall be overthrown!"

Incredibly, these persons who did not believe in YHWH repented—all of them, including the king, who called for a general fast and put on sackcloth and ashes (3:6)! The king recognized that repentance does not guarantee anything. God remains free to accomplish his divine will. The king did everything he could to save his people. Jonah also knew that God was free to do whatever God wanted. For the king, that was a word of hope. For Jonah, it was a word of despair.

What?

Consider the circumstances and the setting of the story. In the time of Ezra and Nehemiah, there was a religious revival in Jerusalem. Part of that revival included a ban on intermarriage. All non-Jewish wives and children were banished. Two great novellas were written to protest this treatment. One was the Book of Ruth, which pointed out that enforcing the law in an earlier day would have meant no King David; the other was the Book of Jonah, with emphasis on God's love for the foreigner.

> *Think About It:* "God cares for the outsider, even when the people who claim to serve God reject all who are different." Who are the Ninevites in our time? What "outsiders" does God call us to care for? Consider such groups as immigrants, ex-convicts, ethnic minorities, the poor, single mothers, the homeless, persons with handicapping conditions. With what message or ministry might God be sending us to them?

The setting of the story is an earlier time in the capital of Israel's main enemy, Assyria, which succeeded in conquering Israel in 721 B.C. So, who would care about Nineveh? It was certainly not Jonah, the spokesman for the people of God. He wanted Nineveh destroyed, just as Ezra wanted all non-Jews driven out of Judah. But God cared about Nineveh, even the animals (4:11). The point was not how wicked they were, but that they too could repent and turn to God.

The message is simple enough! Outsiders were more open to God than the insiders. The Book of Jonah asked the reformers to examine their own situation and ask about what they were doing to helpless women and children. They were reminded that God cares for the outsider, even when they did not. Although the Book of Jonah was preserved, we have no indication that the message of this writing was heeded in Judah. Can we hear God asking us to welcome the outsider and to have compassion for sinners?

Psalter: Psalm 62:5-12

This lesson is a great statement of faith about God's presence with us. Verses 5-7 say, on the one hand, there are all those people who are against us, all those situations that depress and worry us. On the other hand, there is God—who is our rock, our fortress, our refuge.

All these metaphors are military, but they are about defensive and not offensive strength. They deal with protection, not attack. The psalmist has great confidence in God's care for him. These verses also remind us to wait in silence. There is something powerful about being quiet before God and waiting expectantly to see what God will do.

The psalmist shares his experience and confidence with all people. God is a refuge, not just for those of high or low status, but for everyone, in all times and places. God's power and kindness work together to care for and to defend all God's people.

Epistle: 1 Corinthians 7:29-31

The immediate context of this passage deals with marriage. Paul is urging the Corinthians to remain unmarried. Why? Because the time is short; Jesus will return at any time. The early church believed that Jesus would return in glory during their lifetime. This belief led many to quit their jobs and leave their families, to prepare themselves for Jesus' return (a practice that has continued sporadically for centuries). The Corinthians do not seem to be caught up in such a drastic response—but Paul apparently was.

Keep Your Focus

Since the time is short, Paul says, keep your attention focused on what is most important. Do not get caught up in worldly affairs. This can mean all kinds of things, but the specific example Paul uses here is marriage. The call is to focus all one's energy and devotion on God. Here is the reality: if you are married, Paul says, your attention is either divided between God and family, or one is neglected for the other. For Paul, God's agenda is primary. The best solution, Paul says, is to stay single. If you are already married, however, you must still focus on the Lord.

> **Think About It:** Paul says that Christians must live detached from the world. Do you have a house, a car, a mortgage, credit cards, a retirement plan, investments? How can we live responsibly in the world without becoming so attached to possessions and comforts that they obscure our devotion to God?

Paul listed things people should give up to keep their focus on God. If you are married, live as though you are not. Do not mourn, rejoice, act as if you owned anything, or or become enmeshed with worldly concerns. Obviously, one will have to buy groceries, report to work, and perform other activities related to the world; but Paul says this must not become our focus. Do not get caught up in all that, because the time is short. The world is passing away, so we can live without being involved with it.

Interim Living

This whole passage, with its lack of concern for possessions, fits with the early Christian detachment from the world. Many of the earliest Christians took it upon themselves to try to live like Jesus. For them, this meant being a poor, celibate, wandering preacher.

Paul knew that not all the Corinthian Christians could do that. They needed to participate, to some degree, in the economic and social life of their city. The key for Paul was that they not get all wrapped up in the details of economic and social life because it was all temporary. He encouraged them to live for the eternal.

Gospel: Mark: 1:14-20

Jesus began preaching: "Believe in the good news." What is the good news (gospel)? It comes in two parts: an announcement and an appeal. The announcement is simple: The time is fulfilled and the reign of God is at hand. The appeal is equally simple: Repent and believe the good news. Both are incredibly profound.

The Time Is Fulfilled
The Greek word for "time" here is *kairos,* which means a special kind of time, not measured by watches or calendars. It is what we mean when we say things such as, "the time was just right for that." Time is fulfilled because God has come in and begun to establish God's realm.

We have trouble understanding the "kingdom" because our experience of kingdoms is limited to the British royal family and their struggles to stay relevant. In terms of our cultural and political experience, it might be more accurate to refer to God's reign as "the absolute rule" of God. Most kings in Jesus' day were absolute monarchs with little legislative restriction of their powers. They ruled, period. Jesus is proclaiming that the time has come when God will rule in every human life and throughout human society.

Repent and Believe
Our word *repent* comes from a French root that means to "rethink." Rethink your life. Are you satisfied with who you are and what you are doing? Are you restless for more of God and meaning and joy? Then rethink what you are doing and where your attention is focused. Turn to a new life. Why? Because the Kingdom is at hand.

But what about the good news? There is a difference between the good news Jesus preached and the good news about Jesus. We think of Jesus as crucified and risen Savior when we hear "gospel." When Jesus began preaching, that was all in the future. His good news was that God was breaking into human life and beginning the Kingdom. Life could never be the same again.

Follow Me
One of Jesus' early public acts was to call disciples. There is power in a call. For example, how easy is it for us to ignore a ringing telephone? Even if caller

ID identifies someone we prefer not to talk to, it is hard to ignore the phone.

> **Think About It:** The good news Jesus preached was that God was breaking into history, and the world would never be the same again. What are signs that God may be breaking into our world?

Similarly, it was hard for those Galilean fishermen to ignore Jesus, even in the circumstances.

Mark describes this as a totally spontaneous act. He mentions no prior contact between Jesus and these fishermen. One minute they were mending their nets, trying to make a living; the next minute Jesus was calling them away from all they had ever known—turning their backs on the world!

We are skeptical about calls. We want to ask Jesus: Whom did you say you represent? Can we see some identification? Can you come back later? These fishermen really heard Jesus. With only a glimpse of who he was and the authority he carried, they left everything to follow him.

The heart of all evangelism is "follow me" (or "come and see"). Jesus says, Do not worry about all the theological nuances—follow me. The disciples did just that, leaving everything behind them. They went against their cultural heritage, their economic self-interest, even their common sense.

Remember, the call to discipleship is for all people, not just for Peter and the other disciples, not just for clergy. All of God's people are called to follow Jesus and to live out his life in the world.

Study Suggestions

A. Reflect on an Image

Invite participants to sit quietly with their eyes closed. Ask them to imagine a footprint (any kind, anywhere). Then ask them to imagine that footprint on a poster with the caption, "The sign of God is that we will be led where we did not plan to go." Introduce today's theme that God works in our lives to lead us to new adventures.

B. Face Up to God's Call

Read Jonah 3:1-5, 10 and the commentary on pages 70–71. Ask: Based on what you know about the story of Jonah, how would it have been a protest against the zeal of Ezra and Nehemiah? Is it likely that Ezra's followers could accept the message of the Book of Jonah?

Consider the story. Ask: How did God work in Jonah's life? How did God work in the lives of the people of Nineveh? What does *repentance* mean to you? Does repentance bring any guarantees? How could the same truth about God's freedom be a word of hope for the king and a word of despair for Jonah?

C. God Both Calls and Cares

Read aloud Psalm 62:5-12, and review the commentary on pages 71–72. Ask: Why be silent before a God who protects us? Why does the psalmist want to share his experience of God with all the people? If you were going to tell others about God in your life (or the life of your church), what would you say?

D. Keeping Our Focus on Jesus

Read 1 Corinthians 7:29-31 and the interpretation on pages 72–73. Point out the immediate context about marriage. Ask: Why did Paul want people to remain single? How can you focus on Jesus and still take care of your family? What other barriers do we face in trying to keep our focus on Jesus?

In addition to marriage, Paul warns of the dangers of getting tangled up in worldly affairs. What worldly concerns compete with living a Christian life?

E. Hear and Tell the Good News

Read Mark 1:14-20, and review the commentary on pages 73–74. Discuss the key words and ideas: "the time is fulfilled," "Kingdom," "repent," "good news," "appeal," and "announcement." Ask: Is it possible to repent if we don't know the Kingdom is at hand?

Review the call of the disciples. Ask: How might you respond to a total stranger calling you to repent or to follow? What are the challenges in following Jesus today?

F. Put It All Together

Ask participants to think again about the footprint poster. Ask: What have you learned today about God's presence in your life? about God's call to go "where you did not plan to go"? Close by singing "Where He Leads Me I Will Follow" or "Jesus Calls Us" and asking God to help us deepen our commitment to being Jesus' disciples.

Lections for Fourth Sunday After the Epiphany

T Old Testament: Deuteronomy 18:15-20

HE heart of the message in Deuteronomy is that Israel is to be different from the other nations. Particularly they are not to try to discern God's will in ways that the pagans do—they are to listen only to the prophets. An Israelite prophet was not someone who predicted what would happen in the distant future. Rather, the prophet was one who proclaimed what God was doing in the present and in the immediate future and what God demanded of the people, God's covenant partners.

A Prophet Like Moses

Moses reminded the people that they had requested a prophet, and God had promised to provide one or more (the Hebrew can be read either way) like Moses. God would give words to the prophet, and the prophet would speak all that God commanded. Since they feared death from direct contact with God (18:16), Israel was to learn God's will through the prophet.

False Prophets

There were two kinds of false prophets (verse 20). The first was the one who spoke falsely in the name of YHWH, like the court prophets in the story in 1 Kings 22 of Micaiah (who alone spoke the truth). The other was the prophet who spoke in the name of other gods. One of Deuteronomy's major concerns was that Israel would give allegiance to other gods. (Deuteronomy was written to combat this major problem in Israel's history, which was occasioned by their living amongst other tribes and city states that practiced other religions.)

Deuteronomy 18:21 raises the critical question of how to "recognize" the authentic word of God among the conflicting claims of many prophets. How do we know which is the true voice? Verse 22 gives the answer: an authentic word comes true. The answer seems almost like a circularity. But the author of Deuteronomy believed that history is in God's control. What will happen is announced and effected by God's word. So the criterion of true prophecy is truth, the correspondence between the prophet's word and the realities of history, which may take a while to unfold. As the familiar proverb says, "The truth always comes out."

> *Think About It:* How do we recognize truth in what we read and hear? How would we recognize God's voice? What criteria do we use for testing the voices? (Consider the fourfold guidelines of Scripture, tradition, reason, and experience, which can be used to inform and evaluate the validity of each other and all sources of knowledge.)

The Prophet Like Moses Again

Moses was the model for future prophets (see 18:15, 18). The key authentic prophetic ministry is that prophets were the messengers of God's word. Amos perhaps said it best for all the other prophets: "Surely the Lord GOD does nothing, / without revealing his secret / to his servants the prophets. . . . / The Lord GOD has spoken; / who can but prophesy?" (Amos 3:7-8).

By the time of Jesus, there was a fairly consistent expectation that the messiah would indeed be a prophet like Moses. The community at Qumran (the people of the Dead Sea Scrolls) said there would be three messiahs: a king like David, a priest like Aaron, and a prophet like Moses. In John's Gospel, the priests asked John the Baptist if he were "the prophet," meaning the prophet like Moses. John and his community clearly saw Jesus as the fulfillment of this expectation of the prophet.

Psalter: Psalm 111

This is a hymn of praise, celebrating God's goodness. The psalmist identifies several of God's good works for special praise and thanks. God causes these acts to be remembered and celebrated. God provided food—both the manna and quail in the wilderness and all daily food. God secured the people's place within the family of nations. God established and maintained the covenant and honored it faithfully—providing reliable precepts to guide individual and community life, saving and restoring the people, upholding stability and justice.

We can count on God to be faithful; that is, consistent and unfailing. We can count on God to be just; that is, to care for the poor, the weak, the oppressed. God cares for people. To acknowledge this is the foundation of all wisdom. To praise God is our everlasting charge.

Epistle: 1 Corinthians 8:1-13

One of the Corinthians' major questions of Paul was, "Can we eat food offered to idols?" In the ancient world, the foreign temples also doubled as butcher shops. A worshiper brought an animal to be sacrificed; it was slaughtered, and part of it was burned as a sacrifice. The rest was offered for sale in the meat market, usually located conveniently near the temples.

The problem was the relationship between eating this meat and loyalty to pagan gods. Were those gods real? If so, would eating these sacrificial leftovers be a form of second-hand worship? Would having a meal with this food be idolatry? There was a faction in the Corinthian church that prided itself on its saving knowledge. They knew those gods had no real existence, nor would there be any adverse effect from eating the meat.

There were others whose faith was not as strong. They were faithful converts to Jesus but still feared the power of the old gods and of the lure into old ways that the sacrificial meat could represent. The situation was not helped by the "strong" making fun of those who were not sure and pushing them to let go of their caution.

Don't Hurt Partners

Paul acknowledged that the idols were not real and that food itself is morally indifferent. But if this or any other knowledge creates a feeling of superiority, it hurts the community. Ridiculing some members of the church for their individual scruples is a "stumbling block" (8:9). If we focus on our knowledge, he says, we may destroy the conscience of the weaker member.

> **Think About It:** How do we show sensitivity to the scruples of persons that differ from our own?

Being "weak in conscience," in Paul's thought, refers to "self-consciousness" or experience. Those who are unenlightened or inexperienced in the faith need more support and encouragement. Paul stresses the responsibility community members have for one another—grounded in love and in the "one God, the Father, . . . and one Lord, Jesus Christ, through whom are all things and through whom we exist" (8:6). Treating our partners with kindness and compassion is the most important knowledge to possess.

Liberty and Sin

We all want freedom to live out our faith. Liberty can become a problem, however, if our actions lead a weaker brother or sister astray. Paul cautions the congregation that the "strong," those with firm convictions, must feel some sympathy for the scruples of the "weak." Elevating knowledge over love runs the danger that "those weak believers for whom Christ died are destroyed" (8:11). The key to Paul's argument is in 8:13: "If food [or anything else I do] is a cause of their falling, I will never eat meat." To "sin against members of your family" is a sin against Christ.

Gospel: Mark 1:21-28

In some ways, this story almost contradicts Paul's argument to the Corinthians. Jesus certainly overrides the religious scruples of his contemporaries, for the sake of doing good; but kindness and compassion lie at the heart of boh passages.

A Sabbath Healing

The setting is the synagogue on the sabbath, a day when no work could be done. But there was a man with an unclean spirit, and Jesus healed him. Oral tradition allowed for healing on the sabbath, in case of an emergency. If the situation could wait until Sunday, the healing was considered unnecessary work. The leaders of the synagogue judged that Jesus had acted improperly. Of course, they were not the ones who needed healing.

The heart of the story, however, is not the miracle, but "a new teaching—with authority." Jesus' authority is not something extrinsic, given by virtue of an office. His authority is derived from who he is (verses 22, 17). And, there is a delicious irony in the setting of the story. Jesus confronted and defeated the powers of evil in a place of worship.

Dealing With Demons

The "unclean spirit" means that the man was somehow ritually unclean because there was an alien spirit within him (1:23). The common designation for this kind of affliction in Jesus' day was demon-possession. Interestingly, it was the demons who recognized Jesus and trembled. Before Jesus did anything, the demons confronted him and demanded to know what he was going to do to them: "What have you to do with us . . . ? Have you come to destroy us?" (1:24). In a single command, Jesus silenced and banished them.

Taking Authority

The crowds insisted that Jesus had a powerful authority. The inference is that the scribes raised questions and were skeptical. The scribes were not evil men. They were learned scholars who read and interpreted the Scriptures. Their vast knowledge commanded respect, and people listened to them.

> **Think About It:** Jesus had a different kind of authority than the scribes. What was the source of his authority?

Jesus had a special kind of authority—the authority of his person. The Gospels point out the difference between his authority and that of the scribes and Pharisees, without defining what that difference is. Clearly Jesus had authority over the demonic powers. This was a more-than-human authority. For him to be able to command the demons and have them obey him in fear meant one of two things. Either he was a "Prince of demons" or he was divine. The Gospels flatly deny the first option, so this authority over demons is Mark's declaration that Jesus was the Son of God.

Who Is This Man?

After Jesus rebuked and cast out the demons, the people were filled with amazement. They recognized "a new teaching—with authority!" The teaching was action, not words, but the principle was the same. The key was the authority. Who was this, that even the demons obeyed him? The implicit answer was that this was the Son of God. Jesus' power, or authority, came from God at work in him.

No wonder the people went out and spread the story. Soon all of Galilee would know about the rabbi Jesus, who spoke and acted with such authority that even the demons obeyed him. Even in the gossip would be the implicit question, "What's going on here? Who is this?" as people rushed to see for themselves.

So even this little miracle story forces us to face the basic questions of our faith. Who is this Jesus? What do we do about him?

Study Suggestions

A. Reflect on the Week

Ask persons to think of one time this week when they were able to recognize God doing something in the world. Ask them to have that incident clearly in mind and then give God thanks for it.

B. What It Means to Be Different

Ask: Have you ever been in a situation where you were different, so different that you stood out? Maybe you were the only person of your ethnic, economic, faith, or age group, or held and voiced convictions different from the majority.

After several people have told their stories of being different, point out that Moses told Israel they should be different from those around them. Read aloud Deuteronomy 18:15-20. Ask: In what way did Moses ask Israel to be different? Refer to the commentary on pages 76–77.

C. Examine the True Prophet

Ask: What is the "true" prophet? What is the prophet's role? How can you tell if you are listening to a true prophet? Who are the false prophets, and how do we recognize them? Who are some contemporary prophetic voices?

D. Honor Your Fellow Christians

Read 1 Corinthians 8:1-13. Ask: What is the plot? What circumstance is Paul describing in the Corinthian church? Write responses on the chalkboard or on a large piece of paper.

Form small groups and ask everyone to review the commentary. Ask one group to use that information and the Scripture to identify the theological plot. What is God doing here? The second group will note the human interactions. What are persons' actions, attitudes, and feelings? Have a third group consider the potential consequences of expressing the liberties of the "strong" and the "conscience" of the "weak." When groups have shared their findings, discuss as a large group: What do you bring to this passage? What do you think God wants us to do about this passage?

E. Discuss Scruples and Behavior

The focus of this passage is on the practical implications of faith. That is, if some optional behavior is a stumbling block to another, I will voluntarily restrict myself. Ask: What are some things we say, do, or believe that are known stumbling blocks to others? What might we avoid doing to protect others whose faith may be weaker than ours? How do we practice kindness toward persons who are easily offended?

F. Praise God

Read Psalm 111. Ask: Why does the psalmist say we should praise God? What evidence of God's presence with Israel is provided by the psalmist?

G. Reflect on Authority

Read Mark 1:21-28 and the commentary on pages 79–80. Ask: What kinds of authority do you see in the story? What kind of authority is valid for us? How would we react if someone came in preaching a new message, doing things in an entirely different way, or challenging all the existing structures of authority?

H. Put It All Together

Ask: In today's lections, what examples do we see of God's acts in human history? Close by singing a doxology and asking God to help us discern and follow divine authority in our lives.

Lections for Fifth Sunday After the Epiphany

T Old Testament: Isaiah 40:21-31

*T*HE Book of Isaiah includes prophecies that speak to events spanning two hundred years in the history of Israel and Judah from about 742 to 539 B.C. As previously mentioned, the book divides roughly into three historical settings: Chapters 1–39 (First Isaiah) contain oracles from Isaiah of Jerusalem during the reign of four Judean kings; Chapters 40–55 (Second Isaiah) address the concerns of Jewish exiles in Babylon; and Chapters 56–66 (Third Isaiah) are directed to the exiles who have returned home to rebuild.

Exile

Jerusalem was razed and sacked by Babylonian soldiers in 587 B.C. The Temple was destroyed, and the leaders of the community were taken to Babylon. The exiles thought God had abandoned them, saying "my way is hidden from the LORD." Isaiah 40:27 may be a fragment of a communal lament, similar to complaints against God found in some psalms and in the Book of Lamentations. The memory of the forced march to Babylon may be implied in the phrase "youths will faint and be weary, and the young will fall exhausted" (verse 30). The exiles were flagging in their faith, especially when they saw the grand processions honoring Marduk, Babylon's chief god. If the might of a god were to be measured by the fortunes of his people in battle, perhaps YHWH was not so powerful after all.

Creator and Lord of History

Second Isaiah reassures the exiles that God controls the grand sweep of history and cares about the situation of all God's people. The rhythm that rises and falls through the poetry of this passage echoes in the events themselves and underlines his point. The great Babylonian Empire, at the height of its power under Nebuchadnezzar when Jerusalem was destroyed, would in turn fall to Cyrus of Persia in 539 B.C. God "brings princes to naught, and makes the rulers of the earth as nothing" (40:23). From God's perspective people look like grasshoppers—even the greatest of monarchs. Every nation's course through history stands under the sovereignty and judgment of the Almighty God. All will rise and fall in their time.

Second Isaiah tells the people they can count on God to save them because God created the whole world. God "stretches out the heavens like a curtain" (40:22). Moreover, God controls the heavenly host and can call out the stars by name. Astral bodies such as the sun, moon, and stars were closely connected to the chief gods of Babylon. The prophet undercuts belief in these other gods with rhetorical questions that increase in intensity: "Have you not known? Have you not heard? Has it not been told you from the beginning?" (40:21). These questions recall the traditions passed to the people through prior generations of Torah reading and Temple worship. No idol fashioned in silver and gold by artisans, God is creator and lord of history!

> **Think About It:** "My way is hidden from the Lord." Have you ever felt abandoned by God? At what times has your faith flagged? What word, sign, act, or relationship has helped you overcome these feelings and recover your confidence in God's presence and power?

If they keep faith and wait for God to act, says the prophet, God will renew their strength. They shall "mount up with wings like eagles" (40:31). The image of eagles' wings recalls God's words to Moses at Sinai in Exodus 19:4: "You have seen what I did to the Egyptians, and how I bore you on eagles' wings and brought you to myself." God will bring the exiles back home in a new exodus in which God's glory will be revealed and the people's lives will be restored (Isaiah 40:3-4).

Psalter: Psalm 147:1-11, 20c

This psalm opens with an imperative: "Praise the LORD!" This is the second of a group of five psalms that close out the entire book, all of which begin and end with "hallelu-yah" (praise the Lord!). Why praise God? Because God is bringing the "outcasts" (NIV: "exiles") back to Jerusalem. God provides food for all creatures. Notice how the psalmist piles up a long list of verbs that describe how God acts, such as *gathers, heals, prepares.* Steadfast love characterizes God's actions toward Israel and all creation. Given this overwhelming graciousness, all the hearer can do is praise: "How good it is to sing praises to our God" (147:1).

This psalm may have predated the Exile to Babylon and refers to previously exiled Israelites taking a religious pilgrimage to Jerusalem. Given its placement at the end of the Psalter, however, and the way it summarizes themes of many other psalms, the present version speaks to postexilic Judah. Now safe in Jerusalem, the people could look at the scars of exile and say, "[God] heals the broken-hearted, and binds up their wounds" (147:3).

The command, "sing to the LORD" (verse 7) recalls Miriam's invitation in Exodus 15:21, the oldest song of praise in the Hebrew Scriptures. Psalm 147 gathers up the story of Israel from Exodus until now.

Epistle: 1 Corinthians 9:16-23

This passage comes in the middle of Paul's argument with the Corinthians about material support for him and Barnabas. Other apostles, soldiers, vinedressers, shepherds, and priests all got paid for their labor. According to the law of Moses, even an ox should not be muzzled while treading out the grain (9:9). Yet Paul made no claim for anything from the Corinthians.

Slave of God

Why? Did Paul like being a martyr? No, he wanted to remove every obstacle to belief in the gospel in case some hearers assumed he was preaching for personal gain. Besides, if he had a choice, he might claim some reward. But he was merely a slave of God. Ever since Jesus confronted him on the Damascus road, Paul felt compelled to preach the gospel. His language here recalls Jeremiah 20:9: "If I say, 'I will not mention [God],' / . . . within me there is something like a burning fire / shut up in my bones.")

Servant of All

Paul extends the imagery to describe his relationship to those he hopes to win for Christ: He is their slave as well. Here he echoes the words of Jesus in Mark 10:44: "Whoever wishes to be first among you must be slave of all." Paul's servitude shows itself in following the practices of those he seeks to win. He observed Jewish traditions when among Jews; he was not observant when with Gentiles. For example, Paul had Timothy circumcised so as not to offend church leaders in Jerusalem; yet he violated Pharisaic practices by eating with Gentiles. When among the "weak" (the excessively scrupulous), Paul abstained from food sacrificed to idols in order not to offend them. Paul voluntarily limited his "rights" to material support and free behavior for the sake of the gospel. His critics called him "inconsistent." He replied that he was free in all things except his obligation to God.

Paradox of Servanthood

By describing himself as a "slave," Paul is countering the notion that faith confers privileges or spiritual gifts about which to boast. Setting an example of self-discipline, he demonstrated the paradox of servanthood: We are most free when under obligation.

Gospel: Mark 1:29-39

This passage is preceded by the first public act of Jesus' ministry in which he exorcised a demon from a man in the synagogue at Capernaum. That set the stage for Jesus' entire ministry: The Gospel of Mark is a story of intense struggle between Jesus and the powers of evil. When Jesus healed Peter's mother-in-law of a fever, the demonstration of his power continued. By nightfall of the sabbath, when people were free to travel, the whole city was at the door.

More Than a Miracle Worker

This passage summarizes representative scenes from Jesus' early ministry. By using words such as *all, whole, many,* and *everyone,* Mark stresses the immediate and broad impact Jesus had in Galilee. Yet Jesus insisted he was more than a miracle worker; he had "come out" to proclaim the good news of God's reign. "Come out" has multiple meanings: Jesus had come out from his hometown of Nazareth (geography); he had disclosed who he was (identity); and he had come from God into the world (origin). His full identity was to remain hidden, however: He commanded the demons to be silent.

Throughout the Gospel of Mark, Jesus commanded demons, the people he healed, and his disciples not to tell about him (1:44; 3:11-12; 5:43; 7:36; 8:30; 9:30). Why did he teach and perform miracles in public if he did not want people to know who he was? Throughout the Hebrew Scriptures, a sense of mystery attends any manifestation of God's presence and power. Also, ancient peoples believed that if someone knew and spoke your name, it gave that person power over you. Jesus could not allow others to "name" him if he was to retain his integrity and power.

> **Think About It:** Jesus could not allow others to name him if he was to retain his integrity and power. To what extent do you allow others to name, and thereby define and limit, who you are?

Most important, the "messianic secret" was Mark's way of showing that Jesus' true nature could not be fully understood until after his suffering, death, and resurrection. Most people wanted the benefits of following a wonder worker without accepting the claims of discipleship. Jesus stated three times (Mark 8:31-38; 9:30-32; 10:32-45) that he had come to serve and to suffer; any who followed him must be willing to do the same.

Model of Service

After the healing, Peter's mother-in-law got up to cook and serve a meal for them. In so doing she provides an example of the spirit of Jesus' teaching in 10:43: "Whoever wishes to become great among you must be your servant." Mark wants to undercut all self-exaltation that will hobble the disciples.

Jesus Prays

The next morning, Jesus arose very early and went off to pray in a "deserted place." The setting recalls his forty days in the wilderness. Every new demonstration of his power presents him with the temptation to misuse it, so he must return over and over again to prayer. Jesus spent time alone in prayer at Gethsemane, where he wrestled with his final temptation.

Searching for Jesus

Peter and the others came looking for Jesus, reporting that "everyone is searching for you" (Mark 1:37). Their motive is unclear: Do more people need to be healed? Does the crowd hope to be entertained by further miracles? Luke's account supplies a motive: "they wanted to prevent him from leaving them" (Luke 4:42). Elsewhere in Mark, persons searching for Jesus often had hostile intentions, as when the Pharisees sought to test him or when the authorities came to arrest him. Here, Jesus simply moved on.

Study Suggestions

A. Praise the Lord

Read Psalm 147:1 as an invocation. Sing a hymn praising God as creator, like "How Great Thou Art" or "Creating God, Your Fingers Trace."

B. Consider God

Form two groups. Have one group review Isaiah 40:21-31, Psalm 147:1-11, and the hymn for references to God as creator; have the other group review descriptions of God as comforter. Note the verbs and adjectives that support these images. Report findings to one another. Discuss: How do we experience God as both powerful and caring? In human experience do these two qualities tend to reinforce one another or come into conflict? How do we harmonize them? Give examples of how God is active in these two ways in our lives, our community, and our world. How can we exercise power in caring ways?

Invite participants to remember times spent out-of-doors when they felt the vastness and beauty of God's creation. Create and recite a group litany. After each memory is voiced, respond with "How glorious is your name in all the earth!"

C. Know God as Comforter

Ask group members to recall times when they felt bone-weary (like the Israelites in Isaiah 40:21-31). Compare major sources of stress in ancient and modern life. What causes our exhaustion? How does God give us strength? Share experiences of spiritual disciplines that renew vitality and serenity.

D. Examine Servanthood

Review 1 Corinthians 9:16-23 and the commentary on pages 84–85. Invite participants to share reactions to the idea of being a slave. List examples of how slavery is still practiced in our time (as with sweatshop labor or in the Sudan). Define Christian servanthood. What is the difference between slavery and servanthood? How can we serve without inducing guilt, dependency, or resentment in others? What aspects of church organization and leadership present obstacles to servanthood?

Describe Paul's relationship to the Corinthian church as implied in 1 Corinthians 9:16-23. What had he given up for them? What did he expect from them? What can we expect from our church leaders? What do we owe them?

Read the hymn, "Make Me a Captive, Lord," as commentary on Paul's words. Ask participants to name ways they voluntarily renounce their rights for the good of others, such as parents, children, spouses, workers, citizens, or the less fortunate.

E. Explore Healing

Compare Mark 1:29-32 with other stories of Jesus' healing touch (Mark 5:21-24, 35-43; and 9:14-29). What similarities do you note? What differences? How do we explain why healing sometimes takes place and sometimes does not?

F. Pray With Jesus

Review the portion of the commentary on Mark 1:29-32, "Jesus Prays." Jesus needed times of prayer after periods of intense activity to remain clear about God's call. Reflect on these questions: What has God called you to do? How do you stay focused? When and where do you take time to pray?

H. Close With Comfort and Conviction

Gather into a closing circle, holding hands. Invite members to share their reflections aloud as they are comfortable. Sing "Make Me a Captive, Lord." Ask them to pray silently for others in the group, both now and during the week. Read Isaiah 40:31 aloud together as a benediction.

Lections for Sixth Sunday After
the Epiphany

T Old Testament: 2 Kings 5:1-14

HE prophet Elisha towers over the other characters in the first half of
Second Kings, a figure of miraculous powers and broad political influence. The
protégé and successor of Elijah, Elisha purified water, fed the famine-stricken,
healed the sick, advised military campaigns, and dethroned kings. His fifty-year
ministry took place in Samaria during a period (850–800 B.C.) of recurring
warfare between Israel and its neighbors: Aram, Moab, and Ammon.

Naaman Seeks Help
In today's passage, Elisha is matched with another strong figure, Naaman,
commander of the Syrian army to the north, who earlier had led a successful
raid against Israel. Second Kings 5:1 suggests that Naaman even had gained
God's favor in that "by him the LORD had given victory to Aram." Yet
Naaman suffered from the dread disease of leprosy. An Israelite slave girl
whom the Syrians had taken captive told Naaman that there was a prophet
in Israel who could heal him.

Naaman went to Israel bearing gifts and a letter from his king, which the
king of Israel took as pretext for another raid. Elisha told the king of Israel
to send Naaman to him. Naaman's impressive entourage stopped at Elisha's
house, where a messenger directed the Syrian to bathe seven times in the
Jordan River. Affronted, Naaman stormed away. But his servants then prevailed on him to obey the prophet's instructions, and he was healed.

Give God the Glory
Several themes emerge from this passage. First, the story underlines
Elisha's impressive spiritual powers—he healed Naaman at a distance with a

simple verbal command. Second, the passage shows that God is not subject to swaggering egos or national pride. Naaman, the mighty warrior, had to humble himself to receive healing. And the Israelites had to accept God's action in healing an enemy of Israel. God's concern was not bound by national borders or human egos. The humbling of Naaman was heightened by the fact that his healing pivoted upon the counsel of his lowly servants—twice! Finally, the passage gives glory to God, by whom Naaman was victorious in the first place. God (working through his servant Elisha) is the primary actor in this passage.

> **Think About It:** God's concern was not bound by national borders or human egos. How does this challenge our patriotic loyalty to our nation above all others? our attachment to particular leaders who "can do no wrong"? our belief that our locality is "God's country"? our preoccupation with ourselves and our personal well-being with less regard for the welfare of others?

In the verses that follow, Naaman converted to worship of the God of Israel. His conversion underscored the meaning of Elisha's own name ("God is salvation"). In later generations, Jews who were exiled in Babylon would draw comfort and strength from this story of the foreign official who came to worship YHWH.

Elisha and Jesus

Christians saw Jesus as a powerful prophet like Elisha, for Jesus replicated or exceeded several of Elisha's miracles—feeding a crowd, raising a child from the dead, and healing a leper. In fact, Jesus cites the healing of Naaman as an indictment of his hometown of Nazareth and as a justification for his own far-reaching ministry: "There were also many lepers in Israel in the time of the prophet Elisha, and none of them was cleansed except Naaman the Syrian" (Luke 4:27). God would reach out to Gentiles and outcasts through Jesus, even though some of his own people would not receive him.

Psalter: Psalm 30

Psalm 30 conveys the psalmist's thanksgiving to God for deliverance from death. Facing severe illness and death threats from enemies, he cried out to God and God saved him. The verb in verse 1, "drawn up," refers to the act of drawing water from a well. Similar vertical imagery is used in verses 3 and 9 to speak of going down to the Pit. (The words *Pit* and *Sheol* were used interchangeably to describe the realm of the dead.) Since God has "brought up" his soul from death, all the psalmist can do is praise: "I will extol you, O LORD."

The psalm suggests, in fact, that praise of God is the true purpose of human existence. That assumption underlies the fine sarcasm in verse 9: "What profit is there in my death? / . . . Will the dust praise you?" This implies that it is in God's self-interest to heal the supplicant; but on a deeper level, the psalmist is reminding us why we were created in the first place—to glorify God.

In verse 4, the psalmist interrupts his testimony to urge the congregation to join him in praise. The superscription to the psalm indicates it was used during the Feast of Dedication (Hanukkah), which celebrated the restoration of proper worship to the Temple. Though couched in the words of an individual, this psalm offers a fitting vehicle for corporate praise after a national crisis: "You have turned my mourning into dancing." It shows the spiritual power unleashed when a whole community speaks what God has done for them.

In verse 6, the psalmist confesses that his initial prosperity had given him a false sense of security. Confident in his own resources, he had forgotten God. His illness caused him to reassess the true source of his strength.

Epistle: 1 Corinthians 9:24-27

Continuing his exhortation on the importance of self-discipline, Paul makes a comparison the Corinthians would have understood immediately: he urges them to exercise the same self-control as do athletes in training. Corinth hosted the Isthmian Games, one of four important Greek athletic competitions. The Corinthians would have been familiar with the rules of the games and with the long, rigorous training required of athletes.

Paul uses the analogy of athletic contests several times in his letters: Galatians 2:2; Philippians 3:12-16. He reminds young Timothy that "no one is crowned without competing according to the rules" (2 Timothy 2:5). Though Paul's image is apt, pious Jews had ambivalent feelings about the athletic contests because the games were often affiliated with pagan deities and athletes competed in the nude. This metaphor is an example of how Paul tried to "become all things to all people" (1 Corinthians 9:22), using something from Gentile culture to help the Corinthian Christians grow in faith.

Eyes on the Prize

Notoriously lax, self-indulgent, and boastful, the Corinthians needed a bracing of their wills. Paul promises that the prize they will obtain at the end of the Christian race would not be the perishable athlete's wreath made of laurel or wilted celery, but the lasting prize of a life in Christ Jesus.

The Bodily Temple

Some Christians have taken Paul's phrase, "I punish my body and enslave it" (literally, "I give myself a black eye") to justify neglecting or debasing their bodies. A few, like European flagellants in the Middle Ages, engaged in masochistic spiritual practices such as severe fasting or scourging. Paul's exhortation here should be read alongside his glorification of the body in 1 Corinthians 6:19: "Do you not know that your body is a temple of the Holy Spirit within you?" Paul urged the Corinthians to follow his example of self-mastery so they, too, could share in the blessings of the gospel.

> **Think About It:** How might you exercise healthy bodily habits in order to glorify God?

Gospel: Mark 1:40-45

Mark's opening chapter establishes Jesus' authority and sets the scope of his ministry. Having been baptized and tempted, Jesus preached and called disciples, cast out demons and healed diseases; then he cleansed a leper.

A Climactic Cleansing

The cleansing climaxed Jesus' early ministry because people in that day considered lepers as good as dead. Leprosy was seen as a highly contagious, ritually contaminating disease. The law of Moses could do nothing to help lepers, only protect others from them. Lepers were quarantined and required by law to wear torn clothes and to cry out, "Unclean, unclean," whenever anyone approached. (See Leviticus 13–14 for rules regarding leprosy.)

A Remarkable Response

The leper came to Jesus begging to be made clean, declaring his faith that Jesus could heal him. Jesus' response was remarkable in several ways. First, Jesus did not draw back. Second (verse 41), Jesus felt a strong wave of emotion. Some manuscripts describe this as "pity" or "compassion," similar to his reaction to the crowd in 6:34, who were "like sheep without a shepherd." Others record that Jesus was "moved with anger." Was Jesus angry at the leper for approaching him? at the horrible disease that had caused such suffering? at the religious authorities who had been unable to help the man? Given Jesus' strong reaction to the demon in 1:21-28 (Jesus rebukes, silences, and exorcises it), his anger is probably directed at the leprosy itself.

> **Think About It:** Jesus extended the boundaries of God's love to include the outcast. From whom do you draw back? Who are social outcasts in our day? How might we touch them with God's love?

The third remarkable thing about Jesus' response to the leper is that Jesus touched and healed him. Risking ritual defilement, Jesus extended the boundaries of God's love to include the outcast. Yet he instructed the man to follow the prescribed practice of the law: "Go, show yourself to the priest, and offer for your cleansing what Moses commanded, as a testimony to them." This shows that Jesus honored the law, an important point for Mark to make, since the next chapter shows Jesus in conflict with the religious leaders.

Secrecy Versus Disclosure

Jesus also "sternly warned" the man to keep quiet about his healing. This warning, delivered with more great emotion (literally, "roared at" or "snorted"), continued Jesus' practice of trying to keep his identity secret until his true nature was revealed by his suffering and resurrection. But the man at once blurted out the healing. This tension between secrecy and disclosure is seen throughout the Gospel. Jesus did not want to be seen merely as a miracle worker. The greater the miracle, the more likely people would misunderstand him.

Messianic Fever

It is no wonder the people mobbed Jesus (1:33, 37). Expectation of the Messiah, inflamed by the troubled times, had been brought to fever pitch by the preaching of John the Baptist. Jews were looking for God's Anointed One, who would defeat evil powers and restore the rule of God. Exorcism of demons and curing of epilepsy were signs of God's power.

To cleanse a leper fulfilled another expectation of the Messiah. The disciples of John the Baptist asked Jesus point-blank, "Are you the one who is to come?" Jesus replied, "Go and tell John what you hear and see: the blind receive their sight, the lame walk, the lepers are cleansed, the deaf hear, the dead are raised, and the poor have good news brought to them" (Matthew 11:4-5). Partly hidden and partly revealed, the Messiah was known by what he said and did.

Study Suggestions

A. Open With Praise

Form two groups. Read Psalm 30:4-5 responsively, alternating parts halfway through each verse, when the idea is repeated.

B. Explore the Life of Elisha

Invite group members to read 2 Kings 5:1-14 aloud, assigning different members the voices of the different characters: narrator, slave girl, Naaman, king of Aram, king of Israel, Elisha, and Naaman's servant. After the reading, invite participants to reflect on hearing the story this way. What struck you during the reading? What tensions did you notice among the characters? How were the tensions resolved?

Read "Give God the Glory" on pages 88–89. Ask members to think about recent stories in the news. List incidents in which someone has been healed in a surprising way, someone mighty has been humbled, or tensions between two nations have been eased. How is God at work in these events?

C. The Body and Self-Control

Have group members list the athletic activities in which they have participated. Discuss: How did these activities help you learn self-control? What parallels do you draw between athletic training and Christian practice?

Look closely at 1 Corinthians 9:24-27 and the commentary on pages 90–91. What is the point in Paul's sports analogy? If athletes will train so vigorously for a modest reward, to what length does Paul suggest Christians should go to "win the prize in Christ"? What does this mean for your devotion and discipleship?

D. Consider Illness and Prosperity

Review the last paragraph under Psalm 30 on page 90. Invite members to reflect silently on times of illness or trouble in their lives. Ask: Did the crisis cause you to reach out for God in a new way? How did your priorities change as a result of the difficulty?

E. Compare Jesus and Elisha

Read Mark 1:40-45 and 2 Kings 5:1-14. Compare the two healing stories. How was each accomplished? How does the method meet the needs of the person being healed? What does the method of healing say about each prophet?

Review what you know about the ministries of Elisha and Jesus. Using the commentary and ideas from group members, compare their ministries. What did they do that was similar? different? How was Jesus more than a prophet?

F. Push Out Boundaries

Make the following headings on chalkboard or large sheet of poster paper: family, church, workplace, community, nation. Under each heading list groups of persons who are outsiders or outcasts in each setting. Brainstorm ideas on how to push out the boundaries of concern in each category. What did Jesus do to welcome outcasts? What might we do?

Roleplay what might happen if a homeless person, an ex-offender, or one of another race came to your fellowship time or worship service.

G. Close With Prayer

After singing "Help Us Accept Each Other," close with a "bidding prayer" during which the leader names the following groups of persons, allowing spaces of silence in between: the sick, the grieving, the disabled, the outcasts, and those struggling with addictions. Have members pray silently for God's blessing on each group as they are named. Conclude with the Lord's Prayer.

Lections for Seventh Sunday After the Epiphany

T Old Testament: Isaiah 43:18-25

THIS passage is directed to the exiles in Babylon between 545 and 539 B.C. who thought God had forgotten them. They despaired of ever returning to their homeland; yet this passage holds promise.

Announcement

Today's lection contains an announcement (43:18-21), an accusation (43:22-24), and a pardon (43:25). God is about to do a new thing, the prophet announces; it is already springing forth. What is it? A "way in the wilderness" (43:19).

Because the preceding verses alluded to the Exodus (43:16-17), scholars believe this "new thing" refers to a new "exodus," a joyous return to Palestine from exile. As in the first Exodus, God would provide water for the refugees in the wilderness so they do not die of thirst. In fact, there will be rivers in the desert, a powerful image for people from an arid land. Wild animals will "honor" God (43:20) and not harm the travelers, who will journey in safety and joy.

Think About It: "See, I am doing a new thing!" (verse 19, NIV). Do you sometimes get trapped in old patterns and practices? What "new thing" might God be trying to do in your life? your church? our society? the world?

The New Exodus

In this new exodus the vision of abundant water and cosmic harmony echoes both paradise (Genesis 2) and "the peaceable kingdom" (Isaiah 11:6-9). The prophet skillfully evokes earlier traditions of Creation and the Exodus to describe what God will soon do on behalf of the people; yet the new thing will be so

94

remarkable that even the old deliverance will pale in comparison (43:18), causing the people to forget their complaints (43:22) and burst forth with praise (43:21).

Accusation

The announcement of the new exodus is followed, however, by an accusation couched in the legal language of the courtroom. God accuses the people of Israel of misdirected worship. The order of the words in the original Hebrew makes the point: "Not to me did you bring your sheep for burnt offerings; it was not I whom you honored with your sacrifices" (43:23). Perhaps the accusation is of hypocrisy and injustice as in Amos 5:21-24—the people bring offerings to God while oppressing the poor. Or perhaps the charge is idolatry or religiosity, making sacrifices to pagan gods or substituting empty ritual acts for genuine devotion to God.

Thus, instead of serving God with their offerings, the people expect God to serve them, a meaning conveyed by a wordplay with the Hebrew verb 'bad (to serve or to work) in verses 23b and 24b. Though they have complained of feeling burdened by God's expectations, they have actually burdened God with their sins. Their misguided worship has brought their own suffering upon them. This message is consistent with earlier prophets who predicted the Exile as God's righteous judgment against a sinful people.

Pardon

Yet God forgives them, not because they are worthy or repentant, but because God is gracious. "I, I am He who blots out your transgressions for my own sake" (43:25). This language of self-disclosure echoes God's revelation of his name to Moses ("I AM WHO I AM") in Exodus 3:14. Here God manifests the divine self through unmerited pardon. The same God who delivered Hebrew slaves out of Egypt will bring the sinful but forgiven exiles home.

Psalter: Psalm 41

Psalm 41 begins with a beatitude, a statement of God's blessing upon those who show concern for the poor. Verses 1-3 promise deliverance, protection, happiness, and health from God. The beatitude gives the psalmist confidence that God will heal his illness (41:4-9). He considers himself one who shows concern for the poor and thus can expect to share in the blessings of God's reign.

The psalmist prays twice for healing (41:4, 10), confessing his sin and asking God to be gracious. His plea is even more poignant because his enemies are gloating over his misfortune, gossiping about his impending death. Even a close friend has deserted him. Though the psalmist sounds slightly para-noid, popular theology of that time held that illness was a sign of God's dis-favor. His frustration with his enemies boils over in a desire for revenge: "Raise me up, that I may repay them" (41:10). He is comforted by the thought that their failure to defeat him is a sign of God's favor.

Although the psalmist's assumption that God would condone revenge makes us uncomfortable, his less-than-admirable feelings remind us that God's concern for the poor means justice. Those who oppress others will be held accountable.

Psalm 41 concludes the first of five sections of the Book of Psalms. Psalm 1:1 praises the blessed for being open to God's wisdom, while Psalm 41 com-mands concern for the poor. Thus love of God and love of neighbor, a main theme of the Torah, frame this portion of the Psalms.

Epistle: 2 Corinthians 1:18-22

In this passage, Paul is explaining to the church at Corinth why he did not visit them after leaving Macedonia as he had first promised. The Corinthians, whose church was established by Paul about A.D. 50–52, appear to be jeal-ous of Paul's affections. Paul's critics there have accused him of "vacillating" (1:17) in relation to them.

The "Yes" of God

Paul responds to their attack by reminding them of his special regard for them ("you are our boast"—1:14) and then by affirming what is most impor-tant: an unambiguous proclamation of the gospel of Jesus Christ (1:19). Paul makes a profound statement of faith in verse 20: "In [Jesus Christ] every one of God's promises is a 'Yes.' " This affirmation is similar to Romans 1:1-2 where Paul states that Christ is a fulfillment of God's promises "through his prophets in the holy scriptures."

By shifting the argument in this way, Paul turns the attention from his per-sonal defects to the faith that binds them all together. He recalls the word "Amen" ("so be it") that the Corinthians speak aloud during worship (1:20). That word can only be spoken, Paul says, through the power of Christ to the glory of God. In this way Paul moves past their criticism and his own defen-siveness to describe what God is doing in their midst.

God at Work

Paul uses four verbs in verses 21-22 to describe God's work: *establish, anoint, seal,* and *give* the Spirit. The words *seal* and *anoint* recall the act of baptism. When Paul speaks of giving the Spirit, he uses the image of "a down payment" or "earnest money," suggesting that even greater things will come.

Although the word *trinity* is not used by Paul, the passage is thoroughly trinitarian. The persons of the godhead—God, the Son of God, and the Spirit—are named.

As a last thrust, Paul declares that he postponed his visit in order to spare them pain. Having earlier sent them a stinging letter (either lost to us or included as portions of the letters we have), Paul did not want to visit again until tensions eased. He concludes in 2:4 by again professing his "abundant love" for them in Christ.

Gospel: Mark 2:1-12

Chapter 2 begins a new section of Mark's Gospel, one that reflects the mounting opposition of religious authorities to Jesus. Five conflict-ridden scenes illumine key issues in Jesus' ministry about which he makes an authoritative pronouncement. Each scene demonstrates a central truth about Jesus. The section also addresses the early church's question of why Jesus, who brought good news to the people, was met with hostility and abuse.

Teaching About Forgiveness

In the opening scene, verses 1-12, the issue is whether Jesus has the authority to forgive sins. The teaching about forgiveness is conveyed during a dramatic healing. Having returned to his home in Capernaum after a time in the country, Jesus was surrounded by a crowd. Four friends of a paralyzed man lowered him on a pallet through the roof. (The writer was not familiar with Palestinian architecture. He assumed a roof of tiles that could be easily removed and replaced.) When Jesus told the man that his sins were forgiven, some scribes present accused him of blasphemy. Only God can forgive sins, the scribes were thinking, which is indeed true. Reading their minds (a sign of divine power in itself), Jesus answered their question with a question: Which is easier, to forgive sins or to heal?

It is unclear what Jesus meant by this question. Was he implying that forgiveness was harder than physical healing? Was he trying to get them to think about the relation between sin and illness? Jesus told them that the Son of Man (himself) had authority to forgive sins, and he told the paralyzed man to get up and walk. He walked.

Faithful Friends

When the paralyzed man was brought before him, Jesus commended the four friends for their faith. In this story, faith is evidenced by determination and ingenuity. Their faith helped bring about healing for their friend.

Think About It: Has the faith of another ever been instrumental in your healing or growth? Have you helped bring healing to someone else?

The Shadow of the Cross

The scribes, who with the Pharisees functioned as interpreters of the Mosaic law, charged Jesus with blasphemy. This was a serious charge, punishable by death (Leviticus 24:16). The charge of blasphemy will be hurled at Jesus again in Mark 14:64 during his trial before the Sanhedrin, the council of Jewish leaders. Thus the shadow of the cross fell upon Jesus as early Chapter 2 in the Gospel of Mark.

Who Is This Jesus?

Jesus' own self-designation was "Son of Man." This term has two uses in the New Testament. One use is simply a circumlocution for the word *I*. The other use relates to the divine figure who comes from heaven to establish God's rule on earth. Scholars are divided on how the term *Son of Man* is being used in this passage.

We know, however, that when the scribes said "no one can forgive sins but God alone," Jesus would have agreed. His argument with them was that he believed he did have authority from God to forgive sins. (The early church later claimed this same power to forgive sins in Jesus' name.) Mark presents the scribes' comment about Jesus as ironic—they said something true about Jesus without even knowing it. Mark gives us a paradoxical portrait of Jesus in this passage—a lowly, "common" fellow, yet God's representative.

Study Suggestions

A. Open With Assurance

Read in unison Psalm 41:1-4. Reflect on the ways God has guided and sustained you this week.

B. Examine the Exodus

Read Exodus 15:22-27, Isaiah 43:18-25, and "Announcement" and "The New Exodus" of the Isaiah commentary on pages 94–95. What themes in the Exodus passage recur in Isaiah? What new elements occur? What does God expect from the people (Isaiah 43:21)?

C. Make Confession

Read Isaiah 43:22-25, and review some prayers of confession and pardon in your hymnal or worship book. Have participants write a prayer confessing the sins that God accuses the Israelites of committing in Isaiah 43:22-24. Then write words of pardon based on Isaiah 43:25. Read the prayers aloud. Discuss: What parts of the confession speak most powerfully to you? What does it mean to receive the word of pardon from the church?

D. Characterize Paul

Review 2 Corinthians 1:18-22 and the commentary on pages 96–97. How would you characterize Paul's relationship with the Corinthians based on this passage? (Read a few verses before and after the passage for the context.) How would one of Paul's critics describe him? Are Paul's arguments persuasive?

E. Rely on God's Promises

"In [Jesus Christ] every one of God's promises is a 'Yes,' " Paul says in 2 Corinthians 1:20a. Ask: How is Christ a positive influence in your life or others in your church? What is the "Yes" you have received from Christ?

F. Consider the Poor

Psalm 41:1 says, "Happy are those who consider the poor." Make an inventory of the ways you care for the poor: as an individual, a church member, a citizen. Which of these involve direct contact with the poor? What benefits have you experienced when caring for the poor?

G. Renounce Revenge

Review Psalm 41:5-10. What does the psalmist want from God? Does God grant prayers that are motivated by revenge? What is the Christian's response to psalms seeking revenge and expressing blood lust (41:10; 139:19-22; 137:8-9)?

H. Imagine Healing

Invite members to close their eyes while listening to Mark 2:1-12 and to imagine themselves as the paralyzed man. Read the passage slowly, then invite them to meditate on these questions, leaving time for silence after each question: What does it feel like to be helpless on the pallet? taken up to the roof and lowered down? What does Jesus say to your friends? What does he say to you? Of what sins would Jesus need to forgive you? How do you react when the scribes object? What does Jesus say to them? What does it feel like to be told to stand up? What is it like to feel your legs underneath you again? How do the others in the crowd react? What do you say to God afterwards?

I. Close With Prayer

Review the themes of these lections: devotion to God versus complaining; giving thanks versus seeking revenge; standing up for the gospel versus waffling; challenging authority for good versus playing it safe and doing nothing. Encourage members to pray silently for strength and courage to do the faithful thing. Then sing "Stand Up for Jesus."

Lections for Eighth Sunday After the Epiphany

Old Testament: Hosea 2:14-20

$\mathcal{A}$CCORDING to Hosea 1:1, the ministry of Hosea spanned three decades and five kings in the eighth century B.C. Hosea prophesied in Israel during a time of political instability, economic oppression, and indifferent religion. People worshiped the Canaanite storm-god, Baal, in addition to YHWH. Hosea's ministry ended with the fall of Israel's capital, Samaria, in 721 B.C. Later generations understood his words to mandate the religious and moral reforms of King Josiah and to explain the devastation of the Babylonian Exile.

Marriage as Metaphor

In the first three chapters, Hosea presents marriage as a metaphor for God's relationship with the people, picturing God as the husband of a promiscuous wife. Hosea uses his relationship with his own wife, Gomer, described in 1:2 as a "wife of whoredom," to reflect God's abiding love for Israel despite its unfaithfulness.

In 2:1-13, God/Hosea tells Gomer's children to beg her to repent, threatening to disown them and punish her (2:2-4). He says he will strip her naked, withhold food and water, isolate her from her lovers, and allow animals to destroy her vineyards (2:3-12) because she made offerings to pagan gods ("the Baals"—2:13).

After punishment will come a time of reconciliation in the wilderness, described in 2:14-20. God/Hosea will "allure" her and speak tenderly to her, restoring her vineyards (2:14-15). She will respond ardently to him, and no longer speak of the Baals (2:16-17). God will create a new covenant with her and the whole creation so that she need not fear destruction (2:18). It will be

100

a remarriage, the man giving five virtues as the bride price for her: righteousness (personal morality), justice (social equity), steadfast love (dependable compassion), mercy (tender forgiveness), and faithfulness (loyal devotion) (2:19-20). She shall "know" the Lord—a euphemism for sexual intimacy (2:20). The husband later claims the children, whose paternity he had earlier doubted, as his own (2:23).

Problems With Hosea

Though intended to convey the patient and forgiving love of God in the face of Israel's sinfulness, Hosea's daring nuptial metaphor poses problems for the modern reader. It assumes the unequal gender relations of ancient Israel in which women's sexual fidelity was rigidly enforced to ensure legitimate heirs for her husband. The metaphor depicts a father using his children as pawns in a conflict with his wife. It employs violence and shaming as methods of altering behavior. The scene equates evil with the female character. The absolute faithfulness of the husband to the faithless wife might be construed by some to represent an abusive relationship.

Hosea's metaphor effectively conveys his utter horror that the people of Israel would jeopardize their relationship with YHWH by making offerings to other gods. The word of hope from this Scripture might be that *God* restores the relationship after it has been broken, promising that the new covenant will never end: "I will take you for my wife in faithfulness" (2:20). The wilderness setting of 2:14 echoes the Exodus story when God delivered the people from slavery. God takes the initiative when sinful humanity cannot.

> *Think About It:* In Israel, an adulterous wife would be put to death. Hosea depicts God saving the woman from death and restoring the marriage. Does Hosea's overall picture of God offer you hope and healing? How does Jesus' image of God compare with Hosea's? What draws you into relationship with God?

Psalter: Psalm 103:1-13, 22

Unlike many psalms created for use in Temple worship, Psalm 103 has an inward focus. The psalmist addresses his own soul rather than the congregation: "Bless the Lord, O my soul, / and all that is within me, / bless his holy name" (103:1). The word "all" recalls the *Shema*: "You shall love the Lord your God with *all* your heart, and with *all* your soul, and with *all* your might" (Deuteronomy 6:5, italics added). The psalmist is honoring God with every particle of his being.

Realizing how often we forget God, the psalmist exhorts himself to remember all that God has done for him (103:2-5) and for his people (103:6-

13). The list of benefits begins with forgiveness. We cannot appreciate God's bounty when we are still separated by sin. The psalmist remembers how God has healed, redeemed, crowned, and satisfied him. His gratitude is so profound that he feels young and strong again, like an eagle, as in Isaiah 40:31: "they shall mount up . . . like eagles."

The next section recalls God's central act on behalf of Israel, their deliverance from oppression in Egypt. Psalm 103 spoke powerfully to the exiles in Babylon who needed to be reminded of God's care and forgiveness. The prophets had been saying the Exile was God's judgment for their apostasy; they needed to hear that God "will not always accuse, nor will he keep his anger forever" (103:9). Verses 8-13 affirm that God will remove their sins as far "as the east is from the west" (103:12). God will have compassion on them like a father for his children (103:13). The psalm concludes in verse 22 with an invitation for the whole creation to join in blessing God.

Psalm 103 combines individual thankfulness and communal memory, majesty and intimacy in a song of praise.

Epistle: 2 Corinthians 3:1-6

Paul pursues two themes here: defending his leadership and contrasting the old and new covenants. His opponents, who appear to have come to Corinth with letters of recommendation from the Jerusalem church, had been challenging Paul's authority. Paul proceeded carefully. If he did not respond to their charges, he seemed weak; if he defended himself, he would sound self-righteous. Moreover, in refuting his opponents, he could not seem to attack the Jerusalem apostles whose recommendation they carried.

A Letter of Recommendation
Paul's response was brilliant. He began by voicing his opponents' own charge of "commending" himself to them (3:1), thus disarming them. Then he described the Corinthians themselves as *his* letter of recommendation. Their Christian witness was all the credential he needed. Moreover, Paul wrote, as a "letter of Christ" (3:3) they have been written not with ink but by the Spirit. So Paul was merely the scribe or carrier of the Spirit.

Here Paul is making an important theological statement: competence in ministry comes from God, not human ability. This undercuts undue emphasis on personal charisma and spiritual gifts.

Written on the Heart
Paul's image of the Corinthians themselves as a letter of Christ written upon the hearts recalls Jeremiah 31:31, 33: "I will make a new covenant with the house of Israel. . . . I will put my law within them, and I will write it on

102

their hearts." Echoing Jeremiah's contrast of the covenant made at Sinai on stone and the new covenant on the heart, Paul declares himself to be a minister of that new covenant in Christ. The "letter" of the old covenant deals death, because it cannot empower; but the "Spirit" gives life and empowers righteous living. Paul continues the theme of the superiority of the new covenant in Chapter 3, as well as in Galatians 3:19-29 and Romans 7:7–8:17.

Gospel: Mark 2:13-22

These verses continue the challenge mounted by Jesus' opponents in the Gospel of Mark. He was here questioned on two issues: his contact with sinners and his disciples' failure to fast.

The Call of Levi

The first challenge came just after the call of Levi, which resembled the call of Peter, Andrew, James, and John in 1:16-20. In these earlier call scenes, men engaged in respectable occupations heard Jesus say, "Follow me," and dropped everything to follow. The difference here is that Levi would not have been seen as a proper candidate for a disciple. Tax collectors were regarded as unscrupulous collaborators with the Roman government, who often hiked the excise taxes for their own profit. Since meals were an important setting for business and social contacts, Levi would have attended meals hosted by Gentiles, contrary to strict Pharisaic legal practice.

Eating With Sinners

Not only did Jesus call Levi to follow him, he also sat down to eat with Levi's friends—described as "tax collectors and sinners." A "sinner" was one who deliberately disregarded Jewish law, those whom Psalm 1 warns against: "Happy are those / who do not follow the advice of the wicked, / or take the path that sinners tread, / or sit in the seat of scoffers" (Psalm 1:1). Sinners are contrasted with the righteous, whose "delight is in the law of the Lord" (1:2).

When the scribes of the Pharisees, a sect especially concerned with ritual purity, saw Jesus with tax collectors and sinners, they asked why he did this. (Notice how the *disciples* are put to the test here.) The Pharisees' insistence on rigorous personal holiness was intended to keep the Jewish community intact in the midst of foreign influence from pagan culture. Jesus' contact with sinners was viewed as dangerous assimilation.

> ***Think About It:*** Jesus' disciples were confronted about his behavior. How would you respond about your devotion to his actions and principles?

Jesus answered with a well-known proverb and a statement about his mission: "Those who are well have no need of a physician. . . . I have come to call not the righteous but sinners" (Mark 2:17). Levi and his ilk were exactly the ones for whom Jesus had come. Jesus reached out to sinners with God's grace.

What About Fasting?

The second challenge to Jesus was a question about fasting. Although not required by law, Pharisees fasted twice a week. Apparently Jesus and his disciples did not observe religious fasts. What kind of holy people were they? Jesus responded with an analogy: Wedding guests cannot fast while the bridegroom is with them, can they (2:19)? The image of a wedding banquet conveyed the sense of joy of those who had gathered around Jesus. The revolutionary nature of their community is expressed by the next sayings (1:21-22). Jesus, the new wine, is bursting the old wineskins!

There would be time for fasting, however, Jesus said, when his opposition hardened and he was "taken away from them" (1:20). This prediction was taken to heart by the early church, which observed a fast on Wednesdays and Fridays.

Table Fellowship

Given the importance of meals in those times and Jesus' practice of dining with disciples, it is not surprising that issues around eating were crucial topics in the early church. Jesus told two parables that expressed the salvation of God in the image of a banquet (Luke 14:16-24; Matthew 25:1-13). Moreover, every shared meal with his disciples became an acted parable of the reign of God, finally expressed in the Last Supper. Mark 2:13-22 shows us that more important than feasting and fasting is to make all welcome at God's table.

Study Suggestions

A. Open With Praise

Recite together Psalm 103:1-5. Recall and share how God has blessed you in the past week.

B. Make Some Metaphors

Metaphors employ a familiar word or image to represent an abstract idea. What is the difference between literal and figurative language? How does figurative language help us understand God?

Read Hosea 2:14-20 and the commentary on pages 100–101. Review how Hosea uses marriage as a metaphor for Israel's relationship with God. How do understandings of marriage in ancient Israel and modern America differ? What concerns do you have about Hosea's metaphor?

Form two groups, and have members brainstorm other metaphors besides marriage for our relationship with God (such as parent/child or shepherd/sheep). Scripture, hymns, prayers, and personal experience all yield metaphors for God. Choose several metaphors and reflect on them with these questions: What does the metaphor say about God? about us? Whose experience does the metaphor assume? Who is left out?

C. A Letter of Recommendation

Read 2 Corinthians 3:1-4 and the commentary on pages 102–103. Why is Paul defending himself? What does he mean by: "You yourselves are our letter"?

Pretend that someone has called into question the leadership of your congregation. What would the "letter of recommendation" look like that is written on your hearts? What do others "read" about Christ from your life? How does your lifestyle witness to your faith in Christ?

D. Remember God's Blessings

Review the list of things God has done for the psalmist in Psalm 103:1-5. Make your own list of what God has done for you, being sure to include material as well as spiritual blessings.

Review Psalm 103:6-13. How has God blessed our nation? Are any of the things we count as "blessings" obtained at the expense of others? How can we share our blessings with others?

Sometimes we advise each other to "count your blessings," like the psalmist does in 103:3-5. What is the purpose of recounting God's blessings?

E. Study the Gospel

Form three groups. Have each group retell the events of Mark 2:13-17 from one of the following points of view: Levi's friends, the disciples, the scribes. Ask: How does Jesus unsettle their assumptions about themselves? about the other groups?

Reflect on what kinds of persons attend your church. Are people in your church trying hard to be better than persons outside the church? Are "notorious sinners" welcome? If we teach our children to be careful when choosing friends, what does it mean to keep company with Jesus, who "came to call not the righteous, but sinners"?

The scribes challenged Jesus indirectly through his disciples. The disciples had to assess their loyalty to Jesus. When have you been challenged on being a Christian? How did you respond?

Review Mark 2:18-20 and the commentary on "What About Fasting?" Poll the group: Do you fast? Why or why not? What does fasting accomplish? Why is it so difficult in our culture?

F. Close With Singing

Sing a hymn of gratitude (such as "Count Your Blessings") or a hymn of challenge (such as "Where Charity and Love Prevail").

Lections for Transfiguration Sunday

T Old Testament: 2 Kings 2:1-12

HIS episode brings to a close the ministry of Elijah, a beloved Jewish prophet. Elijah had distinguished himself in God's service by opposing the worship of the Canaanite deity Baal promoted by Jezebel and Ahab. He also had worked great wonders in God's name (such as the resuscitation of the son of the widow of Zarephath). Such an extraordinary agent of God could have no ordinary end. The focus of this passage is not simply on Elijah's ascension into heaven while still alive but also on the "passing of the mantle" from Elijah to Elisha, whom God had already designated Elijah's successor in 1 Kings 19:16.

A Double Share of Spirit

In the sober procession to the place designated by God, Elisha followed his master with a loyalty that overrode Elijah's explicit commands to stay behind (2 Kings 2:2, 4, 6). Elisha requested that he receive a double share of Elijah's spirit (2:9). By this he did not mean twice as much of God's power as Elijah himself had. Rather, he was referring to the inheritance practices of ancient Israel. Traditionally the eldest son received two shares of the parents' estate as compared to the single share received by each of the other sons. He asked that the symbolic act that Elijah had used originally to call Elisha (1 Kings 19:19) now be made real in his appointment as heir to the powerful, principal prophet.

He was granted his petition, even though it caused him deep grief to lose his mentor and friend (2 Kings 2:12b). When Elisha used Elijah's mantle to part the waters of the Jordan just as Elijah had done on his way to his departure site (2:8), the company of prophets bore witness that Elisha was indeed worthy to be Elijah's successor (2:13-15).

The Eschatological Prophet

The lack of a real ending to the story of Elijah's ministry invited speculation in Jewish folklore concerning Elijah's potential role in the ongoing story of God's acts on Israel's behalf. The Old Testament closes with the announcement that God "will send you the prophet Elijah" to prepare the people before the day of God's visitation. By turning the hearts of parents and children to one another, Elijah will avert the "curse" of God's judgment (Malachi 4:5-6; see also Sirach 48:10).

> ***Think About It:*** Who have been spiritual mentors in your life? How did they pass on to you the benefits of their experience and wisdom? Have you been able to become a mentor to someone younger than you? Of what did your mantle consist?

This week's Gospel lection will draw on this tradition, as does the passage that immediately follows it (Mark 9:10-13). There Jesus, answering a question about this Elijah tradition raised by the disciples, claims that Elijah has in fact already fulfilled his end-time ministry in the person of John the Baptist, whose fate at the hands of Herod confirms that the Messiah must also suffer.

Psalter: Psalm 50:1-6

This psalm has been connected with Israel's ceremony for covenant renewal. This important ritual focused on the reading aloud of Deuteronomy to the worshipers assembled in the Temple, the offering of sacrifices repeating the inauguration of the covenant with God, and the rededication of the whole people to keep God's commandments.

The psalm was to be read at dawn to begin the ceremony, so that the sunrise would add impact to the worshipers as they considered God shining forth from Zion with fire "all around him" (50:2-3). It summons heaven and earth to bear witness to the acts about to transpire, just as Moses had called heaven and earth as witnesses the first time the book was read (Deuteronomy 31:28; 32:1). The language of fire and tempest recalls the natural disturbances that accompanied God's first appearance to the people in Exodus 19:16-19.

The remainder of the psalm reminds the hearers that God has no need of sacrifices. The people's first aim must be to offer thanksgiving to God and to fulfill the promises made by their parents and ancestors—to keep God's covenant faithfully. Doing so pleases God and will result in God's speedy rescue in the day of trouble. The wicked are warned not to become comfortable with sin on account of God's silence. God will break in to judge the sinner and deliver those who are steadfastly committed to keeping God's law.

Epistle: 2 Corinthians 4:3-6

Paul wrote Second Corinthians after some troubling developments in his relationship with the Corinthian Christians. These believers were already given to weighing one preacher over another and forming "fan clubs" around favorites (1 Corinthians 1:10-13; 3:1-9). Some teachers had arrived who were more than happy to play to this tendency to Paul's detriment. They challenged the worth of Paul's message and criticized his weaknesses—not to mention the disgraces to which he was being subjected. After a member of the church openly challenged Paul when he made a brief visit after writing First Corinthians, Paul retreated and wrote a "painful letter" now lost to us (2 Corinthians 2:1-4). That letter hit the congregation hard, since they had begun to rekindle their appreciation and love for Paul. But the battle was far from won.

Rival Teachers

In this brief passage, Paul attacks the rival teachers and the values they were promoting. Those preachers merely preached themselves, basing the appeal of their "gospel" on their own fine speech, classy appearance, and "spiritual" demeanor. Paul, however, refused to proclaim himself, but only proclaimed the crucified and risen Lord. As to his trials and hardships (see 4:7-15), these were signs of his service for Christ. Far from disqualifying himself in their eyes, his sufferings should earn him their gratitude and loyalty since he endured them for the sake of his congregations and the gospel.

Think About It: On what basis do you judge the character and contribution of others and yourself? How might this differ from how God judges?

The gospel Paul preached (and not the opponents' domesticated message) ultimately separates "those who are being saved" from "those who are perishing" (2:15; 4:3). If people (including rival teachers) did not find God's wisdom in the cross of Jesus, this was because they had fallen prey to the deception perpetrated by Satan ("the god of this age"). In Jesus, rejected and shamed by the world but honored by God, one sees the world for what it really is. The true messenger and disciple surely will not betray the message by appealing to worldly values to gain acceptance.

Gospel: Mark 9:2-9

The Transfiguration is an enigmatic story. Jesus spoke with Moses and Elijah, but we are not privy to their conversation. (Luke 9:31 provides only a brief conjecture.) Peter's suggestion went nowhere, arising from befuddlement rather than insight. The mystical moment passed as suddenly and quickly as it had come, and the four men simply returned to their ministry.

God's Authentication of Jesus' Way

The significance of this event emerges from the "voice from the cloud" (9:7). God's voice is heard only twice in the Gospel of Mark: at Jesus' baptism and at his transfiguration (see Mark 1:9-11). In both places God identified Jesus as the "beloved Son." In the first event, God attested that he is "well pleased" with Jesus, and now God commands the hearers to listen to Jesus. This is an important moment in Jesus' ministry, in which God again breaks in to uphold Jesus' teaching and example, to demonstrate that the one who follows and obeys this Jesus will also be pleasing to God.

The context in which this episode is set, namely in the midst of Jesus' three passion and resurrection predictions (8:31-32; 9:30-32; 10:32-34) and his teachings on discipleship (8:34-38; 9:33-37; 10:41-45), is significant. As Jesus disclosed the disgrace and abuse that was about to be inflicted on him, God disclosed the honor that belongs to Jesus the Son—an honor that would remain undiminished in the Passion and be vindicated in the Resurrection.

The disciples were learning that, while the path of discipleship leads one into conflict with the values of the world, that path stands approved by God. The early interpretation of this event in 2 Peter 1:16-19 confirms this understanding, adding that the direct revelation from God and manifestation of Jesus' honor give Christians assurance that their hope for entering God's kingdom is secure.

> **Think About It:** Have you had to cope with contempt or pressure from others because you were committed to doing what Jesus called you to do? How did you maintain your self-respect and commitment?

Peter, James, and John witnessed the honor and glory that belong to the Son. The momentary change in Jesus' appearance revealed the glory that was the Son's before his incarnation, to which he would return at the Ascension. The revelation of his glory makes Jesus' teachings on servanthood (Mark 10:45) all the more striking. If the Glorious One was willing to set aside his rightful claim to "be served," how much more should the disciples renounce any such claims and seek to be like their Lord.

The Beginning of the End Time

To some, Jesus' conversation with Moses and Elijah carries special significance, for both were expected end-time agents of God. Moses' central role in God's first deliverance of God's people all but necessitated giving him a part in the end-time sequel. In an oft-quoted rabbinic passage, we read that God said to Moses, "Just as you devoted yourself to the service of my people in this world, so also in the time to come when I bring again Elijah the prophet to them you will also come with him." Some think the "two witnesses" mentioned in Revelation 11:3-11 are Elijah and Moses, who bravely stand in the end time against the beast and the wayward inhabitants of the earth. The unrecorded conversation between Jesus, Elijah, and Moses, therefore, may signify that the final interventions of God in human history were set in motion in the earthly ministry of Jesus.

Study Suggestions

A. Encounters With God

Begin by reading Psalm 50:1-6 responsively. Then review the commentary on the psalm (page 107), and invite members to name the signs of God's presence and power that they see in the world around them (verses 1, 6) and the covenants they have made before God (such as baptism, confirmation, marriage—verse 5). Ask: How do our encounters with God strengthen us to remain faithful in our covenants?

B. Taking on the Mantle

Conduct a dramatic reading of 2 Kings 2:1-12, assigning parts for a narrator, Elijah, and Elisha. Ask the others to be the group of prophets. Note that Elijah had known that Elisha would be his successor since the time of 1 Kings 19:16 (as did Elisha, 19:19). Then ask: What might have been gained or lost through Elisha's witnessing Elijah's ascension? What was the impact on Elisha and his career to see the heavenly chariots? on Peter, James, and John to experience the Transfiguration?

Ask members if they have had (or been) a mentor as Elijah was for Elisha. What influence did the mentoring relationship have on your faith and discipleship? How can you help guide the faith journey of a younger disciple as you have been guided?

Comment that Jesus calls us to observe and follow him as closely as Elisha followed and watched Elijah. Ask members to reflect on what wisdom they long to learn from Jesus, or what quality or power they want him to impart to them. How strenuously have they sought that gift? How can group members support one another in following Jesus more closely and faithfully?

C. See Jesus in a New Light

Read Mark 9:2-9 aloud. Summarize Mark 8:31–9:1 to provide the context for the story. Using the commentary on pages 108–110, explain the significance of Moses and Elijah appearing in this story. Ask: Why did Peter, James, and John need to see this sight and hear this voice?

Review the commentary under "God's Authentication of Jesus' Way." Invite members to tell of a time when they failed to follow Jesus and permitted themselves to be influenced by the opinion of others. Ask: How does the Transfiguration story aid in our struggle to choose obedience and witness?

Read aloud 2 Corinthians 4:3-6 and the commentary on page 108. Ask: How has the light of Christ broken the hold of "the god of this age" (NIV)

110

in your life? Discuss the questions in the "Think About It" box, and also: How can we give responsible feedback to each other in the church without passing judgment and becoming defensive? How can evaluation contribute to our spiritual growth?

D. Tie It Together

Discuss the common themes in today's lections—the transforming power and energizing motivation of spiritual visions, the demands of discipleship, the need for and nurture of the mentoring relationship. Ask: How will these emphases help strengthen your faith journey?

D. Close With Song and Prayer

Sing the Transfiguration hymn, "O Wondrous Sight! O Vision Fair," and pray for guidance and strength to be faithful disciples.

LENT

Lections for First Sunday in Lent

*T*Old Testament: Genesis 9:8-17

*T*HE story of Noah and the Flood is one of the most familiar stories of the Bible, especially to children. But it is not a children's story. As the story goes, human wickedness had piled up so high that God threw in the towel, packed up a starter kit for a new beginning, and eradicated the entire creation that God had made "good" at the start.

The First Covenant

Noah's first sacrifice immediately after the cataclysm had a profound effect on God. God decided never again, on account of human evil, to interrupt the course of "seedtime and harvest" (Genesis 8:22) with global catastrophe. God gave Noah and his family a short series of commandments concerning the basic groundwork for a peaceful and civil society, from which the rabbis would later derive the so-called "Noahide laws" considered to be binding on all humanity (Genesis 9:17; see Acts 15:19-21).

God then promised Noah's family by means of a solemn covenant that God would not destroy the earth and all creatures "by the waters of a flood" (Genesis 9:9-11). This speech echoes Genesis 6:17-18, where God first announced the intention to destroy "all flesh" by a flood.

From the standpoint of one form of biblical theology, this covenant begins God's "salvation history," God's determination to redeem humanity and to call for repentance and a right response. The sign of the covenant, the "rainbow," may be more than a meteorological phenomenon since the same Hebrew word also denotes the "bow" of war. The image of the divine bow is familiar in the Babylonian mythology of the ancient Near East, which identified a constellation as the bow that gave the god Marduk victory over Tiamat. Here, in contrast, the bow is hung in the sky as a sign of the determination of the "One God" never to make war on humanity or creation again.

It is significant that God's covenant is not only with Noah and his family but also with "every living creature" (verses 10, 12, 15, 16) and "all flesh that is on the earth" (verse 17). The God who created all of life is now committed to preserve and protect that life.

> ***Think About It:*** God is committed to preserve and protect every living creature. What does this say about our responsibility as children of God to preserve and protect all of creation?

The End-Time Judgment

The covenant promised the maintenance of the natural order as long as earth endured, but this was not "forever." The rainbow was not a sign that God's patience toward injustice and human evil would be limitless. Jesus saw in the "days of Noah" a parable of things to come (Matthew 24:36-39); and the early Christians read the Flood story as a prototype for the last days (see 2 Peter 3:5-7), the final "shaking" and "removal" of created things (Hebrews 12:26-27).

The passages interpret this covenant in the context of another day breaking in against human injustice and evil. This time judgment would not be merely an interruption of the natural order by a flood, but the destruction of the natural order by the end-time conflagration (2 Peter 3:7). Just as there was a new beginning with Noah, so God's creative power would again have the final say in a new beginning after this end-time cataclysm.

> ***Think About It:*** This time judgment will be the destruction of the natural order by the end-time conflagration. What is your response to the oppression, violence, and abuse occurring across the globe? How would the spirit of Jesus address this?

Psalter: Psalm 25:1-10

This psalm is an artfully composed acrostic poem, each two-line unit beginning with a subsequent letter of the Hebrew alphabet. This device, besides providing an accepted artistic frame (like rhyme in English poems), may have aided memorization as the devotee learned the "A, B, C's" of prayer.

This prayer describes the plight of the person who is committed to keeping God's law, knowing that it is the path to peace and safety but also finding two obstacles along the road. First, there are "enemies" who wish to increase their honor by bringing shame to the worshiper, who find profit in the downfall of a fellow human being.

Second, there are the worshiper's own sins—those transgressions against God's law that undermine confidence that all is right between oneself and the

One who alone can make one secure. The psalmist confesses that God's ways are right and prays for forgiveness and deliverance.

Epistle: 1 Peter 3:18-22

First Peter was written to (mainly) Gentile Christians in Asia Minor (modern Turkey). Their conversion meant leaving behind participation in idolatry, eliminating their appearance at civic festivals, public temples, private dinners given by non-Christians, and even political and business meetings. The non-Christians around them had been trying to shame, cajole, abuse, and intimidate them into returning to a more acceptable way of life—one that showed due piety to the imperial gods and solidarity with fellow citizens. First Peter was written to encourage these Christians to persevere in the face of unjust suffering, taking care to live virtuous, respectable lives so as never to give unbelievers a just cause to persecute them.

The Example of Christ

The example of Christ is central to the author's strategy for encouraging his readers. In Jesus, they can see their own future, the author asserts. Jesus endured unjust suffering rather than abandon faithfulness to God, and in the end God vindicated his honor and exalted him above every temporal and spiritual power (3:18, 21). So the believers who faithfully followed Jesus now, not intimidated by the unjust suffering inflicted by unbelievers, would arrive at "honor" and the "imperishable inheritance" (1:47). Such loyalty to Jesus was only fitting, because his sufferings were all "on [their] behalf" (3:18; 1:18-20).

"To the Spirits in Prison"

The author combines with this a secondary theme, introducing Jesus' "proclamation to the spirits in prison" and the ark as a prefiguration of baptism. Who were these disobedient "spirits," and what was Jesus' proclamation? Some say they are the souls of the human beings destroyed by the Flood, now being given an opportunity to hear the message of salvation. First Peter 4:6 would tend to support this reading if it refers to the same event. Another view regards these "spirits" as the fallen angels of Genesis 6:14, to whom Jesus proclaimed his victory over all the evil they spawned on the earth. In favor of this reading is the well-documented Jewish belief in these "watchers," whose children (the "giants") became demons after death. Stressing Jesus' triumph would also better suit the author's argument.

The Flood story provides an interpretive framework for understanding the believers' situation. Noah obeyed God and thus his family was "saved through the waters" of the Flood; similarly, the believers have joined themselves to God (and removed themselves from a godless world) through baptism, which supports their plea to God for vindication and deliverance. This is their path to salvation, insured by the resurrected Christ.

Gospel: Mark 1:9-15

Early Christians saw John the Baptist as the messenger who would prepare people for the Messiah's visitation. Mark combined two key texts (Malachi 3:1 and Isaiah 40:13) in his introduction—both of John as the "voice crying out" in the desert (Mark 1:3) and also of Jesus as the one whose way was prepared by the messenger (1:9).

Wilderness as Proving Ground

John's ministry took place in the wilderness around the Jordan, calling people out from the cities and villages of Judea to the desert to renew their commitment to God. The wilderness is an important symbol for Jews of their formative experiences in the Exodus story, the location of their years of wandering and of experiencing God's providence. In Isaiah's prophecies, the wilderness was also the royal highway Israel had to traverse as it returned from exile in Babylon.

Later readers, divorced from the context of exile abroad, would continue to hear of the "way of the Lord" in the desert and associate it with the end-time renewal of Israel. Going out into the wilderness was a way of seeking to be purified and thus prepared for the coming Messiah. So, several first-century messianic pretenders led people out into the desert in the expectation of a new crossing of the Jordan. They would take possession of the land corrupted by Romans and Hellenized Jews as a restored and free Israel.

Jesus, God's End-time Agent

Jesus came out to the Jordan to pioneer Israel's renewal. The one "who will baptize with the Holy Spirit" first submitted to the "baptism of repentance" in solidarity with the people of God. His role in this renewal is made immediately clear in the divine disclosure that followed. As Israel was once called God's son (Hosea 11:1) in the wilderness, so now Jesus was called God's beloved Son, affirmed and approved by God. Last week we read about the only other place in Mark where God "spoke" this same message. The way of discipleship (following Jesus) is the "way of the Lord," the way to the renewal of God's people.

The Gospel of Mark briefly presents Jesus' temptation by Satan, his living in the desert with the untamed beasts for forty days, and his being served by angels. With these few strokes, Mark depicts Jesus enacting the same experiences as Israel during the Exodus—tempted to turn from following God, homeless and exposed to the elements and beasts, but also finding God's help at every turn.

The Kingdom Will Come

Jesus returned from the desert to the villages of Galilee to preach the good news. Note that Christians did not invent the word *gospel* (Greek: *euangelion*); rather, this term had been used to describe the accession of the emperor Augustus. Jesus' message was an apocalyptic one: God's reign, which would succeed all earthly kingdoms, had come near (see Daniel 7 and Mark 13:14, 26). Now it was imminent. Its assumed proximity made the present time a critical opportunity for preparation by repentance and the renewal of righteousness in the land.

> **Think About It:** How do you use the present time to prepare to meet Christ? Does this remain a living hope in your life?

Study Suggestions

A. Enter God's Courts

Read Psalm 25:1-10 responsively. Then invite members to assume a stationary bodily pose reflecting their attitudes and feelings in response to phrases in the psalm like "I lift up my soul," "in you I trust," "know your ways," "for you I wait," and "steadfast love and faithfulness." Have group members respond verbally to each person's "statue," in terms of the feelings it evokes in them.

B. Beginning Lent

Comment that this is the first Sunday in Lent and that the four lections are chosen with that in mind. Explain that Lent is the forty-day period between Ash Wednesday and Easter (not counting Sundays) that traditionally has been used as a time of preparation for baptism and of special personal and corporate study, self-examination, penitence, and spiritual renewal. Note that the penitence theme is especially prominent in today's passages, and ask participants to watch it and point it out as each lection is discussed.

C. The Resolve in the Rainbow

Read Genesis 9:8-17. Note that the bow is visible mainly to God, not humans (see 9:13-16). Why? Set the passage in context using the commentary on pages 114–15. Ask: What does the Flood story tell us about God? Discuss the questions in the "Think About It" boxes.

Read aloud 2 Peter 3:3-10, an early Christian commentary on the Flood and God's promise of restraint. Ask: Does this passage still provide a meaningful view of history and a real hope? Why or why not? How might our awareness of God's purposes influence our mission to the world?

D. Weather the Floods

Read 1 Peter 3:18-22; then set the passage in its historical and social context using the explanation on pages 116–17. Explore together the two alternatives for interpreting 3:19-20. Which seems more viable? What would each reading tell us about Christ's work on behalf of the people of God?

The author draws an analogy between the ark passing through the flood waters to safety and the Christian passing through this age to safety in God's realm through baptism. Ask: How does this interpretation of the ark relate to our baptism? Explain the social setting of First Peter. Ask: Is there some specific instance where obeying Jesus' voice has led to rejection by your peers or colleagues? How can we assist or support Christians in other parts of the globe who face persecution for their faith?

E. Renewing the People of God

Invite a volunteer to read Mark 1:9-15. Invite members to share their thoughts about (1) why Jesus was baptized and (2) what the desert, the setting for 1:2-13, signifies. Inject ideas from the commentary (on pages 117–18) into this conversation as appropriate.

Ask: Have you ever had a wilderness experience in which your commitment to follow God was refined and confirmed? How did this affect your views of and relation to God's promised future and the present world? Invite volunteers to describe their experiences and the effects.

F. Closing Meditation

Read Mark 1:15, and comment that Jesus summons us to repent and to believe the gospel. Invite members to reflect silently on: For what do you need to repent this Lenten season? How does your daily life reflect trust in God? How might your life change as you engage in repentance and deepen your trust? Sing softly the Lenten hymn, "Lord, Who Throughout These Forty Days."

Lections for Second Sunday in Lent

O Old Testament: Genesis 17:1-7, 15-16

OF necessity, the lectionary editors were rather selective with this story (as was Paul, one suspects), omitting the gift of the land and the emphasis on circumcision, both signs of the covenant. The full chapter shows a definite structure, alternating between covenant promise and covenant sign: YHWH made promises to Abraham (17:18); God instituted the rite of circumcision as the sign of the covenant and determinant of who belonged to the covenant people (17:9-14); God made promises concerning Sarah (17:15-22); Abraham had himself and every male of his company circumcised in obedience to God (17:23-27).

The Making of Covenant

A covenant is a form of relationship between a higher (in this case, YHWH) and a lower (here, Israel) party, in which the former takes the initiative in "establishing" (verse 7) the nature and terms of the pact. In this agreement, the specifics included the promise to make Abraham "numerous" (17:2; see 12:2; 15:5), the progenitor of many peoples (17:4).

A sign of the covenant is that Abram was given a new status and a new name—Abraham, which means "ancestor of a multitude." Similar to the covenant with Noah, this is an enduring relationship (verses 13, 19), dependent on the steadfast love of God, not on human faithfulness.

The form of Genesis 17:17 resembles ancient Near Eastern documents in which a king made a grant of land to a loyal vassal and his descendants, often in perpetuity. Even the phrase "walk before me" (verse 1) is found in these documents, as the king acknowledged that the vassal had behaved loyally in every way—no deceit or disloyalty but complete honesty and allegiance.

Sarah Included

God specifically named Sarai as the co-progenitor of this people (17:15-16, 19, 21) and gave her a new name—Sarah, which means "princess." In Genesis 16, Abraham had produced an heir by Hagar, but now learned he would have another son, through God's blessing of his wife, Sarah, who also would be ancestor to rulers and nations.

> ***Think About It:*** Sarah was named a co-progenitor. What do you think it meant for the writer, who lived in a patriarchal society, to provide Sarah such a high social status?

The Land, a Perpetual Holding

The lection omits verse 8, which has YHWH giving the land of Canaan to Abraham and his offspring in perpetuity. Later, the prophets declared God's judgment on Israel for their idolatry and oppression and said they were being sent into exile as punishment—an exile from which they returned, only to be driven out again. Do you think a God of love and justice, the God of Jesus, would continue to keep a people in a place who deliberately violate that love and justice in their treatment of long-time inhabitants?

A Promise Fulfilled

The promise to Abraham and Sarah included Israel's neighbors—the Ishmaelites and Edomites back then and the Arabs today—all of whom trace their lineage back to Abraham.

The early Christians regarded this promise to Abraham to be fulfilled as people from many different Gentile nations came to call on the one God together with Jews in the church (see Romans 4:11-12). The last component of the promise was that God would be God to Abraham and his offspring, calling for a mutual and perpetual commitment between the descendants and God.

Psalter: Psalm 22:23-31

Psalm 22:1-21a is familiar to many as the psalm often read on Good Friday because of Jesus' cry from the cross (Matthew 27:46). The impact of the first half of the psalm on the Passion narratives of the Gospels is deep: the taunt of the spectators, the piercing of hands and feet, the parching thirst, the casting of lots for clothing (see John 19:23-29; Matthew 27:35-44).

The psalm is a liturgy conducted between one who is falsely accused and the priest. The complainant is in the odd position of not being able to prove his innocence. His opponents are not able to prove his guilt beyond a reasonable doubt. So the accused must endure a cloud of suspicion and slander.

Since a human court cannot resolve the issue, the complainant comes to the sanctuary and places his case before YHWH and pleads for vindication. The priest offers a word of assurance. If he is righteous, God will vindicate him (verse 8). Taking courage from the promise of vindication, the complainant declares the time will come when he will praise God in the congregation—when his innocence is established by God (verses 21b-31).

Epistle: Romans 4:13-25

Paul wrote his letter to the Roman Christians to serve a number of ends. First, he wished to acquaint them with his message (and reply to circulating slanders) so they would support his missionary endeavors to the western part of the Empire. Second, he wished to resolve the tensions that had arisen between Jewish and Gentile Christians, arguing that both must welcome each other as full and honored members of God's family.

Abraham, Parent of All

Abraham is central to Paul's case that the boundaries of the people of God are circumscribed by trust in God rather than by circumcision. In Romans 4:9-12, Paul demonstrated his case by citing chronology: Abraham was "reckoned righteous" by God after he believed God's promises (Genesis 15:6) but well before he received circumcision (17:26). So Paul is able to refute the claim that only ethnic Jews and circumcised Gentile converts belonged to Abraham's family and inheritance. Paul then expressed a wider vision of how God made Abraham the "father of many nations." Abraham is the parent both of those who trust God apart from being circumcised (the Gentiles) and of the circumcised who also follow Abraham's example of trust in God (the Jews) (Romans 4:11-12, 16-17, 19).

Think About It: How does the level of our trust in God enable or limit our discipleship?

A Covenant for Many Nations

By placing "works" and "trust" in opposition to each other, Paul expressed his conviction that a trusting response to the generous and faithful God, rather than the work of circumcision, makes one a part of God's people and heir of God's promises. Circumcision was for him (as indeed for most first-century Jews and Gentiles) a mark that separated Jew from Gentile and established a religious boundary. This violated the nature of God's promise to make Abraham the father of many nations, which included Gentiles. Paul looked finally at the nature of Abraham's trust: Abraham knew God to be capable of acts far beyond what humans thought possible, and this trust energized his obedience at every turn.

Gospel: Mark 8:31-38

Three times in Mark's Gospel we find the pattern of Passion prediction, misunderstanding, and teaching on discipleship (8:32-38; 9:30-37; 10:32-45). The repetition of this pattern provides the central chapters of Mark with their structure and shows the importance he and his community attached to these themes, as they illumine the nature of Jesus' messiahship and the character of true discipleship (following this Messiah).

Who Is the Messiah?

First-century Jews held several views of who the messiah would be and what he would do. One concept saw in the messiah a revolutionary warrior who would expel the Roman oppressors, restore control of the land to the inhabitants, and rule the people of God in righteousness. This appears to be the model with which the first disciples were working (see Mark 10:37 and Acts 1:6). Jesus' messianic program—to die shamed and rejected, then rise again—was not a model ever conceived for the messiah by any other Jewish group. The early church's creative interaction with the Old Testament prophets and psalms created this new paradigm after the reality had been observed and experienced.

Peter had good reason for opposing Jesus' announcement of his messianic program. Aside from caring about his friend and teacher, it had obvious, unwelcome implications for discipleship. Their leader's suffering and execution had no place in their plan for how God would redeem Israel. The reaction of Peter to Jesus' words reflects the rejection of the apostolic proclamation in the mission of the church.

So Jesus had to teach them the true nature of his mission—and of their discipleship. His announcement that all who would follow him must "deny themselves and take up their cross" was calculated to shock the hearers into recognizing the difference between common expectations and the new reality God had made known in Jesus. Jesus was the fulfillment of divine promise rather than the answer to human expectations.

An Alternative View

Jesus' mission would redefine all concepts of greatness and precedence, indeed all definitions of being a success and enjoying quality of life. What it means to "take up a cross" and "deny one's self" is clarified in the later two teachings on discipleship, even as the Passion predictions become more descriptive. It means renouncing attempts to better one's position, as the world sees betterment, and tak-

> **Think About It:** Self-fulfillment and self-gratification are central values in our culture. How do these values fit with Christian discipleship? How does each set of values shape our lives?

ing up the role of a servant to all (9:35; 10:43-44) instead of trying to bring others under one's control. The cross is not merely an unpleasant burden—as in "we all have our crosses to bear"—but a way of life.

The Life of Discipleship

Discipleship—choosing to put Jesus' vision and teachings before one's own desires and preferences—is always costly. Jesus saw two ways of responding to this cost of discipleship. One can cut one's losses, get back one's life in this world, and dissociate oneself from Jesus and his "unpopular" mandates; or, one can accept these losses, dissociate one's life from the world's models, and boldly identify oneself with the values, calling, and mission of Jesus. Discipleship is not the safe or smart path as the world construes security and savvy; it is the only way to be faithful to Jesus and the God he represents.

Study Suggestions

A. Proclaim God's Deliverance

Read Psalm 22:23-31 in unison. Highlight the emphasis in the psalm on bearing witness to God's favors and timely help. Invite members to bear witness to one another by sharing times when God answered them in their need.

B. The Covenant With Abraham

Read aloud Genesis 17:1-7, 15-16; and set the passage in its historical, literary, and religious context, using the commentary notes on pages 120–21. Abraham had been looking for the fulfillment of these promises all his life, but this promise came only in his one-hundredth year. Ask: What does this say about God's timing and our often impatient human response? What is the significance of the report of God's making a promise to the woman Sarah? What is your response to the "Think About It" question regarding Sarah's status? What did/could Abraham's descendants do to void the promise in verse 8?

God called Abraham to "walk before [God], and be blameless" (17:1). Remind the participants of the meaning of this phrase in ancient Near Eastern covenants. Ask: Does this openness and single-heartedness reflect your walk before God? What might God be saying to you about your discipleship during this Lenten season? (Make this a time for confession, rededication, and prayer.)

Abraham was trusting and faithful to God, apart from his doubt and laughter at the improbability of aged Sarah conceiving. Ask: Do we tend to wait for assurance about God's promises before stepping out in faith, or do we follow God's way with the trust of Abraham? What helps or hinders our trustful walk?

C. Share the Faith of Abraham

Read Romans 4:13-25, and review the commentary on page 122. Ask: What was the point of Paul's relating the gospel to the promises to and response of Abraham? What is the connection between Abraham's trust in God (and the thrust of his hope) and that of the Christian (and the content of our hope)? Examine 4:17-25 carefully. Ask: What is the nature and source of our hope? How does our trust influence our life choices?

D. The Call to Discipleship

Ask a volunteer to read Mark 8:31-38. Ask: What were the common messianic expectations in that day? Why did Jesus' announcement of his messianic future meet with resistance from Peter? Now read the explanation on page 124. What would have been the hearers' response to an invitation to "take up a cross"?

Ask: How are we seeking to secure our lives in this world, to build up our lives as American culture views security and success? What tensions do we feel between these goals and Jesus' call to discipleship? What specific issues are we currently facing in this regard? How can we as a group help and support one another in these struggles?

E. Synthesis

Discuss how each of these lections helps us understand what it means to "walk before the Lord and be blameless." The Old Testament, Epistle, and Gospel lections share as a common presupposition the necessity of trusting more in God than in the world's promises and values and of stepping out in faith to take risks in Christ's service.

F. Close With a Lenten Reflection

State that, since Lent is a time for self-examination, the closing moments will be devoted to quiet reflection on what changes in our lives might be needed as we grow in this trust. Then close by singing "Jesus Calls Us O'er the Tumult."

Lections for Third Sunday in Lent

F Old Testament: Exodus 20:1-17

*F*OR many, the Ten Commandments provide a reliable shorthand definition of what it means to be a good or moral person. YHWH did indeed set these ten laws apart from the rest by speaking them to the people directly rather than through Moses. The absence of specific penalties for transgression also gives them a character of absoluteness. They feature prominently in summaries of the law or right living in Jesus and Paul (see Matthew 19:17-19 and Romans 12:9-10), suggesting that they did enjoy a special status as cardinal rules within the Torah. We must remember, however, that for the devout Jew the Torah was of one piece. The dietary, purity, ceremonial, legal, and moral commands were all to be observed rigorously and equally.

A Demanding Law

Despite the fact that many ancient law codes prohibited murder, adultery, theft, and perjury, the Ten Commandments are not a universal law. They constitute the beginning of the covenant stipulations imposed by God specifically upon the Israelites, the people God had delivered from slavery and whom God was leading through the Sinai desert.

Some commands actually came to distinguish the Hebrew people from all their neighbor nations—the prohibition of idols, the refusal to recognize any deity besides YHWH, and the abstinence from all work on the seventh day. God called this vassal people to absolute loyalty as well as to absolute respect. They were not to encroach upon the great "I AM WHO/WHAT I AM" with limiting visual representations or to abuse God's name by swearing false oaths or by presumptuously invoking God's name to curse others.

Interpersonal and social relations were also placed within the sphere of loyal response to God. Thus Israel was perpetually called to honor parental instruction and to return to them in their old age the care they gave in their youth. The prohibitions of murder (excluding war and capital punishment in Israel, at least), adultery, stealing (including kidnapping), and perjury, all insure basic rights within the covenant community. The final commandment stands apart from the rest by moving from external actions to internal motivations that threaten a neighbor's enjoyment of life and property.

A Law That Lives On

Some Christians may question the normative value of these laws that Jesus came "not to abolish but to fulfill" (Matthew 5:17). The benchmark set by Jesus and the apostles for the church was much higher and deeper than these commands (see Matthew 5:21-48 and Colossians 3:5-17).

Think About It: Jesus taught a radical internalization of Exodus 20:12-14 in Matthew 5:20-32. What does this say about the type and level of faithful living called for by Jesus? How well do the Ten Commandments provide guidance for living today? What moral dilemmas do we face that are too complex to be resolved by the direct application of these laws? (Abortion, stem cell research, capital punishment, cloning, and physician-assisted suicide, among others, may be mentioned.) Are there ethical issues we have to decide even when there is no clear direction from Scripture as to what is right and what is wrong? How do we do this?

Moreover, Paul explicitly placed Christians under the norm of the Spirit rather than the Torah (or any part of it; see Romans 8:25, 13-14; Galatians 5:16-26). The results, in terms of guidelines for behavior, often overlap, but that is because one God stands behind both.

Psalter: Psalm 19

This psalm speaks of the revelation of God in creation and in Torah. It has much in common with the wisdom traditions of Israel and is usually classified as a "wisdom" psalm.

Creation, especially the blazing sun and the night sky, displays the greatness, majesty, and honor of God (God's "glory"). It becomes a topic in Jewish wisdom tradition that the one God can be known from God's works, even though the Gentile nations fail to lift their eyes from the creature to the Creator, thereby falling into idolatry (Romans 1:18-23). The first half of this psalm (verses 1–16), therefore, invites those who do know God to delight in the reflections of God's imagination and the awesome marvels of God's natural world.

Torah displays the way to live before such a God, to participate, in effect, in the harmonious ordering of the cosmos that bears united witness to God's greatness and goodness. The psalm teaches an appreciation for God's law as the revelation of what is good, beneficial, and truly pleasant for human beings. Christians can certainly share this appreciation even while seeking to conform to the Spirit of God and image of Christ rather than the written code of Torah. Not surprisingly, the two pursuits remain deeply complementary.

Epistle: 1 Corinthians 1:18-25

In Paul, the place where God's wisdom is found shifts away from Torah to the cross of Christ. The Corinthian converts had been socialized into the values of Greek culture from their birth—particularly artful public speaking, impressive self-presentation, and physical beauty and strength. In short, they were taught to value appearances, honoring those who made a good showing and seeking to make their own claim to honor based on externally visible qualities. Bringing this mentality with them into the church, they were prone to compare and evaluate their teachers and each other.

A Stark Contrast

Paul confronted this mentality with the gruesome image of the cross of Jesus, where the radical difference between God's wisdom and human wisdom, between God's evaluation and human evaluation, makes itself known. The Crucified One has no visible strength or beauty, puts on no fine display, and yet brings the power of God into human history. This shows the unreliability of visible criteria of worth. Moreover, the Crucifixion was intended by humans to label Jesus' way of life as ultimately undesirable. The worldly-wise displayed Jesus as an example of how not to live. Again, God overturned human evaluations. By raising Jesus from the dead, God set a seal of approval on that life as an honorable one and worth emulating. One's honor and best interests are thus divorced from visible, external criteria and served best by living to please God.

Paul thus drew sharp contrasts between what is wise according to the world and what is wise according to God. There is no comparison between these perspectives, for God is vastly greater than the world so that God's folly is wiser than the best human wisdom. The world's wisdom does not lead to a relationship with God and even prevents us from recognizing God's revelation in the cross. The Corinthians were challenged to leave

Think About It: What values from American culture do you bring to your understanding of being a Christian? Do you find yourself calculating and choosing what is beneficial according to the world's standards or in terms of what is best before God?

behind the values and conventional wisdom of the dominant culture and to embrace God's values in their own choices and behaviors.

Gospel: John 2:13-22

The cleansing of the Temple occurred near the end of Jesus' ministry in the other three Gospels, but John places it near the beginning. Some suggest that Jesus did this same action twice, but such harmonization is not necessary. Stories about Jesus circulated for thirty years before the first Gospel was written. Each Evangelist gives an order to the sayings and stories and thereby interprets Jesus. The chronology of events in the several Gospels serves the theological purpose of each writer. The location of cleansing the Temple in the Fourth Gospel was a particular emphasis to the understanding of Jesus' ministry.

Keeping Worship Pure

John presents Jesus throughout his Gospel as the one who perfects the worship of God and brings his followers into pure worship. John places this episode at the outset of Jesus' ministry, thereby highlighting Jesus' efforts to raise the level of first-century Jewish worship (as in the purification rites in 2:1-11 and the worship of God in spirit rather than in a specific location in 4:19-26).

In all four Gospels Jesus is seen to be appalled at the practice of selling animals for offering sacrifices and the setting up of currency exchange booths (since the offerings were to be made only in Tyrian silver shekels) within the Temple precincts. Conducting profane business in sacred space was regarded by Jesus as defilement and exploitation. We might also remember that this trade was conducted in the court of the Gentiles. This use made it impossible for Gentiles to come to the Temple to pray (Mark 11:17). The messianic expectation was that all nations would flow to the Temple to worship God.

The Demand for a Sign

When he was challenged by the authorities (an example of Paul's claim in 1 Corinthians 1:22 that the leaders "demand signs"), Jesus pointed away from the edifice as the place where God's favor is gained and toward a temple of a different sort. The only sign Jesus gave was his own resurrection after the authorities had destroyed "the temple of his body." This will be the proof (the sign): that God has

Think About It: How do secular concerns threaten to defile Christian worship? Do you share Jesus' zeal for the sanctity of worship and the protection of worshipers? What practices make it difficult for strangers to join in the worship of God?

authorized Jesus to reform, redefine, and even replace existing religious observances and institutions. By calling Jesus' body "the temple," John has Jesus begin to invest within himself the important religious symbols and institutions of the parent religion—a constant theme of John—culminating with the replacement of the Passover with the Passion.

Zeal for God's House

Only John notes that Jesus also drove the animals from the Temple. Just as John distinguished the true worship of God as that which happens "in the spirit" rather than in a particular place, he may also be hinting at the rejection of animal sacrifices. (Perhaps this could be in favor of the sacrifices of praise, thanksgiving, and repentance, or hinting at Jesus' own sacrificial death.) John's point is that whoever clings to Jesus retains a grasp on all that was meaningful under the old covenant now brought to its purest form. This was a much-needed message, as Jewish Christians found themselves excluded from the synagogues.

The Scripture (John 2:22) the disciples remembered after the Resurrection may be Psalm 69:9, which is quoted in John 2:17. This psalm speaks of one who bears insult and abuse for the sake of God's honor, is persecuted for his "zeal for God's house," but who is ultimately vindicated by God.

Study Suggestions

A. Open Up to God's Revelation

Sing "For the Beauty of the Earth" or "Let All the World in Every Corner Sing." Ask participants to close their eyes and call to mind an experience of earth or sky that opened them up to the wonder of God. Then form two groups and read Psalm 19:1-6 antiphonally. Ask each person to prepare silently for the hour by asking God for illumination and for guidance in thought and speech. Then finish Psalm 19:7-14 antiphonally.

B. The Ten Commandments

Ask group members to name the Ten Commandments (write them on poster paper or chalkboard). Now read the full text from Exodus 20:1-17. Consider the range of behaviors covered by each commandment (refer to the resources in the commentary on pages 126–27 for a guide). Ask: What roles do these commandments play in Christians' lives? Is this a sort of minimum (or maximum) code of conduct? Also discuss the "Think About It" questions.

Read Matthew 5:20-32, Jesus' own commentary on two of these commandments. What is Jesus doing with these commandments? Are we to keep the Ten Commandments or Jesus' interpretation of the law? Which is more demanding and why?

Are Christians bound in God's sight to keep the whole Torah, just the Ten Commandments, or some other set of rules for living? Read Romans 8:2-5 and Galatians 5:16-26. How might these texts influence our answer to this question?

C. World Wise, Heaven Foolish

Ask a volunteer to read 1 Corinthians 1:18-25, and then review the commentary on pages 128–29. Ask: In light of Paul's conviction that the present age was passing away, why would it be dangerous and self-deceptive for the Corinthian Christians to judge people by quality of appearance? How does Jesus, the crucified redeemer, turn worldly criteria for assessing honor and success upside-down?

We remain influenced by Corinthian values: In what ways do we show preference for physically attractive or charismatic people (and aversion toward those whose appearance is less appealing)? What cultural criteria (American or other) for success and worth drive our life choices and guide our choices of relationships?

D. God's Pure Temple

Conduct a dramatic reading of John 2:13-22: Two individuals will read the roles of Jesus and the narrator, while the rest of the group may read the part of the "Jews" (meaning the religious authorities). Ask: Why did Jesus respond to the moneychangers as he did? How do concerns about money and secular agendas threaten to pollute our worship of God?

John often employs a materialistic misunderstanding of Jesus' words to lead to a correct understanding. Toward what kind of understanding of *temple* is John leading? What is the significance of labeling Jesus' body as "the temple"? This passage calls into question all material or architectural understandings of *temple*. How does an understanding of the real nature of the Christian temple (whether Jesus' body or the gathering of Christians, also called the body of Christ) enrich our life of worship and discipleship?

E. Pray

Form groups of three, asking each group to identify prayer concerns and then pray for one another's needs and spiritual aspirations as Lent progresses and Holy Week approaches. Then form a large circle, holding hands, and recite the Lord's Prayer together.

Lections for Fourth Sunday in Lent

N Old Testament: Numbers 21:4-9

NUMBERS tells a story of generational transition. It begins with the Exodus generation of Hebrews in the Sinai wilderness. Freed from bondage, they are in the midst of a forty-year (the biblical number of years in a generation) sojourn, having been transformed from slaves to nomadic tribes.

The Faithful Lose Faith

Numbers is also a story of lost faith. In Chapters 1–10, the Hebrews were docile and orderly, faithfully fulfilling their rules and duties. In Numbers 11, however, they began to rebel and grouse about their hard life and lack of food and water, wishing they were back in Egypt (even in slavery) where things were familiar and dependable.

Their rebellion came to a climax in Numbers 13 and 14. At the command of YHWH, Moses sent spies into Canaan in hopes they could enter and settle down in more fertile surroundings. The returning spies reported Canaan as "a land of milk and honey." They also reported that an invasion of Canaan was not feasible. Thus, the people had to continue on in their nomadic existence. It would require a new generation, schooled in the desert, to muster the fortitude to cross the Jordan. None of these ex-slaves would be able to settle in the Promised Land.

Near the end of their wandering, when most of the Exodus generation had died, a new breed had replaced them who were to casting envious eyes toward the lush fields of Canaan. Numbers 21:1-3 reports that when the king of Arad, a fortified city-state in the Negeb desert, tried to stand in their way, his towns were

> **Think About It:** Verse 3 (NIV) says: "The LORD . . . gave the Canaanites over to them. They completely destroyed them. . . ." How has Jesus changed our understanding of God from that of Numbers?

132

sacked and their people annihilated by this fierce desert band. Credit for the victory was ascribed to YHWH, who had now become a war god similar to the gods of other peoples of the region. The belief was that victory went to the tribe with the mightiest god.

A Final Complaint

Yet the remaining members of the Exodus generation continued grumbling: Why did you bring us out of Egypt where we had plenty of food and water? We will die here in the desert. Again, they lacked faith in the ability of YHWH to sustain and lead them. Apparently, some at least felt a victory in battle was insufficient evidence.

YHWH sent poisonous serpents that bit and killed. The people interpreted this as punishment for their sin of complaining and pled with Moses to intervene. When Moses prayed, YHWH instructed him to fashion a bronze serpent and put it high on a pole, so when people were bitten they would look up at the bronze serpent and be spared. Thus, the serpent became a symbol of healing and salvation.

> *Think About It:* The Hebrews cried out to YHWH, "Why have you brought us up out of Egypt to die in the wilderness?" When have you wandered in a wilderness (felt forlorn and deserted)? Did you complain? How was God present to you? How did you ultimately respond?

The New Faithful Emerge

In spite of this protest, the people continued on their journey. By Numbers 25, all the old-timers had died. A new generation of hope, born in the wilderness, stood on the eastern edge of the Jordan, looking forward to a new venture rather than back to the time of slavery.

Psalter: Psalm 107:1-3, 17-22

Psalm 107 is an individual song of thanksgiving that may also have been used as a congregational liturgy accompanying a thanksgiving Temple sacrifice. While offering thanks for deliverance from trouble, the psalmist reflects on God's steadfast love. The phrase "redeemed of the LORD" probably was added later to remind postexilic worshipers of the deliverance of exiled Israelites from Babylon and their return to their homeland.

Verses 1–3 are a call to give thanks, followed by four parallel stanzas. Our passage is the third stanza (verses 17-22). All four stanzas have identical patterns: a distressing situation, a prayer for help, God's deliverance, and a thanksgiving.

Contrary to today's culture that promotes self-sufficiency, this psalm's simple but radical message is that human life depends on God. Wise persons will realize that this dependency must be a way of life, not simply an emergency response to trouble. The psalm also declares that the God on whom we rely is steadfast and dependable.

Christians profess that Jesus personified this steadfast love. He fed the hungry, liberated the oppressed, healed the sick, and stilled the storms at sea. Like the psalmist, Jesus calls people to renounce their self-sufficiency and to live under God's sovereignty, depending on and being grateful for God's steadfast love.

Epistle: Ephesians 2:1-10

At first glance, this New Testament letter appears to have been written by Paul to one or more Gentile churches somewhere in his mission field. However, several important literary and theological characteristics of the letter lead most scholars to believe that it was written by a later writer, perhaps a disciple of Paul. Pseudonymous writing was typical and respectable in the ancient world. This letter may give us a glimpse of second-generation Christianity, written perhaps about the same time as the Gospel of John.

New Occasions

Our passage is a faith statement of this unknown second-generation writer. Like Paul, he states that before Christ, people were dead because they followed the inappropriate desires of the flesh and senses—that is, because of their sins (verses 1-3). He also announced that God in infinite, generous mercy and love offers the gift of salvation to those who trust.

> **Think About It:** "By grace you have been saved," declares the writer of Ephesians. What does God's grace (unmerited favor) mean to you personally? What is salvation for you?

Paul had preached that Jesus would return during the lifetime of first-generation Christians to save all believers. He spoke of those who are being saved (1 Corinthians 1:18) and of those who would be saved "in the day of the Lord" (5:5). He talked about salvation as both a present and a future reality and about two time periods: this age and the age to come.

Changed Beliefs

What new situation did the Ephesians face that caused the writer of this letter to reinterpret Paul? The second-generation Ephesians had shifted their world-view. They no longer lived in the temporal tension between the time of Jesus' death and the time of Christ's return. Instead, they lived somewhere between their pre-Christian (earthly) and their Christian (heavenly) identities—a spatial rather than a temporal dualism. Obviously, a new interpretation of salvation was required. The writer of Ephesians, though careful to locate ultimate resurrection with Christ in the future (2:5), reinterprets Paul for them. He claims that by God's grace (God's gift) believers have been saved; however, salvation is not yet complete. Believers live in the "already here but not quite yet" reality of God's saving action in Christ.

Gospel: John 3:14-21

Tradition says the Gospel of John was written by "the disciple whom Jesus loved." Mid-second-century theologians identified this "beloved disciple" as John, the son of Zebedee. However, the beloved disciple is identified by relationship, never by name, so he remains anonymous. The Gospel was likely written around A.D. 80–90.

A Painful Separation

One obvious difference between John and the other three Gospels is the level of conflict portrayed between Jesus and fellow Jews. Scholars believe the tone reflects more of the situation when the Gospel was written than conditions when Jesus actually lived. When John was written, Christians proclaimed Jesus was Christ (Messiah). Jewish authorities reacted by rejecting Christians' claims and expelling believers from synagogues. Jewish Christians were experiencing a painful separation from their Jewish communities. It is important to remember that when John refers to "the Jews," he means not the whole Jewish community of all times and places, but the late first-century synagogue authorities who were antagonistic to Christianity.

Answering an Unbeliever

In John's mind, Nicodemus (a Pharisee and leader of the Jews) may represent those synagogue authorities. Prior to these verses, Nicodemus had come to Jesus at night to question him. He indicated that he knew Jesus had "come from God" because of the signs he did, thus implying a positive acceptance of Jesus as a prophet. Jesus answered that no one sees God without being "born from above." Nicodemus understood him literally—"born again"— and asked how that could be.

Jesus responded with a metaphor: Just as Moses lifted up the serpent in the wilderness to save the Israelites from death, so must the Son of Man be lifted up so those who believe may have eternal life (verses 14-15). John uses a word here that means either "lifted up" or "exalted." Jesus must be lifted up on the cross; that raising (Crucifixion) is a moment of exaltation (Resurrection and Ascension). Using irony, John offers an image (the cross) that seems to humiliate, but really exalts.

Believe or Perish

So, does "born from above" mean born of God through Jesus' resurrection? Partly. Jesus' resurrection is the means, the catalyst, that makes possible being born from above. John 3:16 adds the rest of the answer. Being "born from above" means being born of God's love. But God's love needs a response: Being born anew happens only if one believes and receives God's gift.

For John, God's loving gift of Jesus begins the judgment of the world because the very presence of Jesus in the world confronts each person with a decision: believe and be born from above—or do not believe and perish. The judgment comes in the making of that decision. We condemn ourselves if we do not believe (verses 17-21).

This passage must be understood not only as Jesus' statement but also as the confession of faith of John and his community. Like the writer of Ephesians, John also faced new situations and provided his community with new interpretations of Jesus' death and resurrection. John proclaimed that Jesus' appearance had drastically altered the world. Now there could only be believers who had new life from above and unbelievers who were spiritually dead. Jesus' appearance in the world had given life to those who believed. But his appearance had become self-judgment on those who did not. There was no middle ground.

> **Think About It:** Jesus told Nicodemus that unless one is born from above one is unable to see the realm of God. How do we gain spiritual vision in order to see the things of God?

Study Suggestions

A. Discuss the Bronze Serpent

Cut thin strips of paper. Find a long pole. Decide how to attach the strips to it. Ask: What are things that poison our lives? Write each one on a separate strip of paper. Stick the strips on the pole and call out the poisons. Discuss: How does naming the poisons and hanging them up in a visible way aid in our healing?

Review Numbers 21:4-9 and the commentary on pages 132–33. Discuss the questions in the "Think About It" boxes with reference to the Israelites' complaints in the wilderness and their view of YHWH as a powerful war god. Then read 2 Kings 18:4 and ask: Can you think of instances in your experience where a positive symbol has become a problem? How might the saving power of the cross (or the Bible) become an object of worship like the bronze serpent? How do we guard against worshiping the cross (or the Bible or the church or a beloved pastor)?

136

B. Discuss "Born From Above"

Invite two people to give a dramatic reading of the spoken dialogue between Nicodemus and Jesus in John 3:1-21, omitting phrases like "Jesus answered" and "Nicodemus said to him." Ask: What is this Gospel story telling us? What does being "born from above" mean? How does John 3:16 sum up both elements needed to be "born from above"? (Refer to the commentary on pages 135–36 as necessary.)

C. Discuss Changing Beliefs

Read aloud Ephesians 2:1-10 and the review interpretation on pages 134–35. Ask: How does your understanding of salvation change if you view it as only a future event or as an "already here/not completely accomplished" event? What does it mean to you to know that you are being saved by grace through faith?

D. Tie It Together

Ask: What do the four lections say about God's saving actions? What are the different means God uses? (In Numbers, the serpent is God's saving symbol. In the Psalm, God's "word" heals and saves. In Ephesians, God's grace through the gift of Jesus saves. In John, it is believing, being born of God from above, that saves.) In each case, what is the thing from which God saves?

Ask: What do the passages say about God's nature? (God is forgiving, steadfast, gracious and merciful, loving, and saving. In Numbers, God is also punishing; but in John punishment comes as a natural result of our unbelief, not from a vindictive God.)

Summarizing the main points of the lesson, what do you feel God is calling you to do or to be? How will these insights help you grow and mature in faith?

E. Offer and Claim Assurance

Read Psalm 107:1-3, 17-22 responsively. Look at all four stanzas of the psalm. Review the commentary on the psalm as needed (pages 133–34). Ask: What are the distressing situations? the prayers for help? How does God heal? What thanksgiving is offered? What does it mean to be dependent on God as a way of life?

F. Receive Grace

Close by singing "Amazing Grace" and giving thanks to God in prayer for the saving grace that touches and transforms our hearts and lives.

Lections for Fifth Sunday in Lent

T Old Testament: Jeremiah 31:31-34

*T*HE Book of Jeremiah is a story of destruction and grief and also of restoration and hope. It is mostly about God's people who lived in the city-state of Judah, which was created when the empire created by David dissolved after the death of Solomon in 922 B.C.

Destruction and Grief

After three hundred years of living in a hostile environment and facing conflicts with Israel and other surrounding city-states and larger empires, Judah now encountered even more fiercely troubled times. Egypt and Babylon were vying for control of the area. Finally, in 605 B.C. Judah was forced to become a vassal state of Babylon, paying tribute in return for protection. When the protection turned into domination, Judah responded with three separate revolts. Following each rebellion Babylon invaded, deporting more leaders and members of the upper classes to Babylon. During the third invasion in 587 B.C., Babylon destroyed Jerusalem and its Temple, ravaged the land, and exiled a large portion of the population.

Changing Message

Jeremiah prophesied during Judah's troubled times. Before Babylon conquered Judah, Jeremiah warned of coming destruction: Judah would be destroyed unless the people repented of their idolatry and injustice. When Babylon finally assumed control of Judah, Jeremiah preached submission: Babylon was God's instrument to punish the people for breaking the covenant, so they should accept their lot. After Babylon's fall, Jeremiah preached hope: God would restore the covenant with the people. Some of these changes in the prophetic message can be attributed directly to Jeremiah; it is unlikely that the exiled Judahite community adapted

138

Jeremiah's message over the years to speak to their changing needs and circumstances.

God's Heart-Written Covenant

Our passage is one among many oracles of comfort, restoration, and hope (Chapters 30 and 31). Jeremiah said that the people's hardships were due to their ancestors' sins. The old Mosaic covenant (Exodus 20:1-17)—made in the Sinai wilderness after the Exodus from Egypt—had been broken over the centuries (see Jeremiah 11:3-4). God's later unconditional covenant with David in 2 Samuel 7:10-16 (in which YHWH had promised to be Israel's God and to secure Israel's throne forever) had led the people to a false confidence and growing unfaithfulness to God's ways. This led to the invasion, conquest, and Exile (Jeremiah 31:27-30).

As the people neared the end of their punishment in exile, YHWH promised a new covenant. This time God's law would be written on the people's hearts so they could truly follow it. Furthermore, God pledged to forgive and forget their sins. By implication God also promised that the covenant would endure forever (31:31-34). What is new in this covenant is the God-given ability to obey God. Faithfulness, the real foundation for an everlasting covenant, would now be possible because people would no longer need to be taught the law; they would know it in their hearts. The new covenant would hold up because it would bring an inward transformation.

> **Think About It:** God's people experienced a tension between their confidence that God would always be their God and their struggle to obey God's law, the foundation of that covenant. How do we live between the twin dangers of despair and presuming upon God's grace?

Psalter: Psalm 51:1-12

Psalm 51 is a confession of sin and a plea for God's mercy. Although it is attributed to David in the tenth century B.C., it is found in a section of psalms written four hundred years later in postexilic times. Though the language is personal, it may well have been used in public worship as a communal confession and word of assurance. It is one of seven "penitential psalms"—so called because the early church saw a special note of contrition in them.

After confessing sin and recognizing the depth of human guilt (verses 1-5), the psalmist pleads for forgiveness and restoration to relationship with God. He acknowledges that God alone can bring about that reconciliation: teach me wisdom in my secret heart; create a clean heart in me; put a new and sturdy spirit within me. Acknowledging both human sinfulness and God's steadfast saving actions, this prayer psalm is a Lenten invitation to us to be restored or reconciled to God.

Epistle: Hebrews 5:5-10

This sermon-letter was sent by an anonymous writer to second-generation Christians who were experiencing a faith crisis. In a very sophisticated argument, the writer of Hebrews offers them a Christology: Jesus is "a merciful and faithful high priest" who makes an atoning sacrifice of his life for the sins of the people (Hebrews 2:17).

Christ as High Priest

Hebrews 5:1-5 describes the twin credentials of a priest: he must be both of the people and of God. The writer notes that Jesus Christ meets the second credential: He did not glorify himself, but was appointed by God who named him Son (5:5). Then, since his Jewish Christian readers would know that Jesus did not meet the first criterion (he was not of the priestly line of Aaron—see Exodus 28:1), the writer offers them another model of priesthood, Melchizedek (5:6), who was a Canaanite priest-king during the days of Abraham.

When Abraham's nephew Lot and others from Sodom and Gomorrah were captured during a local war, Abraham went into battle and rescued them (Genesis 14:13-20). When Abraham returned, Melchizedek blessed him in the name of his (Melchizedek's) Canaanite god. Abraham acknowledged the blessing by giving him a tithe of the recovered goods. Centuries later this incident was recalled when YHWH addressed an Israelite king as "a priest forever according to the order of Melchizedek" (Psalm 110:4)

By referring to Melchizedek's priesthood, Hebrews implies that Jesus' priesthood is legitimized through Abraham (not through Aaron) because Abraham acknowledged (through the tithe) that YHWH and Melchizedek's god were the same and that the order of Melchizedek antedates Aaron's order.

Obedient Suffering

> **Think About It:** John offers a distinctive view of Jesus' death, a theology of relational atonement. How do you understand the meaning of Jesus' death? How does your understanding open your heart to the salvation offered you by God in Christ?

Having legitimized Jesus as priest, the writer of Hebrews then describes his priestly role. Jesus is "the source of eternal salvation" (verse 9). He became that source because he learned obedience through suffering on the cross. (Suffering is the choice to accept avoidable hardship in order to accomplish a good that cannot be obtained if one chooses to avoid sacrifice.)

Gospel: John 12:20-33

This passage has traditionally been viewed as Jesus' last public dialogue, the end of his ministry. However, Gail R. O'Day (*The New Interpreter's Bible,* Volume IX, page 681), proposes that Chapters 11 and 12 are "the prelude to Jesus' hour" rather than "the conclusion of Jesus' ministry": a bridge between stories of Jesus' ministry (John 1–10) and stories of his death and resurrection (John 13–20).

Prelude to Jesus' Hour

The "prelude to Jesus' hour" began with the raising of Lazarus in Chapter 11, which served as catalyst for the synagogue authorities' determination to kill Jesus. Mary's anointing of Jesus, which happened in the shadow of that decision, connected that fateful decision with the Passover. Jesus' entry into Jerusalem came the next day.

The Greeks' arrival confirmed the Pharisees' fears that the people were indeed turning to Jesus (12:19). Their arrival hints at God's promise of universal salvation and the church's future mission beyond the Jewish world. This glimpse of the future marked the advent of Jesus' hour of death (12:23). The arrival of the Greeks thus pointed toward a future that required Jesus' death. But why was Jesus' death required? Jesus says in verse 24 that his death (a dying seed) will bear much fruit (the new faith community).

Three Atonement Theologies

Theologians refer to reflections on Jesus' death as "atonement theology." Three possible interpretations of the cross are usually offered: ransom, sacrifice, and moral influence. In the ransom view of atonement, Jesus' death is viewed as a payment to redeem humanity sold into the slavery of sin under Satan's power. In sacrificial atonement, Jesus' undeserved death is seen as a necessary sacrifice to wipe out human guilt and sin. Out of love for the world, God the Father sacrificed the Son. In moral influence theology, the cross is a political and religious scandal; but Jesus' death reflects his deep integrity. Therefore, Jesus becomes an example for human moral behavior.

A Fourth View

Biblical commentator Gail O'Day says that none of these three views of atonement explains John's understanding of Jesus' death. She thinks John believed in a relational theology of atonement. Jesus' death was necessary because it results in the formation of life-giving community: a single dying seed bears much fruit (verse 24). Nurtured by this community, disciples "serve Jesus" (verse 26), leading to restored relationship with God.

In this relational theology of atonement, Jesus' death is not a ransom or a sacrifice that makes amends for human sin. Nor is Jesus' willingness to die for his friends an example for us. Instead, Jesus' death is a gift given to restore relationship and to reveal the power and promise of God's love. In this view, the saving power of Jesus' death resides, not in the cross, but in us—the community gathered as a result of his death. It lives in the work we carry on as we serve Jesus.

Think About It: John offers a distinctive view of Jesus' death, a theology of relational atonement. How do you understand the meaning of Jesus' death? How does your understanding open your heart to the salvation offered you by God in Christ?

At various periods in the life of the church, the questions Why did Jesus die? and What does his death mean? have received different answers. Each theory draws on cultural analogies that help explain the meaning of Jesus' death for us.

Study Suggestions

A. Explore Heart Covenants

Make three red paper hearts per participant. Ask them to write quickly on the paper hearts three things that are "written on their hearts." (A special Bible verse? their strongest image of God? a memory of an encounter with God?) Ask: Who writes on your heart today? Is it easy or hard to recall and live out things written on your heart?

Read Jeremiah 31:31-34 together, and review the commentary on pages 138–39. Look up the Mosaic covenant (Exodus 20:1-17) and the Davidic covenant (2 Samuel 7:10-16). What are the differences? similarities? What makes the covenant promised in Jeremiah new? What is the covenant made with us in Christ?

B. Write a Modern Psalm

Assign one verse of Psalm 51 to each participant to paraphrase quickly, reflecting his or her own experience. Read the new verses aloud in order. Ask: What does this psalm say to you about sin, forgiveness, and reconciliation with God?

C. Explore Obedient Suffering

Read Hebrews 5:7-9, and review the commentary on page 140. Ask: What do these verses mean to you? Why is it sometimes necessary to choose suffering in order to bring about a higher good?

D. Explore "Jesus' Hour"

Read John 12:20-33, and review the interpretive material on pages 141–42. Ask: What is "Jesus' hour"? What is the significance of the Greeks visiting Jesus? Have class members divide a sheet of paper in half. Read John

12:24 again. On the left side, draw the literal image (dying seed planted gives forth fruit). On the right, draw what Jesus meant (the dying seed is his death; the fruit is the new faith community). Ask everyone to hold up their drawings at once for others to view without comment.

E. Tie It Together: Atonement

Review the four interpretations of atonement described on pages 141–42. Discuss the "Think About It" questions, and urge members to indicate how their understanding of Jesus' death has been modified during their lifetime.

Ask: What Bible verses illustrate these atonement theologies? (sacrifice: high priest metaphor, Hebrews 5; moral influence: Jesus, the pioneer, Hebrews 12:2; relational: dying seed/much fruit, John 12:24; ransom: 1 Timothy 2:6).

List these quickly beside the key words. How do each of these insights into the meaning of Jesus' death describe God's love and mercy for us? Which image is most helpful to you?

F. Tie It Together: Reconciliation

Ask: What are the "heart" images in Jeremiah 31:31-34 and in Psalm 51? What do they say about God and reconciliation? Who initiates reconciliation? Refer to the commentary (pages 138–39) as needed. (Both lections acknowledge that God initiates reconciliation, forgiving us our sin.)

Summarize the main insights from the session. Ask: How will these insights influence your faith? As a result, is there anything you feel God is calling you to do or to be? How can these passages help you mature as a Christian disciple?

G. Closing

Sing "O Church of God, United." Pray for openness to God's reconciling love as the week remembering Jesus' Passion approaches.

Lections for Passion/Palm Sunday

Old Testament: Isaiah 50:4-9a

*O*UR Old Testament verses are from Second Isaiah (Chapters 40–55), written by an unknown prophet who lived and preached in Babylon in the 540's B.C. His audience in exile must have had serious doubts about whether they were still in YHWH's favor. Second Isaiah reassured them that God still had compassion for them. Like Jeremiah in our last session, Second Isaiah preached consolation and hope that God's punishment was coming to an end and that the people would soon be restored to their homeland.

Suffering Servant

Our passage is the third of four servant songs found in Isaiah. The speaker is the servant. Some biblical interpreters identify this servant as the nation Israel; others believe the servant refers to an individual—either the prophet Isaiah himself or a servant-leader who will arise in the future. Christians believe this prophecy about a suffering servant was fulfilled in Jesus, which is the reason this lection is used on Passion Sunday.

God has given the servant the tongue of a teacher (verse 4). In Hebrew, the word translated as *teacher* means "of those who are taught." The servant who teaches is taught. When he is persecuted for his faithfulness, the servant does not resist or rebel but submits to the suffering and insults (verses 5-6). He sets his face "like flint"; that is, he is just as stubborn as his adversary. He is confident he will not be disgraced or shamed because God is near. The three questions in verses 8-9a—about contending, adversaries, and guilt—are all versions of the servant's confidence that God would vindicate him before his enemies.

In verses 10-11, Isaiah questions who will ultimately follow and obey the servant. Most will be disobedient and walk in darkness. But the servant—having received daily instruction, submitted to judgment during the dark period, and suffered physical pain and insults for his faith—now knows God's plan of punishment and restoration. Therefore, the servant can teach those who still fear God to walk in the light of God's fire.

> **Think About It:** "God has given me the tongue of a teacher, / that I may know how to sustain the weary with a word." Is your voice a guide to the weary? What is your message? What does the idea of the teacher being a listener and learner say to you about being a disciple of Jesus Christ?

Redemptive Suffering

We find here in Isaiah (as with Hebrews in our last session) an emphasis on obedience through suffering that leads to salvation. If we identify the servant as the nation of Israel, then Israel was required to suffer, not only for its own sins but also because its sacrificial suffering would be redemptive even for foreign peoples (53:5).

If we identify the servant as an individual who will arise in the future, our verses might be a prophecy about the messiah-king for whom the Jews were hoping. Christians read this passage in Second Isaiah as a prophecy about Jesus who came as a servant-teacher, who suffered in order to reveal the divine plan of judgment and restoration of God's people, and who then taught people to walk in the light.

> **Think About It:** What is the difference between suffering that is redemptive and unavoidable pain that is not? How was Jesus' suffering redemptive? What can you do to turn your suffering and that of others around you to redemptive ends?

Psalter: Psalm 31:9-16

Psalm 31 is a universal lament—speaking of a typical situation in confessional tones but without specifics. Because of this generalization, the lament psalms speak to a variety of situations.

The most prominent feature of Psalm 31 is its constant alternation between petition and trust: an expression of trust (verses 3-8) precedes the plea in 9a. The plea is followed by an extended lament over physical and social distress (9b-13). Then trust in God is again expressed (14-15a), followed by another plea for deliverance (15b-16).

This psalm is a prayer for deliverance from enemies. Imagine the circumstances of the one praying. Perhaps he is being scorned and avoided because of a physical or mental affliction. Or perhaps she is being oppressed by society for her faithful stance on some issue. Perhaps the psalmist is expressing the pleas and affirmations of trust of the faithful Israelites in exile. As we enter Holy Week, we hear echoes of Jesus' prayer in Gethsemane or on the cross. Whatever occasion the writing of this psalm, the composer knew the kind of opposition that leads to the cross.

Epistle: Philippians 2:5-11

Paul founded a church in the city of Philippi, a Roman colony in the province of Macedonia, during his second missionary journey, about A.D. 52. Later, when this church learned that Paul was imprisoned, they sent prayers and gifts. This letter is Paul's response.

An Early Christian Hymn

In our verses Paul quotes one of the earliest Christian hymns. Stanza one (2:6-8) describes Jesus' action. Jesus Christ relinquishes heavenly status and becomes fully human and obedient to the point of death. He does not consider equality with God something to be seized (as in a robbery) but rather as a gift from God. The phrase "even death on a cross" may be Paul's own addition. It certainly reflects his emphasis on "Christ crucified."

Stanza two (2:9-11) describes God's action. God exalts Jesus, giving him the name "Lord" (master), denoting power and status. Every knee must bend—a recognition of Jesus' high status. Finally, it urges giving glory to God by confessing "Jesus Christ is Lord"—the church's earliest creed.

Example or Reminder?

Why did Paul quote this hymn in the middle of appeals for unity and steadfastness among the Philippians? If we translate verse 5 as "Let the same mind be in you that was in Christ Jesus," Paul is holding up the example of Jesus Christ to teach how Christian community is formed. Since Jesus gave up all, the Philippians too are called to suffer.

Paul also advises: "Let the same mind be in you that you have in Christ Jesus" (NRSV, footnote). Paul is reminding them they are a community that acknowledges Christ as Lord. Jesus Christ is the ground and object of faith rather than a model for faith. This exhortation calls his readers to work out their own salvation and reflects a relational theology of atonement.

Christians have sometimes used the first translation erroneously—to admonish wives to submit to abusive husbands, or slaves to submit to masters, or all of us to acquiesce to injustice. This rendering reminds any who hold status and power in our society that it is the powerful, not the powerless, who who must learn to become servants. We must create solidarity with the oppressed rather than urge them to endure injustice.

146

Gospel: Mark 15:1-47

It is assumed by most scholars that Mark is the earliest Gospel and was written no earlier than A.D. 70—not quite forty years after Jesus' death. Because the writer assumed his readers would not be familiar with Jewish customs (and because he himself seems unfamiliar with them), most scholars believe this Gospel was written by an unknown Gentile Christian to other Gentile Christians in the Roman Empire. They think early Christians tried to identify this Gospel with Mark, a companion of Peter, because it was not written by one of the twelve apostles.

Today we look beyond Jesus' triumphal Palm Sunday entry to his final days and death (often called the Passion narrative). Mark's Passion narrative has a consistent theme of mockery and betrayal.

Many Betrayers and Mockers

Chapter 14 reports how the Jewish authorities plotted Jesus' death. Judas betrayed him. His disciples deserted him. The Sanhedrin tried him stealthily. After witnesses gave false and conflicting testimony (normally this would have been grounds for dismissal of charges against the accused), the council finally asked Jesus, "Are you the messiah?" When Jesus answered, "I am," the chief priest accused him of blasphemy. Now, based on Jesus' own words, they had a capital case. The council condemned him to death. At the same time, in the courtyard below, Peter was questioned by an unnamed servant girl, answered falsely, and denied Jesus.

Today's lection begins the next morning when the religious leaders handed Jesus over to Pilate (the secular authority). Pilate questioned Jesus; but when he refused to answer, Pilate was left with a dilemma. He knew jealousy had caused the priests to accuse Jesus, so he tried to find a way out. He offered to release "the King of the Jews" to the crowd, following his custom of freeing a prisoner during the Passover. However, the authorities pressed the crowd to ask instead for Barabbas (a murderous rebel from a recent insurrection).

When Pilate asked what they wanted him to do with Jesus, the incited crowd shouted, "Crucify him!" Pilate handed Jesus over to Roman soldiers who mocked and tortured him. He was crucified between two bandits who also mocked him. When Jesus uttered his last words "Eloi, Eloi, why have you forsaken me?" bystanders misunderstood and mockingly waited to see if Elijah would save him.

Few Faithful Witnesses

The last acts came from outsiders. Many of Jesus' women followers faithfully watched the Crucifixion from a distance as "proper women" would have done in those days. Two of them also witnessed Jesus' body being laid

147

in the tomb. They had been with Jesus all during his ministry but entered Mark's story only after the male disciples had deserted and denied Jesus. They are a symbol of hope: not everyone deserted Jesus at the end.

A Roman soldier—another outsider—recognized Jesus as God's Son and became a witness. Then Joseph of Arimathea, a respected member of the Sanhedrin who had voted for Jesus' death (14:64), apparently had a change of heart and boldly asked Pilate for his body in order to bury it—which should have been done by Jesus' absent disciples.

Jesus' Last Words

While Luke emphasizes Jesus' confident faith on the cross and John his triumphant spirit, Mark notes his abandoned feeling: "My God, my God, why have you forsaken me?"—the poignant lament of a righteous sufferer. Yet, this despair was also a hopeful prayer offered faithfully to his God.

Think About It: Many people participated in the undeserved death of Jesus. What part would you have played if you had been there? What part have you played in modern undeserved deaths?

Study Suggestions

A. Explore Redemptive Suffering

Read Isaiah 50:4-9a together and review the commentary on pages 144–45. What are the different ways this "suffering servant" passage is interpreted? How does it reflect the life and death of Jesus?

B. Identify Enemies and Responses

Ask: Who are our various enemies? Make a list of enemies on poster paper as participants name them. How do we respond to enemies? Make a second list of various responses.

Read Psalm 31:9-16 in unison Ask: Who was the enemy? How did the psalmist respond? How does this psalm reflect Jesus' life? our lives?

C. Betrayers and Witnesses

Review Mark 15:1-47 and the interpretation on pages 147–48. Form six small groups. Assign each a role in Mark's Passion story: priests and scribes, crowd before Pilate, bystanders at the cross, Roman soldiers, absent disciples, women followers.

Imagine you are at the trial before Pilate. Look around you. Who is missing? (Encourage group members to call out answers to all these questions from the perspective of their assigned role.) Why are you at the trial? What do you say? Why did you do or say what you did?

Now imagine you are at the Crucifixion. When you look up at Jesus on the cross, what do you say to the dying Jesus?

148

Discuss: What do each of the groups represent in terms of faith or lack of faith? (Possibilities: the women—faithful discipleship; centurion—conversion; crowd and bystanders—ignorance, easily swayed; priests and scribes—keepers of tradition; absent disciples—human doubt and frailty.)

D. Stand With Jesus

Read the commentary on Mark (pages 147–48). Compare Jesus' last words in Mark 15:34 with his last words in Luke 23:46 and John 19:30. What are the differences? How do the words from the cross reflect the Gospel writers' understanding of who Jesus is and why he died?

E. Explore an Early Hymn

Read Philippians 2:5-11 aloud as an early congregation might have done. (Leader reads verse 5; participants join in at verse 6.) At verse 10, actually bow or kneel. Then rise again on verse 11. Notice that this early hymn never mentions the Resurrection, only Christ's highly exalted status.

Recall the four atonement theologies studied in the last session (sacrifice, moral influence, ransom, and relational). Ask: If Paul quoted this early hymn as an example for the Philippians to follow, which atonement theology does it illustrate? (Moral influence; it asks the Philippians to suffer like Christ.) If Paul meant to quote the hymn to remind them, which atonement view does the "reminder" explanation illustrate? (Relational theology; it reminds the Philippians that their community emerged because of the death and resurrection of Jesus Christ.)

F. Profess Your Faith

The earliest Christian creed, found in Philippians 2:11, professes that "Jesus Christ is Lord." Today, Christians profess our faith in many different ways: Jesus Christ is sovereign. Jesus Christ is savior of the world. Christ is the Son of God. Jesus is the way, the truth, and the life. Christ is my redeemer. Jesus is the example for my life. Christ is reconciler. Christ is liberator. Ask: What one sentence could serve as your profession of faith? Who is Jesus Christ to you?

Summarize the insights from today's session. What insights have helped you grow in faith? What more is God calling you to do or be?

G. In Closing

Sing "Dear Jesus, in Whose Life I See"; then invite members to offer brief prayers asking God to lead them to make a deeper commitment to Jesus Christ during this Easter season.

EASTER

Lections for Easter Day

First Lesson: Acts 10:34-43

*W*RITTEN by Luke, Acts is the only New Testament book to tell the story of the early church. The writer traced this story from the church's earliest origins in Jerusalem and Judea to the vast Roman Empire. He focused primarily on the church's mission to Gentiles and the spread of the gospel.

Two Visions

Our verses are part of a longer story (10:1-48) about how this mission to the Gentiles began. Cornelius, a Gentile centurion and therefore "unclean" in Jewish eyes, had a vision in which God told him to send for Peter at Joppa. As Cornelius's messengers approached, Peter was having his own vision of a large sheet filled with food. A voice said, "Eat"; but Peter protested that he did not eat food that was ritually unclean. The voice responded, "Do not call anything impure that God has made clean" (10:9-15, NIV).

While Peter was puzzling over this vision, the Spirit told him to go with Cornelius's messengers, for they were from God. When he met with Cornelius, Peter recalled (with some exaggeration) that it was unlawful for a Jew to associate with a Gentile, but that God had shown him he should not call anyone "impure or unclean" (10:28, NIV).

Peter's Sermon

After Cornelius recounted his own vision, Peter spoke. His sermon showed his new understanding of God's impartiality: God fully accepts all people on equal terms. Therefore God's people can fully accept one another fully within the body of Christ and in ordinary social relationships. Peter is generally viewed as the apostle who initiated the mission to the Gentiles. The mission is about God's actions through Christ. Peter acknowledged the Jewish roots of Christianity but insisted that God was sovereign of all, not just of Israel.

When God clearly conferred the Holy Spirit on the Gentiles in a manner similar to Pentecost (10:44-48), Peter challenged anyone to deny them water baptism (the initiation rite that admitted persons to Christian fellowship). Hearing no dissent, he had them baptized in the name of Jesus Christ. Peter remained with them for several days, signifying his full acceptance of them. Cornelius is generally viewed as the first Gentile convert to the Christian faith.

> **Think About It:** How is this story is related to the Easter story? How can the conversions of Cornelius and Peter also be seen as a kind of resurrection from the dead—Cornelius from the death of unfaith and Peter from the death of prejudice? What kinds of death do we need to be raised from?

A Double Conversion

Peter's new understanding of God's impartiality suggests that his conversion to a Gentile mission was as crucial to the story of emerging Christianity as was Cornelius's conversion to the Christian faith. This double conversion may hold a lesson for the church today in the midst of contentious controversies. How might we break through painful deadlocks by accepting the need for conversion on all sides of an issue? What disagreements currently troubling the church might be resolved, or at least healed, in this way?

> **Think About It:** "Do not call anything impure that God has made clean" (10:15, NIV). What or who are you prone to call "unclean" or "sinful"? How does Christ enable us to regard fellow humans from a divine rather than human perspective?

Psalter: Psalm 118:1-2, 14-24

Psalm 118 likely was sung originally during festival worship, perhaps to celebrate a national victory. The speaker may have been a king. The psalm came to be used at Passover, recalling the Exodus). It also has echoes of the Exile, implying that, because of God's steadfast love, future deliverance may still come in postexilic times.

In verse 22, the "rejected stone, chief cornerstone" image is a proverb that has been applied in many ways in Scripture. Using stone mason images, Isaiah 28:16-17 referred to Zion as the cornerstone or foundation of faith; one tests one's faith by the plumbline of justice and righteousness. In Mark 12:10-12, Jesus quoted Psalm 118:22-23 at the end of a parable calling people to decide for or against him. The priests and scribes listening assumed the parable was told against them.

The implication of future deliverance can be seen in Matthew 21:42-43. Jesus quotes Psalm 118:22-23, saying the stone is the rule of God that will be given to those who produce godly fruits. In Acts 4:11, Peter identified Jesus as the stone rejected by the builders (religious authorities).

Epistle: 1 Corinthians 15:1-11

Paul wrote this letter about A.D. 54 to a church he had founded three years earlier in Corinth, a prosperous urban center that was ethnically, culturally, and religiously diverse. The Christian congregation in Corinth probably mirrored the city's diverse population: Gentiles and Jews; persons of diverse financial and social status. This was a fledgling Christian community in the midst of a pagan society. Small groups of believers scattered around the city probably came together regularly for worship and a common meal.

Paul wrote to respond to several spiritual matters the Corinthians had raised and to verbal reports of social disorders within the congregation. Their diversity may have been a factor in these problems, for Paul pleaded with them to live in unity and harmony, following Christ's example.

The Corinthians and Resurrection

One of the spiritual problems in the Corinthian congregation was that some members believed they were already reigning with Christ in glory (4:8). They lived in the present. They did not believe in the resurrection of the dead.

Paul reminded the Corinthians of the good news he had already preached and urged them to hang on to his message: Christ died for our sins, was buried, was raised, and appeared to various disciples and then to Paul himself. Paul thus claimed apostleship, though he felt it was undeserved because as a Jew he had once persecuted Christians.

The core of Paul's argument about resurrection follows in 15:12-58. He insists that if the Corinthians do not believe in and hope for the resurrection of the dead, they are denying Christ's resurrection and thus rejecting the foundation of their faith (15:12-19). He reminds them that resurrection is still a future event. He urges them to remain steadfast while waiting for the final transformation (15:20-58).

Think About It: "Hold firmly to the message that I proclaimed to you." What core message of the "good news" do you hold firmly? How does this influence your decisions and behavior?

An Early Creed

Paul is probably repeating an early Christian creed in verses 3b-5, one which offers good news about God's redemptive activity in Jesus Christ. It stresses that he died, was buried, was raised, and was made visible. In John (see pages 155–56), two pieces of that creedal formula (was raised, was visible) are expanded into the narrative of Mary Magdalene meeting the risen Jesus at the empty tomb.

Gospel: John 20:1-18

While the four Gospels vary in their accounts of Jesus' death and resurrection, all four agree on one thing: In the early darkness of the first Easter morning, Mary Magdalene went to Jesus' tomb. She was at the cross when Jesus died and was also at the tomb to witness the Resurrection. Gospel writers do not discuss this display of faithfulness; they simply report it as an essential part of the story. Variations in the rest of the Easter story suggest that the early Christians knew many Resurrection stories and that the Gospel writers selected from among these stories as they wrote.

Mary Magdalene's Reputation

In the other Gospels two or more women came to the tomb, but in John Mary Magdalene came alone. She was the woman from whom Jesus had exorcised seven demons (Luke 8:2).

Christian tradition has portrayed her as a sinful woman or prostitute. This portrait does not come from the Gospels but developed later in church history. Instead, in the Gospels, as we see in John 20:18, Mary Magdalene was the first witness of the risen Christ and the first disciple to proclaim the good news: I have seen the Lord!

Witnessing the Empty Tomb

Mary Magdalene was also the first witness of the empty tomb (verse 1). After seeing it, she rushed to Peter and the beloved disciple and offered the only logical explanation: someone had stolen Jesus' body. Her confusion here reflected a pre-Resurrection world that could make nothing of an empty tomb except grave robbing.

On hearing the news, Peter and the beloved disciple returned with her to the tomb. We know nothing about Peter's response. We only know that the beloved disciple looked and believed. But what did he believe? He did not yet know about the Resurrection. He believed because he already believed, says one commentator. The two male disciples returned home after noting the empty tomb. In contrast, Mary—who knew nothing of the Resurrection either—stayed behind. Where earlier she was confused, now she grieved: "I do not know what they have done with my Lord."

Called Into Resurrection Reality

Mary met someone she thought was the gardener. The risen Christ said to her: "Woman, why are you weeping? Whom are you looking for?" (20:15); but his words did not penetrate Mary's grief. She was still focused on the empty tomb, the

Think About It: "I have seen the Lord [the risen Christ]." What words or actions do you use to witness to the Resurrection? What resurrections have you experienced personally in your life?

missing body. Only when the "gardener" gently spoke her name did the reality of the Resurrection break through her grief. This intimacy changed her world; now she understood: She had seen the Lord!

The First Post-Resurrection Lesson

When Mary tried to embrace the risen Christ, he told her not to hold him. This should not be read as a harsh rebuke, but rather as Christ's first post-Resurrection teaching: He could not and would not be controlled or held to preconceived standards or expectations of who he was. The lesson was that we must leave Christ free to offer us his fullness.

Christ urged Mary to spread the news of his resurrection and of the new life with God and one another now available to everyone. Mary's proclamation that she had seen the risen Christ is the core of the Easter gospel. She was the first to recognize the risen Lord and the first to tell others. She became the first disciple in the post-Resurrection world, the first of the Easter People.

Study Suggestions

A. Examine the Cornerstone

Place a large stone and hang a mason's plumbline where participants can gather around them. Ask five people to read Psalm 118:22-23; Isaiah 28:16-17; Matthew 21:42-43; Mark 12:10-12; and Acts 4:11.

Ask: Who is the cornerstone? the rejected stone? the builder? What have the builders rejected? What does the plumbline represent? (twin criteria for testing faith: justice and righteousness) Who becomes the new cornerstone? (Jesus or the new faith community that carries on Jesus' work?) How does God transform the rejected stone into the keystone of divine purpose? (through the Resurrection and the new faith community). Refer to the commentary on pages 153–54.

B. Explore Double Conversions

The concept of God's impartiality was well established in Jewish thought. Deuteronomy 10:17 states that "the great God, mighty and awesome, . . . is not partial and takes no bribe." However, God's impartiality is given new meaning in Acts. By declaring no one profane or unclean, Peter breaks through a religious barrier that kept Jews and Gentiles apart and unequal.

Read Acts 10:34-43 and the commentary about it on pages 152–53. Ask: What was Peter's conversion? Cornelius's conversion? How did these conversions transform the lives that were touched by the event and the early Christian community?

Identify controversial or divisive issues in the church today. Ask: What kinds of double conversions might help the church to model God's impartiality on those troublesome issues? What will help all parties become more open to conversion?

C. Discuss the Empty Tomb

When Mary saw the empty tomb, she was confused. She searched for the missing body and grieved over her loss. She could not let go of the "body" until she met the risen Christ. Review John 20:1-18 and the commentary on it on pages 155–56.

Ask: Have you ever lost something (or someone) very important and not known where it was located? Why is that so disturbing? Are you holding on to a "body" (people or things) that you need to release? How can your faith help you relinquish what you need to let go of?

D. Call Out Our Names

Have each participant introduce himself or herself by full name. Include maiden, married, or professional name; nickname; say "Mary, daughter of Emma," "grandson of Manuel"—whatever reflects one's full identity.

Ask: What is the power of being called by name? What happened to Mary when Jesus called her by name? (See John 20:16-18.) How does being addressed intimately lead to discipleship?

E. Make a Faith Statement: Tie It Together

Paul passed on the core of his faith in 1 Corinthians 15:3b-5. That model of faith has four parts: Christ died, was buried, was raised, was made visible. List these four parts on paper or chalkboard. Look at affirmations of faith printed in your hymnal or worship book—especially at the lines that focus on Jesus.

Invite participants to use the four-part model as a guide and to write their own personal statement of faith. Give them time to write, then invite volunteers to share statements. Ask: What affirmations offered new insight to you about the nature of Jesus Christ? What do these statements call you to do or to be? What insight do today's lections provide on the meaning of Easter? How do they help you grow as a disciple of Christ?

F. Read, Share, Pray, Sing

Read responsively Psalm 118:1-2, 14-24. Share one or two of the faith statements from Activity E. Then close by singing the group's favorite Easter hymn and asking members to voice their response to this session in brief personal prayers.

Lections for Second Sunday of Easter

First Lesson: Acts 4:32-35

OUR verses from Acts make up the second of three summaries about the community life of the first believers. (See also 2:42-47; 5:12-16.) The early Christian community is described as a unified fellowship that involved worship and study, regard for the presence of the Spirit, internal harmony and solidarity expressed in concrete concern for one another, and sharing possessions. Luke sketched an idealized communal goal that inevitably met with real dissension and conflict. The practice of sharing possessions seems unique to the Jerusalem church.

> **Think About It:** "Now the whole group of those who believed were of one heart and soul." Although some Christians live communally today, how might all Christians share in the needs of others? As the whole people of God, how do we strive for unity and harmony?

Sharing Possessions

Acts 4:32-35 emphasizes property-sharing in a way that offers us a model for how Christians are to relate to one another. Marks of a Spirit-filled community include not only sharing possessions but also almsgiving and showing hospitality. This generalized picture is then made more concrete with an example found in 4:36-37. A property owner, Barnabas, sold a field. In solidarity with the community, he brought the money and laid it at the apostles' feet so that they might distribute it to those in need.

A negative example of hoarding then follows. In 5:1-11, Ananias and his wife Sapphira attempted to deceive the church leaders by holding back some of the proceeds of property

> **Think About It:** They died because they lied. What is destroyed in a community by dishonesty? How does honesty build community?

158

they had sold. While all of the gain was at the disposal of the couple, they died because they lied about the extent of their gift.

Psalter: Psalm 133

Psalm 133 is a "song of ascents," most likely referring to the ascent of pilgrims who sang these psalms on their way up to Jerusalem from the coastal plain or the Jordan valley. The psalm begins with concern for individual family harmony or unity. One commentator says the psalm offers us a vision that families are like anointed high priests leading worship. In this vision, the anointing oil represents peace, health, joy, and hospitality; dew is symbolic of blessings of "life forever" through descendants.

Another commentator suggests that, although the psalm begins with individual family unity, it really. is an appeal for the national reunification of Israel with Judah. The dew of 9,000-foot, snowcapped Mount Hermon represents the dream of people from the north "flowing" down to the lower mountains of Zion (Jerusalem), the worship center of Judah, bringing unity to the people.

Both interpretations of the psalm move quickly from the harmony of individual family to a much broader image of the unity of God's people. Ultimately, the psalm seems to say, the whole people of God is the crucial institution, not the individual family unit.

Epistle: 1 John 1:2–2:2

The writer of First John is addressing an internal conflict in the Johannine Christian community early in the second century A.D., at least ten to twenty years after the Gospel of John was written for the same community. Some members had departed from the community's traditional beliefs about Jesus and their high ethical standards. They did not believe that Jesus was fully human and were not practicing love toward one another.

Instead of the usual greeting found in most New Testament letters, First John jumps headlong into the issues in his prologue (1:1-4). He pauses only momentarily to let his readers know that a faithful restatement of the Christian heritage—which they had heard "from the beginning"—is possible. He alerts readers that he intends to adapt traditional beliefs to the new needs of the community without abandoning the content of the tradition.

Having alerted his readers to expect new interpretations, First John asserts in verse 2 that his opponents are wrong. The eternal "word of life" has been made present in the earthly life of Jesus; that is, Jesus is divine and fully human. Then in 1:3-4, he introduces the importance of participating in full community—in practicing love for one another—in order to have full fellowship with God and Christ. First John presents an image of God as faithful, caring, and righteous. The term *Father* conveys God's personal and caring nature typical in a healthy family.

Walking in Darkness or Light

In the four-verse prologue, the writer was rather lofty and vague. Now in verse 5 he becomes more specific, introducing the subject of sin to expose his opponents' errors. He opens with the axiom: "God is light and in him is no darkness at all," a statement that the opponents would have accepted. But he immediately follows this traditional proclamation with sayings that identify progressively worse sins: from lying (1:6), to deep self-deception (1:8), to gross misrepresentation of God (1:10). These three verses expose the increasing depth of error in the opponents' thinking about Jesus and about fellowship with God.

Verses 7 and 9 offer assurances to those who recognize the presence of sin in their lives and confess it to God: If we walk in the light, we will have unity with one another and forgiveness from God. This fellowship is not a mystical experience or a sterile, intellectual exercise; rather, proper communion with God is identified by the quality of our relationships with others—by the way we walk in the light. This involves both owning up to sins that destroy community and striving for deeper fellowship with one another.

Who Is the Advocate?

In 2:1-2, we are offered further assurance: If we do sin, we have an advocate with God—none other than Jesus Christ. Although verse 2 seems to represent sacrificial atonement through Jesus for the sins of the world, the word *advocate*—which comes from the Gospel of John—adds another dimension. In the Gospel Jesus promises his disciples that when he departs he will send them another advocate—the Spirit—to remain with them (John 14:16-17). Legally, an advocate is one who speaks for or pleads another's cause. Technically this implies a legal defender; theologically an advocate is a reconciler. Jesus, through the Spirit, works on our behalf to bring reconciliation with God.

> **Think About It:** The mark of fellowship with God is the quality of our relationship with others. If we fall short, there is One who helps reconcile us with God and one another. Does the quality of our harmony with others in God's family reflect a full fellowship with God? If not, what can we do?

Gospel: John 20:19-31

On Sunday evening, many of Jesus' followers (not just the Twelve) were meeting behind locked doors for fear of the authorities. Jesus appeared among them and offered them peace—fulfilling a promise (14:27). When he showed them his wounds, they joyfully recognized the risen Christ—fulfilling another promise (16:22).

The Church Is Born

Once they recognized Jesus, he again offered them peace; now they could receive it. Then he commissioned them to continue the work God had sent him to do: "As God has sent me, so I send you." He "breathed" the Spirit into them to empower them to continue his work. *Breathed* reminds us of God breathing life into the first human being in Genesis. It reminds us that this is a new creation, that those who believe receive new life sustained by the Spirit. This story differs from Acts where the Spirit descends, not on the Resurrection night, but fifty days later. For John, the Resurrection directly and immediately results in the formation of the Spirit-filled community.

The Work of the Church

Jesus told the newly commissioned community that they have the power to forgive or retain sins (verse 23). What does he mean? Since his words are addressed to the entire faith community, forgiveness of sins is the work of the community, not just its leaders. Also, forgiveness of sins is Spirit-empowered. Finally, since the community's work is an extension of his work, the forgiving and retaining of sins must be seen in light of Jesus' teaching and actions about sin. What he says in the Gospel of John is in contrast to our common understanding of sin and forgiveness.

Usually we understand the word *sins* to mean specific acts of moral wrongdoing or lawbreaking (see Matthew 18:15-18; Mark 11:25; Luke 11:4). This view may be what leads the church to believe that it should judge, punish, penalize, or ostracize others from the community of faith. In John, however, Jesus says that sin is a theological failing. Sin has to do with our relationship with God, not our particular behavioral transgressions. Sin is a failure to believe in God or to witness to our belief in God. To *retain sin* means to remain (or cause someone to remain) blind to the revelation of God in Jesus. Thus, neither individuals nor church are arbiters of right and wrong.

We also usually understand *forgiveness of sins* to mean giving up anger or resentment, pardoning, overlooking a transgression, or giving up the right to punish someone for a wrong. But in John to *forgive sin* means to witness to God's identity as seen in Jesus. This witnessing brings the other to a moment of either belief (forgiveness) or unbelief (self-judgment and alienation from God).

If we combine Jesus' command in John—to forgive the sin of others rather than retain it—with his earlier charge to "love one another" (13:34), we begin to see what John means. The church's mission is to forgive (to witness) and to love one another as Jesus and God love us.

A Brief Note About Thomas

Thomas, who was not present, said he needed to see and touch the risen Lord in order to believe. Christ forgave Thomas's sin (unbelief) by offering himself (thus witnessing to God). He gave Thomas exactly what he needed, urging Thomas to move from unbelief (not doubt or skepticism) to belief. Thomas exclaimed: "My Lord and my God!" (verse 28), acknowledging that to know Christ is also to know God (14:7).

We have wrongly labeled Thomas as the only doubter among the disciples. He was no different than the others who did not believe until they saw the risen Christ—nor from us. We too must find forgiveness (the witness of God's identity as seen in Christ) to be moved to believe.

Study Suggestions

A. Sing the Resurrection

Sing "Christ Is Alive," stanzas 1 and 5.

B. Envision Christian Community

Cover a long table with paper. Gather colored markers. Print across the paper: "Now all the believers were of one heart and soul. Everything they owned was held in common. How good it is when kindred live together in unity!"

Quickly read Acts 4:32-35, Psalm 133, and the commentary on pages 158–59. Then sketch ideas, images, or symbols of unity, community, and sharing possessions all around (and lightly on top of) the printed words on the table banner. When done, ask: What possessions do we personally share or hoard? What would it mean for our local church to share possessions responsibly? How can the church concretely express unity and also deal honestly and openly with disagreements among us?

C. Examine the Work of the Church

Read John 20:19-22, and review paragraphs 1 and 2 of the commentary. Discuss: What is the commission that Christ gave his followers on the night of his Resurrection? What does it mean to you to carry on Christ's work?

Read John 20:23. Review paragraphs 3–6 of the commentary. Ask: What work does Christ give the disciples? How do we usually understand the word *sin*? How do you personally understand the difference between *sins* as moral transgressions and *sin* as a theological shortcoming?

If we understand sin as theological failing, who judges and punishes? What is the ministry of the church in this view? How does Christ's command to love one another fit with this "theological failing" view of forgiving sin?

Read John 20:24-29 and "A Brief Note . . ." on page 162. How is Thomas like the other disciples and like us? How is believing different from knowing?

D. Walk in Darkness or Light

The second-century Johannine community struggled to understand sin. First John uses images of walking in darkness or light to talk about this struggle. Read 1 John 1:6-10 and the interpretation on pages 159–60. Ask: What are the three examples of "walking in darkness"? Are these sins "moral transgressions" or "theological failings"? What are the three examples of "walking in the light"?

Review 1 John 2:1, John 14:16-17, and the commentary on page 160. Ask: Who is the advocate? What does the advocate do?

E. Explore Fellowship

Ask: What qualities of fellowship have we seen in our four lections? (Possible responses: communal living, sharing possessions; family unity, harmony; forgiveness of sin; advocacy of the Spirit; Spirit-filled, loving, carrying on Christ's work of witnessing, retaining or forgiving sins.)

Ask: What do these images of fellowship say about our commission as disciples of Christ? What questions do you have about John's view of sin as theological failing?

F. Renew Your Commission

Stand facing one another in two lines. Turn to the hymn "Sois la Semilla" ("You Are the Seed") or another hymn about commissioning and discipleship. This hymn expresses Christ's commission to us today; he is the one speaking in the song. Read the three stanzas responsively. Everyone reads the refrain at the end of the third stanza. Consider how the lections have called us to discipleship. What is God now asking us to do or to be?

Close by singing "Breathe on Me, Breath of God," stanzas 1 and 2, and asking the Spirit to empower us for faithful discipleship.

Lections for Third Sunday of Easter

First Lesson: Acts 3:12-19

THE context for today's lection is the healing of the crippled beggar at the Beautiful Gate outside the Temple courtyard. Peter and John invoked the name of Jesus, and the man was healed. When the previously lame man began leaping and praising God, he attracted a crowd. Peter and John spoke to the curious onlookers.

"Why Do You Stare at Us?"

Do you not just love that question? The crowd wanted to know what was going on. Peter told them not to gawk; this was not some trick or magic, it was nothing they had done by their own power (3:12). It was the God of their ancestors who had performed the miracle. In the healing, God had "glorified his servant Jesus" (3:13).

The servant reference reminds us of Isaiah 52:13–53:12, the greatest of the servant songs. The believers in Jerusalem identified Jesus with the "suffering servant" figure, the servant of the Lord chosen to suffer and redeem. The healing just performed glorified Jesus; the suffering and Resurrection glorified Jesus even more.

> **Think About It:** The *servant* was *glorified*. Do you see a contradiction between these two words? A servant is humble; to be glorified is to be exalted. What insight is given in justapositioning these opposite concepts? when referring to Jesus? What truth does this paradox provide?

The Holy and Righteous One

"The Holy and Righteous One" was another title ascribed to Jesus. By naming Jesus holy and righteous, Peter was condemning the decision of the Sanhedrin to seek Jesus' execution by the Romans. Peter proclaimed that, in the Resurrection, God had vindicated Jesus. This was a direct challenge to the Jerusalem authorities. If Jesus were righteous, why did they condemn him? Their condemnation of a righteous man earned them the judgment of God. These were "fighting words." Speaking in the Temple, Peter took the risk of being accused of blasphemy as Jesus had been.

Faith, Power, and Repentance

Acts 3:16 is a confused and confusing verse, which is obvious from reading the verse. It seems to mean something like, "Because this man believed in Jesus' name, the name itself has made him strong." (Remember that Peter had healed the man by saying, "In the name of Jesus Christ of Nazareth, stand up and walk.") The faith through Jesus healed him. Note: this is not faith in Jesus or about Jesus. It is faith through Jesus; that is, faith itself is a gift of grace.

Think About It: Many Jews believed in the resurrection of the just. In their mind, Jesus was not a righteous man. To claim that God raised him from the dead was to question their understanding of righteousness. How did Jesus redefine the meaning of *righteousness*?

The word *rulers* in Acts 3:17 could refer to the civil authorities or to the high priestly community. But it could also refer to the "principalities and powers," the rulers of the heavens, according to popular thought. In either case, the inference was that the rulers thought they were dealing with Jesus but did not realize what power Jesus truly wielded. They did not know who he really was.

Finally (verses 18-19), Peter calls on his listeners to "repent." Repentance is an act of acknowledging that our lives are going in the wrong direction and making an about face. In this case, Peter challenged his hearers to admit they had misjudged Jesus and to ask God to forgive them for causing his death.

Psalter: Psalm 4

The psalmist expresses concern about two real-life issues. One is what other people think (verses 2-3); the other is material possessions, particularly the suspicion that others may have more than we do (verses 6-7). Both are legitimate concerns. They may be even more crucial for the psalmist, who thinks he is being unjustly maligned. The key to the psalm is what other people think of him based on his economic standing. The opinions of others cannot shake his conviction that he is of infinite value because he belongs to God.

Think About It: "The awareness that he belongs to God is what provides the psalmist's identity—and his attitude toward material things." What provides your identity? How does your relationship with God determine your attitude toward material things?

Belonging to God changes one's values, priorities, and lifestyle. So the psalmist says with conviction, "When things go against you, remain confident. Offer yourself to God and trust him." The awareness that he belongs to God provides his identity and his attitude toward material things.

Epistle: 1 John 3:1-7

Who we are makes a difference in the way we live. In my family, we say, "a Gooch does not do that." This is not a snobbish statement but a recognition that, because we belong to this particular family, there are certain things we choose not to do—because of who we are. In God's family, we say, "a Christian does not do that."

The writer of First John is clear—we are God's children by his love. Like all children, we develop the characteristics of the family. The first of these is "doing righteousness" (verse 7). The norm of righteousness is God's own justice, particularly justice for the poor. The second characteristic is purity—moral uprightness, unimpeachable integrity. In both these ways God's children are like their heavenly parent.

> **Think About It:** "Who we are makes a difference in the way we live." In what ways do you live differently because you are a Christian, a child of God?

Calling and Responsibility

God's children are called to walk in the way of Christ. Neither justice nor purity is a condition for earning God's love. Rather, they are a response to what God has already done in making us children. Purity, for example, comes from our "hope in him" (Jesus). God has not yet shown us what we shall be, but we are God's children now. We are responsible (and responsive) children because of God's prevenient grace.

Sin and Lawlessness

There is an inherent conflict between lawlessness and righteousness (verses 4-7). Lawlessness, in Jewish apocalyptic thought, is a cosmic power, something greater than the sum of its parts, which hates God. Righteousness, on the other hand, is the form in which God's rule over creation is revealed. The writer of First John sees the church's crisis within this apocalyptic framework. This is a reflection of the teaching of "Two Ways" in early Christian thought. One can choose to be either for God or evil, for lawlessness or righteousness. The language is adversarial. The writer is challenging the claims of those who would tempt the church to choose the wrong way.

Sin is a real problem in human life, so there is a real need for Christ to take away sin. For both the writer and us who read him is the reminder that we

166

must take sin seriously. Sin is more than inappropriate conduct, or a "no fault" interpretation of human behavior. Sin is a spirit of rebellion against God. Christ won a victory over the power of sin in the world and in us. The Christian celebrates God's power that overcomes the sin that is in us.

Gospel: Luke 24:36b-48

This passage follows a narrative about one of the most famous walks in history. Two disciples were walking from Jerusalem to Emmaus on the day of Resurrection. Jesus walked with them to the village and then disclosed himself as the Christ. These two hurried back to Jerusalem to tell the Eleven and others of their experience with Jesus.

Evidence of the Resurrection

Jesus offered two evidences of his resurrection. First, he showed his hands and feet to the astonished disciples. This may refer to his wounds, but it may also be that he simply showed the parts of his body that could be seen outside his robe. The second evidence was that he ate in front of them. As he said, a ghost would not have flesh and bones. "Evidence" is important in the New Testament. The apostles testified to "what we saw"; Acts 10:41 identifies these eyewitnesses as those who "ate and drank with him after he rose from the dead."

From about the third century B.C. into the time of the early church, there was debate and confusion about the unity of body and soul. The concept of Plato that the soul was immortal conflicted with the Jewish concept of the resurrection of the body. Rabbis taught that at death, the soul left the body but might return until the body disintegrated; at the messianic age, the body would rise.

Think About It: How do you understand the difference between immortality of the soul and the resurrection of the body?

the body would rise. The death and resurrection of Jesus, whose body and soul remained united with God, developed a system of belief that moved beyond both Jewish and Greek beliefs.

The Fulfillment of Scripture

Jesus reminded the disciples that he told them all these things while still with them. There is, therefore, a mystery about the resurrected Jesus. He appeared to them, but he was no longer "with them." Then he opened their minds to understand the Scriptures. The message of Scripture is not always self-evident; one's mind must be opened to grasp the meaning. Luke clearly believed that the Scriptures are rightly understood only in the light of Jesus' death and resurrection. Remember, when the New Testament talks about

Scripture, the reference is always to the Septuagint, the Greek translation of the Hebrew Scriptures.

But what does it mean to "fulfill" the Scripture? The Greek word for *fulfill* means "to make complete, to bring to fullness." So fulfilling Scripture did not necessarily mean making a prediction come true; that would, in fact, be a violation of the integrity of the text. Scripture has to be understood in the light of what it meant for the writer and the original audience. Only after we grasp that message can we look for other meanings as we bring the text into conversation with contemporary life. So "fulfill" means that Scripture is made complete in Jesus. When the Scripture mentions suffering, for example, it is Jesus' suffering that defines what suffering means.

Fulfillment in Mission

Part of fulfilling the Scripture, Jesus says, is that repentance and forgiveness are to be preached to all nations. The greatest of the Hebrew prophets had said the same thing. What is new is that the preaching is done in Jesus' name. This will begin in Jerusalem and extend to all nations (compare Acts 1:8). A witness is one who has seen and can testify to the truth of the gospel. By their own experience, the apostles bore witness to the fact of the Resurrection. By faith, they saw the significance of Jesus' suffering, death, and resurrection and testified to its truth and power.

We are not eyewitnesses to the Resurrection. We have not seen or touched the risen Lord. We do believe the witness of the apostles, and we also know the power of Christ's resurrection. We have seen its power in the life of the church and in our own lives, and we bear witness to it.

Study Suggestions

A. Explore Who Jesus Is

Sing or read together the hymn "Thine Be the Glory," and look for titles for Jesus. Ask: Who does the hymn say Jesus is? Why have Christians historically affirmed both his humanity and divinity?

Read aloud Acts 3:12-19; then call out the words that describe who Peter thought Jesus was, and write them on the chalkboard or a large sheet of paper. What titles does he use? What do they mean? Read the commentary on pages 164–65, and review the background of this passage. Ask: What does repentance mean to you? How is it a response to who Jesus is?

B. Discover Your Own Identity

Ask persons to find a partner, preferably someone they do not know well. Then ask them to describe who they are without saying anything about their work—using adjectives as well as nouns.

Have participants read 1 John 3:1-7. Ask: What does the writer say about our identity? How did we develop that identity? What does our identity have to do with our calling and responsibility? How does this compare with the ways we have just defined our identity?

Read the commentary on pages 166–67. Explore the conflict between lawlessness and righteousness. Ask: What is meant by *sin* in this text? How does this relate to our usual understanding of sin? How is rebellion against God different from wrong conduct?

C. Consider Psalm 4

Have the group read Psalm 4 in unison. Ask: What does the psalmist say about what other people think about us? How do the opinions of others shape our own identities?

D. Fulfill the Scripture

Invite the class to read Luke 24:36b-48 silently, then review the commentary on pages 167–68. Ask: What does it mean that Jesus "fulfilled" Scripture? There may be a variety of understandings, but be sure you include the idea that fulfillment means to "make complete." How do we fulfill the Scripture in our lives? How can our lives make the Scriptures complete in our world?

Ask members what the phrase "resurrection of the body" in the Apostles' Creed means to them. Why does the Creed speak of the body rather than the soul?

E. Draw It All Together

Today's lections speak about identity and responsibility. Ask: What have we heard today about identity, both Jesus' and ours? What have we learned about how we are called to respond to these identities? How are mission, repentance, witness, what others think of us, and material possessions all ways in which we can respond to who Jesus is and who we are called to be?

Close with prayers to accept and act on the gifts and responsibilities we have as disciples.

Lections for Fourth Sunday of Easter

First Lesson: Acts 4:5-12

*A*FTER healing the blind man and calling on the astonished crowd to repent, Peter and John were arrested for "disturbing the peace." In fact, Acts 4:2 says the religious authorities were "much annoyed" at this episode. Today's text records their arraignment before the authorities.

Who's in Charge Here?

The Sanhedrin was a council comprised of priests and scribes that had both religious and limited civil powers. The citadel, located at the Temple, was occupied by Roman soldiers. The soldiers maintained order. The Sanhedrin heard cases brought by the Jewish community. Annas was the high priest from A.D. 6 to 14. Five of his sons and a son-in-law (Caiaphas) succeeded him, but Annas was still the power behind the office. He and Caiaphas conducted the secret hearings that condemned Jesus. "John" might refer to the Jonathan who succeeded Caiaphas as high priest in A.D. 36.

The question the council put to Peter and John is an interesting one: "By what power or by what name did you do this?" It is a question about authority. In ancient psychology, to know the name of a person or a god gave a certain amount of control over them. So the question about the name may also be about power. How can we control whoever gave you the power to do this?

Peter was "filled with the Holy Spirit." This implies that the Spirit filled him in that moment in the same sense the Spirit spoke through Saul, Samuel, Elijah, and Elisha.

Peter Asserts the Spirit's Power

The word *healed* is from the same root as the word *saved*. Healing is a part of salvation; and salvation is involved in healing. Some have coined the word *wholth* to convey this concept. The man was in good health and was saved to wholeness, by the name of Jesus Christ whom you crucified. For Peter to have said these words, he had to be brave indeed! The implication is that, even though the council had Jesus killed, his power and his work could not be stopped, but continued in those who believed in and followed him.

The *stone* refers to Jesus. The *cornerstone* probably means the corner cap-stone that binds two walls together. So, by analogy, it would be Jesus who holds the church together and makes it strong.

There is salvation in no one but Jesus Christ, Peter says. That statement has been a part of the impetus for Christian mission for two thousand years. We have seen ourselves as messengers of an eternal truth, offering salvation to the world while there is still time to grasp it.

Today, many in the church question that exclusivity. They ask: Do we have the right to tell persons of other faiths they are wrong, that only in Jesus will they find salvation? Some advocate the approach of inclusivity (other faiths are valid because they are really Christians in disguise). Others stress pluralism (all faiths reach the same goal). Still others utilize dialogue (we listen and learn from each other, and remain open to conversion). In this context, Peter is clearly asserting that the healing of the man occurred exclusively in the name of Jesus.

> *Think About It:* Is God revealed to humankind through religious expressions other than Christianity? In a world of heightened religious consciousness and tension, what unique claims can we make for Christian faith?

Psalter: Psalm 23

This psalm is so familiar that we seem to read it off the back of our eyeballs. We associate this psalm with funerals and death. But it is really set in the every-day activities of life. It is about getting through the daily routine, finding God's presence in the ordinariness of life. The psalm calls us both to an individual assurance of God working in our lives and to a place with others in the house-hold of God, even when we "walk through the darkest valley" (verse 4).

If we are with God, then we do not have to want for anything. The psalm says to trust God, rather than in our own efforts, achievements, and assumptions. It tells us we should be a part of the family of faith and share community around the table. We belong to God and to one another.

Epistle: 1 John 3:16-24

Jesus showed us what love is. He laid down his life for us. Therefore, we ought to lay down our lives for the community. Jesus' self-giving is not a momentary act of heroism; rather, the writer establishes the idea that self-sacrifice is the way to life. We lay down our lives by paying practical attention to those who lack the basic necessities of life. Love calls us to provide for their needs—this is the durable responsibility of love on the part of the faith community.

The Authentic Life

How do we know our lives are authentic? We check our hearts. In the Bible, the heart refers to the seat of moral and spiritual consciousness. There are two possibilities for us. First, our hearts may condemn us without a full account of the evidence. In that case, an all-knowing higher court (God) overturns the verdict. Second, our hearts may not condemn us because we know we accept the command to believe in Jesus Christ. By faith in him, we are bold to stand before God.

Think About It: First John calls us to a life of loving self-sacrifice, evidenced in working to ensure that all persons have the basic necessities of life. Do you hold to John's practical definition and practice of love? What are you doing to fulfill this call?

How can we live so our hearts will not condemn us? The writer is clear on this. We "walk the walk" as well as "talk the talk." When we pay practical attention to those who lack the basic necessities, we are loving in truth. For First John, love is not an emotion, or an abstract principle; it is a direct action on behalf of those in need.

Prayer and Commandment

We can be bold about our relationship with God. We are in a position to receive from God whatever we ask—provided we keep the commandments. This does not mean that if we are good and keep all the rules, then God will owe us. God's gifts are always given by grace. If we do what is pleasing to God, then we will ask only for those things that God is eager to give us anyway. What is pleasing to God is our living in response to Jesus' command to love.

Personal Commandments

What are the commandments? First, the commandment is personal and theological. We are called to believe in the name of God's Son, Jesus. This means more than paying lip service. It means a commitment to the person of Jesus Christ and to his work and his power in the world.

Second, the commandment is ethical. We are called to love one another. This also means more than paying lip service. Loving means being aware of one another, being open and vulnerable to one another, faithfully serving one another. It also means something very practical—becoming responsible over the long haul for those who have needs that we can help meet.

Gospel: John 10:11-18

Jesus identifies himself as the Good Shepherd and then draws on Old Testament metaphors to explain what he means. The "good," or "model," shepherd is described in Ezekiel 34:11-16. The good shepherd cares for the sheep, rescues them, and feeds them; he tends the weak, injured, and lost. When Jesus identified himself as the Good Shepherd, Jesus meant he was fulfilling God's promises and doing God's work. This is a powerful statement to a hostile audience who had to recognize that they were not doing the work of the shepherd, even though they held the office.

The "Bad" Shepherd

The good shepherd gives his life for the sheep. The hired hand in verses 12-13 is reminiscent of the bad shepherds in Ezekiel 34:3-6, 8-10; Jeremiah 23:1-3; and Zechariah 11:15-17. The kings of Judah did not die for their people; rather, they asked their people to die for them. By contrast, the good shepherd is ready to die to protect the flock.

The Good Shepherd Knows . . .

Jesus knows his own (those who believe), and they know him. A shepherd knew his own sheep and could easily sort them out of a mixed flock when his sheep responded to his voice rather than the voice of an unfamiliar shepherd. This knowledge is parallel to the knowledge the Son and the Father have of each other. Knowledge here is a category of relationship, not of information—the model for knowledge is the mutual intimacy of the Father and the Son. Jesus is the Good Shepherd because of his relationship with the Father. He lays down his life for the sheep because of this relationship.

The flock whom the shepherd knows is not limited to Israel (or to Christians). All who hear and obey Jesus' voice, however different they be and however much we may not like them, belong to Christ's flock.

We reach out to those who are not of the flock, but who hear the voice of Jesus. We welcome them into the flock, even when they seem not to fit in; then we become one flock, following the one Shepherd. This vision of the unified flock also reminds us of Ezekiel 34:31, where God makes a covenant with all the sheep of the flock.

Jesus' Death

In John 10:17-18, the shepherd metaphor is dropped and Jesus speaks directly about his death and his relationship with God. First, Jesus' death is an act of love. The Father loves the Son who is giving up his life. The Son loves the world, for which he is dying. The love comes from both Father and Son. It is not a matter of a loving Son placating a Father who is outraged at the world's sin; it is a unified action of the Godhead.

173

Second, Jesus' death was voluntary. He chose to die as an expression of love and of his obedience to the Father. He was not murdered; his life was not "taken" from him, but freely given in love.

Third, Jesus' death and resurrection/ascension are inseparable. Jesus' death is an incomplete act of love until the Resurrection and Ascension, when the great work of victory and salvation is complete.

A Part of the Flock

Think About It: What does it mean to live as one of Jesus' sheep? What metaphor other than the image of sheep speaks to you of your relationship to Jesus Christ?

Those who gather around Jesus are members of the flock, who share in the mutual knowledge of the Father and the Son. They gain an identity through Jesus' gift of life. To be a Christian is to be one for whom Jesus is willing to die.

Study Suggestions

A. Reflect on the Week

Ask persons to think quietly about the week just past, then offer their thoughts to God as a prayer.

B. Put Jesus on Trial

Read aloud Acts 4:5-12. Ask: What is the key question here? (The question about authority—in whose name were they teaching the people?) Why is this an important question? What is Peter's response? What is significant about his answer?

Read the commentary on this passage (on pages 170–71). Note that Peter says salvation comes only in the name of Jesus. Ask: What is meant by this claim? Can non-Christians know eternal salvation?

C. Explore True Life and Love

Invite group members to read 1 John 3:16-24 and review the commentary on pages 171–72. Ask: How does the writer define true love? What are the practical implications of this definition? If love is truly defined by how we deal with those who do not have the basic necessities, how is our congregation involved in love? What ministries would help us move toward living that definition of love?

Turn to John's words about whether our "hearts condemn us." Discuss: What sort of belief or action would condemn our hearts? How can we know our lives are authentic?

D. Check Out What You Need

Bring in and display a variety of newspaper and magazine ads. Invite participants to move around the room and look at them carefully. Ask: What are all the ads trying to sell us? (One possible answer is "unhappiness." They try to persuade us that we are discontent without this particular product.) Read Psalm 23. Ask: How does the psalm speak of contentment and satisfaction in life?

E. Live With the Good Shepherd

Form three teams and have everyone read the commentary on the Gospel lection (pages 173–74). Have one team read Ezekiel 34:11-16, another John 10:11-18, and the third Jeremiah 23:1-3 and Zechariah 11:15-17. Ask: How do the texts describe a good shepherd? When Jesus says he is the Good Shepherd, what is he saying about himself?

Consider the shepherd metaphor in terms of church leadership. Ask: What are the implications of the shepherd metaphor for the mission of the church? If we take this metaphor seriously, what should we be doing?

Finally, there is a question of our identity in these verses. A Christian is one for whom Jesus is willing to die. How do you react to that statement? What limits does this put on who is a Christian and who is not?

F. Put It All Together

Ask: What are some common threads in today's lections? (Some possibilities: determining who is within and outside the fold; what is genuinely fulfilling; what is authentic faithfulness; the responsibilities of the shepherd.) What does each lection suggest we need to do about our faith?

G. In Closing

Gather in a circle to sing "The Lord's My Shepherd, I'll Not Want" and to offer brief prayers responding to the import of the session.

Lections for Fifth Sunday of Easter

First Lesson: Acts 8:26-40

*P*HILIP was one of the seven deacons chosen to assist the Twelve in their work (see Acts 6:1-6). At least two—Stephen and Philip—broke the mold of service and became evangelists as well. Philip's first preaching was in Samaria (8:4-25). Jews and Samaritans shared a mutual contempt. Guided by the Holy Spirit, Philip preached to the Samaritans; and the gospel was gladly received by them. In today's lection, Philip was directed by the Holy Spirit to leave Samaria and go to the desert. Being thus led, Philip brought the gospel to another person who was outside the Jewish covenant.

Meet the Ethiopian Convert

The Ethiopian was, indeed, a black African, part of a powerful nation to the southeast of Egypt. He was also a eunuch, one whom the law excluded from the assembly of Israel. Both as a eunuch and as a Gentile, he would have been outside the limits of what the Jerusalem church would consider a proper subject of evangelism. Still, he had been to Jerusalem, either on a pilgrimage or on some official business for his queen. Now he was returning home.

> **Think About It:** "The conversation could be a model for teaching and evangelism in our day." How would you characterize Philip's approach to the Ethiopian? How is it a model for contemporary evangelism?

As his chariot passed by, Philip heard him reading aloud, as was the custom. The passage he was reading was Isaiah 53:7-8, probably in the Septuagint, the Greek translation of the Hebrew Scripture. This incident was the first time we know of that Jesus was identified as the "suffering servant." The conversation between the Ethiopian and Philip is interesting and could be a model for teaching and evangelism in our day: "Do you understand what you are reading?" "How can I, unless someone explains?"

176

Philip Offers His Services

We have some indirect clues as to what Philip said, in addition to telling the story of Jesus. He must have been clear that the gospel was open to persons formerly excluded from the covenant. He also must have taught about baptism, because the Ethiopian felt free to ask if he could be baptized. One ancient text adds (as verse 37) that Philip told the Ethiopian he could be baptized if he believed with all his heart. The eunuch replied, "I believe that Jesus Christ is the Son of God." This simple statement may have been the first baptismal creed of the church.

After the baptism, the Spirit caught up Philip; and the Ethiopian went on his way back to Africa, filled with joy. The Ethiopian Coptic church traces its origins to this incident.

Philip, meantime, found himself carried by the Spirit to the coastal town of Azotus, near the city of Caesarea. He ended up in Caesarea, which was apparently his home, and had a long ministry there. Paul stayed with him on his last journey to Jerusalem (Acts 21:8). Caesarea was the seat of the Roman government in Palestine. The work of the Spirit through Philip expanded the boundaries of the Christian community.

Think About It: How is the Spirit at work in the world today to bring unbelievers into the church? How must we respond to those whom God has made part of the church?

Psalter: Psalm 22:25-31

Psalm 22 is dear to the church because Jesus prayed the opening verse as he hung on the cross. This would have meant to his Jewish listeners that the entire psalm was on his heart.

Our passage is about praising God, even in suffering; for God is present with us and shares our pain. We always live in the presence of death. This passage turns that idea upside down by saying that death lives in the presence of life. Life is greater than death; life overcomes death. The payment of vows is a typical part of thanksgiving. It involved an offering and sharing a sacrificial meal with the poor, who because of God's presence will "eat and be satisfied" (22:26).

Epistle: 1 John 4:7-21

We learn to love from our parents and other significant adults. The same is true for Christians: We learn to love from God our Parent. Without God's love as the model and source of power, we would never be able to love. Verse 8 tells us it is God who defines love, not the other way around.

God's love was revealed to us in the sending of the Son (verses 9-10).

Through him we are able to live—and love. Jesus is God's only Son, the unique one through whom true life and true love are possible for the community that believes in him. How do we know love? We know God loves us because God sent the Son to bring us love and life. Jesus came into the world to free us from sin. The God who could have condemned us because of our sin chose instead to free us from it. This is truly an act of love.

Because of God's love, Christians are called to live in new ways (verses 11-12). Because God loves us, we are called to love one another. We are not called to love just the people who are easy to love. We are called to love the persons we had rather hate, ignore, or shove aside. Our relationship with God is tied up in this love. We have never seen God; but if we love one another, that love is a sure sign that God is among us. God's love finds expression and maturity among Christians when we love one another.

The Test of Love

The Spirit is also a sign of God's love and presence among us: "We know that we live in him and he in us, because he has given us of his Spirit" (4:13, NIV). The Spirit is given to the church to help us better understand (1) ourselves and (2) our relationship with God. We live in God's love, but there is an important limitation: No matter how intimate our relationship with God, we are not God; and we dare not take on ourselves the prerogatives that belong to God alone. The inclination to love originates in God.

The church testifies to its own experience. It has seen God sending the Son as Savior and recognizes that God lives in whomever confesses Jesus as God's Son. The commands to believe and to love are complementary, each completing the meaning of the other (4:14-16a).

Think About It: We dare not take on ourselves the prerogatives that belong to God. What prerogatives of God do we or the church sometimes try to assume? What happens when we do this?

The character of God's love is to bring hope to the world. God is love, so to live in love is to live in God. God pours out divine love on the church so that we may be bold in the day of testing. The hope of confidence in the face of judgment and despair is also a characteristic of the church. One need not fear if God's love is present and active, and we are promised that it is.

Finally, John reminds us that love for God and love for neighbor are inextricably linked. How can we love God whom we have not seen if we do not love our brothers and sisters whom we have seen?

Gospel: John 15:1-8

Jesus redefines the traditional symbol of the vine—first in relationship with God, then in relationship with the people of God. In this passage, Jesus, not Israel, is the vine—the middle ground between God (the gardener) and the community (the branches). God is the source and power for all of Jesus' work. Jesus is the true vine because he comes from God.

The Relationship of Vine and Branch

The gardener (God) prunes the vine so it will bear fruit. The branches that are not producing are cut off; the productive branches are pruned back so they will bear superior fruit. The author is clear that the unproductive branches are not outsiders who have nothing to do with the community; rather, they are those persons in the community who do not bear fruit in love.

The community has been "cleansed" by the word (verse 3). *Cleansing* is the same word as *pruning* in verses 1 and 2; it means staying in relationship with Jesus and his word. The required obedience is not just verbal assent. It is a quality rooted in the depths of one's being. The statement, "to hear is to obey," expresses the heart of Jewish consciousness.

If we are not obedient to the word, we have never really heard the word. By the same token, if we do not do what Jesus says, we are not in relationship with him. This relationship is the key to bearing fruit; without a relationship with Jesus, disciples cannot live in love, and thus cannot bear fruit.

Jesus said, "I am the vine, you are the branches" (John 15:5). "I am" is a statement both of self-identity and of relationship with God, since it is a way of saying the divine name. Jesus claims for himself not only an intimate relationship with God but also the very nature of God. We have already seen this in his statements about being the true vine and his Father being the vine grower. Now he links the identity of the community with his own identity (verses 5-8). Note the implications of the metaphor. Branches have no life without the vine. Lifeless branches are either thrown away or, more thriftily, used for fuel.

There are two results of the intimate relationship with Jesus. First, if we ask God for anything out of that intimacy, it will be given us. The key is to ask out of intimacy with Jesus, which would preclude asking for anything that is wrong. Second, the sign of discipleship is bearing fruit, that is, doing works of love. In John's model, this means that we care for our brothers' and sisters' needs. This, Jesus says, is how we glorify God.

The Model for Community

In John, interrelationship and mutuality identify the community. There are no free-standing individuals in the community but rather branches that circle and support one another. The fruitfulness of the branch does not depend on its own effort but on the nurture provided by the vine. Thus, in the church community members are known for the acts of love they do in common with all the other members in union with Christ. This notion is not really new, because the Jewish community saw itself as a whole community ruled by God.

Think About It: God holds all members of the community accountable to one standard. To what kinds of norms do we try to hold members accountable? How can we build agreement on one common standard?

God determines what is fruitful. God holds all members of the community accountable to one standard. This community does not celebrate individual gifts but the mutual working out of love. The mark of a faithful community is not who its members are, but how it loves.

Study Suggestions

A. Reflect on Easter

Easter Day was several weeks ago, but we are still in the Easter season in the church year. Ask group members to think quietly about Easter and how it has been a reality for them this year. Ask: Where have you experienced the power of the Resurrection in your life? Then invite any who are willing to tell of an experience.

B. The New Creation by the Spirit

We talk a lot about "pushing the edges" or "pushing the envelope." Ask: What does that phrase mean in the business world? (It usually has to do with taking risks, doing things in new ways, daring to do something differently.)

After some discussion, invite persons to read Acts 8:26-40, looking for ways in which the power of the Spirit redefined the boundaries. How did the church learn to incorporate the new situation created by the Spirit? How has the Spirit redefined the meaning of the church for you?

C. Learn to Love

Ask: How do we learn to love? Read 1 John 4:7-21 aloud. Ask: How does John say we learn to love? How do we know love? What is the difference between learning to love and knowing love?

The writer says that, because of God's love, we are called to live in new ways (verses 11-12). What new ways do you think the writer had in mind? (Primarily loving our neighbors and caring for their needs.) In what new ways is God calling us to live because of God's love for us? (Allow time for silent reflection before moving on.)

Note that there is an important limitation to living in God's love. No matter how intimate our relationship with God, we dare not take on the prerogatives that belong to God alone. Review the commentary on page 178, then ask: What do you think this means? What prerogatives belong to God alone? Which of these does the church sometimes try to assume? What happens when we do this?

D. Pay Our Vows

Remind participants that Easter is about rejoicing and thanksgiving. Invite them to read Psalm 22:25-31, which reminds us that love is greater than death. Use the commentary (on page 177) to point out what "payment of vows" meant to the psalmist and his religious culture. Ask: In what forms do we pay our vows of thanksgiving? Is providing food for the hungry a form of thanksgiving? What else?

E. Prune the Vine

Ask gardeners for stories about pruning. Then ask: How does knowledge of this metaphor help us understand the meaning of the text?

Read John 15:1-8. Focus the discussion on the vine and the branches (15:5-8). Ask: What does this metaphor say about our relationship to Jesus? about the model for the community?

F. Draw Things Together

Ask: How does the baptism of the Ethiopian, First John's call to love all members in God's family, and Jesus' metaphor of the vine fit together? What is the picture of unity provided in all these lections?

Close by joining hands, singing "Jesus, United by Thy Grace," and praying for a sense of unity in Christ and new strength and wisdom to "push the edges."

Lections for Sixth Sunday of Easter

First Lesson: Acts 10:44-48

*T*HE immediate context for today's lection is Peter preaching to Cornelius, a Roman centurion, and his household (see lection for Easter Day). Cornelius sent for Peter, asking to hear the good news. Simultaneously, Peter had a vision, which convinced him that God declared Gentiles no longer unclean; therefore Peter should not view them as unclean. The larger framework for the lection is the struggle in the Jerusalem church over the nature of their mission. Were they sent only to Israel, or was the gospel intended also for Gentiles?

Perhaps several years before Paul preached to the Gentiles, under the guidance of the Holy Spirit, Philip and Peter proclaimed the gospel to persons who did not belong to the traditional community of faith. The narrative reveals the struggle of the church over issues related to exclusion and inclusion, the traditional past and the open future.

God Loves Them?

When Peter went to visit the home of a Roman officer (10:17-24), he took with him a group of disciples. Peter could have gone alone, but he sensed the need for witnesses to see what God had directed him to do. The disciples who accompanied him were amazed in the midst of Peter's preaching. The Holy Spirit was poured out on the Gentiles (10:44). Are we not sometimes amazed to discover that God loves people we do not like? What does it take to open us up to see things and people from God's perspective?

Baptism With Water

Peter's question is interesting: "Can anyone withhold the water for baptizing these people who have received the Holy Spirit just as we have?" Water and the Holy Spirit have been inextricably linked in the history of baptism in the church. To this day, some branches of the church insist that one must witness to having received the Spirit before being baptized, while others assert that baptism is a work of grace whenever it occurs, and thus the Spirit is bestowed in the laying on of hands at baptism.

Think About It: How is the Spirit present in the sacrament of baptism? Does the Spirit work within the sacrament? Does the Spirit work apart from the sacrament?

By the end of the first century, at the latest, water baptism was seen as a necessary condition for being admitted into the church. The two elements begin to come together in Peter's question. Since these Gentiles already have the Spirit, can we deny them water baptism? That is, how can we deny them membership and the rites of the church, if God has already blessed them?

Think About It: Can we deny membership in the church to someone whom God has blessed? What other times in the history of the church has that question been important? What does the question mean in the contemporary church?

In this story, Peter admitted the Gentiles to fellowship—and church membership—because the Spirit had given a clear sign that he should. The Spirit's work released Peter from any obligation to consult with the church at Jerusalem, although that did happen later (Acts 15).

Baptism and Nurture

That Peter and his friends remained in Caesarea for several days (verse 48) should not go unnoticed. The drama and excitement of becoming part of the church, or the initiation into the church, needs to be followed by intentional nurture on the part of the church. Peter stayed so that these new converts could learn more about the faith.

Psalter: Psalm 98

This is one of the enthronement psalms, which carries the basic message that God reigns. It was written during the time of the Babylonian Exile when Second Isaiah was active. The messages of both are similar: justice and righteousness are the essence of God's will for and action in the world. For us, justice and righteousness are motivated by faithful love. Perhaps the most familiar

Think About It: Salvation (personal) and justice (social) are inseparably linked. Both are motivated by faithful love. How does your salvation experience (God's faithful love for you) move you to acts of justice in the world (your faithful love for others)?

version of Psalm 98 is the Christmas carol, "Joy to the World," by Isaac Watts.

183

Epistle: 1 John 5:1-6

The argument in this passage of First John is both complex and simple. It is a circular argument, but the author was not trying to win debate points. He was trying to speak to a faith community about the importance of love and its implications for our daily lives. Here is how it looks in outline:

1. Everyone who believes Jesus is the Christ is born of God.
2. We respond to God's love by loving God's children.
3. We know we love God's children when we love God and carry out God's commands.
4. We know we love God by keeping the commandments.
5. God's commandments are not difficult to keep.
6. When we keep them we can conquer the world.
7. We win the victory through our faith.
8. The one who believes that Jesus is God's Son conquers the world.

Faith—Belief—Faith

The statement begins with faith/belief and ends with faith/belief. We are born of God—and able to conquer the world—when we believe that Jesus is the Christ, God's Son. The writer presents the essential core of the Christian message. Now let us move in reverse from the last point. We believe; we win the victory through our faith. We conquer the world when we keep God's commandments (point 6). Is this a contradiction? Can we conquer by both faith and keeping the commandments (works)? For this author, the answer is "yes," because keeping the commandments is an expression of faith and love.

> **Think About It:** The way to love is by caring for others. What are the latest statistics for your community and state on persons who do not have enough to eat, basic medical care, a proper place to live, or a decent education? In what ways are we called to love these children of God? How is our love for God demonstrated by our ministry to persons in need?

We know we love God by keeping the commandments (point 4), which mandate us to love God's children—in response to God's love for us—by doing concrete works and giving to those in need. For John there is a direct connection between faith and good works. For all who love God, good works are easy to do (point 5).

To take the argument a step further: The key to keeping the commandments is being united with God in love. When we love God, the commandments are easy—a joy not a burden. Belief in Jesus is not a matter of intellectual assent but the focus of our lives. If we believe Jesus is God's Son, we have both a model and a source of power for living in love. We have a model because we see how

184

Jesus lived and cared for us. He is our source of power because he is the Son of God.

Children of God

That is who we are—God's children. There is a dignity about us, an unshakable status that we did not and cannot earn. We are God's children; God chose us in love. This provides us with incomparable worth. The key to that worth is that we not claim it for ourselves but recognize and honor our worth.

Gospel: John 15:9-17

"If You Love Me Like I Love You . . ."

That is what the children's song says, but the reality is a bit more complex. The church defines love by the love that the Father and the Son have for each other. This same love is expressed in the church. The Son loves the church in the same way that the Father loves the Son—completely, without reservation or condition. We are able to love God because God loves us; this is the love we are called to live out in the world. In biblical language, "complete" joy means our joy is perfect—everything joy could possibly be—because of the love that comes to us in Christ.

How Do We Live God's Love?

Verses 12-17 focus on what it means to live out the love that God and Christ have given us. Verse 12 sets the theme: We are to love one another as Christ loved us. Then verse 13 makes the most explicit statement in the entire Gospel about how we love as Jesus loved. The model of love is Jesus' own death, laying down one's life for one's friends. Paul said the same thing (Romans 5:6-8), expressing amazement that anyone would die for the sake of even a good person. Yet Christ died for us as sinners! John says that Jesus died for the sake of those he loved—the whole world.

In Greek the word meaning "friend" (John 15:13) shares a common root with the verb meaning "to love"; so "friends" are "those who are loved." Lazarus was Jesus' friend, and John 11:5 says that Jesus loved Lazarus (as well as Mary and Martha). Even the idea of friendship is grounded in Jesus' love. To be Jesus' friend and to love Jesus are synonymous, since both *love* and *friendship* are defined as keeping his commandments (14:15, 21, and 15:14). Jesus is now calling his disciples "friends" rather than "servants" (15:13). He has kept nothing of God's love from them/us.

Election and Mission

God chooses and calls certain persons to be his own. The disciples' place with Jesus is a result of his initiative, not theirs. The relationship is always an act of grace. We are in the church because we are called by God through Christ, not because we decided to be. In the United States, membership in the church is often thought to be a matter of individual choice. The text states otherwise: God chooses us to be the church.

> **Think About It :** We tend to use the term *friend* loosely, even calling casual acquaintances *friends*. If we reserved the word *friend* only for those we truly love, how large would be our circle of friends?

God chooses us for the divine mission—grounded in Jesus' gift of his own life. God does not choose us for privilege and power. God chooses us for sacrifice, service, love, and caring. God chooses us to give our lives in response to God's choice.

Answers to Prayer

The final guarantee of the community's union with the Father and the Son was Jesus' promise that their prayers would be answered (verse 16). Jesus prayed to God in full confidence that he was heard and would be answered; disciples can pray with the same confidence. Prayers are answered so readily because the disciples share in Jesus' relationship with the Father. This is further evidence that they are Jesus' friends.

These verses contain God's eternal message through the Son in the church. God lives in the Son and in the church, which lives in communion with God through living out the love command.

Study Suggestions

A. The Unity of the Church

Open by singing "In Christ There Is No East Or West." Ask the group to note how the themes of the hymn parallel the themes in this week's lections.

B. Peter's Experience of God

Draw on the commentary on pages 182–83 to set the context and framework for today's Acts passage. Summarize the story in Acts 10:17-43, and review the study of Acts 10:34-43 done on Easter Day. Then read today's lection aloud.

Ask: How did the Spirit redefine the boundaries for the church? How does God continue to redefine and change our boundaries?

Comment that many denominations see baptism as the moment when one becomes a full member of the church, including baptized infants. Ask: If bap-

186

tism is the act of initiation into church membership, how does this act redefine the limits on inclusivity for the church?

C. Explore Belief, Love, and Action

Read 1 John 5:1-6. Ask the group to summarize the argument in these verses. Write their outline on a chalkboard or a large sheet of paper, then compare it with the one given on page 184. How are they alike and how different?

Ask: Why do you think the argument begins and ends with faith/belief? What is the relative importance of faith and doing good works? Is it really true that "the way to love is by caring for the needs of others"?

D. Justice and Righteousness

Read together the hymn, "Joy to the World." Ask: What is this hymn about? The broader emphasis is on God's righteousness, love, and justice. What do the two songs (Psalm 98 and "Joy to the World") say about justice? about righteousness? about love?

E. Explore How to Live God's Love

Read John 15:9-17 and the interpretation given on pages 185–86. Ask: What does this text say is the source of love? How are we able to love at all? What does it mean for us to lay down our lives for our friends? Is it easier to die than to live a life of service to others?

Finally, When Jesus says that living in his love means our prayers will be answered, is this a *quid pro quo* (an equal substitution)? How do we explain it when prayers of persons living in Christ's love are not answered as they would want?

F. Identify Major Themes

Ask the group to lift up common or major themes in these lections. Write these words on a chalkboard or a large sheet of paper. (Inclusion of outsiders, baptism, faith and works, and unity in love and mission might be mentioned.) Ask: In what ways do these insights call us to do or to be something new?

G. Close With A Litany

In a spirit of prayer, call out each of the themes listed earlier. After each is read, have group members respond with the refrain, "To this end, help us to be faithful, O God."

Lections for the Ascension
of the Lord

First Lesson: Acts 1:1-11

*L*UKE'S account of Jesus' post-Resurrection appearances continues in Acts 1. Luke 24:50-51 tells of Jesus' final actions on earth. He led the disciples out of Jerusalem to Bethany, blessed them, stepped aside, then disappeared into the heavens. Acts, which like Luke's Gospel, is addressed to Theophilus (either a general term for a "lover of God," or an actual person), begins with a reference to this final event when Jesus gave "instructions through the Holy Spirit to the apostles he had chosen" (1:1, NIV).

Jesus' Resurrection Appearances

The Gospel describes Jesus' Resurrection appearances as all happening on Easter Day, but in Acts this is expanded to forty days. His activities included signs, wonders, appearances, and teachings given to his followers. These are detailed in Luke 24 (verses 44-49), which also envisions that the reign of God will continue (Luke 22:16, 18, 28-30); but in Acts 1:6, the disciples expressed confusion as to what its nature will be.

Prior to the Ascension, Jesus was at table with his companions (1:4). He told his disciples to stay in Jerusalem, which reinforced his previous statement that their evangelistic activity would commence there (Luke 24:47).

The baptism of water practiced by John the Baptist is again contrasted with the coming baptism of the Spirit (Acts 1:5). (See last week's discussion of this matter in connection with the Acts 10:44-48 lection.) This is an obvious reference to the Pentecost event to be described in Acts 2.

On a different occasion, the disciples asked when Jesus would be bringing in the Kingdom (verse 6)—probably reflecting their expectation of him as a military or political messiah. In his reply (verses 7 and 8), he rebuked them for wanting to know too much and explained that the coming reign of God required patiently waiting for and accepting God's gift of the Spirit. Then, empowered by that Spirit, they would have their hands full moving out to share the good news, first in Jerusalem, next in Palestine, and then to the regions beyond.

Details of the Ascension

Then come the details of the Ascension. It happened on the Mount of Olives (verse 12), in the presence of the apostles as eyewitnesses (verses 2 and 9), and attested to by two persons in white (verse 10), which indicated their unusual status. The apostles were told that their friend Jesus who had now left them would return again in like manner (verse 11). This reminds us that Jesus himself had predicted the return of the Son of Man (Luke 21:27)—a possible reference to the vision in Daniel 7:13-14. The apostles were to stop wasting their time looking up into an empty sky; so they returned to the upper room in Jerusalem to pray, select a replacement for Judas, and prepare for the momentous tasks lying ahead.

Need for Quiet Time

Jesus' sudden, dramatic departure, coming immediately after his promise of the Spirit and missionary charge, must have impressed on the disciples that his presence among them had had world-shaking significance and that their responsibility to make this known was staggering. They no doubt needed some quiet time in the upper room to let all this sink in and begin to gear themselves up for what lay ahead.

Think About It: They went to prepare for the momentous tasks lying ahead. What would it mean to you if, in a six-week period, you had lost your best friend, feared for your life for being associated with him, been astounded by his return, been challenged to share his message with a hostile world, and now seen him disappear into the sky? When have you been amazed by the activity of God in your life? How did you respond? How have you shared this story with others?

Psalter: Psalm 47

While this psalm was composed as a battle hymn, in which Israel gives YHWH credit for their military conquests, Christians now associate it with the Feast of the Ascension because it celebrates God as sovereign over all the earth. Of its two calls to praise, the first (verse 2) has a patriotic motif and the second (verse 7) a more religious emphasis. Both stanzas end by mentioning YHWH's enthronement (verses 6, 10b). The first was used for carrying the ark of the covenant through the city (verses 2-5) and back to the Holy of Holies (verse 6-7), the second when emissaries from vassal states came bearing tribute to Israel's kings (verses 8-9). Today, Jews recite this psalm seven times before blowing the *shofa*r (trumpet, ram's horn) announcing the new year.

As to the historical origins of the psalm's imagery, shouting and hand clapping (verses 1-5) were done during ceremonies highlighting military or political accomplishments (see Joshua 6:16, 20; 1 Samuel 10:24; 1 Kings 1:39-40). The phrase "the Lord, the Most High" is first found in Genesis 14:18-20; the name "Great King" was ascribed to Assyrian and Babylonian rulers (Isaiah 36:4, 13; 2 Kings 18:19, 28). Trumpets were often sounded during political events (see Joshua 6:20; 2 Samuel 15:10; 1 Kings 1:39; Psalm 81:4). Verse 9 is one of the few mentions of Abraham in the psalms (see Isaiah 51:2, which also refers to Sarah) and makes him and his god YHWH sovereign over all kings and armies. (Compare Genesis 12:1-3, where Abraham is seen as the fount of God's blessing to all nations.)

> **Think About It:** How does this association of Jesus' ascension with political and military exploits relate to his rejection of the political form of messiahship, such as in his statement to Pilate, "My kingdom is not of this world" (John 18:36, NIV)? How do you correlate phrases like "king over all the earth" (Psalm 47:2, 7) with the God of compassion and the servant Jesus who washed the disciples feet?

Epistle: Ephesians 1:15-23

This passage contains a thanksgiving for the readers' faith and love (verses 15-16), an intercessory prayer for their enlightenment (verses 17-19), and a celebration of Christ's ascension and enthronement on high (verses 20-23). The writer first tells the Ephesians that he expresses gratitude to God in his prayers for their firm belief and compassion to their sisters and brothers. He also prays that God will continue to guide them into new truth, wisdom, and awareness of the hope of glory that awaits them.

Dominion Over All Things

The writer then affirms that Christ's resurrection and ascension give proof of God's mighty power. The symbolism here comes from Psalm 110:1 (see Romans 8:34; Acts 2:33-35) and Psalm 8:6 (see 1 Peter 3:22). This language, which may have been used in an early Christian hymn, combines reference to the Resurrection and Ascension, which have happened, with Christ's dominion over "all things" (Ephesians 1:22), which is still to come. The risen and exalted Christ is

> **Think About It:** Christ is head over everything for the church. Why do you think the early church emphasized Jesus' kingship when his earthly life and teachings had embodied humility, healing, and servanthood?

made "head over everything" (verse 22, NIV; like God, see 1 Chronicles 29:11). The writer also makes the point that Christ's sovereignty is for the sake of the church and that it is the church, not the cosmos, that is his body and fullness (Ephesians 1:22).

Gospel: Luke 24:44-53

Luke 24 begins with the empty tomb (verses 1-12), continues with Jesus' mysterious encounter with two disciples on the road to Emmaus (verses 13-35), moves to his appearances back in Jerusalem (verses 36-49), and concludes with his benediction and ascension (verses 50-53). The story is familiar: Christ is raised, his followers fail to recognize him, he upbraids them for their doubts, they eat together, he expands their understanding of Scripture, they are astonished and delighted at the new insight he brings. One interesting twist in verses 36-43 is the emphasis on the physical nature of the resurrected Christ. Luke has him show his hands and feet, ask them to touch him (verse 39), and eat fish (42-43).

> **Think About It:** The physical nature of the resurrected Christ is emphasized. Why do you think Luke stressed Jesus' physical body in these Resurrection stories? Remember that he also suddenly appeared and then vanished in the Emmaus story. Does this suggest a spiritual rather than a physical body? Why are both the physical and spiritual represented in this narrative?

Between Easter and Pentecost

The relationship between Jesus and the religion of his Jewish contemporaries, found throughout Luke's Gospel, is seen here both in the emphasis on Jesus' death and resurrection as fulfilling the Hebrew scriptures (verses 44-46) and in the stress on Jerusalem as the point from which outreach to the world is to begin (see Acts 1:1-6; Isaiah 2:3). The message to be spread in this mission is repentance and forgiveness of sin (Luke 24:47; see Acts 2:38; 3:19; 5:31; 11:18; 17:30). Empowerment for this mission will come from the Holy Spirit, for which they are to wait in Jerusalem (Luke 24:49; see Acts 1:4-8). The apostles, like ourselves, are abiding between the joy of Easter and the infilling and commissioning of Pentecost.

Jesus Christ Is Lord!

The Gospel of Luke is emphatic in its belief that the risen Christ ascended into the heavens after forty days. This was their way of asserting that the Jesus whom they had followed and loved was indeed the Messiah of God, was reigning with God, and would return to establish his rule over "earth as in heaven." They were saying that Jesus the rabbi was Christ the redeemer

> ***Think About It:*** Jesus Christ Is Lord! What do you mean when you affirm your faith in these awesome words? What dimensions of faith are expressed by the human Jesus, the saving Christ, and the reigning Lord? These dimensions are often called Jesus as prophet, priest, and king. Why are all three important?

and Lord of the universe. It is these basic tenets of faith that we likewise affirm on Ascension Day. Jesus Christ is Lord!

The basic meaning of Ascension Day is that Jesus Christ is not only a human prophet, teacher, and healer who dwelt on earth two thousand years ago, but also the transcendent Christ who came from God, returned to God to reign over all creation, and will come again in glory. The early Christians expected his return soon; today we await the completion of his work of creation, redemption, and judgment in a variety of ways. Some leave the fulfillment all up to God; some see the signs of an imminent end; some "work for the night is coming, when our work is done";

> ***Think About It:*** How do you wait and/or work for the coming of Christ and the fulfillment of his purpose?

some believe his second coming is fulfilled when he enters and transforms human hearts and lives.

Study Suggestions

A. Recite the Creed

Begin by asking the group to stand and repeat the Apostles' Creed. Write on chalkboard or a large sheet of paper the words, "He ascended into heaven, and sitteth at the right hand of God the Father Almighty; from thence he shall come to judge the quick and the dead." Read the comparable sentence from the Nicene Creed, which adds the phrases, "he will come again in glory" and "his kingdom will have no end." State that it is this belief, grounded in this week's lections, that is the basis for today's observance of Ascension Day.

B. Form Groups

Divide into four groups, assigning each one of the four lections. Have them read the passages and the commentary material on pages 188–92. Ask them to discuss the general questions below and the "Think About It" questions specific to each lection. Ask each group to select a recorder/reporter who will share its findings with the total group later on. The study questions that apply to all four lections are: (1) What is the central teaching in this passage? Put the key idea in one sentence. (2) Why was this idea important to the writer and first audience? (3) How is this idea helpful to us in growing our Christian faith and life? (4) What is troublesome about this passage and idea? (5) How might we resolve the issues it raises? Write these on a chalkboard or a large sheet of paper so the groups can refer to them as they discuss the questions.

C. Report Back

When the groups have finished, ask the four reporters to take seats together as a panel. Pose the five questions one at a time, asking each reporter in turn to share hir or her group's thinking on one question before going on to the next. After all four have reported on the first question, invite the whole group to express their thoughts on it, before continuing with question two, and so on. Introduce the "Think About It" questions into the discussion at relevant points.

D. Compose an Affirmation of Faith

Send participants back into the small groups. Each group is to write a sentence expressing their belief in the doctrine of the Ascension in words that are (1) faithful to the original intent of these Scriptures and (2) meaningful to "your people," however they choose to identify their people.

E. Reach a Consensus Statement

Have representatives from the groups (the same or different persons) return to the panel, share their affirmations, and work through to a consensus affirmation on which all can agree. Write this up on a chalkboard or a sheet of paper. If the group finds it impossible to agree, comment that this is not uncommon in the church and ask how Christians should feel about and handle such basic disagreements. Recall the classic statement, "In essentials unity, in nonessentials liberty, in all things charity." Ask whether they think the doctrine of the Ascension is an essential. Emphasize that a more important basis for the unity of the church may be spiritual and relational rather than doctrinal.

F. Affirm Spiritual Unity

Close with a brief moment of worship. Sing an Ascension hymn, such as "All Hail the Power of Jesus' Name" or "Jesus Shall Reign." Read Psalm 47 responsively, possibly using a sung response. Recite the Apostles' Creed, substituting the Ascension sentence developed by the group. (If no consensus was reached on this, use instead an impromptu prayer of confession acknowledging differences but affirming mutual acceptance and respect.) End with the benediction from Romans 15:13: "May the God of hope fill you with all joy and peace in believing, so that you may abound in hope by the power of the Holy Spirit."

Lections for Seventh Sunday of Easter

T First Lesson: Acts 1:15-17, 21-26

THE first readings since Easter have come from the Book of Acts rather than from the Old Testament in order to tell the story of the disciples after Jesus' resurrection. Acts continues several emphases from the Gospel of Luke: the fulfillment of Scripture, the work of the Holy Spirit, and the importance of prayer. The two-volume work was written about A.D. 70–90 in vivid and elegant Greek by a well-educated Gentile Christian who consulted the Septuagint, the Greek translation of the Hebrew Scriptures.

As we have seen, the opening verses of Acts describe the Ascension, when the risen Christ was taken up into heaven. Having been instructed by Jesus to wait in Jerusalem for the baptism of the Holy Spirit (1:4-5), the eleven remaining disciples were praying with others in the upper room.

Peter emerged as a leader immediately and dominates the first half of Acts, thus fulfilling his commission (Luke 5:1-11; 22:31-32). He declared that they must choose a twelfth disciple to replace Judas. Jesus had promised that the Twelve would sit at table in the God's realm and judge the twelve tribes of Israel (Luke 22:30). The number *twelve* signifies wholeness.

Peter interpreted the Scriptures for the gathering (as had Jesus on the Emmaus road in Luke 24:27), explaining that the Holy Spirit spoke through David in the Psalms to predict the fate of Judas. Luke has Peter citing Psalms 69:25 and 109:8 to prove that Judas's place must be given to another (Acts 1:18-20).

Credentials and Commission

Peter then stated the qualifications for being an apostle: he must have been with Jesus since the baptism of John until the Ascension. The commission for

194

the apostles is stated twice in this first chapter of Acts, once by Jesus—"You will be my witnesses in Jerusalem, in all Judea and Samaria, and to the ends of the earth" (1:8)—and once by Peter—"One of these must become a witness with us to his resurrection" (1:22). The commission begins both a geographical and a theological progression: Their witness will proceed from Jerusalem to the whole Roman Empire and from Jewish to Gentile converts.

The group selected two persons who met the criteria—Joseph Barsabbas (Justus) and Matthias—and prayed that God would show them whom to select. The method they used to discern God's choice was casting lots or rolling dice. The lots were cast and Matthias was chosen. He is never mentioned again. Matthias was important in order to complete the quorum.

Casting lots to reach a decision seems strange to modern readers; yet this practice was seen as one of the ways in which God revealed the divine will. Questions were posed, requiring a yes or no answer. Seekers would put marked stones in a vessel and shake it until one stone came out to answer the question. In the Old Testament, lots were used to apportion the land of Canaan on a random basis among the twelve tribes (Joshua 14:2) and to appoint the first king of Israel (1 Samuel 10:20-21). Proverbs 16:33 states, "The lot is cast into the lap, / but the decision is the Lord's alone."

> ***Think About It:*** "Casting lots was seen as one of the ways in which God revealed the divine will." What methods do we use to determine what God wants for our lives? How can we be sure the guidance we receive is really from God? (Consider the classic guidelines of Scripture, tradition, reason, and experience that can be used to mutually test and inform one another —and our decisions.) Do we see God making the choice—or us? In some situations, is a random choice the best way to decide?

Psalter: Psalm 1

Psalm 1 contrasts two ways of being in the world—the way of righteousness and the way of wickedness. Righteous persons, who delight in God's law, will prosper like a fruitful tree planted by streams of water. Jeremiah used similar language (17:7-8), promising that those who trust in God need not fear drought. But the wicked will perish like chaff blown in the wind. Persons who scoff at those who rely on God (Psalm 1:1) will be excluded at the judgment (1:5).

The opening beatitude ("Blessed is . . . ," NIV) sets the tone for the whole Book of Psalms. Blessing comes from centering oneself in God's word, from living in dependence upon God rather than upon our own human powers. The contrast between blessedness and wickedness is typical of the Wisdom Literature (Job, Proverbs, Psalms, Ecclesiastes). Although it is peppered with

Think About It: Righteousness
is not adherence to laws but
reliance on God's love. What
is the relationship between
righteousness and right conduct or moral behavior? What
function do laws or rules have
in guiding right conduct?
What is the source or motivation for righteousness?

exhortations about right and wrong, it teaches
that righteousness is not so much perfect
adherence to moral laws as it is reliance upon
God's faithful love.

Jesus, and later Paul, picked up the theme of
reliance upon God, particularly in hungering
and thirsting for righteousness (Matthew 5:3-
11) and in the image of Jesus Christ dwelling in
the believers' hearts, rooting and grounding
them in love (Ephesians 3:16-17). Those who
trust in God will have deep resources to sustain
their lives.

Epistle: 1 John 5:9-13

The three letters of John share language and many themes with the Gospel
of John. Scholars are divided on whether the Gospel writer was also the author
of these epistles. Most believe that a church leader who identified himself as
"the elder" (2 John 1) re-applied the teachings of the Gospel for his own community besieged by false teachers and persecution about A.D. 90–110.

Testimony

The Gospel theme stressed in 1 John 5:9-13 is the nature and work of
Jesus Christ. "Testimony" (or "witness"—5:9) translates the Greek *mar-
turia,* from which comes the word "martyr." Martyrs testify to Christ with
their lives. John 1:6-9 tells how John the Baptist came "as a witness to testify" to Christ. Jesus told the disciples they are to testify (15:27), promising that the Holy Spirit will help and comfort them (14:26-27; 15:26).

Three Witnesses

In Jewish law, two, preferably three witnesses were required to validate
a testimony (Deuteronomy 19:15). First John 5:6-8 declares that the true
nature of Christ is testified to by three witnesses: the water, the blood, and
the Spirit. John may have meant the water of Christ's baptism, the blood
of the Crucifixion, and the prompting of the Holy Spirit. Or, he may have
been referring to the testimony of the soldier who pierced Jesus' side and
saw water and blood gush out (John 19:34-35). Either way, he wants to
show that Jesus had been called by God, had
truly died, and was raised from the dead.
First John made this argument against those
who held that Jesus had been only a spirit
and not fully human.

Think About It: What con-
vinces you that Jesus is the
Son of God?

196

The writer states that human testimony (like the soldier's) is superseded by God's own witness to Christ (1 John 5:9), which is made in the hearts of believers (5:10) and by the gift of eternal life (5:11). God's word is valid testimony in itself. If we do not believe it, John says, we make God a liar (5:10). The life believers experience in Christ is a foretaste of the life to come.

Gospel: John 17:6-19

Jesus' prayer in John 17:6-19 on the eve of the Crucifixion is the theological climax of the Gospel. After concluding his teaching in Chapters 13–16 and washing the disciples' feet, Jesus prayed for his disciples, knowing he would soon be taken away. In the prayer, Jesus looked back to what he had accomplished, anticipated the cross, and prepared the disciples for what they must do. Jesus prayed for them in confidence that God would grant what he asked because he and God "are one" (17:11). The prayer provides a glimpse of the intimacy between God and Jesus, modeling that intimacy for the faith community.

Before moving into his intercessions, Jesus made clear to whom the disciples belonged—God. "They were yours, and you gave them to me" (17:6). Jesus interceded for them because they belonged to God and not to the world. Here *world* (Greek *kosmos*) refers to the constellation of evil powers hostile to God, not to be confused with "creation" or "earth." Jesus had "guarded" (17:12) them like a good shepherd watches over the sheep (10:1-5, 11-15); but once he was gone, they would be vulnerable to the world.

Three Intercessions

Therefore, Jesus asked God to do three things for the disciples: protect them from division (17:11), guard them from the "evil one" (17:15), and sanctify them in the truth (17:17). The first petition asks that believers will experience the same mutual love that exists between Jesus and God, a oneness that brings joy (17:13; 15:11). This echoes Jesus' teaching after the foot washing: "By this everyone will know that you are my disciples, if you have love for one another" (13:35).

The plea for protection includes a curious phrase repeated twice: "Protect them in your name that you have given me" (17:11, 12). Throughout the Gospel, Jesus speaks about himself with the words "I am," such as "I am he" in 8:24 and "I am the light" in 8:12. Jesus' self-identification echoes the divine name revealed to Moses on Sinai, "I AM WHO I AM" (Exodus 3:14). Jesus shares in the character and identity of God; to dwell in that divine nature is the disciples' best protection.

The second petition takes seriously the ever-present power of evil in the world (17:15). The prayer assumes they can be protected spiritually from

Satan, but will not be exempt from suffering and persecution (17:14; 15:18-20). Though this prayer has no parallel in the other Gospels, the second petition recalls "Lead us not into temptation" in the Lord's Prayer (Matthew 6:13, NIV).

Jesus' third petition, "Sanctify them in the truth," suggests the missionary work the disciples will pursue; for *sanctify* means to "set apart for a sacred work or duty." As God is holy (Matthew 5:9), the disciples are to be holy. They will bear the name of God in the world (John 20:21).

A Prayer for Us

Though John 17:6-19 depicts Jesus in prayer for the disciples prior to his passion, 17:20 makes clear that the prayer extends to later generations of believers. In the last decades of the first century, Christians faced increasing persecution, which Jesus prayed would not tear them apart as a community or cause them to falter in their faith.

> **Think About It:** Jesus asks God to protect the disciples from division and evil and to sanctify them in the truth. What does your church need from God? What would you like Jesus to pray for you?

Once Jesus ascended to heaven, the community of faith became the way that God's love is made incarnate in the world. Therefore, they have to be united, strong, and holy.

Study Suggestions

A. Pray for Discernment

Begin by singing "Break Thou the Bread of Life" and praying for discernment and wisdom as you study and seek to understand today's Scriptures.

B. Consider Commission

Identify several real or imagined tasks to be carried out during your time together (taking the offering, reading Scripture, taking the roll, and so on). Then have group members in turn roll a pair of dice to discover what their jobs will be. Discuss the advantages and disadvantages of designating leaders and assigning tasks by chance. Ask: How does God choose disciples today? How do we make responsible decisions?

Review "Credentials and Commission" in the commentary, and read aloud Acts 1:15-17, 21-26. Ask each group member to jot down his or her reflections on personal commissions or callings, using these four questions: (1) What have you seen God do? (2) Whom should you tell? (3) Where does God want you to go? (4) What qualifications equip you? Invite participants to share what they have written—first in pairs and then with the entire group—and to make a commitment to encourage and support one another in being faithful to their commissions.

198

C. Talk About Testimony

Assign different groups to study Deuteronomy 19:15-21 and John 15:26-27 concerning testimony. Ask: How do we discern truth? Why is truth-telling important in community life?

Re-read 1 John 5:9-13 and the interpretation given on pages 196–97. Ask: Have you ever heard or given a testimony (as in a lay witness mission, an evangelistic service, in conversation with a friend)? How did it affect you? How did others respond? How might you do it differently next time?

D. Explore Psalm 1

Ask group members to list phrases from Psalm 1 that identify the "way of the wicked" and the "way of the righteous" and then to review the commentary on pages 195–96. How does Psalm 1 offer a different view of dependence and relationship from the typical North American notion of self-sufficiency? Discuss the questions in the "Think About It" box.

Consider (outdoors, if you wish) how a tree's roots go deeper the taller it becomes. Meditate on what it means for you to be "rooted" in God's love. What is required to maintain this sense of rootedness?

E. Compare Prayers

Compare John 17:11b-17 and Matthew 6:9-15. Ask: What similar words or concepts do you notice? What differences? What does Jesus want for the disciples (and us) in each prayer? What is the impact of considering "world" as the realm of evil? How do we differentiate the good from the evil in our world? How do we live responsibly in the world so as to enjoy its benefits, resist temptations, contend against evil, and struggle to right injustices?

Rewrite the Lord's Prayer as if Jesus were praying this prayer for the disciples. Rewrite John 17:11b-17 as if the disciples were praying it for themselves.

F. Reflect on Christian Unity

Read John 17:11 aloud. Form three groups to reflect on the quality of relationships between Christians in: (1) your church, (2) the churches of your community, and (3) the world. What expressions of unity do you see? What divisions? What specific things can you do in each arena to foster unity within the body of Christ?

G. Close With Prayer

Join in praying the Lord's Prayer together, followed by your rewritten version of John 17:11b-17 from Activity E.

Lections for the Day of Pentecost

*T*HE Day of Pentecost celebrates the empowerment of Jesus' disciples by
First Lesson: Acts 2:1-21

*T*HE Day of Pentecost celebrates the empowerment of Jesus' disciples by
the Holy Spirit fifty days after Easter. The Christian holy day is often called
the birthday of the church and may be celebrated with balloons, cakes, banners, red clothes, crimson vestments, and candles.

Acts 2:1-21 describes the disciples gathered in Jerusalem with a multitude
of other Jews for the Jewish festival of Pentecost, the Feast of Weeks, one of
three annual pilgrim festivals to the Holy City. The feast was observed at the
beginning of the wheat harvest (Leviticus 23:15-21), fifty days after the Feast
of Unleavened Bread. Having been told by the risen Christ to remain in
Jerusalem until they received "power from on high" (Luke 24:49), a large
group of disciples were "all together in one place" (Acts 2:1).

Suddenly a great wind shook the house and tongues of fire fell upon them.
Luke says the disciples were "filled with the Holy Spirit" (2:4), just as Jesus
was after his baptism (Luke 4:1). The Spirit, which had descended as a dove
at Jesus' baptism, came here in wind and fire. Fire accompanied other manifestations of the divine presence in the Scriptures, such as the burning bush
when Moses received his call (Exodus 3:2) and the pillar of fire that accompanied the people of Israel in the wilderness (Exodus 13:21).

The Gift of the Holy Spirit

The experience of the Holy Spirit described in Acts 2:1-21 fulfills promises and predictions given in both Luke and Acts: "He will baptize you with
the Holy Spirit and fire," John the Baptist said of Jesus in Luke 3:16. Jesus
promised the same at the beginning of Acts: "John baptized with water, but
you will be baptized with the Holy Spirit not many days from now" (Acts
1:5).

The Holy Spirit conferred the ability to speak in other languages so the

200

disciples could be understood by all the Jews in Jerusalem, who had come from all over the Mediterranean world and spoke a variety of languages. This had the effect of reversing the Tower of Babel experience, in which separate languages confused and blocked communication (Genesis 11:1-9). The visiting Jews heard—each in his or her own language—the disciples tell about "God's deeds of power," culminating in the life, death, and resurrection of Jesus Christ.

Peter interpreted the event for them as a fulfillment of Joel 2:28-32, the pouring out of God's Spirit before the final judgment. The purpose of this display of the power of the Spirit was salvation: "Everyone who calls on the name of the Lord shall be saved" (Acts 2:21).

Power for the Church

The gift of the Holy Spirit equipped the nascent church for ministry and witness. Peter, who once denied knowing Jesus, spoke boldly to the crowd, some of whom may well have cried "Crucify him" fifty days before. Peter would lead, teach, and heal, in the name of Jesus, and would soon be joined by Stephen, Philip, Barnabas, Paul, and others. The manifestation of God's power at Pentecost met a mixed reception, much like Jesus' first sermon in Nazareth (Luke 4:22-30), suggesting that the church would soon be persecuted as Jesus had been.

Think About It: Where do you see the power of the Holy Spirit manifested in your life and in your congregation? (Possibilities: in vibrant worship, evangelistic outreach, fervent prayer, prompting to service, bold speech for Christ, mutual care and support, action for justice, inclusive acceptance, visionary ministries.) How do you recognize the Spirit's presence and power? How do you respond? What have been some Pentecost-like events in your life and that of your church?

Psalter: Psalm 104:24-34, 35b

Psalm 104 praises God as creator of a marvelous world. Verses 24-27 open today's portion of the psalm with an exuberant reference to the great variety of sea creatures, from small creeping things to Leviathan, the giant sea monster, whose diverse beauty gives glory to God. It is as if the psalmist is standing on a cliff overlooking the water, flinging his arms wide to its expanse and exclaiming: "Yonder is the sea! There go the ships! And Leviathan!" (verses 25-26).

The psalmist then reminds his hearers that all of these creatures depend on God for their food and life-sustaining Spirit: "When you open your hand, they are filled with good things" (verse 28b). The implication is that humans depend on God just as closely.

Verse 30, celebrating God's creative spirit, connects to today's Pentecost theme, the work of the Holy Spirit. Recalling Genesis 1:2 and 2:7 and pointing forward to John 1:3, this verse testifies that the Holy Spirit was with God in creation—in the wind that God blew over the face of the deep and in the breath of God that filled the lungs of Adam and Eve. Psalm 104:24, "In wisdom you have made them all," evokes a related picture of the pre-existent Spirit as Wisdom, an aspect or manifestation of the Almighty.

These verses also model the ongoing work of the Holy Spirit in new works of creation—art, industry, nature. The Holy Spirit, the original artist and architect, now works within human beings to form an ever-changing world, an act that elicits exuberant praise (verses 31-34, 35b).

Epistle: Romans 8:22-27

In the Letter to the Romans, a mature Paul distills two decades of his teaching and writing for the church at Rome. Written just before his trip to Jerusalem with the collection for the saints (between A.D. 54 and 57), the letter's basic premise is that the gospel "is the power of God for the salvation of everyone who believes" (Romans 1:16, NIV).

Waiting for Future Glory

In Romans 8, Paul explores the tension between the suffering caused by sin/persecution and the future glory that will come when God's saving purpose is fulfilled. Paul describes this time of waiting as "groaning" with labor pains (8:22-23), an image Jesus also used of the transition between the old and new age (Mark 13:8).

Think About It: Some transitions are accompanied by "groaning" and waiting. Have you ever experienced a time of intense waiting as in the birth of a child or the return of a loved one? What do those memories suggest about the urgency of Christian hope and expectation?

Not only do Christians wait, the whole created world longs for God to set all things free from evil powers (what Paul calls "bondage to decay," Romans 8:21). The coming of the new age will restore humanity's original glory and unity with creation, blighted by sin since the garden of Eden (Genesis 3:17-18). Believers will be fully revealed as what they are: children of God. Until then, they wait with patient perseverance, for "perseverance produces character, and character, hope" (Romans 5:4, NIV adapted).

The Work of the Holy Spirit

In keeping with Pentecost Sunday, Romans 8 also emphasizes the work of the Holy Spirit. The present power of the Holy Spirit is a pledge or down payment on the future glory Paul describes. Chapter 8 describes the Spirit as manifested in several ways: It "dwells in you" (8:9); it "[bears] witness with our spirit that we are children of God" (8:16); and it "intercedes for the saints" (8:26-27). Paul assures believers that even their clumsy, inarticulate prayers will be conveyed by the Spirit to a God who knows their hearts, adopts them as children, and will answer their prayers consistent with the divine will (8:26-27).

Gospel: John 15:26-27; 16:4b-15

What would the disciples do once Jesus was gone? How would they keep from buckling under the pressure of persecution? Jesus reassured them in John 14–16 that they need not fear because the Holy Spirit would come to help them.

The immediate context of this teaching about the Holy Spirit is the Last Supper after Jesus had washed the disciples' feet (13:1-20) and alerted them that they would soon be leaving for the garden of Gethsemane (14:31). Knowing that Judas would be coming with a cohort of soldiers, Jesus wanted to prepare the disciples for his arrest and crucifixion, and for the persecution to follow.

What Is a "Paraclete"?

Jesus promised in 14:16-17, 26; 15:26-27; 16:7-11, 12-15 that he would send the "Paraclete"—translated "Advocate" (NRSV) and "Counselor" (NIV)—to the disciples. The Greek word, *paraclete*, used as both noun and verb by John, has several meanings, such as "to exhort and encourage" and "one called to the side of." An *advocate* is a defense lawyer, one who makes a formal argument on behalf of another in a court of law. The disciples would need such an advocate when they were questioned by the authorities as Jesus was (15:20). Jesus promised that the Holy Spirit would "testify" on their behalf (15:26) and "prove the world wrong" about him (16:8).

Paraclete has also been translated as "Helper," "Comforter," and "Counselor." "Helper" was the common usage of the Greek word. "Comforter" conveys the sense of consolation that the disciples would be given in their grief, a translation that accords with John 16:7. The translation "Counselor" pulls together several of these meanings of encouragement, guidance, support, and comfort.

Telling the Truth

John used another phrase to describe how the Holy Spirit would be at work among the disciples—as the "Spirit of truth" (16:13). The ability to discern and tell the truth is crucial, as in "You will know the truth, and the truth will make you free" (8:32). The disciples need to be guided by the "Spirit of truth" just as the psalmist prayed, "Teach me to do your will, / for you are my God. / Let your good spirit lead me / on a level path" (Psalm 143:10).

The disciples, who would face the full wrath of "the ruler of this world" (John 16:11), would need the ongoing guidance of the Spirit. They could trust the Spirit because it would speak only what was given it by God (16:13), just as Jesus only spoke what God gave him (16:15).

A Difficult Moment

Jesus showed great sensitivity to the disciples' feelings in that difficult moment. He understood that they might have quit asking him questions out of a sense of sorrow and foreboding (16:5-6). He cut short his teachings because they "cannot bear them now" (16:12). Anticipating their grief, Jesus cared for them as for bewildered children, saying that it was to their advantage that he should go away because then the Spirit would come (16:7).

> **Think About It:** Jesus advised his disciples that "it is to your advantage that I go away." Would you have found this comforting? What would you have wanted to hear from Jesus at that time?

Jesus' words help us understand the work of the Holy Spirit who continues in ministry to us in the physical absence of Jesus. What Jesus had done the Holy Spirit would do: teach, guide, defend, comfort, help. By the power of the Spirit the disciples would be equipped to witness for Jesus in a hostile world.

Study Suggestions

A. Read the Psalm and Sing

Read Psalm 104:24-34, 35b responsively. Sing a hymn about the marvels of God's creation, such as "God Who Stretched the Spangled Heavens."

Invite participants to share times they have experienced the glory of creation, particularly on or near the ocean. Have any been on a whale watch or gone snorkeling near a coral reef or experienced the surf crashing on the rocks? Does our delight in God's creation call us to preserve our environment?

B. Explore the Holy Spirit

Form four groups, assigning each group one of the lections for today. Have them read the Scripture and review the commentary on their passage. Ask: What does the Holy Spirit do in this passage? What is the effect on human beings? How are God's purposes accomplished?

Have groups report their findings. Make a master list of all of the ways the Holy Spirit is shown to be at work in today's lections. Invite group members to share previous knowledge about the work of the Holy Spirit from other

Scriptures and from their own experience. Look up the passages in addition to the lections that are mentioned in the commentary material.

C. Investigate the Paraclete and Spiritual Gifts

Discuss how you see the gifts of the Spirit (not limited to the biblical lists) at work in your lives, your group, and the world. What are the most dramatic gifts (perhaps loving persons too difficult to love) and the most subtle (perhaps helping behind the scenes). Ask: How do you feel about dramatic manifestations of the Spirit? What do they add to the life of the community? Note the ways you see the Holy Spirit at work in your congregation. Give examples of persons who seem to be Spirit-filled or Spirit-led. Ask: Are there any ways you see the Spirit at work that are not written on the master list? (Remind class members that every Christian receives the Spirit at baptism.)

Review the different translations of the Greek word *paraclete* from the commentary on page 203, and take time to explore the meanings associated with each one. Ask: Which seems most compatible with the context? How do you see the Paraclete guiding you?

Read Acts 2:12-13, Luke 4:28-30, and John 15:18-19. Ask: What do you think prompted the resistance to Jesus and the disciples? When have you observed resistance to an outpouring of the Holy Spirit?

D. Experience Pentecost

Ask three or more persons who know a language other than English to obtain before the session a copy of the Bible in that language. Have them read aloud Acts 2:14-21 from their versions at the same time the English translation is read. Ask: What was it like to hear the different translations? What does this suggest about the first Pentecost?

E. Study Romans

Read Romans 8:22-27 aloud, and review the commentary on pages 202–203. What are Paul's main points in this passage? For what do believers wait? What image does Paul use for the time of waiting? What help do believers receive? Look up Galatians 5:22-23 for a related verse that details the "fruit(s) of the Spirit."

F. Close With a Prayer Hymn

Conclude by singing together the praise chorus, "Spirit of the Living God, Fall Afresh on Me." Invite participants to use simple, impromptu movements to accompany each phrase as they feel led.

SUNDAYS AFTER
PENTECOST

Lections for Trinity Sunday

Old Testament: Isaiah 6:1-8

*T*HIS vision of God's glory came to the prophet Isaiah in the year King Uzziah died (about 742 B.C.). Uzziah's long and prosperous reign had taken the federated city states of Judah to their greatest heights since Solomon; but Uzziah had been stricken with leprosy, creating a national emergency. The visions and oracles of Isaiah of Jerusalem (First Isaiah) are contained in Chapters 1–39 of the Book of Isaiah. He prophesied from 742 to 701 B.C. during the reign of four kings: Uzziah, Jotham, Ahaz, and Hezekiah (1:1).

The Vision of Isaiah

While worshiping in the Temple, Isaiah "saw" the Lord, an astounding assertion given the Old Testament belief that no one could see God and live (Exodus 33:20). Actually, Isaiah's vision was only a marginal yet inspiring glimpse—more than enough to overpower him and change the course of his life. What he said he saw was a high throne, the hem of a vast robe, and seraphim—six-winged heavenly beings in the shape of serpents. The seraphim hid themselves with two of their wings while calling out praises to God. The doors of the Temple shook, and the room filled with smoke, manifestations of the divine presence that are reminiscent of Moses' experience at Sinai (Exodus 19:18).

A People of "Unclean Lips"

Isaiah believed he was lost (or that he must fall silent—the phrase can be translated both ways) because he was a "a man of unclean lips" among an unclean people. "Unclean lips" suggests sinfulness and defilement in contrast to the holiness and majesty of God. Throughout his ministry, Isaiah would upbraid the people for lying, cheating, and oppressing the poor. Jesus later stressed that "it is not what goes into the mouth that defiles a person, but it is what comes out . . . evil intentions, murder, adultery, fornication, theft, false witness, slander" (Matthew 15:11, 19).

A seraph touched Isaiah's lips with a coal from the altar, cleansing him from sin, which enabled him to say, "Here am I; send me!" (Isaiah 6:8). This vision demonstrates that it was God who inaugurated Isaiah's ministry. Isaiah's vision presents the image of God as a king with his minions, a powerful ruler who had absolute control over the lives of his subjects. The Book of Isaiah contains many other images for God such as father, mother, shepherd, warrior, and potter.

Trinity Sunday

The Gospel writer, John, believed that what Isaiah really saw was a vision of the glory of Christ (John 12:41). In the last speech of Acts (28:25-27), Paul names the voice in Isaiah 6 as the Holy Spirit. Following these leads from John and Luke, later Christian commentators have seen Isaiah 6:1-8 as an expression of the Trinity in which the Father, Son, and Holy Spirit are all present. The cry of the seraphim still resounds in the sanctuary when we repeat their words of the Great Thanksgiving during Holy Communion.

> **Think About It:** Isaiah upbraided the people for lying, cheating, and oppressing the poor. Jesus named other sins that defile. For what sins would Isaiah or Jesus upbraid us today—as individuals? as a nation? What would correspond in our time to the external (what goes into the mouth) versus the internal (what comes out) reasons for condemnation/approval and rejection/acceptance of persons? (Consider for externals: skin color, language, dress, hair style, tattoos; for internals good/ill will, honesty/deceit, generosity/greed, caring/ignoring.)

> **Think About It:** Isaiah's vision presents the image of God as a king. There are many other images for God in Scripture. How do you think of God? Which are closest to Jesus' picture of God?

Psalter: Psalm 29

Psalm 29 calls on members of the heavenly council to give glory to YHWH. Like Isaiah, who had a vision of hovering seraphim, the psalmist imagines the "heavenly beings" who surround God's throne, commanding them to "ascribe" to God what rightfully belongs to God. These heavenly beings, "sons of God," were understood as semi-divine beings that had been adopted as servants of YHWH. The opening verses assert that now God alone reigns!

God Reigns

The next seven verses paint a powerful picture of how God's awesome sovereignty is revealed in natural phenomena. The voice of God is heard in the storms that rise up over the Mediterranean Sea and electrify the Syrian desert (29:3-4, 7). The power of God uproots trees and shakes the mountains (29:5-6, 8-9). The psalmist recreates the terrifying sensations of an actual storm by repeating "the voice of the LORD" seven times, each phrase like a clap of thunder. Verse 9a can also be translated "causes the deer to calve"; ancient people believed thunder could induce labor. The strong and violent verbs in the psalm—"break, flash, shake, whirl"—culminate in the one-word utterance, "Glory!" (29:9).

These verses call to mind other theophanies (powerful manifestations of God's presence), such as the earthquake and wind that presaged God's appearance to Elijah in the cave (1 Kings 19:11-12). The psalmist uses the skin-prickling power of the thunderstorm to evoke awe for almighty God.

Psalm 29:10 may be a sideways thrust at the Canaanite storm god, Baal, who was often pictured enthroned over the water. God, at whose command the flood waters rose and fell (Genesis 6–8), reigns supreme. In the final verse the psalmist asks that God's awesome power be used to strengthen and help God's people.

Epistle: Romans 8:12-17

In this densely packed paragraph, Paul describes life in the Spirit and how the believer is changed by faith in Christ. Using a style of argumentation common among Greek philosophers (diatribe), Paul draws sharp contrasts between flesh and spirit, life and death, slavery and adoption. His strong rhetoric asserts a radical new reality: "There is therefore now no condemnation for those who are in Christ Jesus. . . . [Christ] has set you free from the law of sin and death" (8:1-2).

When Paul contrasts "flesh" and "spirit," he does not mean that the human body is inherently evil. Rather, he sees "flesh" and "spirit" as two different spheres of power that act upon human nature. To "live according to the flesh" (8:12) means a system of values opposed to God's will, as when healthy sexual desire is perverted into lust. Life in the Spirit is led by God, to whom we cry out with words of intimate affection ("Abba"—"Papa").

The Family of the Trinity

This passage was chosen for Trinity Sunday because it describes the work of all three persons of the Trinity: Christ restores us to right relationship with God (8:1); the Holy Spirit leads us (8:14) and bears witness in our hearts (8:14,16); the Father adopts us as children and heirs (8:14-17). Paul is more concerned with describing what the Godhead does than with its identity. The equality, mutuality, and interdependence within the Trinity form the nucleus of a new family into which all believers are adopted.

Is this adoption conditional on our suffering for Christ as verse 17 seems to suggest? The phrase translated by the NRSV, "if, in fact," can also mean "if indeed" (NIV), or "since." Elsewhere in his writings Paul puts no condition on salvation except faith in Christ (see 5:1). Perhaps he is taking it for granted that the believer will experience persecution for the faith.

Gospel: John 3:1-17

In this rich and complex passage, the spiritual seeker Nicodemus gets more than he bargained for. Jesus turns a clandestine tutorial into a personal challenge, confronting Nicodemus with a profound exposition of Jesus' own work and the requirements for believers.

Who Is Nicodemus?

Nicodemus's relationship to Jesus was ambiguous. He was a Pharisee, a group often criticized by Jesus. Nicodemus sought Jesus, but only at night, a cautious foray reminiscent of the waffling King Zedekiah who consulted Jeremiah under cover of darkness (Jeremiah 37:17-21). Nicodemus flattered Jesus, calling him, "Rabbi," and asserting that he had "come from God." Though Nicodemus had come secretly, presumably to avoid detection by his peers, he spoke somewhat arrogantly, as if for the whole council: "We know . . ." (John 3:2). His questions seem combative, "How can anyone . . . ?" (3:4). Later in the Gospel, however, Nicodemus would defend Jesus when Temple police came to arrest him (7:50-52) and would help anoint Jesus' body for burial (19:39-40).

Attracted to Jesus, but still deeply committed to the Pharisaic world-view, Nicodemus was not ready to become Jesus' disciple. Jesus' complaint may have been that Nicodemus's faith was based on amazement at Jesus' signs (3:2) rather than on understanding. Jesus did not trust those who only wanted to see miracles (2:23-24).

> **Think About It:** Are you sometimes hesitant to declare allegiance to Christ? Whose criticism do you fear? What helps overcome your resistance?

The Kingdom of God

This passage recasts several traditional terms from the other Gospels such as "kingdom of God" and "Son of Man." Jesus uses the conversation with Nicodemus as a springboard for teaching, a pattern that occurs elsewhere in John (see 4:1-26). Jesus teaches that the realm of God can be entered only by those who have been "born *another*." The Greek phrase has a double meaning lost in English translations that must choose either "born from above" or "born again." Jesus intends both meanings. The believer experiences rebirth through baptism by water and spirit (3:5), and new life comes from above

(3:3). Through baptism, we are given access to the realm of God. The power of God is mysterious and unpredictable: "The wind [or "spirit," another word with a double meaning] blows where it chooses, and you hear the sound of it, but you do not know where it comes from or where it goes" (3:8).

The Son of Man

This passage also reinterprets the title Jesus most often used for himself, "Son of Man." The Son of Man is the one who descends from heaven and will ascend to heaven (3:13). The cross bridges the gap. Jesus compares his crucifixion to when Moses lifted the serpent to convince the people that God could be trusted (John 3:14; Numbers 21:9). Both events demonstrate God's power to deliver and command belief.

To "lift up" (John 3:14) also means "to exalt," a third word with a dual meaning. Jesus will be exalted in the Crucifixion. An early Christian hymn (Philippians 2:5-11) expresses the same truth. The outcome is eternal life for those who believe, but death for those who do not (3:15, 18). Jesus softens this harsh either/or language by proclaiming God's ultimate purpose of saving the world (3:17).

Though spoken in conversation with Nicodemus, who may well be "everyman," Jesus' words were also reassuring to the early Christians whose faith was being challenged by antagonistic Jewish leaders: "God so loved the world that he gave his only Son, so that everyone who believes in him may not perish but may have eternal life" (3:16).

Study Suggestions

A. Open With Singing

Sing a hymn to the Trinity—"Holy, Holy, Holy!"

B. Explore Images of God

Display traditional symbols of the Trinity such as an equilateral triangle or three interlocking circles. Observe where such symbols are in your sanctuary in furniture, stained glass, or paraments. Ask: What do these symbols suggest about the nature of the Trinity? How do you understand the doctrine of the Trinity? What phrases or images would you use to explain "God in three persons" to a non-Christian?

Read Isaiah 6:1-8 and review the commentary on pages 208–209. Try to imagine the vision of God that Isaiah saw. Then brainstorm a list of images for God from the Scriptures and from your personal experience. Ask: Which image has the most meaning for you? Why? Which image do you resist? Why?

C. Compare Flesh and Spirit

Read Romans 8:12-17 and review the commentary on pages 210–11. Make a two-column chart on poster paper or the chalkboard, labeling the first column "Flesh" and the second "Spirit." Ask for examples of contrasting values or behaviors appropriate to each column such as lust/love, greed/generosity, and caring/ignoring. Discuss the outcome and effect of each contrasting behavior—on both self and others. Read Romans 8:13 aloud.

Some Christians believe that the human body is evil, a source of temptation and sin. Do you agree? What, do you think, should the church teach about body image, health, and sexuality?

D. Form a Family

Review "The Family of the Trinity." Draw a circle and place a triangle within it representing the Trinity. Draw a larger circle around it, and write the names of each group member in the outer circle. Discuss what it means to be together in the family of God. How should we treat each other? How do the members of the Trinity model our relationships?

E. Experience God's Power

Form two groups. Recite Psalm 29 as a choral reading, with groups reading alternating verses. Ask: When have you experienced a powerful storm? What happened? Can a fierce storm still fill us with primal fear and awe?

F. Learn With Nicodemus

Review John 3:1-17 and the interpretation on pages 211–12. List the key terms in this passage—*kingdom of God, eternal life, rebirth*. Define each one. Ask two members to roleplay the dialogue between Jesus and Nicodemus. Let them read the dialogue from the Scripture or put it in their own words. Ask the observers: How did hearing the roleplay enhance your understanding of the passage? What would you ask Jesus if you could?

Invite class members to share testimonies about how they came to profess faith in Christ. How did confessing faith in Christ seem like a new birth?

Read John 3:8 aloud. Have participants think about the wind—how it moves things without being visible itself. Where do we see the result of the wind of the Spirit?

G. Close With Prayer

Invite members to write prayer concerns on sticky notes and post them on the Trinity triangle (Activity D). In a prayer circle, ask the Holy Spirit to move and act upon each concern named.

Lections for Sunday Between
May 29 and June 4

V Old Testament: 1 Samuel 3:1-20

ERSES 1-10 of this lection are discussed in the Old Testament commentary for the second Sunday after the Epiphany (pages 64–65). We pick up the story with verse 11. The boy Samuel had responded to the voice of God in the middle of the night with the words advised by the aged Eli: "Speak, for your servant is listening" (verse 10).

What God had to say to Samuel—or to Eli through Samuel—was not good news. Once it became become widely known, people would be astounded, their "ears will tingle" (verse 11). God was fed up with the apostasy and blasphemy of the priest Eli's sons, and the soft-hearted permissiveness of their father (verses 11-13). They would no longer be able to rely on his priestly functions to protect them (verse 14). His dynasty was doomed.

> **Think About It:** In your prayer moments, what proportion of the time do you devote to speaking and how much to listening? Do you practice disciplines of meditation and contemplation that allow space for the Spirit to break through and touch and move you? What practices have you found helpful that you can share with others?

Giving the Bad News

This message frightened Samuel. He could neither go back to sleep nor muster the courage to return to Eli and give him the bad news (verse 15). But first thing in the morning, Eli wanted to know; so Samuel had to

> **Think About It:** God was fed up. What in our lives and society corresponds to this situation—weak and corrupt leadership at some levels, permissiveness reigning throughout the culture, lack of vision and direction, some

214

tell him. Eli knew it was the truth, took it in stride, and resigned himself to his fate (verses 16-18). The die was cast. God would do what God would do.

The upshot of the story was that Samuel was groomed to replace Eli as God's chosen instrument of prophecy and leadership. His fame spread and from north (Dan) to south (Beersheba); all came to trust and follow him (verses 19-20). In the time of Eli the voice of God had been dimmed by the people's waywardness, and the leadership lacked vision to point the way out of the moral morass they were in (3:1). But now, under Samuel, a new day was dawning. Hope and vitality were returning. The will of God would be heeded and followed once again, and there were prospects for a brighter future.

aware that a change is needed but hesitant to speak out, the will of God clear to those with ears to hear? With what might God be fed up in our time? What signal is needed today to make some "ears tingle"?

Think About It: Was there nothing Eli could do to remedy the situation? Do you ever feel that standards of public and private morality have fallen so low there is no possibility of recovery?

Psalter: Psalm 139:1-6, 13-18

See the commentary for the second Sunday after the Epiphany (pages 65–66).

Epistle: 2 Corinthians 4:5-12

After pointing up the honesty and openness with which he has carried out his ministry and the blindness of unbelievers to the truth of the gospel (verses 1-4; see the Epistle commentary for Transfiguration Sunday on page 108), Paul in this passage first stresses that the focus of his preaching is not on himself, but only on "Jesus Christ as Lord." This phrase may well have been an early Christian creed (see Romans 10:9; 1 Corinthians 12:3; Philippians 2:10-11)— a precursor of the present-day statement of faith to which all member communions of the World Council of Churches subscribe—"Jesus Christ, God and Savior."

Think About It: The creed of the early Christians was "Jesus Christ is Lord," that of today's Christians is "Jesus Christ, God and Savior. Do these phrases express the heart of your faith? Do they communicate the Christian gospel meaningfully and effectively?

A Slave for Christ

In the service of this gospel, Paul counts himself nothing more than a "slave" (Greek *doulos*; see 2 Corinthians 1:24; 12:15) of those he has led to Christ

215

(verse 5). This humility and dedication are in sharp contrast to his critics and adversaries, whom he charges with dominating and mistreating the Corinthian congregation (see 11:20). His readers can readily see the truth of this claim of servanthood, for the impact of Paul's ministry has shown them the clarity of the gospel, illuminated their minds, and enabled them to see the glory and goodness of God in the revelation of Jesus Christ (verse 6; see verse 4 and Genesis 1:3).

The transforming gift of the gospel, though, is housed in fragile containers ("clay pots"). Human beings—both Paul and his readers—are frail and unworthy vehicles for embodying and communicating the wonder of God's grace. Paul had only recently been made aware of this through an experience in Asia Minor, when he had to face up to the contrast between his own weakness and the greatness of God's power (see 1:8-11). This paradox is also seen in Paul's awareness of God's entrusting to mere fallible humans the awesome and demanding task of spreading the gospel—which he sees as God's power to save (Romans 1:16) and Jesus' redeeming love manifested on the cross (1 Corinthians 1:17-2:5).

The Cross: Symbol of Shame or of Grace

To unbelievers the cross was a symbol of torture and shame. When Paul and the Corinthians identified with it they were "tarred with the same brush" and faced with the same risks. But Jesus has transformed the cross to become a symbol of God's redeeming grace (Romans 1:16) as expressed in Christ's sacrificial death (verses 7, 11; see Romans 5:6-11; 2 Corinthians 5:14). The result is that though they (we) may be persecuted, bewildered, troubled, and wounded, they (we) cannot be devastated, depressed, or made hopeless (verse 8-9). For the dying Jesus became the risen Christ, through whom we are given a life and a hope that overcome all obstacles (verses 10-12).

> **Think About It:** The cross was a symbol of shame, but Jesus made it a symbol of grace. What do you think of when you see a cross—on an altar, a steeple, or a chain around someone's neck?

We are troubled but not destroyed. Where do you turn for help and encouragement in such circumstances? When have you felt defeated and downcast? What brought you through the crisis? Does the Resurrection offer you hope at such times, or is it for you mainly a promise of eternal life?

Gospel: Mark 2:23–3:6

These two stories describe incidents in which Jesus came into conflict with the religious authorities over sabbath traditions. In these instances he and his disciples lived out his dictum in 2:27-28 that persons take priority over precepts, that morality is a matter of responding to human need rather than obeying the rules. The "Son of Man" (which can be taken as either a messianic term applied to Jesus or simply a reference to Jesus' identification with humanity) has sovereignty over the sabbath (representing the law—conventions, customs, regulations, habitual expectations).

In the first episode (2:23-28), Jesus supported his followers in their violation, for reasons of hunger, of the sabbath regulations forbidding all work—in this case the reaping, winnowing, threshing, or cooking of grains. In his defense of their actions Jesus cited an incident from 1 Samuel 21:1-6 in which David, trying to escape from danger, stopped at the tabernacle in Nob and requested food. None was available except the shewbread ("bread of the Presence"; see Exodus 25:23-30)—twelve long loaves on a table in the Holy of Holies, which were an offering to God. Only the priests were allowed to eat it (Leviticus 24:9) and then only when it was stale and needing to be replaced. But because he was hungry, David and those with him were justified in eating this sacred bread, thereby showing that even in the Hebrew Scriptures human need was more important than legal requirements.

> **Think About It:** Morality is a matter of responding to human need rather than obeying the rules. What instances of this choice have you faced? What guided your decision? Did you meet opposition or criticism for what you chose? What is your attitude toward Christians who insist on maintaining traditions that produce harmful consequences?

In the next instance, it was Jesus himself who violated a sabbath tradition by doing "work"—healing a man with a withered hand (3:1-6). Pharisaic tradition clearly prohibited medical treatment on the sabbath, except in life-threatening cases. Fractures, cuts, sprains, wounds—all could receive only emergency first aid; but long-term remedies had to wait until sundown or the next day. A crippled hand was clearly not an emergency; it was a "pre-existing condition" that was no more critical today than yesterday or tomorrow. But the man was in need; Jesus was there; the love and power of God were available. So Jesus acted.

He also used the occasion as a teaching moment. He knew the Pharisees would disapprove of this act of compassion and this incensed him. How could they be so blinded by the minutiae of their tradition that

> **Think About It:** "So he confronted [the Pharisees]." Why do you think Jesus deliberately challenged these powerful men, knowing where they stood, how they would react, and what they might do to him? Have you had occasion to take such stands for the right? What sustained you in this choice? What was the result? Would you do the same again?

they could not see the intent and heart of God's law—the love of neighbor! So he confronted them with a question: What is God's purpose: to do good or harm, to save or destroy (verse 4)? Again they had no answer; again the barrenness of their prescriptions was exposed; again their hearts were hardened and their resentment inflamed. So they resolved to do away with him and went off to scheme with their allies the Herodians (powerful men who supported Herod Antipas) about how to accomplish this (verse 6).

Study Suggestions

A. Begin With Prayer

Ask members to sit with open hands turned upward as you pray for guidance and openness to the leading of the Spirit in today's study session.

B. Speak, for Your Servant Is Listening

Read 1 Samuel 3:1-20, and review the commentary both here (pages 214–15) and for the second Sunday after the Epiphany (pages 64–65). Form three groups, asking each to discuss the "Think About It" questions in one of the boxes on pages 214–15—on contemplative prayer, moral decay and social change, and God's will and our responsibility. After each group has reported, invite participants to share their personal experiences related to the issues raised.

C. Make a Creative Response

Distribute colored construction paper, markers, scissors, and tape. Ask each person to create a collage or drawing expressing his or her feelings about the matters just discussed. When finished, form two concentric circles facing each other and have members move slowly and silently in opposite directions holding their creations for one another to view. Then post them on the wall. When all have returned to their seats, invite verbal responses.

D. "Jesus Christ Is Lord"

Read 2 Corinthians 4:5-12, and review the commentary on pages 215–16. Note that this phrase may have been an early Christian creed, and point out the statement of faith of the World Council of Churches. Allow a few moments of silence for each member to formulate a phrase that expresses the core of their faith. Then have them call these out and write them on chalkboard or a large sheet of paper. See if the group can come up with a consensus statement that reflects their basic conviction. Then ask them to evaluate it in light of how well it communicates to their friends and associates outside the church.

E. The Cross as Symbol

Hold up or point to a cross in the room. Ask: What does this symbolize to you? What did it mean in the first century? How did Jesus transform the meaning of the cross, and how did Paul interpret it? What is the difference between wearing or displaying a cross as an ornament, understanding the cross as representing Christ's death for our salvation, and taking up one's cross as Jesus called his disciples to do? At which of these levels of discipleship are we?

F. Troubled But Not Destroyed
Read 2 Corinthians 4:8-9. Ask: How do you respond to this? When have you felt this way? What is the source of this tenacity, courage, and hope?

G. Love Over Law
Review the Gospel lection and interpretive material on pages 216–18. Discuss the questions in the two "Think About It" boxes. Point out how Jesus' emphasis on care for human need over obedience to precepts was in keeping with the strand of Jewish tradition represented by the David story and the proclamations of the prophets about justice for the poor and oppressed. Focus on manifestations of legalism and moralism in our church and society today. Note how civil disobedience is consistent with Jesus' attitude toward the law. Ponder together why Jesus chose to confront the religious authorities this way.

H. Draw Things Together
Ask members to identify central themes in today's lections. Consider these possibilities: response to God's leading (Samuel), the cross—Christ's redemptive sacrifice (Paul) and Jesus' move toward the cross by confronting the powers through putting love over law (Mark), affirming our faith (the creed), and God's power holding us firm (2 Corinthians 4:8-9).

I. In Closing
Read Psalm 139:1-6, 13-18 around the group, one verse per person. Sing "Lord, Speak to Me."

Lections for Sunday Between
June 5 and 11

Old Testament:
1 Samuel 8:4-20 (11:14-15)

*L*AST week's young boy Samuel, full of hope and promise, had now become an old man. Eli's two sons had betrayed their priestly office in idolatry and corruption. Now history was repeating itself, and Samuel's sons—like Eli's sons—had likewise stooped to taking bribes and undermining the integrity of the judicial system (verses 1-3). The pattern of charismatic leadership of the judges period had decayed to the point where the people and their leaders (elders)—looking around them at neighboring nations—were demanding a more ordered and centralized system—a monarchy. Citing Samuel's advanced age and the corrupt behavior of his sons, they suggested that he was no longer fit to rule and declared that a new leader—this time a king—would solve all their problems (verses 4-5).

Samuel, reluctant to give up the old, familiar way (and perhaps also his status in it), was displeased by their request; so he turned to God in prayer for advice (verse 6). The account has God telling him that the people's desire for a king was a rejection not of Samuel but actually of God—just the latest in a long line of rebellions going back to their wilderness sojourn. Apparently resigned to the change, God counseled Samuel to accept it too, but to caution them of the hazards of a monarchy (verses 6-9).

A Catalog of Pitfalls

Verses 10-18 then spell out these dangers—coming from either observations of the failings of their neighboring kingdoms or an insertion by a later writer of accounts of the actual sufferings of Israel under Solomon's autocratic rule. Their sons would be taken from peaceful domestic occupations and drafted into the army and the war industry (verses 11-12). Their daughters would become servants in the royal household (verse 13). Their lands and orchards would be confiscated and incorporated into an expanding royal estate (verse 14). Their produce would be taxed to maintain the royal establishment (verse 15). Their slaves and domestic animals would be compelled to work for the king (verse 16). In the final indignity, they themselves would be forced into servitude to the king (verse 17). They would then realize their mistake and scream in protest, but it would be too late. They had made their bed and now must lie in it; God had acceded to their request and now would turn a deaf ear to their entreaties (verse 18).

Think About It: When have we (as individuals or a nation) wanted something very badly, been given what we thought was a green light, disregarded warning signs, and rushed pell-mell into it only to realize too late that we were headed for disaster? Why does God (as in this case) allow us to make such mistakes? How can we discern the hidden pitfalls in what looks on the surface like a promising venture? What precautions might we take to avoid these negative consequences? What parallels do you see between the situation of Samuel and the Israelites and that of our country today? (Consider conditions on the military, economic, social, and religious fronts.)

But their minds were made up. They wanted to be like other nations. The attractions of order, security, and military conquest outweighed the potential loss of civil liberties and domestic comforts that Samuel was warning them about (verses 19-20). So Samuel took God's advice, bowed to their wishes, sent them home (verse 22), sought out Saul (Chapter 9), anointed him privately as king (10:1), assembled the people at Gilgal, and "made Saul king before the Lord" and the assembly. A great celebration was held, with appropriate sacrifices to YHWH, and Saul and all the people were content—for the time being (11:14-15).

Psalter: Psalm 138

This is a psalm of thanksgiving hearkening back to a situation of need from which the psalmist has been delivered (verse 3). The praise seems to be offered in a heavenly court (verse 1), before which the psalmist sings, bows, and gives thanks (verses 1-2). His will not be a lone voice of thanksgiving for long, though, for soon he will be joined by the songs of all earthly royalty (verses 4-5) giving praise for God's glory. And well they should, since YHWH's "preferential option for the poor" and judgment on the high and mighty is well known (verse 6).

The writer then expresses his confidence in God's guidance in trouble, protection from enemies, deliverance from difficulty, guiding purpose, and everlasting steadfast love (verses 7-8a). In the last line, the tone of praise shifts to a fervent petition. In spite of all his confidence, the psalmist urges God to be sure to continue "the work of your hands."

> **Think About It:** The psalmist shifts from praise to petition. What is the balance in your prayers between thanksgiving and requests?

This could refer to sustaining the works of creation, but in light of the preceding verses it more likely means the preservation of the poor and lowly who are completely dependent on God for their survival and well-being.

Epistle: 2 Corinthians 4:13–5:1

Having claimed the treasure (God's grace) in clay jars (human finitude), affirmed a faith that surmounts persecution and despair, and voiced confidence in the power of life over death (4:7-12—last week's lection), in today's passage Paul confesses his faith in the invisible and eternal. He begins by quoting Psalm 116:10 to assert that his ministry is based in faith (verse 13). Paul's use of the pronoun "we" suggests that he wants his readers—both the Corinthians and us—to share his belief in the Resurrection and salvation to come (verse 14; see 1 Corinthians 15:24-28; Romans 6:3-5; 8:18-25, 28-30).

> **Think About It:** When you face trials, does your inner life keep you going, or do discouragement and depression get in the way of your relationship with God? How do you maintain your spiritual disciplines to cultivate hope at such times? How can you support others who are facing difficult times?

All his ministry endeavors were intended for the readers' benefit and could thereby influence wider and wider circles of potential converts. Thus, gratitude would be multiplied among the faithful and God would be glorified (verse 15; see Romans 5:19-21).

A Blessing in Disguise

Apparently, Paul was facing a severe trial—whether a physical ailment or vicious opposition we do not know. But he was not letting this get him down. Even though outwardly the going was tough, inwardly his spiritual life was vibrant and growing (verse 16). His tribulation was transitory and bearable; he even saw it as a blessing in disguise, since it was helping to equip him for the next life (verse 17).

> **Think About It:** How do you think about death—your own and that of loved ones? What gives you hope? What do you believe about life after death?

With the eyes of faith Paul could see beyond the visible and temporal to the invisible and eternal (verse 18). He knew that his physical body ("earthly tent") would sooner or later wear out or meet a violent end but was confident that God would provide him with a spiritual body ("house not made with hands") in which he would live forever. Again, by saying "we" Paul is including all believers in this faith and promise (5:1).

Gospel: Mark 3:20-35

The focus of today's Gospel lection is on Jesus' relationship with his family. They did not understand his purpose or who he really was; Jesus' relationship with committed disciples took priority over blood ties. To read this section properly, combine verses 19b-21 with 31-35 and take verses 22-30 separately. Verses 19b-21 give the reason for Jesus' unwillingness to accompany his family in 31-35.

A House Divided

In verse 21, the phrase "to restrain him" implies that his family was concerned for his physical safety. "Gone out of his mind" indicates that many thought Jesus was crazy because his teachings and lifestyle were contrary to the Jesus they knew. The writer's purpose in inserting verses 22-30 at this point is to emphasize that Jesus was not possessed by an evil spirit. Rather, it was God's Spirit that guided him. The name "Beelzebul" probably refers to the Canaanite god Baal. By casting out "the strong man" (verse 27), Jesus had demonstrated that he had power over Satan ("the ruler of the demons"). "The house can be plundered" is a reference to the collapse of the power of evil due to Jesus' influence for good. "A realm/house divided against itself cannot stand" (verses 24-25).

> **Think About It:** "A house divided against itself cannot stand." Jesus argues that evil and good oppose each other and that his exorcisms demonstrate he serves the forces of good. Is it possible to serve good and evil simultaneously? How do we serve the good?

The Unforgivable Sin

Interpreters have given many meanings to the "unforgivable sin" (verses 28-30). Whatever sin is the current anathema gets labeled as unforgivable. But here it clearly means the refusal to acknowledge the presence and activity of the Holy Spirit, instead blaspheming by calling God "unclean."

> **Think About It:** "Interpreters have given many meanings to the 'unforgivable sin.'" How have you customarily understood this statement? What would be some present-day examples of deliberately or mistakenly confusing the activity of God with that of evil? Would a loving God really refuse to forgive any sin, no matter how heinous? Does pardon for sin enable us to avoid all of sin's consequences?

Who Are My Mother and Brothers?

> **Think About It:** "Whoever does the will of God is my brother and sister and mother." Note the emphasis on *doing* rather than believing. What characterizes a true Christian—belief or behavior? Have you had the experience of being misunderstood, criticized, or even rejected by family because of your Christian commitment? of feeling closer kinship with fellow disciples than with blood relatives?

Verses 31-35 are one of only two references to Jesus' family in Mark. Both here and in 6:1-6, they are portrayed as "outsiders" who are not in tune with Jesus' calling. Jesus' rejection of his family here may seem harsh; but they had not accepted his mission, and he took this occasion to affirm those who had made the choice to follow him. For Jesus, true kinship in the realm of God was of the Spirit and was demonstrated by living according to God's will. One's relationship with God is seen in deeds of faithfulness, not in one's religious birth certificate.

Study Suggestions

A. Begin With Praise
Sing "God of Many Names," then read Psalm 138 responsively. Invite members to name the things they can praise God for this day. Give the background on Psalm 138 found on pages 221–22. Discuss the significance of God's "preferential option for the poor" and the questions in the "Think About It" box.

B. Wanting a King
Read 1 Samuel 8:20; 11:14-15, and review the commentary on pages 220–21. Read Deuteronomy 17:14-20, noting that this could be a reference to Samuel and/or to the commission of all prophets to speak God's truth regardless of the consequences. Discuss the "Think About It" questions. Ask: Does God ever yield to a lesser good in response to human desire or willfulness? For contemporary parallels consider: the personal desire for acclaim or advancement vs. the need for humble, unrecognized service; a people's desire for comfort and accumulation vs. needs for housing, health care, and a living wage; a nation's desire for revenge vs. the need to seek peace with justice and protect human rights and civil liberties.

C. Inward Faith and Outward Difficulty
Read aloud 2 Corinthians 4:13–5:1, and review the interpretation on pages 222–23 Discuss the questions in the "Think About It" boxes. Invite members to tell of times when they were facing troubles and feeling downhearted. What helped them maintain or recover a vital relationship with

God? Ask: How can we create a climate in this group so persons will feel free to share their struggles and seek our support? How can we sense when persons are feeling this need? If appropriate, take time to pray with a class member who has expressed his or her present struggle.

D. Jesus and Family

Read aloud Mark 3:19b-21, 31-35, and 22-30 in that order, citing the reason given on page 223 for this re-ordering. Ask: Why was Jesus so hard on his family here? Discuss the questions in the "Think About It" box on doing versus believing. Invite members to share their experiences with nonbeliever family members compared with their relationships with persons in the family of faith.

E. A House Divided

Re-read Mark 3:24-25, and refer to the context in verses 22-27. Discuss why some thought Jesus was "out of his mind." Explore the questions in the "Think About It" box on division. (Possible contemporary parallels: a family of both believers and non-believers; one who professes to be a disciple yet lives in affluence while giving only minimally to church and charity; a church that claims to be inclusive yet discriminates on the basis of race, class, or criminal status; and a country that pledges allegiance to "one nation, under God, indivisible, with liberty and justice for all," but supports repressive regimes, imprisons two million of its citizens, and fails to provide adequate food, shelter, and health care to many.

F. The Unforgivable Sin

Review Mark 3:28-30, and the explanation on page 223. Discuss the related "Think About It" questions. Ask participants to share times they felt they had committed an unforgivable sin. What helped them through this spiritual crisis? Discuss: Is sin a condition, an attitude, or an act? What makes it unforgivable—its gravity or our refusal to repent? Is there any sin God will not forgive? How does your answer reflect your concept of God?

G. In Closing

Join hands and pray for forgiveness for our sins and divisions as individuals and as a people.

Lections for Sunday Between
June 12 and 18

T Old Testament: 1 Samuel 15:34–16:13

*T*HIS lection begins with Samuel's regrets over Saul's inadequacies as a monarch and YHWH's regrets over having made Saul king in the first place (15:34-35). It is preceded in Chapter 15 by an account of Saul's failures to obey what the writer believed to have been YHWH's orders, thereby precipitating the need for a change of command in Israel.

Chapter 16 begins with YHWH sending Samuel out, equipped with oil for anointing and a calf to sacrifice, to the household of Jesse in Bethlehem to look for a new king to succeed Saul from among Jesse's sons (verses 1-3). Samuel was fearful of Saul's retribution should he learn of Samuel's actions (2a), but he did as YHWH commanded. Unlike the selection of Saul, which seemed almost accidental, this time YHWH made the selection.

There were several similarities in the two anointings. Both were done in secret—this time, though, Samuel did not tell the anointed one, David, why he was being anointed. Neither assumed the throne immediately after being anointed. Both Saul and David tended animals—Saul tended donkeys and David, sheep—and hence were of rather lowly social status. Saul had said he was from an insignificant tribe and clan (9:21). David was a mere lad—the youngest of Jesse's sons—and at first was out tending the flocks and not even considered by his father a possibility for Samuel to meet. This theme of the youngest and least probable later becoming God's chosen was first seen in Hannah's song (2:8) and reached its apex in Jesus, born in a stable to a Galilean peasant girl but exalted by God and given "the name that is above every name" (Philippians 2:6-11).

In both stories Samuel's power as an oracle is called into question. His advice to reject the monarchy had been repudiated by the people (see last week's lection, 1 Samuel 8:4-20), and here he made the mistaken assumption that the first son shown him by Jesse must be YHWH's choice, because he was handsome (16:6-7).

God Looks on the Heart

YHWH chided Samuel for making a snap judgment based on externals, but curiously when David was selected the only favorable characteristic mentioned was his good looks (16:12). The writer's point is still well-taken, however. We humans are often prone to base our choices and decisions on superficial, transitory factors—appearance, size, cost, popularity, immediate return—but God sees beneath the surface to the heart of things—purity of motive, strength of character, quality of devotion, depth of commitment. The implication is that Samuel—and we—should pay more attention to these intangibles as well.

> **Think About It:** "God does not see as mortals see; they look on the outward appearance, but God looks on the heart." What instances can you recall when your judgment was based on superficial factors, only to learn later that the inner reality was more important? How can we avoid making snap judgments? (Consider such things as the advice of wise consultants, prayerful reflection, thoughtful observation over a period of time, and analysis of performance.)

In this instance, the outcome was that Samuel followed YHWH's counsel, anointed David in front of his more likely brothers (how resentful they must have felt!), and left for Ramah. And the writer comments—probably from hindsight—that David was possessed with the power of God's spirit from that time on.

Psalter: Psalm 20 or Psalm 72

Psalm 20 is a "royal psalm" offered as a prayer for victory by a priestly chorus prior to a battle. In verse 1, calling on the "name" of YHWH is a prayer for divine protection, extended from the Temple on Mount Zion (verse 2; see 1 Kings 8:17). That God also dwells in the "holy heaven" is affirmed in verse 6. On the eve of the battle, the king goes to the Temple to make his offerings (verse 3; see 1 Samuel 7:9; 1 Kings 8:44-45) to YHWH to assure protection and triumph. The priests' song assumes the coming victory celebration, with battle flags flying (verse 5).

The idea of a holy war, in which victory was assured—regardless of the number of enemy horses and chariots—just because God fights on our side (verses 7-8; see Judges 7:2), had its origins in the period of Israel's tribal confederacy (1250–1000 B.C.). To compute relative strength would betray a lack of faith in the power of YHWH, so the priests express confidence that in

God, "they are brought to their knees . . . , but we [will] rise up . . ." (verse 8, NIV). Christians have transformed this psalm into a prayer for God's help in spiritual and moral struggles against the power of sin.

Psalm 72 is a coronation hymn written by court poets for the elevation of a crown prince ("son," verse 1) to his father's throne. The prayer is for the new king to have long life (verses 5, 15), be supported by the people's prayers (verse 15b), and rule with justice for the poor (verses 2, 12-14). The poet anticipates that the new king's reign will bring prosperity and fair treatment for both the citizens and the land (verses 3-4, 6, 16), and conquest over enemies (verses 8-11) who will pay much tribute and make him rich (verses 10, 15).

The River (8b) was the Euphrates. In verse 10, Tarshish (in southwest Spain; see Job 1:3), the isles (in the Mediterranean), Sheba (southern Arabia), and Seba (Ethiopia) represent the far reaches of the king's hoped-for domain.

Christians may view this psalm as a song of adoration to Christ, the Son of the living God. It also defines an understanding of the purposes of a competent society.

Epistle: 2 Corinthians 5:6-10 (11-13), 14-17

Paul here continues with the theme of eternal life as a source of confidence and hope in the face of affliction and persecution. The physical body provides a temporary home, but our faith gives us hope that before long we will go to be at home with Christ (verses 6-7). Although the latter home is preferable, in either state the goal is to serve Christ (verses 8-9). Since what we do in our temporary bodies is subject to God's judgment, we try to win persons to Christ's way (verses 10-11a).

These evangelistic efforts are pleasing to God and, hopefully, also to Paul's readers (verse 11b). This will give them occasion to commend his message to their companions who see only externals and neglect their souls (verse 12; note similarity to 1 Samuel 16:7b). Paul's evangelistic zeal ("beside ourselves") is motivated by his love for God, and his sober thought ("right mind") by his love for them (verse 13). The possibility of serving Christ rather than self and the promise of eternal life resulting from conversion are based in Christ's death and resurrection (verses 14-15).

Because of this revolutionary change in the human situation, we no longer see Christ or persons from a one-dimensional human perspective (verse 16). Rather, when persons abide

Think About It: "If anyone is in Christ, there is a new creation" (verse 17a). What are the signs of this radical newness in the Christian life? In conversion, what changes and what remains the same? How is the new creation both instantaneous and ongoing?

in Christ, the old being is transformed; a new being takes its place and a whole new range of possibilities is opened up (verse 17). This is the Christian perspective on human life!

Gospel: Mark 4:26-34

This lection comes in a chapter beginning with the parable of the sower (or soils, 4:1-9), which contrasts various levels of and obstacles to receptivity to Jesus' message in the hearts of his hearers. This story is followed by a statement attributed to Jesus that the purpose of his speaking in parables was to hide the meaning of the gospel from outsiders and keep it secret for believers (4:10-12). This emphasis reflects a later situation in the context of Gentile Christianity (see 1 Corinthians 1:18–3:1, especially 2:7) rather than the openness and clarity of Jesus in proclaiming the simple message of God's love and demands of discipleship (see below, verses 21-25).

Then, in response to a question from the disciples, the parable of soils is interpreted allegorically—probably an explanation developed in the early church (4:13-20). The sayings about parables in verses 21-25 emphasize that Jesus intended them to edify not perplex his hearers. They are encouraged to listen carefully (verses 23-24a), for all truth will be made plain (verse 22), and those who understand a little now will gain still greater clarity as they grow, while those who obstruct or reject the message will lose even the glimmer of light they once had (verse 25).

The Kingdom as a Seed

Then Jesus tells two more parables of the reign of God. The first (verses 26-29) uses the analogy of seed sown in the ground producing grain ripe for the harvest to point to God's realm as a divine mystery rather than a product of human achievement. People must be patient in waiting for it to come to fruition in their lives or in society; they cannot hasten its fulfillment with effort or urging.

The second parable (verses 30-32) points to the miracle of the tiny mustard seed growing into a huge bush big enough to hold birds' nests—but slowly and steadily rather than instantly and hastily. This probably was intended by Mark as a description of the way the Christian movement would develop—from its tiny, insignificant origins into a powerful, world-changing phenomenon. But it can also be understood in terms of the way the seed of the gospel, planted in a human heart or community, can develop and bear fruit in powerful and unexpected ways.

> **Think About It:** God's realm is a divine mystery rather than a product of human achievement. Is it being faithful just to sit and wait for it to come, or are we meant to help prepare for its coming by working for justice and peace? What signs of the realm of God do you "already" see?

The passage concludes (verses 33-34) with another reference to insiders (the disciples) and outsiders (the multitude of hearers). The private teaching of the disciples by Jesus, often done in someone's home (see 7:17; 9:28, 33; 10:42), may reflect the ongoing training of followers in the house churches of the Markan community.

> *Think About It:* The mustard seed (God's kingdom) grows "slowly and steadily rather than instantly and hastily." Do you see signs of its gradual growth, or are you frustrated and impatient that it develops so slowly or even seems to be ebbing?

Study Suggestions

A. Kingdom (Reign) of God

Write this phrase on chalkboard or a large sheet of paper. Explain that today's lections all deal with God's rule. Ask the group what the kingdom of God means to them. List their responses. (Words like *God's dominion, rule, realm; our obedience, discipleship; peace, justice, liberation; inner transformation, final judgment* might be mentioned.) Comment that some prefer the term *reign* because it avoids medieval, authoritarian connotations. Some say *kingdom* to emphasize relational, family aspects. Ask each person to use markers and paper to symbolize their concept of the kingdom (reign) of God. Post these, and refer to both verbal and symbolic responses during the discussion.

B. Criteria of Kingship

Read or tell the story of David's anointing in 1 Samuel 15:34–16:13. Draw on the interpretation on pages 226–27 in explaining its background. Emphasize Samuel's mistake in judging the fitness of Jesse's sons based on external appearances. Read 16:7 in unison. Discuss the "Think About It" questions. Note that Jesus was a descendant of David, which led people to expect him to be an earthly king and conqueror—exhibiting external qualities and establishing a worldly kingdom.

C. Songs of Victory and Coronation

Read aloud either Psalm 20, Psalm 72, or both. Explain their background and original purpose, noting that such psalms came out of Israel's tribal confederacy and monarchy, when rulers fought ruthlessly, held dominion absolutely, and gained great power and wealth, upheld by gods (like YHWH) who fought, dominated, and were praised for their power and glory—except that YHWH expected Israel's rulers to deal justly and to defend the poor. Ask: How does this concept of kingship compare with Jesus' teaching about the kingdom/reign of God? Considering the origin of many psalms, why do Christians continue to use them in worship?

D. A New Being

Read aloud 2 Corinthians 5:6-13, then have the group read verses 14-17 in unison. Explain the background from the commentary on pages 228–29. Note that here again we find the contrast between the temporal and eternal, and inner and outer criteria. Discuss the "Think About It" questions. Also ask: How does the focus here on the new creation relate to the reign/kingdom of God as Jesus spoke of it? Is it primarily inner or outer? eternal or temporal? already here or yet to come? or both?

E. Parables of the Kingdom

Introduce the Gospel lection by reviewing the material that precedes it in Mark 4, drawing on the background on pages 229–30. Ask: What is a parable? (It is a short story illustrating a single point; a teaching device using surprise or reversal and leaving hearers free to draw their own conclusions.) Why did Jesus teach in parables? Why does Mark state parables were given by Jesus both to clarify and to obscure the truth of the gospel?

Form groups of four to six persons. Assign half the groups to read verses 26-29 and the others verses 30-32. Have all groups discuss these questions, plus the "Think About It" questions related to their parable: What is the main point of this parable? What does it teach us about the reign/kingdom of God? What response does it call for from us? After they report, compare their answers to their phrases and drawings prepared in Activity A.

F. Review, Sing, Pray

Summarize the elements of the reign of God identified in this session. Sing "O God of Every Nation" or "The Kingdom of God." Pray for sensitivity to signs of the Kingdom, obedience to God's rule, and dedication to Christ as lord.

Lections for Sunday Between June 19 and 25

Old Testament:
1 Samuel 17:(1a, 4-11, 19-23) 32-49

*T*HE story of David and Goliath, beloved to many since childhood, begins the adult drama of David's rise to power in Israel. Handsome, brave, and resourceful, David appeared at a time of crisis for Israel. The Philistines, coastal neighbors to the west, bolstered by a thriving economy and a monopoly on the manufacture of iron, had massed an army on Israel's border about fourteen miles west of Bethlehem.

The Philistine army was championed by a giant warrior, Goliath, whose taunts had stung the Israelites for forty days (17:16). King Saul, whose earlier victories against various enemies had earned him great praise (14:47), had since lost God's favor and could not break the military impasse.

David Versus Goliath

The story dramatizes the contrast between David and Goliath, who was huge—6' 9" or 9' 6" depending on the text one follows—a hardened warrior heavily-armored. David, "just a boy" (17:33) who could not bear the weight of regular armor, had only a shepherd's staff, sling, knapsack, and five stones. (It must be noted that 2 Samuel 21:19 provides a very different account of the death of Goliath.)

The telling difference, however, did not have to do with military equipment. David invoked the name of "the LORD of hosts, the God of the armies of Israel" (17:45). Five references in Chapters 16–18 state that YHWH was with David (16:18; 17:37; 18:12, 14, 28). This battle was really between the God of Israel and the gods of the Philistines (17:43, 45). The theological purpose of the outcome: "that all the earth may know that there is a God in

232

Israel" (17:46). The storyteller makes a point that the psalmist will echo: Soldiers are not saved by sword and spear, but by the power of God alone (17:47; Psalm 20:6-8).

Holy War?

The context of the story of David and Goliath is a "holy war," seen by the combatants as a righteous cause led by YHWH. The verses that follow this passage recount the gory aftermath of David's slung stone: the beheading of Goliath and the slaughter of the Philistines. (Consider, however, 2 Samuel 21:19.) Though neither David nor the storyteller question that vanquishing and massacring the Philistines is God's will, modern Christians may wonder in the light of this century's atrocities whether God condones war and military conquest, whatever the cause.

> **Think About It:** The battle was between YHWH and the gods of the Philistines. Do you believe with David and the storyteller that God fought with David and the Israelites and brought them victory? When nations are in conflict, what are the alternatives to war? What, if anything, justifies Christians participating in war?

A New Hero

First Samuel 16–17 is part of a history that legitimizes David's rise to kingship in Israel. David, the underdog, the insignificant youngest son of a farmer and shepherd, was immensely popular with the people, who identified with his marginal status and admired his many talents. The common opinion was that he "knows how to play the harp . . . is a brave man and a warrior . . . speaks well and is a fine-looking man. And the Lord is with him" (16:18, NIV). Chapters 16–17 interweave two different accounts of how David came to the attention of Saul—as a musician (16:14-23) and as the slayer of Goliath (17:31-58). Whichever came first, the historian wants us to understand that God had chosen David to replace Saul.

Psalter: Psalm 9:9-20

In this prayer of lament, the psalmist exhorts the congregation to praise God's mighty deeds and pleads with God to save the afflicted. Shifting moods abruptly, the speaker alternates between thanksgiving and petition, confidence and despair, personal experience and the fate of nations.

Though such shifts seem jarring, they were typical of lamentation, interconnecting personal need and political comment. The psalm may have been used in communal worship after the Exile, a mixed time for the Israelites: Though free to worship in the restored Temple, they were still under foreign rule. The psalmist notes gleefully that wicked persons and nations will suffer the fate they have imposed on others (9:15).

The psalm pleads on behalf of the oppressed (9:9), with whom the psalmist identifies, who are also described as "afflicted" (9:12), "needy" (9:18), "poor" (9:18), "innocent" (10:8), "helpless" (10:8), and "orphan" (10:18). The Hebrew root behind most of these terms literally means those "bent low." This group of words refers to those who are bowed down by suffering, as well as those who humble themselves to worship God.

One scholar describes petitions such as those in Psalms 9 and 10 as a "class action appeal." God has a special concern for the poor, a concern also articulated in covenant laws (Deuteronomy 15) and by the prophets (Isaiah 3:13-15). Jesus would later proclaim God's blessing upon the same group: "Blessed are you who are poor, for yours is the kingdom of God" (Luke 6:20).

Epistle: 2 Corinthians 6:1-13

In this passage, Paul appeals to the Corinthians to trust him and accept his leadership. Like an ardent lover, he declares all the things he has done for them: suffering for them (6:4-5), boasting about them (7:4), and renouncing their material support (6:3; 1 Corinthians 9:12). He wants them to return his affection (2 Corinthians 6:11-13) and be reconciled to God (5:20). Paul's opponents, Jewish Christians who insisted that all Christians must be circumcised and follow Mosaic law, have undermined Paul's teaching and swayed hearts away from him.

"What I Did for Love"
Paul fights back with all the persuasion he can muster. He evokes a sense of urgency in verse 2 with a quotation from Isaiah 49:8, adding: "Now is the acceptable time; see, now is the day of salvation." He enumerates nine different kinds of suffering he has endured (6:4-5), breaking the travails into groups of three for increased impact: (1) general sufferings—"afflictions, hardships, calamities"; (2) sufferings inflicted by others—"beatings, imprisonments, riots"; and (3) self-imposed sufferings—"labors, sleepless nights, hunger" (fasting).

Paul repeats and expands this list in 11:23-28, this time culminating with mention of "the daily pressure of my concern for all the churches" (11:28, NIV). All this he has done because he loves them: "Our heart is wide open to you" (6:11).

Suffering and Virtue
Paul links the endurance of suffering with a virtuous life, saying that he and his fellow-workers live by purity, patience, and kindness (6:6-7). This list of virtues resembles the fruits of the Spirit in Galatians 5:22-23. Paul further suggested that appearances are deceiving; though treated as "impostors," he

and his co-workers are "true." The other paradoxes he mentions in verses 8-10, such as dying/alive, sorrowful/rejoicing, and poor/rich, contrast outward appearance with true inward reality, a theme we have seen in previous lections. The mature Christian responds to tribulations with spiritual grace that defies the world's wisdom. That Paul lived through all these tribulations and paradoxes with such grace makes his argument all the more compelling.

Gospel: Mark 4:35-41

This lection poses a question about Jesus that the entire Gospel seeks to answer: "Who then is this?" In Chapters 1–3, Mark shows us an inspired figure who can heal, exorcise, and teach. Today's passage underlines Jesus' divine nature, for in the Old Testament, it was only God who could command the deep (Genesis 1:2; Exodus 15:19). Throughout the Gospel, Mark builds evidence for the climactic witness of the Roman soldier at the Crucifixion: "Truly this man was God's Son!" (Mark 15:39).

To the Other Side

Spent after teaching the large crowd (4:1) and instructing his disciples about the parables (4:33-34), Jesus told the disciples to "go across to the other side" (4:35). He directed them to sail east across the Sea of Galilee to a predominantly Gentile region known as the Decapolis, a group of ten cities. Why? To rest and escape the crush of the crowds (3:9)? To spread the good news beyond the boundaries of Israel (5:1, 20)? The Scripture offers no motive; they simply go.

The obscure phrase that they took Jesus with them in the boat "just as he was" implies that Jesus made no special preparations for the sea journey, perhaps not even leaving the boat after teaching. The phrase heightens the feeling of urgency in the story (an urgency that permeates the Gospel of Mark), as well as suggesting Jesus' complete trust in God to provide whatever he needed. His attitude of trust was revealed even more dramatically when he slept right through the storm.

Will We Drown?

Storms develop quickly on the Sea of Galilee, a large freshwater inland lake. Wind is funneled by the surrounding mountains down upon the water, whipping up six-foot waves. The disciples, seasoned fishermen, knew the power of a storm at sea. What they did not know was the power of the man asleep in the boat. They awakened and reproached him: "Do you not care that we are perishing?" Their words echoed Psalm 44:23: "Rouse yourself! Why do you sleep, O LORD?" Jesus "rebuked" the wind and silenced the waves (the same way he handled the unclean spirit in Mark 1:25). His action replicated Psalm 104:7: "At your rebuke [the waters] flee." Jesus then rebuked the disciples for their lack of faith.

Fear and Faith

Jesus' question, "Have you still no faith?" suggests that since they had seen his healings and exorcisms, they should emulate his trust in God. Perhaps they would come to know that "for God all things are possible" (Mark 10:27). For now, all they could say was, "Who then is this, that even the wind and the sea obey him?" (4:41).

This is the first of three scenes on the water in which Jesus challenged the disciples' lack of faith and understanding. In 6:45-52, they were in the boat "straining at the oars against an adverse wind" (6:48). When they saw him walking on the water, they cried out in fear. He said, "Take heart, it is I; do not be afraid." In 8:14-21, they were worrying about not having enough food in the boat—right after they had seen Jesus feed four thousand people. "Do you not yet understand?" he asked them. In Chapter 5, he told the synagogue leader, Jairus, "Do not fear, only believe" (5:36). Jesus demonstrated that he was powerful to save in every circumstance.

Think About It: Jesus asked the disciples, "Why are you afraid? Have you still no faith?" When are you most likely to be afraid in your journey of faith? How does Jesus help in such situations?

The early church took this image to heart during times of persecution. Early Christian art depicted the church as a small boat on rough seas. Danger from water was a symbol for all the troubles that beset a believer. "Peace, be still" became their assurance that, after the storm, all would be well.

Study Suggestions

A. Open With Psalm and Prayer

Begin by reading Psalm 9:10-11 in unison, then praying for God's guidance in this study session.

B. Remember David and Goliath

Invite participants to recall when they first heard the story of David and Goliath: in Sunday school? from a children's Bible? in a song or picture? Discuss: How were these childhood stories and songs faithful to the biblical account? What did they leave out? What did they teach?

C. Consider Leadership

Review the commentary under "A New Hero." Read the First Samuel lection, plus 2 Samuel 21:19. Brainstorm a list of American leaders such as presidents, politicians, military officials, civic figures, clergy. Form three groups. Ask each group to choose one leader from the list and compare him or her to David. What similarities do you see? What differences?

Together report on comparisons. Discuss these questions: What do we expect of our leaders? What do we do when a leader fails us? What makes a leader—circumstances, ability, training, or what? What are the qualities of effective leadership? How might God be at work through our leaders?

Have participants imagine themselves as members of the church at Corinth. Ask a person to read 2 Corinthians 6:1-13 aloud with dramatic emphasis. What would it feel like to have these words spoken to you? Have the participants write their reactions. Ask: What would you want to say back to Paul? Is it good for leaders to show emotional vulnerability or strong personal feelings? What are the risks? What are the benefits?

Review the first two paragraphs of the commentary on the Corinthians lection. Ask members to identify in the passage places where Paul leads by: (a) example and (b) powerful speech. Invite them to give examples of persons they know who lead by speech and/or example.

D. Practice Virtue

Form two groups. Have Group 1 compare 2 Corinthians 6:6-7 to Galatians 5:22-23; have Group 2 compare it to Ephesians 6:13-17. Have each group compile a master list of virtues/"weapons of righteousness" from their comparison. Ask each to indicate the virtue or spiritual weapon they would most like to have. Ask participants to describe a scenario in which they might employ their chosen virtue or weapon.

E. Be Peter

Ask one person to retell the story in Mark 4:35-41 as if she or he were Peter telling his wife about the incident the following morning. What would the person be thinking? What did he or she learn about Jesus and about God?

F. Make a Hit Parade

The theme of Jesus' mastery over water has inspired a number of nautical hymns, from the 1871 classic, "Jesus, Savior, Pilot Me," to the 1969 pop hit, "Here Comes Jesus" (Sonny Salsbury). List hymns, poems, stories, and so on based on this theme. Ask: What "storms" threaten you? What reassuring word might Jesus speak to you?

G. Compare to Prayers

Compare 2 Corinthians 6:4-10 to other prayers of covenant or commitment, such as John Wesley's "A Covenant Prayer in the Wesleyan Tradition." What common themes or phrases do you notice? When have you found any of these paradoxes true in your own life?

H. Close With Prayer and Singing

Close with the covenant prayer and a nautical hymn such as ("When the storms of life are raging") "Stand by Me."

Lections for Sunday Between
June 26 and July 2

Old Testament: 2 Samuel 1:1, 17-27

*S*ECOND Samuel opens in the dangerous and insecure period between the death of one king and the accession of another. Today's lection focuses on David's reaction to hearing the news of the death of Saul and Jonathan and the defeat of the armies of Israel at the hands of the Philistines. These people lived in the five coastal cities that had been antagonists of Israel since the days of the judges. The news David received in 2 Samuel 1:2-16 differs markedly from 1 Samuel 31:1-8, and these are worth comparing closely.

David's Lament

Rather than rejoice at the death of the man who had driven him into exile, David lamented what the loss of Saul, Jonathan, and the many fallen soldiers meant for Israel. His first concern was for the honor of his people (Israel's "glory"), which stood in jeopardy. David wished that the news would not be proclaimed in Gath and Ashkelon (two of the five Philistine cities), although the news had already reached those places (1 Samuel 31:9-10). It horrified David to think of the enemy being lifted up—extolling their own achievements and praising their deities—at the expense of the honor of Israel and her God.

The Curse

In the second stanza, David pronounced a curse on the mountains of Gilboa because the death of YHWH's anointed king occurred there. The desacralizing of Saul (whose shield would be "anointed with oil no more") called for a corresponding desecration of the place itself. This accompanied the curse upon (execution of) the self-avowed agent of that tragic loss, the

Amalekite messenger (2 Samuel 1:10), who claimed he had done what David had scrupulously refused to do himself (2:15-16). Several times David or his men had had the opportunity to strike down King Saul (1 Samuel 24:6-7; 26:6-9), but David would not allow it. The Amalekite, no doubt thinking he would be rewarded for removing David's barrier to the kingship, lost his life instead.

The Heroes

The elegy recalled the good that came to Israel through Saul and Jonathan, while mentioning none of Saul's mad frenzies, his insane jealousy of David and attempts to kill him, and his eventual rejection by YHWH (1 Samuel 15; see 1 Samuel 28:7-19). What was highlighted was courage in battle—an essential virtue in the ancient world where bloody battles frequently determined whether the people back home could live in safety. Saul's reign was also celebrated as one that brought prosperity to the land.

> **Think About It:** David models for us the nobility of thinking beyond his private gain (the removal of a persecutor) to the communal loss incurred by his people with the death of Saul. Which was more prominent in your thinking when, for example, a rival was fired? when someone with whom you were at odds left your congregation? when a troublesome neighbor moved away?

To Lose a Friend

David's final stanza reflects the value of the loyal friendship of other persons, which was prized, next to siblinghood, as the firmest bond in the ancient world. The relationship between spouses ("the love of women") did not in that time entail the partnership of kindred souls that now is essential to a fulfilling marriage.

> **Think About It:** Loyal friendship was the firmest bond in the ancient world. What is the place of friendship in our world today? Name in your mind your best friends. What do those relationships mean to you? How do friendships begin and develop? How are they nurtured?

Psalter: Psalm 130

The enduring value of the Psalter is especially clear in psalms that give poignant expression to what it feels like to be overwhelmed by circumstances. This psalm expresses hopeful watchfulness in seeking God's help. Whether ill or depressed, persecuted or unemployed, believers find hope here for relief from their distress.

The image the psalmist uses to describe his state—being engulfed by deep waves or submerged in troubles, aptly captures the sense of being overcome. The second stanza articulates an awareness of sin and the impossibility of "standing"—of surviving God's scrutiny or judgment. The petitioner knows he cannot lay claim to God's help by right. Sinfulness denies us this right. The basis for hope is not human worthiness but God's generosity, expressed in forgiveness. This grace puts the sinner in God's debt and evokes the desire to revere, honor, and serve the Almighty.

The third stanza finds the worshiper in a position of watchfulness, looking for God's relief from distress, like a weary sentinel on the city wall looks for the dawn that signals the changing of the guard. Hope comes through recalling God's steadfast love (God's covenant of faithfulness). More than just remembering, the worshipers take heart that God has promised to redeem them from their sin (including the consequences of that sin, such as exile and foreign domination).

Epistle: 2 Corinthians 8:7-15

Paul is remembered as an evangelist, but he was also the administrator of an immense relief effort on behalf of the Christians in Judea. These believers' confession of Jesus as Messiah resulted in their being ostracized; consequently they lost all means of income and financial support. Paul's monetary collection made an important contribution to the unity of the early church. The distinction between Jewish and Gentile Christians would be replaced by brother and sister rushing to the relief of brother and sister in the family of God.

Macedonian Generosity

"The earnestness of others" (8:8) refers to the Macedonian Christians' eagerness to participate in the collection for the poor in Judea, despite their own hard times (described in 8:1-6). The genuineness of the Corinthians' love for God and the household of God would now be demonstrated by their enthusiastic participation in this relief effort.

Paul has set up a kind of holy rivalry, spurring on the Macedonians to act honorably through beneficence by praising the Corinthians' good beginning (see 9:1-5). Further, Paul encouraged the Corinthians to complete their relief efforts by pointing out the exemplary conduct of the Macedonians. He asserted that since we benefit from Christ's generosity, we must honor his example by aiding his family in tangible ways.

An Equality of Resources

Paul encourages Christians to bring about equality of resources within the household of God. This is a major challenge to Western Christians. In fighting so strenuously against the advance of Communism, we have neglected the importance of sharing possessions with those in need. The love of Christ mandates that we should not have excess while others lack daily essentials. Such sharing was central to the kinship ethic that made the early church a caring family. Paul's quotation of Exodus 16:18 (8:15) refers to God's provision of manna in the desert—a reminder that all we have is a gift from God and should be used for the good of all.

> **Think About It:** "All we have is a gift from God; it should be used for the good of all." What does this suggest about the way we spend, buy, save, and give? Could Paul praise us for our "wealth of generosity" (8:2b) as he did the Macedonians?

Gospel: Mark 5:21-43

In this passage we find two closely related healings: a twelve-year-old girl lying at death's door and a woman who had been hemorrhaging for twelve years. In both it is a touch that is specifically sought as the means of healing. Mark is known for the technique of interlacing one story in the middle of another to suggest links of interpretation between the two. While the stories here may have been linked already by the tradition that Mark received, he may also have brought them together himself so that each might shed light on the other.

Mosaic Law and Purity

Jewish society regulated itself largely by the Mosaic law and its unfolding interpretation and application. Leviticus 15:25-31 lays out the restrictions that would have applied to the woman. Her desire for healing was a concern for both physical well-being and also social acceptance.

Those who face chronic illness today may find themselves avoided or rejected because of their condition. For this woman, the law dictated the consequences of her state of being unclean. Her chair and bed would pollute those who used them after her. The Mosaic laws defined the causes of this contamination as well the means for ceremonial cleansing. It was believed that violation of these laws was offensive to the holiness of God and would estrange the community from God.

Mark uses language taken from the early Greek translation of Leviticus to describe her condition as "a flow of blood" (Mark 5:25, RSV; see Leviticus 12:7), calling attention to her state of impurity and the reversal effected by Jesus. The woman's unclean state anticipates the ultimate state of uncleanness (death) faced by the young girl.

She Is Only Sleeping

As the good news of recovery came to the "daughter" whose "faith had made her well," the worst news a parent could hear overcame Jairus: "Your

241

daughter is dead." The hired band of mourners making lamentation when Jesus arrived (Mark 5:38-39) laughed at his suggestion that the girl was not really dead (5:40). But tears and mockery turned to joy when Jesus brought her back to life.

God Overcomes Uncleanness

A theme running through Jesus' healings and exorcisms—his acts of bringing God's deliverance to the people—is that the power of God can overcome uncleanness. Jesus' power to make the unclean clean made the laws of uncleanness moot. Jesus' willingness to enter places regarded by the law as polluting—even his willingness to touch those who were contaminated—expressed God's deliverance in a powerful, tangible way.

> **Think About It:** Ritual purity may no longer be a concern to the modern mind, but we have many other barriers separating us from one another. What lines have you crossed to bring God's touch of love and healing to others?

Just Trust in God

Jesus confirmed the woman's healing, offering a gentle correction that healing came not from any magical manipulation of materials (touching a garment) but from trust in his power to confer such gifts from God. As elsewhere, Jesus tried to restrict the celebration of his healing power by committing Jairus and his wife to silence about the cause of the girl's recovery. His messiahship would be misunderstood if the focus were on the marvels and not on the cross.

Study Suggestions

A. Lament and Hope

Begin by reading Psalm 130 in unison, then explain its meaning by drawing on the commentary on pages 239–40 and that for August 7-13 (see pages 275–76). Invite members to share any circumstances or concerns that so weigh upon them as to make them feel suffocated or "over their heads." These may be intensely personal or may reflect concerns in the world at large. Ask: What does it feel like to wait for God's resolution? What sustains you as you wait? Join hands and pray for one another's concerns, then sing or read Martin Luther's hymn "Out of the Depths I Cry to You."

B. My Gain, Everyone's Loss

Read 2 Samuel 1:1, 17-27, and review the commentary on pages 238–39. Have group members read the other Scriptures listed there for comparison. Ask: Why do you think David responded as he did to the news of Saul's death?

Invite the group to think about people who have been, in whatever sense, their rivals or enemies. Ask: Looking past their differences, are there ways in which God brought about good through them? How would their removal have meant loss for the whole enterprise (whether in a business, community, or a ministry venture)? Also discuss the questions in the first "Think About It" box.

Remind the group of the strong friendship bond between David and Jonathan, and explore the "Think About It" questions about friendship.

C. Mine/Yours and God's/Ours

Read aloud 2 Corinthians 8:7-15, and review the interpretive comments on pages 240–41. Identify the various motivations for giving that Paul provides in this short passage. Ask: What is his attitude toward possessions? What are the implications of this passage for your stewardship practices and those of your congregation?

D. Crossing the Line

Roleplay Mark 5:21-43, assigning these parts: a narrator, Jairus, the woman, Jesus, disciples, and the messengers. Set the scene in context by reading the commentary on pages 241–42. Ask: How does each character show trust and courage?

Discuss the "Think About It" questions. Ask: What is the connection in our society between physical traits or blemishes and social acceptability? How might you be challenged by stepping over previously uncrossed boundaries and reaching out to the rejected with a healing touch?

E. The Touch of God

The lections have all spoken of God's touch in some way—whether waiting for that touch, seeing God's hand at work through someone who is at variance with us, experiencing it through the gift of a sister or brother, or being restored to wholeness and to community in Jesus' name. Invite group members to tell of ways in which they have felt God's touch or have communicated it to another.

Invite participants to share how God has challenged them (perhaps even in this hour) to reach out to another person or persons on God's behalf—to be the vehicle for some blessing God wants them to have through us. Close by praying for one another, that each may fulfill this privileged calling as God directs.

Lections for Sunday Between July 3 and 9

Old Testament: 2 Samuel 5:1-5, 9-10

*D*AVID'S valor in leading the army, together with rumors of Samuel's prophetic word to David, led to his selection as successor to Saul as king by the elders of Israel at Hebron. (Hebron was David's seat of rule for approximately seven years.) The succession crisis was thus brought to an end, and the prospect emerged of a new beginning under David.

The City of David

The reader may be surprised to learn that Jerusalem remained a pagan city until this time. The expulsion of the Canaanites from the land of Israel was a long process left quite incomplete by Joshua and by the judges that followed him. The Israelites lived among the small Canaanite city states for a considerable period after first invading the land. In this passage, we find Jerusalem still a stronghold for the indigenous people, called Jebusites after the Canaanite name for the city—Jebus (Judges 19:10-12).

With a secure water supply, the city was naturally well suited to repulse an invasion. When the Jebusites learned of David's intention to capture the city, they scoffed that "even the blind and the lame will turn you back." David then turned back this taunt onto the Jebusite guards, telling his men to go up to the aqueduct and "attack the lame and the blind, those whom David hates" (2 Samuel 5:8). David clearly meant the boastful soldiers and not the disabled persons in the city. The story also provides an incidental explanation for a later restriction on physically challenged persons from entering the "house," that is, the Temple.

The God of All

Verses 6-8 were omitted from the lection out of sensitivity to those in our Christian family who suffer these conditions. The ancient point of view toward handicapping conditions was obviously a harsh and unaffirming one. The conditions of blindness and lameness were thought to place people at the low end of the scale of performance and contribution and thus be a cause for rejection and ostracism—the special protection of Mephibosheth by David notwithstanding (see 2 Samuel 9:6-13). The terms "the blind and the lame" could be used as epithets or insults; a stigma of divine disfavor was attached to these conditions.

The best remedy for the denigration of the physically challenged in this passage, however, is not to pretend that such passages do not exist; rather, it is to hold them together with the prophetic announcements of God's specific care for the "blind and the lame" (see Isaiah 35:5 and Jeremiah 31:8). These prophecies reverse the prohibition against persons with disabilities and show God's tender heart toward them—the heart we are to adopt.

After David's forces overcame the city's defenses, he made Jerusalem his capital. Jerusalem became "the city of David," the unique possession of his dynasty. He turned it into his own fortified city.

> **Think About It:** The Jebusites placed their security in material fortifications and were disappointed. In what ways have you or your family tried to establish security and stability on dubious foundations (such as job, peer acceptance, or wealth)? What can be said from a biblical perspective of a nation that relies on arms and military means for its security? (This is being written in the aftermath of the events of September 11, 2001, when America has turned to bombs and missiles to retaliate against terrorism, in spite of the warning that violence only begets more violence.) In light of what has happened since then, as well as the biblical vision of turning swords into plowshares, are such methods effective? Return to these questions after studying the Epistle lection.

Psalter: Psalm 48

This psalm shows us just what Zion, or Jerusalem, came to mean to the Jews. Verses 12-14 are especially poignant: The fortifications of Zion are the visible representation of the power and presence of God. So close is the connection that the psalmist can exclaim: "This is God, our God forever and ever."

The apparent strength of its defenses was to be seen as a representation of the strength of God, Israel's "sure defense" (48:3), who manifests divine protection by means of this chosen city (48:4-8). This psalm also provides us with the reason that the destruction of Jerusalem (in 587 B.C. and A.D. 70) would be so devastating to the morale of the Jews, warning them and us of the danger of tying divine realities to material structures.

Epistle: 2 Corinthians 12:2-10

The Corinthian Christians were still very much geared toward evaluating one another and their teachers by worldly criteria, such as physical appearance, eloquence, esoteric knowledge, and flashy charismatic experience. They also tended to compete with one another for prominence within the community; and they expected their teachers to vie with one another, based on such observable criteria. This competition demonstrated to Paul that their eyes were still focused on temporal rather than eternal things, still trying to play the world's game in God's assembly.

Boasting in Weakness

As Paul brought his second letter to a close, he parodied his rivals' presentation of themselves. He claimed to be a better apostle because he had been beaten up more often, or endured more deprivation, or had to run away from an angry king through a window (11:16-33). In mockery of the honor of being the first soldier to scale an enemy wall, Paul boasted of being the first to be let down the wall! His key theme throughout is that he boasted in whatever revealed his weaknesses (11:30; 12:9-10). If he were to point to his own abilities or natural endowments, people would just see the human being. When he pointed to his weaknesses, then people could see the power of God at work in whatever he did (see 4:7-15).

> **Think About It:** With Paul, what you see is what you get. He wanted to be valued only for the spirit of Christ within him. What do persons see in you that reflects the spirit of Christ? Is there variance between what is seen and what is?

Paul, the Visionary

Paul had visionary experiences, but the word from God that he was called to reveal was not connected with such lofty moments of strength that set him apart from other people. He also struggled with God in prayer over his "thorn in the flesh." This "thorn" was some disease or condition that impeded his performance or marred his physical appearance, though obviously it did not prevent his missionary work. This malady was God's remedy for any temptation Paul might have had to judge himself by worldly standards. Rather than valuing impressive physical appearance or proving his merit through great achievement, Paul found his worth in being a transparent vessel through which God's purpose could be seen and others could encounter and learn to trust the grace of God.

246

What You See Is What You Get

Verse 6 is a sobering word. Paul would not have anyone form an opinion of him based on reports of visions or mystical experiences. With Paul, what you see is what you get. He wanted to be valued only for the spirit of Christ in him: If we do not see the fruits of the Spirit and the character of Christ in a person, no other religious claim is of any worth whatsoever (see 1 Corinthians 13).

Gospel: Mark 6:1-13

This passage reports the continuing opposition Jesus faced from the very inception of his ministry. He had been opposed by "some of the scribes" when he pronounced the paralytic's sins forgiven (2:1-12) and by certain Pharisees for healing on the sabbath (3:1-6). There are in Mark five controversies in Chapters 2–3, after which Mark comments that the Pharisees went out and immediately conspired against Jesus with the Herodians, their enemies up to this point (3:6). After slander spread to the effect that Jesus was in league with the devil, his own family sought to restrain him, to protect the honor of both himself and his family in the eyes of their neighbors.

Rejection at Home

Following these early controversies, Jesus returned to Nazareth, a rabbi surrounded by his group of disciples, to teach and exercise his ministry of healing and deliverance—only to be rejected not by strangers but by those who knew him best.

It is difficult to know why the people responded as they did. Some say that his earlier work as a craftsperson made it difficult for people who knew him to accept him now as a teacher of God's way. Nevertheless, Shammai, the founder of one of the two chief schools of rabbis (Hillel was the other), had also been a carpenter.

Is Not This the Carpenter?

A Jewish male is almost always referred to by the name of his father, so that we hear in the description, "the son of Mary," a possible reference to rumors about his illegitimacy (see also John 8:41; 9:29). Perhaps this is an attempt to "bring him down to size," so to speak, within the context of his earlier life as a villager. It may be that his very familiarity—the fact that his origins and early years were no mystery but rather quite ordinary—made it

Think About It: The villagers of Nazareth rejected one they knew well. When has familiarity or a perceived lack of credentials prevented you from hearing a word of God from another person? from being heard by others?

247

impossible for those who had known him growing up to accept him as a teacher and worker of God's wonders.

Finally, we should not rule out the possibility of envy. After all, Jesus had in a short time achieved a fame that surpassed them all. People could either celebrate their famous son and bask in his fame or take offense out of an envious spirit.

The Advance Team

Note that the disciples were witnesses. They were about to set out on a ministry where they would encounter similar rejection. Jesus sent them to proclaim repentance to the towns of Israel and to extend his healing ministry. Traveling in pairs, perhaps, ensured that they could later confirm each other's testimony (see Deuteronomy 19:15).

They were also sent out without any provisions or shelter for the night (that is, without a second cloak or tunic, as mentioned in Mark 6:9). They were to depend wholly on hospitality. When they were welcomed as guests, they were to stay for the duration of their ministry in a given village (so as not to dishonor that first householder by opting for other accommodations later). Wherever they were not received, they were to shake the dust from their feet. Jewish travelers shook the dust of foreign lands from their feet before entering Palestine. The disciples would thereby convey to villagers that they were no longer part of Israel but were a land under God's judgment.

Why did the early church preserve these stories of sending and rejection? First, the mission of Jesus to Israel was an important sign of God's fidelity to God's people (see Romans 15:8-9; Acts 3:25-26). The fact of rejection, however, also prepared the early Christians to encounter and cope with rejection of themselves and their message.

Study Suggestions

A. Remember Holy Places

Introduce Psalm 48 using the notes on pages 245–46, and recite the psalm together responsively, verse by verse. Gather the group by inviting each person to recall a place (natural or human-made) where they have experienced God's strength, presence, or awesome being in a particularly striking way. Ask each member to tell what that place was and what was (or is) conveyed to them of God's reality by the visual impact of that site.

B. Encounter Holy Persons

Invite someone to read Mark 6:1-13. Ask: Why did the people of Nazareth take offense at Jesus? What did the town lose by its response to Jesus?

After the discussion, use the commentary on pages 247–48 to clarify and broaden the conversation. What would acceptance or rejection of the disciples, sent out to carry on Jesus' ministry, mean for the villages to which they went?

Invite members to share what has caused them to be unresponsive to another person who may have been speaking God's word of challenge or hope. Ask: When have you thrown roadblocks in the way of others (intentionally or unintentionally)? Is it more difficult to accept a healing message from family and close friends or from mere acquaintances (or even strangers)? Why or why not?

Ask members to share experiences from the other side—times when they have been unable to get a healing message across. What got in the way? How does this lesson challenge us to be alert for how God's word may come to us? How does it prepare us to accept rejection (and not equate it with failure)?

C. False Security 101

Read 2 Samuel 5:1-10 and the commentary on pages 244–45. Ask: What factors made the Jebusites so confident that David's forces (the "king and his men," a small detachment of the army) would not be able to take the city? What were the Jebusites trusting in for their stability and security?

A recurring Old Testament theme is that the people who trust in armies, chariots, and fortifications are disappointed, while those who trust in God are saved and victorious. Ask: What do we rely on to feel secure? How can we build a more secure stronghold? Also discuss the "Think About It" questions.

D. False Security 201

Introduce the Epistle using the notes on pages 246–47, and invite someone to read aloud 2 Corinthians 12:2-10. Ask: How were Paul's rivals and congregation seeking to establish their worth and legitimacy? What dangers attend a performance- and appearance-oriented estimation of oneself and others? What do we miss by trying to keep up appearances and by encouraging others to hide their weaknesses?

Now turn to the things of which Paul boasted—his various weaknesses, including that mysterious "thorn in the flesh." Discuss: Do you have a "thorn in the flesh" that could be changed from a point of concern or affliction to a point of praise for God's power? When have you seen God's power made perfect in your weakness?

E. In Closing

As a follow-up to last week (Activity E), invite participants to report on ways they have reached out to others. Rejoice where these have been accomplished and continue to pray over those who have not yet had opportunity. Then sing or read together the hymn, "My Hope Is Built."

Lections for Sunday Between
July 10 and 16

Old Testament: 2 Samuel 6:1-5, 12b-19

*D*AVID had decided to bring the ark of the covenant to Jerusalem. Why? Possibly he wished to link his new capital city with the symbol of God's covenant with Israel. God would remind David, however, that God's power could never be made to serve the ends of a human being, but rather the reverse must be true.

The Ark Brought to Jerusalem

The ark was the central piece of furniture in the tabernacle, containing the tablets of the Ten Commandments. When the phrase "before God" occurs in the context of the sanctuary, it seems to refer to the ark. If this be the case, according to some traditions the staff of Aaron that bloomed (the proof of God's choice of Aaron for the priesthood), a pot of manna (a testimony to God's provision for the people), and the book of law were also kept in or near the ark (see Exodus 16:34; Numbers 17:10; Deuteronomy 31:26).

The ark was the very throne on which YHWH was thought to sit in the midst of Israel. As such it was a powerful symbol of God's power in the midst of Israel. It had been carried ahead of the Israelite armies as they defeated their enemies. After the Philistines captured the ark in battle and took it home as a trophy, God wreaked havoc in the temple of Dagon and the Philistine cities of Ashdod and Gath (1 Samuel 5). When some failed to rejoice at the return of the ark, it was thought that YHWH killed seventy of them (1 Samuel 6).

This deadly, sacred power again broke out against Uzzah, who had reached out with his hand to steady the ark on a bumpy stretch of road. His death on the spot reinforced the impression that danger resided in not treating the ark and the God it represented with the utmost reverence and on the exact terms dictated by God. David was afraid of carrying out his original plan of bringing the ark to Jerusalem (in the part of the chapter omitted in the lection—verses 6-12a).

The ark was placed instead in the house of Obed-edom. When the family of Obed-edom prospered while the ark was in their care, David was emboldened to take the ark to his own house (verses 6:12-13). The procession involved extravagant sacrifices, loud music of praise, and even the king, disrobed down to his undergarments, dancing in worship to YHWH. God not only received gifts and praise; everyone was allotted a portion of bread, meat, and raisins (6:19).

Think About It: Why would God's presence entail both promise and danger? What contemporary parallels to the sacred aspects of this story can we legitimately attribute to God today? What meaning do these two aspects have for you?

How to Honor God

The one dissenting voice in the celebration was that of Michal, Saul's daughter, whose marriage to David had no doubt helped to legitimize his rule. In the sequel to today's lection, David went home with the intention of blessing, but instead was reproached by Michal for dishonoring himself in the eyes of his maidservants (that is, even the lowliest of his subjects). David replied that he would not protect his own image in the slightest degree where honoring God was concerned. He depended wholly on God for his standing, not upon image consultants. He was certain that doing so would ultimately mean honor for him.

Think About It: David would not protect his image where honoring God was concerned. In what forms does this tension between burnishing self-image and being faithful to God present itself to us? (Consider dilemmas like what we wear to church, how we budget our money, seeking recognition for acts of charity and service, and other image-building actions.)

Psalter: Psalm 24

David's ceremonial delivery of the ark into the tabernacle at Jerusalem may have been commemorated as an annual festive event during the monarchy, and Psalms 24 and 132 are thought to have been used during such a liturgical reenactment. The psalm is a celebration of God's kingship, established in Creation (verses 1-2) and expressed in the preservation of God's faithful people (verses 3-6), particularly in Israel's battles (hence the military images in verses 7-10). The association of God's sovereignty with God's dwelling in Jerusalem (visibly represented by the ark on procession) is strong in this psalm.

The seas and rivers are symbols of primeval forces of chaos, upon which God founded the order of creation (see Genesis 1:1-2), according to some strains of thought in Israel (learned from their Egyptian, Canaanite, and Babylonian neighbors). Creation was God's victory over the forces of disorder. God's imposition of order on the elements leads naturally to the idea of the moral order ingrained in the human part of creation by God. Israel's religion is based not on manipulation of God but on coming into harmony with God's moral character.

The lifting up of the heads of "gates" and "doors" has been interpreted in several ways. It could be an address to the inanimate portals to pay attention and open up, to the gatekeepers to see who approached and opened the gates, or to the gates enlarging themselves to accommodate the immense but invisible majesty that was passing through them. However it is taken, it is bold language befitting the lofty thought that the Creator was entering into Jerusalem to reside there and benefit its people.

Epistle: Ephesians 1:3-14

The letter to the church in Ephesus opens with this expansive and hymn-like paragraph celebrating God's favor toward the Christian community. The form of the paragraph is that of the "blessing" (*barakha* in Hebrew), something familiar from synagogue liturgies and from Hellenistic-Jewish hymns (see Luke 1:68-75).

God's Purpose for Us

Noteworthy in this blessing is the emphasis on God's "will," "purpose," "plan," and "pleasure," as well as on the end for which God has "destined" the believers. The author offers an answer to the conundrum of life's meaning and purpose in this outline of God's will for humanity. This purpose is summed up in the word *grace*, which signifies here God's desire to bring benefit to humankind.

We have been chosen in Christ to live lives pleasing in God's sight, separated from the sins that have alienated us from God and each other, sealed with the Spirit as the pledge of the wonderful end that God has in store for us. Division between people is to be replaced by unity in Christ.

> **Think About It:** The author explains at length God's purpose for humanity. What do you think is God's purpose for you?

The Practice of Praise

Also noteworthy is the repetition of the phrase "to the praise of [God's] glory" or "to the praise of God's glorious favor" (Ephesians 1:6, 12, 14). In the Greco-Roman world, generosity led naturally and necessarily to the praise of the giver, to the spreading abroad of the virtuous character of the giver by the recipients, and thus to the increase of the giver's reputation. To fail to respond to favor (grace) in this way was to be ungrateful. Having received so many gifts from God as well as assurance of gifts yet to come, the believer is obliged to honor God and live in recognition of God's goodness and generosity (1:12). The second half of Ephesians (Chapters 4–6) outlines at greater length the kind of life that honors God the Giver.

Gospel: Mark 6:14-29

The story of Jesus' ministry pauses as Mark turns to describe the end of John the Baptist's ministry. The transition is provided by Mark's account of several different evaluations of who Jesus is (as in "Who does he think he is!"). This same kind of conversation will lead to Peter's confession that Jesus is the Messiah in 8:27-29. In both places we are told that some people viewed Jesus as John the Baptist raised from the dead. This reinforces the impression we have from the Synoptic Gospels (Matthew, Mark, and Luke) that Jesus' ministry did not gain much recognition until John's had ended.

John's death is presented as a possible explanation for Jesus' miraculous powers (verse 14). The similarity of John's and Jesus' message—a call to repentance—might have contributed to the confusion felt among people who had not personally encountered the two. This bridge allows Mark to tell how John had died.

The Death of the Baptizer

In the course of calling the people of Judea and Galilee to repentance and to observance of God's law, John indicted even the tetrarch Herod Antipas. (Calling him "king" is ironic, since he desired that title but never attained it.) Antipas and his wife Herodias had both divorced their spouses in order to marry one another. This was not the rub. Herodias had been married to Antipas's half-brother Philip, so Antipas had married his half-brother's wife while he was still alive—a union explicitly forbidden in Leviticus 18:16 and 20:21.

No one, in John's view, was above the law. Herodias was especially enraged by John's indictment (6:19), since repentance would mean her repudiation by Antipas. Antipas recognized as well (as we are told by the first-century historian Josephus) the potential such an indictment had for arousing popular resistance to his rule—a rule already rendered unpopular by Antipas's disregard for Jewish law in other matters.

Surprisingly, Antipas only imprisoned John and was even credited by Mark with desiring to protect John from Herodias's desire to have him killed (6:19-20)—the standard way to deal with enemies and rivals in the Herodian household. Herodias's devious plan for getting her way in the end is a well-known aspect of this story (6:21-27).

The Aftermath

> **Think About It:** John courageously stood up for God's standards wherever he saw them flouted, refusing to mute his message to satisfy those who had power over him. When have you been in a situation where you felt you should speak up for God's standards in the face of those who did not want to hear the truth?

Josephus also records that the local population was quite indignant with Antipas for killing John, whom they regarded as an honorable and true prophet of repentance (Josephus, *Antiquities* 18.5.1-3). Three years later, the father of Antipas's first (divorced) wife, King Aretas of Nabataea, invaded Antipas's western territory and massacred his army. The populace saw in this defeat God's revenge on Herod for this crime. Everyone recognized that John died merely because he had spoken the truth: "It is not lawful for you to have your brother's wife" (6:18). But this was a truth that the powerful did not want to hear.

Elijah, John, and Jesus

Mark's purpose in telling this story is to comment on the common belief that Elijah would return (Mark 9:9-12). John is displayed as the returned Elijah. John's fate prefigured the Messiah's death as well as the persecution that would befall the disciples who had to witness to God's truth in a world where it was not welcomed by those in power.

Study Suggestions

A. Lift Up Your Heads

Psalm 24 invites affirmation of God's imposition of order on chaos, confession of sin (failure to align oneself with God's order), and invocation of God's presence to deliver and protect. Read verses 1-2 together; then invite individuals to thank God for what God has done in their lives.

Read verses 3-6 together, and invite group members silently to confess their sins and ask God's pardon. Then read verses 7-10 together, and invite members to share their hopes of what God will do as God "comes in" to your midst. Ask: What is there in modern life that robs us of our sense of reverence and awe? How does this diminish our worship?

B. Paraders of the Lost Ark

Read or tell the story in 2 Samuel 6, drawing on the commentary on pages 250–51. Ask: What did the ark signify for Israel? How do we signify and recognize God's presence in our sanctuaries?

This story shows a deep awareness that God's presence brings great power to bless but also great danger if God's honor is not respected. Ask: What experiences of God's presence have you had that made you aware of the awesome power of this holiness? What impact have these experiences had on your worship and your lives?

Return to the story. Ask: Why did David dance as he did, and why do you think Michal had such a negative reaction? (An ephod fits somewhat like a short loin cloth; if an ephod were David's only garment, he would have been exposed.) Which is more important for the different characters in the story: forgetting about oneself in the presence of God or never forgetting "who one is" and how a proper person behaves? Which takes priority for you? Discuss the "Think About It" questions related to this tension.

Lead the group into a discussion of different kinds and levels of participation in worship (from reserved singing to the raising of hands to swaying and dancing). Ask: What are your attitudes toward these expressions? Can worship be done decently and in order and retain high emotion?

C. God's Plan for You

Read Ephesians 1:3-14 and the interpretation on pages 252–53. Invite participants to list all the elements of God's "purpose," "plan," or "pleasure" in this passage. Ask: What does the author suggest we do if we wish to align ourselves with God's purposes? What goals or activities will characterize the life that fulfills these purposes? What might change in your life for this to be so for you?

What does the benediction (verses 2-3) say about God's desire to show kindness and favor? Invite the group to share honestly their experience of these gifts and how much they value them. Ask: Given the importance of returning gratitude to match the favor shown, to what extent do our lives (our witness, our service, our worship) reflect the value we place on God's gifts?

D. A Costly Accountability

Read Mark 6:14-29 and the comments about it on pages 253–54. Ask: What was John's indictment against Antipas and Herodias? What do you think led him to denounce such powerful people, when letting it slide might have added years to his ministry?

Discuss the "Think About It" questions. How might your reflection in Activity C embolden you in such cases?

E. Drawing It Together

The Psalm, Epistle, and Gospel lections all call us to align ourselves with what pleases God and what God seeks for us. Invite persons to share ways in which they have been challenged today in that regard. Pray for one another to heed that call, then sing "Sent Forth By God's Blessing."

Lections for Sunday Between
July 17 and 23

Old Testament: 2 Samuel 7:1-14a

*D*AVID showed a noble sensitivity at the outset to God's honor. He found it inappropriate that he should dwell in a magnificent palace, while God's ark—the symbol of God's presence—remained in a tent, as it had since the ark was built. David determined, therefore, to build a temple more suited to God's magnificence; and Nathan the prophet initially gave his consent.

Think About It: "It was God's pleasure to dwell in a tent, since God was a God of movement." Does building a magnificent church bring honor to God? The word *house* meant both a building and a household. What meanings do we associate with the word *house* today? What was God's purpose in making a covenant with the house of David?

God's response here corresponded to an earlier response to the people's original request for a human king (namely, Saul). It seemed to mean for God a step away from what God had intended. God was Israel's king; and it was God's pleasure to dwell in a portable tent, since God was a God of movement. God conceded, however, that David's son—not David himself—would be permitted to build a temple for God. Here the writer introduces a pun on the word "house"—as both a building (that is, a palace or temple) and a household (that is, a dynasty). YHWH would do for David what David was not permitted to do for YHWH—establish a "house."

The House of David Begins

The high point of David's story is this oracle of God that legitimizes not only David's rule but also the dynasty of his descendants. Doing so expresses the royal theology that the king is God's son and God is the king's father (see also Psalm 2). Israel's royal ideology stands apart, however, from any ideology that claims divinity for the ruler. The king's position was the gift of God, driven home here by the emphasis on God's generosity toward David, taking him from the lowly status of shepherd and making him king and the founder of a dynasty (2 Samuel 7:8-11).

This ideology also stands in contrast to common Semitic traditions that placed the ruler above law. The king was still subject to God and God's law and still liable to punishment when he transgressed that law. A central element of this oracle, however, was YHWH's oath not to take back his faithfulness from David's house and not to reject it as the ruling line in Judah. God would punish the rulers for wrongdoing, but would not cut off or reject them (7:14b-16).

Would the House of David End?

The course of history appeared to nullify this covenant, as the rule of the house of David was eventually cut off in 587 B.C. by the Babylonian conquest. Confidence in YHWH's oath, however, led to a prominent strain of Jewish messianism. This was the expectation (after centuries of rule by foreigners) that God would raise up a king from the house of David who would restore Israel to its former greatness and even subjugate the Gentile nations under his rule (see Isaiah 11:2-9 and Jeremiah 23:5-8, for example).

Jesus' own Davidic lineage became important to early Christian thinking about his messiahship (see Matthew 1:1; Luke 1:32-33, 69; 2:4; Acts 13:22-23, 34). This reflection connected assessment of Jesus' person and significance with the royal psalms that declared divine sonship and exaltation to God's right hand (see Psalm 2:7 and 2 Samuel 7:14 in Hebrews 1:5, and Psalm 110:1 in Hebrews 1:13; 10:13).

Psalter: Psalm 89:20-37

This psalm recalls God's promises to David and his household in 2 Samuel 7, but not, as the lectionary's selection would suggest, in order to celebrate them. Rather, the context for this psalm is lament and mental anguish as the psalmist and the worshiping community try to hold together God's unfailing oath with their recent experiences.

The psalm reflects the postexilic period after Jehoiachin's capture in 597 B.C., the siege of Jerusalem of 587 B.C., and the exile of key leaders and citizens. The time was ripe to contemplate the sorry condition of Judah, now a perpetual vassal state under Gentile domination, with neither independence nor Davidic king. All the elements of God's actions on David's behalf and of his oath to David remembered in verses 20-37 would be reversed or revoked (verses 38-45).

The psalm ends not with words of assurance or easy answers but with the psalmist entrusting his case to God. The psalmist, and indeed the whole nation, bear reproach for the sake of God's anointed king (either his capture or, later, his perpetual absence from the scene of Judahite politics). Their only hope is that God would remember God's oath and overturn their reproach.

The early Christians, who turned to the Psalter as their hymnal, found the resolution to this psalmist's lament in the resurrection of Jesus; but even this continued to be fraught with tension. Jesus was exalted to God's right hand; but his reign was not yet realized in the world, and his followers still had to bear God's anger against the anointed one (verse 38). Nevertheless, the last word entrusts life's predicament to a faithful God (verse 52).

Epistle: Ephesians 2:11-22

Pious Jews regarded their separation from the Gentile nations as the appropriate, God-ordained response to God's selection of Israel to be God's special possession. Refusal to blend in with the Gentiles was an expression of their loyalty to God and their gratitude for God's revelation to them. The Pauline mission emphasized, however, the end of this separation. Just as God was one, humanity must become one again under the one God (2:13-14).

A New Humanity

Jesus' death laid the foundation for this new humanity in the church. The author underscores the two dimensions of reconciliation effected by Jesus. Both Jew and Gentile were alienated from God, despite the privileges that had belonged to the former. Both are now reconciled to God on the same ground. Jew and Gentile were in fact also alienated from each other (2:11-12). The alienation that had kept them apart by prescribing separation was now abolished, since the promise toward which it had pointed had now come in Jesus (2:15-16).

> **Think About It:** The church is called to model a unity in Christ that is God's plan for all things in heaven and earth. How does your church reflect this unity? What can you do to help break down "walls of hostility"?

Becoming God's Household

The author's language distances the hearers from their pagan past—in terms of time ("at one time," "once"), space ("you who were far off"), and belonging ("without Christ," "aliens," "without God"). "Now" they have come "near" and are "citizens" and "members of God's household."

The author continues to use this language to help Christians respond wholly to God's call for repentance and change of heart, rooting out the old ways and learning new ways of relating and valuing in Christ. An essential element in this newness is in the core of one's identity—a change from "strangers and aliens" to "saints" and "members of "God's household" (2:19, NIV) that is founded on Christ and the apostles (2:20).

Gospel: Mark 6:30-34, 53-56

Last week's reading on the death of John the Baptist was a kind of aside to the main story. Prior to that episode, Jesus had sent out the disciples to proclaim repentance and to extend God's power to heal the sick and cast out demons. When they returned from what was no doubt an extensive and exhaustive endeavor, Jesus greeted them with an invitation to a well-deserved rest, a retreat in the wilderness (6:30-32). This can be taken as a mandate for those in ministry (ordained and lay) to engage in self-care, without which we can easily burn out and become ineffective.

The Crowd Pressing In

Rest, however, was to elude the disciples: crowds had already gathered, raced to their retreat spot ahead of them, and were waiting upon their arrival (6:33-34). Jesus' response was exemplary. He did not see people who were interfering with his plans for a retreat with his disciples, nor did he send them away out of an interest in protecting his personal time with the disciples. Instead, he saw people hungry for healing and teaching about God: "sheep without a shepherd" (6:34).

He set aside the plans for a retreat and instead taught the crowd for the rest of the afternoon. Jesus responded this way not because there was no one else to do the job or because it was expected of him, but because it was where his heart was. Mark says, "He had compassion for them" in their shepherdless predicament. Prayer and personal nurture is one remedy for burnout; but equally vital is a heart of compassion for people, without which ministry is tedious and draining.

Sheep Without a Shepherd

The image of the shepherdless sheep reverberates powerfully with 2 Samuel 7 and other Old Testament texts. Second Samuel 7 speaks of the tribal elders as "shepherding" God's people and presents David—who had been a shepherd before becoming a leader, being appointed by God as "shepherd" (2 Samuel 5:2) of Israel. Ezekiel 34:1-6, 20-24 makes a bridge between 2 Samuel and Mark, as the prophet lamented the lack of a faithful shepherd to care for Israel and predicted God's intervention to raise up "one shepherd, my servant David, and he shall feed them."

Jesus now stepped into the gap to shepherd the people, and indeed fed them in the next passage. Language about Jesus as shepherd stems from the early church's conviction that he was the "son of David" in whom God's faithfulness to his oath to David, and thus to Israel, was fulfilled.

Think About It: How do you look at the people around you? Are they sometimes an annoyance or interruption, or can you see them with Jesus' eyes as hungry and hurting and needing compassion and healing?

A Sacred Rest

Although the lectionary defers the story of the feeding of the five thousand to next week, we note that the disciples did enjoy some rest with the crowds as they all broke bread together on that Galilean hillside. It was a rest shared by all, ever so much richer than the disciples would have known alone.

The Next Crossing

In the lesson for June 26–July 2, we met a woman with a hemorrhage, a woman in the crowd around Jesus when he "had crossed again in the boat to the other side" (5:21). (See also 5:1; 6:45, 53 for the same transitional phrase.) We are told she believed she would be made well if she could "just touch his clothes" (5:28, NIV). Either she was not the only one to have such faith or news of the success of that touch had spread. Yet again, Mark shows the crowd pressing in upon Jesus just to "touch even the edge of his cloak" (6:56, NIV). And Jesus, the good shepherd, healed them all.

Study Suggestions

A. Waiting for God's Faithfulness

Read Psalm 89:20-37 responsively, then review the commentary on pages 257–58. Next, continue reading Psalm 89:38-52 responsively. Invite participants to do what the psalm models: to share their disappointments, their experiences of tension between God's promises and life situations. Then pray for one another's ability to entrust themselves fully to a God who will be faithful in all things.

B. Relying on God's Promises

Read 2 Samuel 7:1-17 and the notes on pages 256–57. Ask: Why might God have been reluctant to exchange a tent for a stone and cedar temple? What did the tent represent that would be lost in a temple? What warning might this speak to Christians who have heavily institutionalized their religion? Also discuss the questions in the "Think About It" box.

Invite different group members to read aloud 1 Kings 15:1-5; 2 Kings 8:16-19; 16:1-3; 19:32-35; 20:1-6. Ask: Did the sin of Israel (and David's descendants) finally overcome God's favor? Did God's promise to David fail? Why did the early church find in Jesus the fulfillment of God's promise and proof of God's faithfulness to David?

The way New Testament writers interpret the Davidic covenant suggests

God's freedom to honor God's promises in God's own way and time. How does this working out of the promise to David over a thousand years help us as we struggle with what seem like unfulfilled promises?

C. One in the Spirit

Read Ephesians 2:11-22 and the comments on pages 258–59. Ask: What did it mean for Jewish Christians to give up their barriers against Gentiles in the church? What did it mean for Gentile Christians to overcome their barriers of resentment against Jewish Christianity? What barriers to exhibiting unity do we face in our congregation? among our local churches? as a global church? How can we begin to live out what we are in Jesus Christ?

Look at the terms used in Ephesians 2:19-20: *strangers, aliens, citizens with the saints, members of the household of God, Christ Jesus as the cornerstone.* Ask: How do you relate to these terms personally? What does it mean to you to be a stranger or a saint, for example? How is God at work in this portion of your identity?

D. The Shepherd's Heart

Read Mark 6:30-34, 53-56 and the commentary on pages 259–60. Ask: Why was it important for the disciples to rest with Jesus? Where do you see signs of people looking for healing or teaching about the spiritual dimension of life? How do you feel toward such seekers (for example, those who browse the self-help, occult, and new age sections of bookstores)? Do you have a heart of compassion for these people, or do you tend to be indifferent or critical? What have you done to share with them the insights you learned from Christ, or to lead them on the way to wholeness in Christ?

E. Visit the Shepherd

Spend some time in silent prayer, inviting the group to seek the guidance or healing they need from Jesus. Ask him to share his heart for the wandering with them. Then close by singing "Softly and Tenderly Jesus Is Calling."

Lections for Sunday Between
July 24 and 30

Old Testament: 2 Samuel 11:1-15

*T*HIS week begins a series of two readings from what has become, next to David's defeat of Goliath, perhaps the most famous episode in David's life. David had been acclaimed king, in part based on his original willingness personally to lead Israel in and out of battles (2 Samuel 5:1-3). The writer's opening words contain a thinly veiled rebuke of David, who at the height of power had forsaken his former valor and left Joab to command his army. David's decision not to share in the fate and lot of his armies left him at home where he did not belong and thus in a position to witness what he ought not to have seen. An ill-timed walk on his roof made David's leisure an occasion for lust.

> **Think About It:** Which was David's greater sin—adultery with Bathsheba (personal and sexual) or abandoning his leadership responsibilities (social and political)?

Bathsheba, Wife of Uriah

Bathsheba was engaged in a ritual purification bath after her monthly period. She was a Torah-observant daughter of Israel and not a loose woman bathing in public view. She was probably bathing in an enclosed courtyard, visible to David only because of the elevation of his position on the roof higher up the hill in his citadel. He summoned Bathsheba to the palace, and they committed adultery. One may speculate whether Bathsheba was willing; the text does not say. Nevertheless, it can be said that women in that society were little more than property and had very little freedom. When commanded by the king himself, Bathsheba clearly had little, if any, choice.

The Faithful Uriah

But the king was not above the law. When Bathsheba conceived, he had to find some way to cover his tracks. Uriah her husband, however, was far too disciplined a soldier, far too committed to his comrades in the field, to "lie with [his] wife" while David's army was at risk in battle. The courage and self-control of this Hittite makes David's lack of self-control and courage all the more shameful. David had enjoyed Bathsheba illegitimately. Uriah, bound by laws of purity for battle (1 Samuel 21:5; Deuteronomy 23:9-14), refused to defile himself. Still intent on a cover-up, David set up Uriah to be killed so he could take Bathsheba to be his wife and perhaps pass off the child as an early but legitimate one.

David's Sin and Repentance

Second Samuel makes no attempt to conceal the sin of adultery and the crime that first robbed Uriah of his wife and then caused his murder. Centuries later, Matthew still names Solomon's mother as "the wife of Uriah" (Matthew 1:6). This is not because the Jews were unable to wink at David's crime, but because David was, in the end, unwilling to maintain the cover-up further and unwilling to keep his heart hardened against God: "I have sinned against the Lord" (2 Samuel 12:13). Israel accepted the penitent, just as God did. David maintained his honor not by maintaining the deception, as human nature might tempt one to do, but by confession and repentance.

> **Think About It:** Israelite culture was one in which open repentance from sin was encouraged, both through the public sacrificial system and through such encounters with prophets as David had with Nathan. Do we in our churches accept the penitent sinner, or do we encourage people to cover up their sins and prevent their healing? (Think of our attitudes toward released convicts, recovering alcoholics and drug addicts, or even the homeless, unemployed, or mentally ill who have simply fallen on hard times.)

Psalter: Psalm 14

This psalm represents the lament of the poor (or those who observe their plight). The psalmist's blanket condemnation of "all" stands in stark contrast to the appearance in verses 4-7 of the "company of the righteous" and "the poor" on whose behalf God intervenes. In his meditation, he castigates those who devour the poor (14:4) and who frustrate their plans and hopes in order to carry out their own agenda (14:5-6).

"Fools" (14:1) are those who live without an awareness of God's commitment to justice for all. They deny God's existence not only with their lips but also with their conduct toward other people. More important than a verbal confession of faith is the fear of God that guides one's conduct in the economic, political, and practical matters of life (14:2). The "fool" may be clever and successful in the eyes of worldly people; the wise person, who truly fears God in word and deed, finds his or her refuge in God.

This tension takes on distinctly nationalistic overtones since those under assault are "my people" (14:4) and since it is the restoration of God's people that is envisioned as God's forthcoming intervention (14:7). Paul's interpretation of this psalm (and others) in Romans 3 is revolutionary in that it undermines any such ethnic claim to being "the company of the righteous" that has a special claim on God's favor. For him, the words specifically address and negate Jewish privilege before God, leveling the playing field between Gentile and Jew.

Epistle: Ephesians 3:14-21

This is the second time the author has shared the contents of his prayers for the hearers (see 1:17-19). In both, the direction is essentially the same, namely that Christians everywhere will understand the immensity of Christ's love, of God's favor toward us, of God's power (particularly to accomplish the divine will), and of the goodness of the destiny God has appointed for those who are "in Christ." He recognizes the danger that Christians will underestimate these things, which will not only impoverish their own lives but also weaken their ability to respond fully and wholeheartedly to God's call.

Jesus' Love for the Believer

Here the focus is primarily on Christ's love for the believer, which the author prays will become the center and source of stability for the Christian's entire life. The images of tree roots and the foundation of a building convey the importance of grasping the immensity of this love—even though this is an attempt at knowing the unknowable. Meditating on the dimensions of this love, however, helps the believer apprehend God's fullness.

> **Think About It:** By the power of God, believers are able to do far more than we can ask or imagine. How have you seen God's power at work in you? When has God done the unexpected or unimaginable in your life?

The doxology (verses 20-21) expresses the desire that honor will come to God by means of Christ and the church. God is honored in Christ through Christ's obedience to God even unto death. God is honored through the accomplishment of God's purposes for creation now in the exalted Christ.

Responding to God's Favor

The Epistle lections for this and the next four weeks continue through Ephesians, turning now from reflection on God's generosity and mystery to

264

the response of Christians to God's favor. By our obedience to God's commands and commitment to doing what pleases God, we make the fitting response of bringing our Benefactor's name into good repute before all people. As the writer shows us, that response is encouraged and supported by our own prayers as well as the prayers of others.

Gospel: John 6:1-21

The lectionary follows John's Gospel for the episodes of the feeding of the five thousand and of Jesus' walking on water, thus enabling us to hear John's extensive interpretation of the meaning of these episodes (6:22-69). For five weeks, the Gospel lessons will remain focused on Jesus' significance as "the bread of life," something the pursuing crowds who hoped for repeat performances of the feeding miracle failed to perceive.

Holy Days

John is rather intentional throughout his Gospel to link episodes in Jesus' life with holidays in the Jewish calendar—Passover, Succoth, and Hanukkah. Often John perceives a connection between the significance of these holy days and that of Jesus' person, deeds, or teaching. Here, the Passover season is the setting—the holiday that recalled God's deliverance of the people from Egypt, and by extension, God's provision of food in the desert. These two are frequently linked in the psalms celebrating the Exodus.

Miraculous Provisions

Jesus led the crowds out from the towns into the deserted areas around the Sea of Galilee, and there through him the people again experienced God's miraculous provision of bread and meat (see, ironically, 6:30-32). Jesus was identified by the people as "the prophet who is to come into the world" (6:14), language recalling Deuteronomy 18:15-18, where God had promised to raise up a prophet like Moses for the people.

By making these connections, John presents Jesus as God's promised agent of deliverance in a new Passover, a new Exodus. It inaugurated a renewed wilderness experience, which was regarded by Jews as a time of special intimacy between Israel and God, in spite of their constant "murmuring."

Those who enjoyed the simple but ample meal provided by Jesus recognized that something astounding had happened. We should not overlook the element of physical hunger here, for the ancient agrarian economy left many at the subsistence level, living from day to day and going hungry many days. The opportunity to have a full stomach would not have been taken for granted.

The twelve baskets of leftovers (more than they started with) is a sign that

Think About It: The crowds acclaimed Jesus on the basis of having their temporal needs met. To what extent are you interested in a messiah who will simply make life smoother in this world?

all had eaten their fill. The unusual experience of plenty for everybody was enough for the crowd to wish to make Jesus king; but, of course, Jesus refused to allow his messianism to be limited to becoming an earthly ruler. He had come to do more than make people comfortable in this life. His mission was to lead them into a broader, unending life with God.

Walking on Water

The sequel to this episode is one of the strangest in the Gospels. While a few people might claim to heal, exorcise demons, raise the dead, and the like, no one can claim to walk on water. Perhaps our minds, confirmed in a scientific worldview, also find the claim that natural law was suspended here for Jesus to be odd, or perhaps even distasteful. Nevertheless, the meaning John gives the episode is clear, as he has Jesus use the divine disclosure formula, "I am" (John 6:20; see Exodus 3:14), to identify himself from atop the waves.

The walking on the sea was a parabolic event. In Jewish allegorical typology, the sea represented death. That Jesus could walk on the water symbolized his victory over death. This triumph over death was also represented in the bread of life. The promise is that all who ate the bread of life given by Jesus could, like him, be raised from the dead (John 6:54).

"I Am He"

Identifying Jesus with God is crucial to John's Christology (see the use of the "I AM" statement in John 4:26; 6:35; 8:12, 24, 28, 58; 10:11; 11:25; 13:19; 14:6; 15:1; 18:5, 6). John believes that Jesus saw himself to be identified intimately with God, and this understanding was amply supported in actions such as this one.

Study Suggestions

A. Protecting the Poor

Begin by dividing the group and reading Psalm 14 antiphonally, verse by verse. Ask: What complaints are raised against the "fools"? Then review the commentary on pages 263–64, and ask: What is the relationship between seeking after God and trying to avoid bringing harm or despair to the poor and less powerful? How are we involved, even indirectly, in devouring the poor to our benefit? What would "seeking God" lead us to do about this?

B. Sin in High Places

Roleplay 2 Samuel 11:1-15, assigning a narrator, a messenger, Bathsheba, David, and Uriah. Ask: In this episode, how do you view David? Uriah?

266

Bathsheba? Now read the commentary on pages 262–63. Ask: What factors increased David's vulnerability to sin? What did David risk by taking Bathsheba? His crime was more than sexual; it violated the rights of Uriah— rights the king was supposed to protect. What happens when leaders betray public trust?

C. Repentance in High Places

Return now to David (but keep your own experiences in mind). Ask: What enabled David later to admit his sin and repent? Does our church help people confess and repent by fostering and modeling forgiveness and acceptance, or does it encourage them to cover it up and maintain appearances? How can we become more of a healing community, and less of a community of hiding?

D. Laying Again the Foundation

Read Ephesians 3:14-21 and the commentary on pages 264–65. Ask: What does the author pray will happen for his readers? Why does he want them to have a fuller grasp of the dimensions of Christ's love?

Ask participants to place themselves in this prayer. Discuss: How fully has this prayer been answered in our own lives? Where are the roots and foundation of our being? What is the source of our strength? How full of God are we (as opposed, perhaps, to full of the world or of self)? How are we living to bring God honor? How can our response to God be more complete?

Form groups of three, and ask them to rewrite the prayer in terms they would use naturally and that make it meaningful and applicable to them. Then have them stand and use their bodies to create a group sculpture depicting their feelings and attitudes in response to their prayer. Have the total group view each small group sculpture in turn, making verbal response to each sculpture in terms of what it evokes in them.

E. More Than Bread

Investigate John 6:1-21 in a fishbowl. Have three persons representing Philip, Andrew, and Jesus discuss what they felt and experienced in these two episodes. The rest of the group will observe. After the three have finished, have everyone review the commentary on pages 265–66. Ask the three: How did you feel in your role? Ask the observers: Why do you think Jesus tested his disciples? Why did the crowd react as they did? What were they seeking? Discuss the "Think About It" questions as a total group.

F. Draw It Together

The lections fall into a well-known liturgical pattern, beginning with self-examination and confession of sin, moving into encountering God's forgiveness and love, then re-entering into God's favor. Close by inviting group members to confess their sins and receive forgiveness. Close by singing "Because Thou Hast Said" and praying the prayers written in Activity D.

Lections for Sunday Between
July 31 and August 6

T Old Testament: 2 Samuel 11:26–12:13a

HE editors of First and Second Samuel incorporated into the text several narratives (such as the Saul narrative and the ark narrative). Nathan's parable of the poor man's lamb is part of the "succession narrative"—a story of God's promise to David to establish his throne forever.

Various accounts eventually were gathered together to describe Israel's change from a loose confederation of tribes ruled by judges to what was described as a small empire ruled by a king. What now appear as First and Second Samuel were shaped over several centuries to describe Israel's failures and the exile of its leaders. The final editors wrestled with how God's plan prevailed in spite of the nation's sins and misfortunes.

Abusive Power

When she learned of her husband Uriah's death, Bathsheba mourned, observing custom. Then David "sent for" and married her. We sometimes romanticize this woman whom David coveted, seduced, murdered for, and married (seeking perhaps to soften David's harsh actions and ignore his sin). In reality we do not know what Bathsheba felt or wanted. She was probably at the mercy of the king's power. We can, however, easily imagine David's response: "Mission accomplished!" But David had not reckoned on God's displeasure. David had wielded power by "sending" people and messages. Now God exerted divine power, "sending" the prophet Nathan to David.

Confrontation and Confession

Nathan's previous message from God to David was a promise of an everlasting dynasty (2 Samuel 7:4-17). Next he delivered God's judgment. He described a legal case for David: A rich man with many flocks kills a poor man's only lamb. David, shocked and angered by the heartless action, told Nathan that the rich man should die and should "restore the lamb fourfold" (12:6; see Exodus 22:1). Nathan immediately made his point: You are the man! David had condemned himself and admitted: "I have sinned against the LORD" (2 Samuel 12:13).

Divine Response

God forgave David, but the sinful affair marked a turning point for David. God's judgment was severe: ongoing conflict, rape, killing, alienation, and conspiracy all would occur in David's house. The pure and powerful David, God's chosen, had fallen.

Throughout Second Samuel the narrator weaves a dramatic theological story tracing how God worked through human events to shape Israel's future. Nathan's parable illustrates how Israel's prophets (God's spokespersons) repeatedly confronted their kings' moral crimes. While other ancient Near East rulers might rule absolutely and capriciously, Israel's king was accountable to YHWH.

Today this story calls those in power to face the ways they abuse their power. It calls the rest of us to speak the word of truth courageously in the face of abusive power. The tricky part is recognizing when we are David and when we are called to be Nathan. The potential to abuse power in pursuit of selfish ends lies within each of us.

> **Think About It:** David abused his power; the rich man abused his. When have you abused your power or position? How did you recognize that abuse? What did you do?

Psalter: Psalm 51:1-12

This psalm is an eloquent petition for God's mercy and cleansing. Like David, the psalmist acknowledges sin and the need for forgiveness. Though the superscription says this psalm was David's lament, scholars believe it was added later to present the psalm against the backdrop of David's story. Both the David/Nathan story and the psalm emphasize human sin. Note how guilt, sin, and sinner dominate in verses 3-11.

Psalm 51 also stresses reconciliation. Like the David/Nathan story it highlights God's forgiveness and grace: God forgives, keeps the relationship intact, and reissues the invitation to be reconciled. Note how images of heart, spirit, and God dominate in verses 12-19. Note also that the reconciled sinner is to become a reconciler (51:12-13).

While this psalm may be prayed individually, verses 18-19 take it to a communal level—Israel's plea for restoration after the Exile. Today, it might be read as the church's plea for forgiveness for many institutional and corporate transgressions. The psalm proclaims that all repentant sinners are justified by God's grace; all are reconciled to God and invited to become reconcilers.

Epistle: Ephesians 4:1-16

Either Paul or one of his flock wrote to the Gentile Christians at Ephesus in the late first century about unity and diversity in the church. If the author was a follower of Paul, he was faithful to Paul's message.

Call to Unity

In Ephesians 4:1-6, the writer appeals to believers to be worthy of their calling "to keep the unity of the Spirit through the bond of peace" (4:3, NIV). "Peace" refers to God's salvation, not just a lack of human conflict. Jesus Christ brought peace by joining two parties (Jew and Gentile) and reconciling them to God (2:14-18). "Bond" refers to that reconciled divine/human relationship. Believers maintain unity by living peacefully (with humility, gentleness, patience, and love) and by remembering that they are bound in unity (one body, Spirit, hope, faith, baptism, and God).

In Unity, Diversity

The writer then reminds believers that they have been graced with Christ-given diverse gifts (verses 7-16). This "one body, many parts" focus is both similar to and different from Paul's statements in Romans 12:3-8 and 1 Corinthians 12:4-30 where Paul stressed general gifts of the Spirit. Ephesians accents leadership functions in an expanding church that was becoming more organized. However, the emphasis is still on members' complementary tasks.

> **Think About It:** Ephesians urged believers to maintain unity of Spirit in the bond of peace. How do you live up to that calling?

Our task is to build up the church until the entire body of Christ reaches a mature harmony (Ephesians 4:12-13). This too echoes Paul's theme that though Christ is the cornerstone, God needs believers (the body) to join in the work of salvation.

This lection presents a tension. On the one hand, believers are called to unity (one body, Spirit, hope, faith, baptism, and God); on the other hand, we are called to honor diversity (one body, many gifts). First-century Christians were concerned mostly about Jewish-Gentile unity and diversity. Today, we face many kinds of diversities in our highly technological and interactive world. How do we live up to our calling today?

270

Gospel: John 6:24-35

The Gospel of John was written sometime after the Jewish Temple was destroyed in A.D. 70 and before 100 when the manuscript was known in Egypt. It was addressed to persecuted Jewish Christians being expelled from their synagogues for their belief in Jesus as the Messiah.

In the Synoptic Gospels (Matthew, Mark, and Luke), Jesus speaks in parables and short sayings about "the kingdom of God." In John, however, Jesus speaks about God through long, difficult dialogues that people often misunderstand. The "bread of life" discourse we study today is one of those complex passages.

Seeking Signs

The day after the feeding miracle, the crowd found Jesus in Capernaum and asked when he got there (verses 24-25). Instead of answering, Jesus focused on their motives in seeking him. The word *sign* recalls two earlier signs (the water-to-wine miracle in 2:1-12 and the offer of "living water" in 4:7-15) where people believed after they saw Jesus' sign and quickly spread the word (4:27-42). This crowd believed only in full stomachs, seeking bread that perishes (6:26).

Receiving God's Gift

After rebuking the crowd, Jesus urged them to "work for" food that endures (6:27). But they misunderstood. He was offering them a divine gift, but they asked how to get bread that would not go stale.

In verse 29, Jesus attempted to recover his original point by redefining *work* as "faith in the one whom God had sent." John sees Jesus himself as the work of God who works God's works. Work is not only what Jesus does; it is also who Jesus is.

The crowd said they would do God's work—believe—only if Jesus first gave them a sign (6:30). They reminded him that Moses gave a sign—manna from heaven (see Exodus 16:1-36 and Numbers 11:1-35). Jesus' assessment was confirmed: They failed to comprehend; they had already been fed with miraculous bread!

In verses 32-33, Jesus tried again. He told them that God, not Moses, gave the bread in the desert; that his offer of bread was the "true bread from heaven." They (not their ancestors) were the recipients of God's true gift. They had already received a sign, if only they would believe. But they said, "give us this bread always" that bread from God would be given over and over (6:34). In verse 35, Jesus corrected that mistake: "I am the bread of life"; if you believe you will never be hungry.

Beyond Signs to Faith

In the Gospel of John a sign is intended to evoke faith but is by itself insufficient grounds for faith. If we look only at the sign, we end up exclaiming,

271

"See what Jesus *does*!"—and looking for more signs. We either believe in Jesus as a miracle worker or reject that miracle worker. But if we look

Think About It: The crowd misunderstood Jesus' sign as well as his explanation. When have you looked for a sign, only to miss it—or interpret it too literally?

beyond the sign to the meaning of Jesus' words, we exclaim "See who Jesus *is*!" Jesus comes from God—himself a sign of who God is. He is the "bread that endures" as God endures. He offers God's gift of life. Signs evoke our faith in God. The proper response is to receive God's gifts and share them, not work for them.

Study Suggestions

A. Create a Faith Banner

Gather colored markers. Cover a table with paper. In the center, print: "Components of a Believer's Life." Randomly add these phrases based on today's lections: "Recognizing Wrongdoing"; "Seeking Forgiveness"; "Receiving God's Gifts"; "Maintaining Unity"; "Offering Reconciliation"; "Honoring Diversity." Invite participants to draw symbols or images reflecting the phrases.

B. Explore Abusive Power

Review 2 Samuel 11:26–12:13a and the commentary on pages 268–69. Ask: What was David's sin? What was Nathan's underlying message about power? (Abusive power has serious consequences.) Who are the Davids today who abuse power? When might we be a David? Who are today's Nathans who speak out against abusive power? When has our church been a David? a Nathan?

C. Pray for Reconciliation

Pray Psalm 51:1-12 responsively. Ask: What is the psalmist's petition? (For forgiveness and restoration.) How is this psalm reminiscent of the Second Samuel story? (See the interpretation on pages 269–70.)

D. Explore Our Common Task

Read Ephesians 4:1-16. Ask: What is the believer's calling? What do *peace* and *bond* mean? How are believers to fulfill their calling? (Review the commentary on page 270 as necessary.) How do you explain the dual Ephesians message of unity (verses 4-6) with diversity (verses 7, 15-16)? How well does our local church and denomination live out this message? How might we do better?

E. Explore Signs and Faith

Read John 6:24-35. Ask: What was the feeding miracle (6:1-15) supposed to do for the crowd? (See the commentary on pages 271–72.) What is the gift? What is the proper response? How does the crowd misunderstand? How is Jesus both the sign and the gift? How do we distinguish between signs of God's gift and the gift itself? John claims that Jesus was the bread of God "come down from heaven" meaning that Jesus was fully divine (see 1:1-2). How do you understand the relationship between God and Jesus?

F. Reflect on a Believer's Life

Review the banner. Our lections pose broad theological themes: judgment, confession, punishment, forgiveness (Samuel and Psalms). Ephesians and John emphasize reconciliation, eternal life, and being called to a common ministry of reconciliation and unity while honoring diverse gifts. Ask: How do you explain God's role in judgment and punishment? What would church life look like if we all fully accepted God's gifts and truly worked for unity-with-diversity?

G. Close With Praise

Joyfully sing "Many Gifts, One Spirit."

Pray: "Great Merciful God, we thank you for your gifts of forgiveness and new life. Great Reconciling God, we will seek unity and peace. Great Giving God, we praise you for your gift of Jesus—your sign of 'bread that endures'—your sign of the 'bread of life.' We praise you for your many diverse gifts that unite us all as your children. Amen."

Lections for Sunday Between
August 7 and 13

I Old Testament: 2 Samuel 18:5-9, 15, 31-33

IN action prior to this lection, David's punishment for abusing power had unfolded. His child born of the affair with Bathsheba had died; his daughter Tamar had been raped by her half-brother Ammon; another son, Absalom, had killed Ammon in revenge and lived in exile for three years. The king had finally allowed Absalom to return to court, but refused to embrace his son.

Absalom's Mutiny

A deeply alienated Absalom patiently schemed to win over David's subjects. Finally, having gained some power, he attempted to seize the throne from his father. A politically weakened David still maneuvered the site of the decisive battle. He divided his army into three groups, assigned each group a commander, and then weakly agreed to remain at the gates of the city to hear news of the battle.

Plea and Predicament

Before sending his armies into battle, David pled with his commanders to "deal gently with the young man Absalom" (18:5). We sense David's predicament: The king had to seek Absalom's death because Absalom was the enemy; the father (belatedly) was concerned for his son's well-being.

Sometime during the battle, Absalom rode under a great oak tree entangling his thick hair in the branches, which suspended him between heaven and earth (14:25-26.) Biblical scholar Walter Brueggemann suggests that Absalom hung "suspended between life and death, between the sentence of a rebel and the value of a son, between the severity of the king and the yearning of the father" (*First and Second Samuel*, Interpretation; Louisville, John

Knox, 1990; 319; quoted in *The New Interpreter's Bible,* Volume 2; 1998; 1336). Witnesses to Absalom's predicament reported it to their commander Joab who pragmatically killed Absalom, the rebellious traitor. David's plea echoed in the wind.

Tension Between Roles

The tension increased as two runners raced from Joab to David with news. The first to arrive, a young Israelite, announced the military victory; but the king ignored it. The father wanted only news of his son. The runner hedged, aware that bad news delivered to the king could result in his own death. The second runner arrived and announced that God had delivered King David from all his enemies. Again the king ignored the victory. The father wanted news of his son. This runner, an African, delivered the message of Absalom's death obliquely, aware that as a foreigner his life held little value for the king. But it was the father, not the king, who responded. David mourned the death of his son and wished he himself had died instead.

The narrator paints a universal tension between the private and public roles of leaders. David's poignant lament in 18:33 expresses intense parental grief. At the same time, the ever-pragmatic Joab considered David's grief absurdly self-indulgent; David had to reestablish his power (19:5-7). Love versus duty—David chose too late and too little.

> **Think About It:** David grieved a rebellious son, but still had a kingdom to govern. When have you felt caught between private and public or professional roles? How have you dealt with this tension?

Psalter: Psalm 130

This psalm is the eleventh of fifteen "ascent songs." The Hebrew word for "ascent" means "to go up" (a hill or stairs). Pilgrims recited these psalms while climbing up to Jerusalem or engaging in a Temple celebration. The psalms reflecting people's daily life (home, spouse, children, extended family, friends) are interspersed with those expressing national concerns—a pattern that would have made sense to pilgrims traveling from various regions toward Jerusalem. Identification with the theocratic nation was the common thread that transcended their diverse lives.

Psalm 130 begins on a personal note. One who has sinned cries out for God's help, knowing he or she could not resist God's remembrance of those wrongs. The next breath recalls: There is forgiveness in you, God. Then, no longer talking to God, the psalmist makes a personal profession of faith. Yet Psalm 130 ultimately is an ascent song with a national concern. It shifts to a direct appeal to Israel to "hope in the Lord" and ends with a universal profession of Jewish (and Christian) faith: God loves steadfastly; God will redeem.

Epistle: Ephesians 4:25–5:2

The writer, having urged Christians to live lives worthy of their calling, now instructs them how to do this.

Do Not Fall Back

The first rules for Christian living are found in 4:25-32. This list is linked to the reminder in verses 20-24 not to fall back into old ways. The writer takes a negative view of Gentiles based on pagan stereotypes: they lied, hated, talked vulgarly, and took unfair advantage of others. He also exhibits an attitude of religious superiority: assuming that Gentile pagans were impure (in contrast to Jewish and Christian concepts of holiness), when in reality, the Stoics, for example, had high ethical standards. We, too, sometimes tend to judge others based on stereotypes or to assume our form of religion is superior.

Regardless of stereotypical assumptions, however, these instructions provide a list of "don'ts" that give good guidance for living: don't lie, steal, speak evil, offend the Spirit, or harbor bitterness, anger, wrangling, slander, or malice. The writer follows up these negatives with a short positive list: be kind, tenderhearted, and forgiving. To be "sealed for the day of redemption" (4:30, NIV) refers to the role of baptism in sanctifying the believer.

Imitate God

The key to all this is found in the final dual recommendation: Imitate God by forgiving (4:32b) and loving (5:2). As "dearly loved children" (5:1, NIV), Christians must imitate God. This phrase reminded readers that through Christ God had included Gentiles as heirs, creating one new humanity from two different groups: Jew and Gentile. (See the account of this union and reconciliation in 2:11-22.) All were created in God's image. And, since love and forgiveness are the two main aspects of God's relationship with humans, to imitate God is to forgive and to love.

> **Think About It:** Ephesians calls believers to imitate God by forgiving and loving. Think of times in your life when you tried to imitate God. How successful were you? What might you do differently the next time you find it a challenge to imitate God?

Gospel: John 6:35, 41-51

This is another section of the long "bread of life" discourse. Last session, the crowd missed the significance of Jesus' sign and misunderstood his reference to "bread that endures." When they asked to be given that bread, Jesus claimed: I am the bread of life. The bread stands before you!

Bold Self-Naming

The "I am . . ." declaration in verse 35 is the first of several such statements where Jesus depicted himself in terms of common objects: bread (6:35, 51), light (8:12; 9:5), gate (10:7, 9); shepherd (10:11, 14); life (11:25; 14:6); and vine (15:1, 5). These metaphors augment the titles in John 1. Together the metaphors and titles suggest that no one image can adequately portray who Jesus is. It seems John intended to expand, not restrict, the ways we understand and approach Jesus.

The Jews' Complaints

Jesus was interrupted by the grumbling crowd (verses 41-42). Here for the first time people were identified as "the Jews," by which John meant the authorities (not all Jews) who were resistant to accepting who Jesus was. He may have meant not only hostile Jewish authorities in Jesus' day but also those in his own time (fifty or sixty years later) who were expelling Jewish Christians from the synagogues because of their faith in Jesus. Either way, these leaders assumed that by identifying Jesus' parentage, they could dismiss his claim to be the bread from heaven.

The Manna

The crowd had mentioned the manna from the Exodus story (6:31). John was reminding readers of the rest of the story by using the word *complain* or *grumble*. These complaining Jews were just like their grumbling ancestors (recall Exodus 16:1-36 and Numbers 11:1-35). They did not see what God was doing!

Living Bread

In 6:43-47, Jesus addressed the grumblers; but instead of responding to their complaint, he restated an earlier point: God's teaching is offered to all; but only those who "hear and learn" will come to Jesus in faith. Jesus repeated their reference to the manna, but changed "our" to "your," thus distancing himself from them and their history. He then made his point with another bit of Scripture: Those grumbling ancestors later died (Numbers 14:21-23; Deuteronomy 1:35). Thus, this crowd who had just been fed miraculously also would die unless they heard and received the true bread of life.

In 6:51, Jesus summarized his point by reflecting the manna miracle, then drew the logical conclusion: I am the living bread

> **Think About It:** Jesus boldly claimed, "I am the bread of life" (verse 35) and "I am the living bread" (verse 51). Does that metaphor for Jesus have meaning for you? How? If it does not, what metaphors or titles for Jesus do speak to you?

come from heaven; eat and receive the gift of eternal life. The phrase *from heaven* can mean either miraculous food or God's gift of the Word. For John, Jesus both offered miraculous food and was the Word who gave eternal life. The reference to bread/flesh reminds us of Jesus' sacrificial death for our salvation.

Study Suggestions

A. Discuss David's Predicament

Read or tell the story in 2 Samuel 18:5-9, 15, 31-33, then review the commentary on pages 274–75. Ask: How would you describe the relationship between Absalom and David? What is David's plea to his commanders? Why did Joab (David's nephew and Absalom's cousin) not honor that plea? What is the predicament that plagues David? How does this speak to us today?

B. Reflect on a Psalm

Read Psalm 130 together, then interpret it from the commentary on pages 275–76 and that for June 26–July 2 (pages 239–40). Ask: How might this psalm reflect David's confession and plea after Absalom's death? Where do you also see the ascent aspect and the corporate dimension? Why do some need to hit bottom before crying out to God? For what do societies need forgiveness? What would repentance look like for a nation?

C. Examine Rules for Living

Read Ephesians 4:25–5:2, and review the commentary on page 276. Ask: Why are these particular rules given to the early Gentile Christians? How do these rules relate to our calling "to keep the unity of the Spirit through the bond of peace" (4:3, NIV)? How does the writer stereotype Gentile pagans? How can we name sinfulness without stooping to name-calling and stereotyping?

This list in Ephesians is reminiscent of Paul's admonitions (Galatians 5:19-21 and 1 Thessalonians 5:12-22) and of earlier lists (Zechariah 8:16-17 and Psalm 4:4). Look up and compare all four passages. Discuss: How are they alike? different? Do the writers use such lists for the same or different reasons? What do they convey about right living? Look up "ethical lists" in a Bible dictionary, and compare these lists to other Greco-Roman ethical systems.

D. Discuss Bread of Life

Read John 6:35, 41-51 and review the commentary on pages 276–78. Ask: What do you think Jesus' statements in verses 35 and 48-51 meant to John's readers? If you were in their place, how might you have received these images? What are other metaphors John used to describe Jesus? (Light of the world, good shepherd, true vine, living water.) What does John's dual emphasis of Jesus as Word from heaven and bread from heaven mean to you?

E. Dig Deeper Theologically

In today's lections some persons and groups are considered less worthy while others are assumed to be religiously superior. Identify the stereotypes and assumptions of superiority in each lection. (Hints: the African runner/King David and Israel; other nations/Israel; Gentile pagans/Christians; Judaism/Christianity.)

Discuss: How are stereotypes and assumptions of superiority an issue of power and control? How do we invite others to Christ without being arrogant? Can God's gifts of forgiveness and eternal life come through other faiths? The psalmist pleads with Israel to hope in God and asserts that God loves steadfastly and will redeem the nation. Ask: How might the psalmist's plea and affirmation about Israel apply to the United States?

F. In Closing

Sing or read together "Become to Us the Living Bread," and close with prayer.

Lections for Sunday Between August 14 and 20

T Old Testament: 1 Kings 2:10-12; 3:3-14

*T*ODAY'S passage concludes the "succession narrative" of God's promise to David of an eternal dynasty (2 Samuel 7). The material in First and Second Samuel and First and Second Kings was shaped by a Deuteronomic editor three hundred to four hundred years after David's reign. To understand today's verses, we must look at events surrounding David's death.

Scandalous Events

In 1 Kings 1, when David's eldest surviving son Adonijah (the presumed heir apparent) declared himself king even before David's death, the prophet Nathan intervened. Nathan urged Bathsheba to remind David of an old promise he had made that her son Solomon would become king. This promise had never been mentioned before, leading us to suspect that Nathan and Bathsheba were conspiring. Real or not, David acknowledged the promise and declared Solomon his successor. In 1 Kings 2:12, the narrator declared that Solomon's kingdom was established, implying that God's promise to David had been fulfilled.

But David's dynasty was not yet firmly established. In the ensuing power struggle, Solomon spared his elder half-brother's life (1:49-53). However, when Adonijah continued to scheme to obtain the throne, Solomon finally killed him and his supporters (1 Kings 2:13-46a). The narrator then firmly concluded (again) in 2:46b that David's dynasty was secured.

This story has no characters to be emulated. Adonijah was ambitious and impatient and also a divisive threat since his supporters came only from the kingdom of Judah. Nathan and Bathsheba schemed to deceive a dying David whose pride would surely not let him admit he had forgotten such a significant promise.

Divine Actions

As a new king, Solomon went to Gibeon (a hill sanctuary seven miles from Jerusalem) to sacrifice (3:3-4). He followed an ancient Near East practice of sleeping in a sanctuary in hopes of receiving a divine message. In a dream, Solomon humbly requested wisdom to govern (judge) rather than selfish, worldly things. We often interpret Solomon's request as an admirable model of faith: seek first the good of God's people. However, in his day people believed that acquiring wisdom led to worldly benefits like longevity, honor, and riches. Solomon was being practical!

The narrator's message underlying the story of Solomon's succession to the throne is theological (rather than moral): God's purposes are worked out in human events, sometimes even through plots and scandals. God is the main actor in this story. God appeared to Solomon with all his human imperfections and invited him to request a gift (3:1-5). God responded to Solomon's imperfect love by granting his request (3:10-13). God summoned Solomon to love and obey (3:14).

Think About It: David's life had been marred by sin, yet God's promise to him was kept. When have you felt that God was working through surrounding events in spite of your shortcomings?

Psalter: Psalm 111

This psalm is an acrostic hymn of praise; each half of a verse begins with a successive letter of the Hebrew alphabet. Acrostic was a pedagogical technique; this is an instructional psalm.

Psalm 111 teaches that true wisdom or knowledge begins with grateful praise and leads to obedience. Praise is to be personal but not private. Those who delight in God will know God's saving work that brings justice to the oppressed. They will study God's precepts (instructions), which are intended to help them maintain justice. They will know that God relates faithfully to them and expects faithfulness in return.

God's work of redemption and the people's work of justice are mutual aspects of the divine/human covenant. God's holiness is not intended to keep people fearful or at a distance; rather "fear of God" involves performance (praise, gratitude, obedience, doing justice). Verse 10 summarizes this radical notion: Wisdom begins with grateful praise and obedience. Those who have wisdom (fear God) will embrace God's commitments and values (will be righteous, gracious, and merciful).

Epistle: Ephesians 5:15-20

This passage offers a third set of instructions for Christian living, which follow from the admonition in 5:6 ("Let no one deceive you with empty words"). They urge us to "be careful" how we live so as not to be led into doing evil.

Live Wisely

In 5:15-16, believers are urged to live wisely, "making the most of the time" (literally, buying up the time). *Time* refers to human historical time, which is labeled "evil." The admonition refers to a common New Testament apocalyptic perspective that historical time would soon be replaced when Christ returned. Until then believers were to live wisely. The writer's feelings were clear: Nothing was more important than living a Christ-like life until Christ came again. (See, for example, 1 Corinthians 7.) This rule in Ephesians may have been taken from Colossians 4:5 where believers were told to conduct themselves wisely toward outsiders, although this passage seems not to be limited to outsiders.

Focus on God

Ephesians 5:17-20 offers two more rules: do not be foolish; do not get drunk with wine. These specific "don'ts" are then rephrased as positive, more general actions: try to discover God's will (or, as in 5:10, try to find out what is pleasing to God); and be filled with the Spirit, giving thanks at all times and for everything.

> **Think About It:** Ephesians urges believers not to be foolish, but to live wisely, imitating God. What rules or guidelines do you follow in order to "live wisely"?

The writer of Ephesians was reformulating familiar Pauline ideas to motivate his Gentile Christian audience to live as renewed persons in Christ. He was urging them to live so they did not harm but rather benefited other people, both fellow Christians and outsiders. The model to be imitated is God: forgive and love.

We may have different understandings today of time and of Christ's return; nevertheless, these admonitions are relevant to us as we try to relate our beliefs about new life in Christ to practical ways of wise living in our twenty-first-century world. We too are urged to imitate God.

Gospel: John 6:51-58

Verse 51 reminds us that we are still exploring the "bread of life" discourse.

Double Meanings

In verse 52, the authorities indicate they have followed Jesus' argument—at least on one level—when they argue about how he could give them his flesh to eat. Taking *flesh* literally, they hear him implying an unthinkable thing. They were still missing the rich symbolism of the bread metaphor.

However, John's readers would not have misunderstood "eating flesh" and "drinking blood." They had already been sharing in a ritual meal based on Jesus' words and acts during his last meal with the disciples. They would have heard his words as a reference to the Eucharist where flesh and blood were symbolized by bread and wine.

Besides using *flesh* to refer to Jesus' body, John uses the word *eat* in two different ways: eating sacramental food—the bread and wine of the Eucharist—and hearing and receiving the Word (Jesus), the bread of life (6:51). For John, word and sacrament are inseparably related.

A Different View

John was writing fifty to sixty years after Jesus' death to a community of Jewish Christians who were being persecuted by the authorities for their belief in Jesus. The holy meal separated them from their synagogue and their Jewish heritage. Biblical commentator D. Moody Smith notes that the Eucharist, like baptism, would have indicated "a clear confession of faith in Jesus, a break with the synagogue, and adherence to the new community of Jesus' disciples"—which John was no doubt urging his Jewish Christian community to do (*Harper's Bible Commentary*, HarperCollins, 1988; 1058.)

John's view of the sacrament emerges only when we compare it to others in the New Testament. In Matthew 26:26-29 and Mark 14:22-25, the blood/wine/cup of the Last Supper is more important than the bread. The cup symbolizes Jesus' death as a sacrifice that established the new covenant (the basis for salvation) with God. John, however, focuses on bread as life, barely mentioning the cup or sacrifice.

Luke draws on a different form of the early liturgy known to Paul. (See Luke 22:14-20 and 1 Corinthians 11:23-25.) Both see the holy meal as remembrance, while John stresses Jesus' presence and relationship. Jesus abides with believers when they eat and drink. Believers receive life through Jesus' presence (John 6:56-57). For John, the sacred meal celebrates a present relationship between believer and Jesus, not a meal of remembrance.

Come to the Table

Some churches today exercise power by controlling who offers and who receives the Eucharist. John challenges that power and access by emphasizing the personal, relational—not the institutional—dimensions of the sacrament. In John, it is Jesus—not his disciples—who distributes bread and fish to the crowd (see 6:11). It is he who offers living bread to believers. The message is clear: all are welcome to come to the table to receive the bread of life.

> **Think About It:** Jesus says "unless you eat the flesh of the Son of Man and drink his blood, you have no life in you" (6:53). What do you experience when you receive the bread and cup at the Eucharist?

Study Suggestions

A. Examine a Scandal

Read 1 Kings 2:10-12. Ask: What scandals surround Solomon's accession to the throne? What is the narrator's point in telling these stories? (See the commentary on pages 280–81.) Who was responsible for bringing Solomon to the throne? What do you think about the narrator's point that God was active in events that brought Solomon to the throne? How do you understand God's role in history? What meaning does the story have for us today?

B. Explore Wisdom

Read 1 Kings 3:3-14. Ask: What was Solomon's request? How do you define *wisdom*? Now read Psalm 111. Ask: How is wisdom defined here? What do those who have wisdom know and do? What is the obedience that God requires? (See 1 Kings 3:7.) What are the mutual aspects of the divine/human covenant? (See the commentary on page 281.) What was Solomon really asking for when he requested wisdom?

C. Explore Wise Living

Review Ephesians 5:15-20 and the commentary on pages 281–82. Ask: What does the writer mean when he urges Gentile Christians to live wisely? What are the two rules in 5:17-18? How is one to be filled with the Spirit (5:19)? How should we respond to what God has done for us (5:19-20)?

How does "wise living" relate to being "imitators of God" (5:1-2)? How does "wise living" in Ephesians compare to "wisdom" in Psalm 111? What does this mean for us?

D. Discuss Double Meanings

Read John 6:51-58, and review the commentary on pages 282–83. Ask: How are flesh and blood understood by the crowd? by John? How is the word *eat* used? (See 6:45, 63, 68. It means to eat sacramental food—bread and wine—and "hear and receive" the Word—Jesus, the bread who brings life.) What is the message of John to his Jewish Christian readers throughout this whole discourse? (Possibilities: Leave your Jewish heritage behind for Jesus, the true bread of life. "Eat" this bread by sharing in the sacrament of the Eucharist and by hearing and receiving the Word of God.)

E. Explore Communion

Form four groups. Give each one of the following: Matthew 26:26-30; Mark 14:22-25; Luke 22:14-20; 1 Corinthians 11:23-25. Ask each group to compare its passage with John 6:51-58 to discover how John's understanding of the Eucharist differs. Identify the several views of the Eucharist. (See the commentary on page 283.) Ask: How does John challenge us to think about an open table for the Lord's Supper, where all baptized persons are welcome?

F. Create Personal Posters

Today's lections focus on three major themes: wisdom, right living, and "eating" the bread of life. Provide paper, markers, and other art materials. Invite participants to create a visual image of these concepts, then to share and discuss their creations.

G. Close With Praise and Petition

Read together Psalm 111:1-3, 10. Sing "Bread of the World in Mercy Broken."

Lections for Sunday Between
August 21 and 27

Old Testament:
1 Kings 8:(1, 6, 10-11), 22-30, 41-43

*F*IRST Kings 8 describes Solomon's dedication of the newly built Temple. The ceremony was similar to that used by neighbors of ancient Israel when they brought an idol to reside in a newly constructed shrine. Verses 1-8 describe the lavish procession that brought the ark to the new Temple. In verses 10-11, the "cloud" represents the presence of YHWH and the "glory" a visible aura surrounding YHWH. Clearly, YHWH was believed to be present. But in what sense?

> *Think About It:* Two Hebrew verbs in verses 12-13 (*tabernacling*—temporarily dwelling—and *enthroning*—sitting, residing, being placed on a throne) are translated as "dwell." Was YHWH originally thought to be enthroned in the Temple like a pagan god in a shrine? Or was the ark a symbol of YHWH's mysterious, moving presence?

Old Promises

Solomon recalled YHWH's promise of rest and a central sanctuary after the conquest of the land (Deuteronomy 12:1-7). He rejoiced that peace was secured and the Temple built. However, by the time the final editing of this story occurred several hundred years later, both Israel and Judah had been invaded, their leaders exiled, and the Temple destroyed. The people had lost both rest and sanctuary. Addressing this calamity, the final editor emphasized that, while the Temple was a house for the name of YHWH (8:29), not even the "highest heaven"—much less the no-longer-existing Temple—could con-

286

tain YHWH (8:20, 27). God's "enthroning" presence meant God's "sovereign" presence.

In his prayer, Solomon also recalled God's promise of an everlasting Davidic dynasty. He praised God's faithfulness, declared God's promise to David fulfilled and appealed to God to keep that promise forever. This part of the story also bothered the final editor/narrator, since no independent king sat on Israel's throne in the sixth century. Had God reneged? No, but the narrator reminded his exiled audience that God's promise had an unmet condition: faithfulness.

Renewed Promise

In his prayer Solomon offered several petitions that all pled for God's presence. Our lection focuses on the one asking God to hear the foreigner—any non-Israelite. Again, the narrator seems to have shaped the old Temple ceremony story to his sixth-century audience, as can be seen in the petition involving images of captivity, divine presence, and repentance (8:46-53). Hope for the captive Israelites lay in their change of heart, which would then allow them to appeal for the forgiveness that was possible because of God's "enthroning" (sovereign) presence.

Think About It: The Temple dedication ceremony evokes images about the nature of God's presence. How do you describe God's presence in your life? When have you been a "foreigner" pleading for God's presence? When the sense of God's presence grows dim, could unfaithfulness be a factor?

Psalter: Psalm 84

In Psalm 84, a pilgrim rejoices to see the Temple, to be in God's presence, and to know that all may find a home with God. Those who are happy (wise) are those whose strength and trust are in God.

Although this psalm speaks of one person's joy, the psalms were not simply prayer-poems of pious individuals. Psalms were collected and used like a prayer book, at least in the postexilic period from 515 B.C. in the rebuilt Temple and synagogues. Psalms formed an instruction manual to reeducate the people about their covenant with God. Exile posed a crisis for a people who had lost its land, Temple, and monarchy. Thus, although our psalm rejoices in worship at the Temple, it also instructs that God's sovereign reign exists apart from Temple and land. Those who are "happy" trust only in God.

Epistle: Ephesians 6:10-20

Ephesians began with a cosmic picture of God's plan (1:3-23) that included all believers (2:1–3:13), and a prayer for wisdom (3:14-21). It then focused on rules for living wisely (4:1–5:21), including instructions for wives, husbands, children, slaves, and masters (5:22–6:9). Today, we examine a final appeal to all believers.

Girding for Battle

Believers are urged to put on God's armor and to stand battle-ready against enemies—not human foes but quasi-demonic powers or evil forces that dominated the world. They are seen as "the devil" (6:11), "rulers," "authorities," and "cosmic powers of this present darkness" (6:12), implying the organized forces of evil.

> **Think About It:** Ephesians called Christians to "put on the armor of God." How do you ready yourself as a Christian and for what?

The armor (6:14-17) believers are to put on includes: (1) Belt of truth: A soldier's belt holds tools for battle. Truth may be defined either in a static Greek sense as "correct knowledge" or in a dynamic Hebrew sense as "faithful, reliable." (2) Breastplate of righteousness: Righteousness, coupled with justification, implies a freedom to move forward among evil forces because one is saved by God's grace. (3) Shield of faith: A shield protected a soldier's body from flaming arrows. With a shield of faith (trust in, reliance on, and fidelity to God) a believer is protected against arrows (blasphemous words). (4) Helmet of salvation: A helmet provided a bubble of safe space. A helmet of salvation implies broadened safety for living, created by Christ's resurrection. (5) Shoes of the gospel of peace: Military shoes were hobnailed sandals or short boots for long marches. Believers are to be roving messengers of the gospel. (6) Sword of the Spirit: A sword was used in close combat. Believers are to use the gospel.

Praying in the Spirit

Verses 18-20 shift from a call to battle to an appeal to pray for the saints, including the writer who is an ambassador in chains (Paul?). This shift implies that though Paul may be gone, believers are to emulate him by continuing the battle against evil.

Meanings Today

For many, putting on God's armor to fight evil forces has deep meaning. For others the war imagery and way of defining evil are problematic. One way to keep unity in a bond of peace (4:3) may lie in restating Ephesians' message in other metaphors.

Gospel: John 6:56-69

Verses 56-58 conclude the bread of life discourse with this restatement: The bread of heaven is not like the manna eaten by the ancestors—they died; but those who eat bread from heaven receive eternal life.

More Complaints

The crowd had complained in response to Jesus' teachings. Now the "disciples" (the large group of Jesus' followers) grumbled about eating flesh and drinking blood, saying, "This teaching is difficult; who can accept it?" (6:60). Jesus challenged their resistance: If this teaching offends you, how will you respond to the ascent of the Son of Man? With that question, John had placed the offensive teaching of Jesus in the context of his whole life. John then left the matter open for readers to decide about the significance of that life—from Incarnation to Crucifixion to Resurrection.

A New Teaching

Because the followers had not understood the word *flesh*, Jesus offered a new teaching: "It is the spirit that gives life; the flesh is useless" (6:63). Yet he had just said, "eat my flesh." It seemed the followers, like the authorities, had heard "human flesh and blood" when Jesus had really meant "the Word become flesh" (John 1:14). Also, "flesh and blood" was a Hebrew formula implying mortality—as contrasted with the immortal Spirit of God.

The point was that flesh without Spirit dies; Spirit without flesh denies the Incarnation; but united they create life. John's whole Gospel proclaims that a divine Jesus became flesh, died, was resurrected, then returned to God.

In this teaching about spirit and flesh, John attempted to counteract a growing misperception within late first-century Christianity that the Communion elements somehow magically contained the key to eternal life. In verse 63, John claimed that flesh had power to save only when bound up with the life-giving, Spirit-filled words—and Word—of Jesus. Jesus' followers were not being asked to eat flesh and drink blood; they were being invited to receive God's offer of Spirit-filled bread that endures.

Always a Choice

Jesus knew not all his followers would accept his teachings. Indeed, some turned away (6:66), accenting one of the themes of Chapter 6: God offers life, but people have a choice. The followers' turning away reflects John's time when some Christians, subject to severe penalties from their synagogues, abandoned their faith.

> ***Think About It:*** John believed that a divine Word became flesh in Jesus, who was crucified, resurrected, and then ascended to God. Peter confessed, "You have the words of eternal life." What do you believe?

Jesus then asked the Twelve if they too would turn away. Simon Peter said he had "heard and learned" (6:45) that Jesus had "words of eternal life" (6:68). Then he confessed his faith: "You are the Holy One of God" (6:69). Peter and the others chose to remain faithful. Yet the next verse (6:70) notes that one would turn away. Again we see the tension between divine initiative and human choice.

Study Suggestions

A. Explore God's Presence

Review 1 Kings 8:1-43 and the commentary on pages 286–87. Ask: What were the two divine promises that Solomon saw fulfilled? What are the two Hebrew verbs that describe God's presence (verses 12-13)? How did the sixth-century editor/narrator of Kings solve the tension between these two notions of God's presence? Why was this important? What was the significance of Solomon asking God to listen to the foreigner? (His reign involved contact with foreign nations; he had foreign wives. This may be an effort to make God universal, not just for Israel.)

The lectionary skips from Solomon's receiving wisdom (last session) to his dedication of the Temple, leaving us with an image of a wise and humble king who fulfilled God's promise by building the Temple. Read 1 Kings 5 for a fuller picture of Solomon. How did his deal with Hiram cause suffering and injustice? (Food taxes and forced labor.) Did the end result justify the means? Does it ever?

B. Pray and Praise

Joyfully read together Psalm 84. Review the commentary on page 287 Ask: What is the ultimate message about those who are "happy"? (They trust only in God, not in temple or church. See verses 5, 7, 12.) How does this psalm's message relate to the Solomon story? (Both reflect an exile viewpoint after the Temple was destroyed.)

C. Explore Battle Imagery

Read Ephesians 6:10-20. Ask: Why are believers to put on God's armor? What are the six pieces of armor, and what do they represent? (See commentary on pages 287–88.) What shift occurs in this lection? What might this have meant to the readers? What was the writer calling his readers to do? What are Christians called to do today? What non-war and contemporary metaphors might be used to convey the main message of this passage?

Ask people to create with markers and paper a symbol or picture that does not use war imagery. Share when finished.

D. Explore a New Teaching

Read John 6:56-69, and review the commentary on pages 289–90. Ask: How does verse 58 conclude the bread of life discussion? What themes are tied together? (See John 6:31, 35, 49-51b.) What is Jesus' new teaching? (See verse 63.) How is *flesh* used in this verse? How do John's and Paul's uses of *flesh* differ? (Paul often used *flesh* to connote an urge to sin.)

Imagine you were with Jesus when he explained this comment on flesh and spirit. Would you have been confused or convinced? Why? Why did some followers turn away from Jesus? (They either heard Jesus wrongly, or they heard him rightly but did not believe him.) Why do people turn away from Jesus today? What does this bread of life discussion in John 6 teach us today about how we present the gospel? (Possibilities: Keep inviting people to engage in dialogue; use meaningful metaphors; repeat as often as necessary; keep restating in new and different ways.)

F. Close With a Hymn

Sing "Let Us Break Bread Together" or "One Bread, One Body."

Lections for Sunday Between August 28 and September 3

T Old Testament: Song of Solomon 2:8-13

ODAY we leave the external Old Testament world of tribal conflicts, royal intrigues, male heroes, prophetic calls for religious reform, and divine judgments. Instead, we enter an internal world of romantic relationship. The strong female voice in this biblical poem suggests, according to *The New Interpreter's Bible,* that the poet may have been a woman who was "assertive, uninhibited, and unabashed about her sexual desires." In contrast, Ruth's and Esther's voices in the Bible are mediated by male narrators, and their contributions are overshadowed by male heroism and male-identified dramas.

Dynamics of Human Love

Early in the poem, a black-skinned woman of an educated elite class longs for her shepherd lover's kisses. Their relationship is forbidden—perhaps because of race, economic class, or age differences. Seeing him, she flirts; he teases. She feigns modesty; he counters. She returns the compliment and fantasizes or reminisces about a rendezvous that leaves her faint with desire. Learning from her experience, she shares with the Jerusalem daughters (girlfriends? critics?) that one must not waken love until it is ready (1:1–2:7). Then in our verses she passionately describes her beloved and his invitation to join him in a daytime tryst (2:8-13). Though tempted, she urges a more cautious nighttime meeting. Expressing a new lover's possessiveness, she declares, "My beloved is mine and I am his" (2:16-17). Here is the halting, lurching, impetuous dance of new lovers.

Although the poem describes a woman's relationship with a man, all lovers, regardless of gender or orientation, will recognize themselves in the man's hesitancy to commit to a relationship as well as in the woman's desire and need to be loved. Anyone whose love for another has met with disapproval will appreciate the hasty and secretive encounters of these two lovers. Ultimately these songs are about the dynamics of human intimacy, love, and commitment.

An Interpretative Challenge

Traditionally, Song of Solomon has been interpreted as a spiritual allegory, either about the love between God and the people of Israel or about Christ and the church (or individual soul). Thus, a parallel is drawn between the relational and physical love between a man and a woman and the spiritual love between God and persons.

Increasingly, however, scholars interpret the Song as secular love poetry. It expresses the tensions of newfound love experienced in an atmosphere of disapproval. It describes mutual love where neither lover dominates the other nor submits to the other. It delights in female sexuality (in contrast to much of the Bible where women's sexuality is assumed to be chaotic, dangerous, and defiling to men).

Think About It: Song of Solomon has been interpreted as an allegory. How do you think of this book—as literally describing a human love affair or speaking symbolically of a spiritual relationship? How can we know when to take the Bible literally and when to look for symbolic meanings? If the Song is about human love, what does this say about the biblical view of sexuality as compared with attitudes often held in the church?

In short, if we read Song of Solomon as it stands, it calls us to reexamine our assumptions about human sexuality and intimacy, including our tendencies to disapprove of certain kinds of loving relationships because they are "different" than the average "approved" relationships.

Think About It: Contrary to much of the rest of the Bible, Song of Solomon celebrates human love and female sexuality. What personal meanings do you find in this poetry?

Psalter: Psalm 45

Psalm 45 is the only psalm of praise addressed to a human being rather than to God. It is probably a wedding song for an unknown Israelite or Judahite king marrying a non-Jewish princess. The psalmist praises the king's handsomeness, his speaking ability, and his military strength (45:2, 6) but notes that all this power and majesty is not for the king's personal benefit. It is for God, whose "throne . . . endures forever and ever" (45:6).

The king is to ride forth on behalf of God's purposes—truth, humility, and righteousness—using his scepter (a symbol of his power and authority) to promote equity and justice. He is to join God as an advocate for the oppressed (45:7).

After describing the king's wedding garments and the elegant setting of the wedding, the psalmist addresses the princess, commanding her to forget her people and submit to her king/husband (verses 10-14). This portrayal reflects the patriarchal understanding of women in the ancient Near East. Her only benefit seems to be that the king will desire her for her beauty. In verse 16, the psalmist again speaks to the king, predicting many sons. The "I" in verse 17 can be read either as the psalmist or as God who will cause the king's name to be celebrated.

Epistle: James 1:17-27

Although classified as a letter because of its salutation (1:1), James otherwise lacks the characteristics of an epistle. It is a collection of essays probably preserved in Palestinian Christianity under the name of James, the brother of Jesus. The author teaches that faith reaches perfection through testing, endurance, and faithful works.

A Proper Perception

Chapter 1, preceding the first essay, provides five of James's basic assumptions. First, we live under a God who exalts the lowly and resists the wealthy and proud (1:9-12). Second, God does not test anyone; persons are tested (tempted) by their own inner desires (1:13-16). Third, God is a constant and generous giver of good gifts, not the tester of people (1:17-18). Fourth, life demands choices. One chooses either the way of the world or the way of faith. Fifth, the way of faith leads to good gifts from God, but one must ask in faith (see 1:5-6). These assumptions, according to James, provide believers with the proper perception needed to profess one's faith and act it out.

A First Response

James calls persons to respond to the word of truth by walking the way of faith. Believers' first response should be listening (be "slow to speak," verse 19) because the word of truth can only save if it is truly received. Believers are to put aside arrogance, desire, rage, and so forth and put on meekness and a listening ear so they can truly hear and be reshaped by God's word of truth.

A Second Response

James then teaches that endurance can produce a "perfect" or real faith, but only if one understands that real faith requires action (verses 22-25). What counts is not learning and speaking the word of truth, but doing it.

Believers are to translate their faith into deeds, such as honest speech or caring for the dispossessed. They are to act out "the perfect law, the law of liberty," which is to "love your neighbor as yourself." The faithful who act will be blessed in their doing.

Gospel: Mark 7:1-8, 14-15, 21-23

Early Jewish Christians probably had to defend their nonobservance of Jewish laws and customs. Thus, Mark's story of a confrontation between Jesus and his opponents over a Jewish purification rule would have interested them greatly.

The Tradition of the Elders

In Mark 7:1-5, Jesus' opponents (Pharisees from Galilee and scribes from Jerusalem) questioned Jesus about why he and his disciples were not living according to the "tradition of the elders." Trying to embarrass him and undermine his authority with the crowd he had been teaching, they questioned Jesus about eating with ritually unclean or unpurified hands, something teachers following the tradition of the elders would never do.

The "tradition of the elders" was an oral interpretation of Israel's ancestral customs. The pious sect of Pharisees considered this "tradition" legally binding on all Jews, even though not all followed it. Mark's rather stereotypical explanation of the purification ritual demonstrate he is not sympathetic to Pharisaic traditions.

Jesus' New Teaching

Jesus first responded to his opponents by quoting from the Prophets and the Law, sources more authoritative than the tradition of the elders. He said his adversaries were people who honored God with their lips (rituals) but not with their hearts. They taught human laws as divine doctrine (Isaiah 29:13). They had abandoned the "commandment of God and [were holding] to human tradition" (Mark 7:8).

Finally, Jesus responded directly to their question about the purification regulation. However, he addressed the crowd, not his opponents, thus resuming his position as an authoritative teacher. He told the crowd that nothing that went into a person could defile (7:14-15). Rather it was the things coming out that defile. Then Jesus privately instructed his disciples, who had not understood this new teaching any more than the crowd did. After further explaining that what went inside a person (food) could not defile (verse 19), Jesus said that defilement or impurity was what came out of people's hearts—namely, evil intentions. He identified these as "fornication, theft, murder, adultery, avarice, wickedness, deceit, licentiousness, envy, slander, pride, folly" (verses 21-22). Jesus called for inner, not outer purity. Since his list included items prohibited by the commandments, Jesus had upheld the law of God that he had just accused his opponents of undermining.

Present-Day Implications

Jesus' new teaching about inner purity calls us to reexamine our tendency to engage in long-held traditions and rituals rather than in the transformation of our hearts. It also challenges our tendency to hold on to human traditions as if they were divinely commanded. Finally, it calls us to reexamine the exclusive stance of our faith communities. This last challenge may be the hardest call of all, if our faith is predicated on an "us-versus-them" understanding.

Just as traditions and purity regulations helped preserve ancient Israel's religious and ethnic identity and faith in a hostile world, so traditions and purity rules help preserve traditional biblical Christian identity and faith today in the midst of a very diverse culture. We, like the crowds following Jesus or like Mark's first readers, are confronted by Jesus. Do we hang on to traditions and rituals and remain exclusive in our thinking in order to protect our traditional faith and identity? Or do we let God open our hearts—even if such action subjects our faith and identify to change?

Think About It: Jesus challenged our tendency to engage in easy rituals rather than in the hard work of opening our hearts. What transformation of the heart might you need to engage in right now?

Study Suggestions

A. Listen to a Love Song

Ask two people give a dramatic reading of Song of Solomon 1:5-7; 2:1-10a, 16-17 (one voice) and 1:8 and 2:10b-13 (second voice). Invite participants to imagine being in an open-air arena 2,500 years ago listening to a public performance of Song of Solomon.

Ask: What dynamics of new love did you hear? How has this poem traditionally been interpreted? (Review and discuss the commentary on pages 292–93.) If we read the poem as a Jewish or Christian allegory of a spiritual relationship between God and persons, what is it saying? If we read it as human love poetry, what assumptions about human love relationships does it challenge? Discuss the questions in the first "Think About It" box.

B. Explore a Wedding Psalm

Read Psalm 45 in unison. According to the psalmist, how should a public leader behave? Can we apply these criteria to leaders in our government (which is not a theocracy like Israel but a secular democracy)? If we do, what standards for their behavior and leadership do they suggest? What does the psalmist admire about the king? about the princess? How is the psalmist's view of women different from the image of women in Song of Solomon? (Review the commentary on pages 292–94 on both passages.) Ask: Does our society always value women's character or ability? Does it ever value their beauty or appearance over their character and ability? What does the church seem to value most about women? How does the Christian emphasis on the worth of all persons as children of God challenge these views?

C. Examine Inner Purity

Read Mark 7:1-8, 14-15, 21-23 and review the interpretive material on pages 295–96. Ask: What was the "tradition of the elders"? What particular part of the tradition did Jesus and the disciples violate? How did Jesus respond to his opponents' question about that violation of the tradition? What did Jesus teach the crowd about purity? What further teaching did he give his disciples? How did Jesus' teaching about inner purity challenge people in his and Mark's times? How does Jesus' teaching challenge us today as individuals, as a local church, and as a denomination?

D. Analyze Perceptions

Read James 1:17-27, and review the commentary on pages 294–95. Ask: What basic assumptions does James make about God? life? faith? Do you agree with the five assumptions that make up James's "proper perception"? If not, what different assumptions do you make? Does James's either/or perception seem too simplistic or arbitrary to you? How would you qualify it? What should believers' first and second responses be after they have properly perceived God's gift of the word of truth?

E. Make Connections

How is James's perception of the "way of the world" similar to Jesus' view of "evil intentions"? If you were to take these teachings to heart, what might you hear God calling you to do or to be differently? (Consider possible changes in attitude, behavior, relationships, commitments.)

F. Close in Prayer and Song

Invite group members to request specific prayers. Then join together to pray for those concerns and for those who rejoice or who struggle in their loving relationships, those who search for the ways to respond to the gifts of their faith, and those who seek to live out of true devotion and piety. Close by singing "Sweet Hour of Prayer," which reflects the spiritual intimacy of Song of Solomon, interpreted allegorically.

Lections for Sunday Between September 4 and 10

Old Testament:
Proverbs 22:1-2, 8-9, 22-23

*P*ROVERBS is an anthology of Israel's traditional wisdom. Some proverbs date back to Solomon's reign during the tenth century B.C. or earlier, others to a later era. However, the collection was ultimately edited after 538 B.C. to meet the needs of postexilic Judah.

Proverbs has two sections: Chapters 1–9 (lengthy wisdom poems) and Chapters 10–30 (short pithy sayings). Our verses come from the second section. The one-line sayings may reflect Israelite peasant traditions similar to African folk traditions. The more literary and more sophisticated two-line parallels were probably written by the scribes, an intellectually elite social class that was the keeper of Israel's wisdom literature.

Think About It: The fear of God is foundational to life. How do you understand the fear of God? How do you relate this to love for God? Is your religious and moral behavior motivated more by fear (awe, reverence) of God or by love (gratitude, affection) for God?

Wisdom writers believed that fear of God was foundational to life. (See Proverbs 14:27.) *Fear* meant awe, reverence, obedience, and proper relationship. Without such fear of God, people walked the way of death. Wisdom or death were people's choices. Wisdom writers believed actions invariably produced certain consequences (life or death), so the wise person should always consider the consequences before acting.

Wise and Foolish Ways

This lection focuses specifically on wise and foolish ways of regarding wealth and power. Verse 1 is a two-line parallel that advises choosing a good name (to be respected and esteemed) over having wealth. Verse 2 observes that the status of wealth is limited; wisdom and righteousness—and God—are placed above it. Verse 8 warns of the potential for leaders to abuse the power that comes with their position. If they sow injustice, they will reap calamity, and their unjust rule ("rod of anger") will fail.

In contrast, verse 9 affirms that those who are generous (just) will be blessed. Verses 22-23 advise the wise not to exploit the poor just because they are poor and not to crush the afflicted at the city gate (where public business and legal matters were transacted) because God defends the poor, pleads their cause, and fights their fight. Verse 23b implies that God will do to wealthy wrongdoers what they have done to the poor—and more.

Choosing One's Way

The Book of Proverbs was intended to persuade persons to engage in certain behaviors and attitudes, either to maintain the existing social order or to refine and restore it. Ancient Israelites were urged to maintain the existing economic order so that each person had a share of the land and the wealth it produced (see 22:28). Today these proverbs on wealth remind us that when some of us (persons or nations) accumulate excessive goods or use more than our fair share of natural resources, we deprive others of what is due them and what they need for their livelihood. These verses remind us that all wealth gained by wrongdoing, injustice, or excessive accumulation stands condemned by God.

Think About It: Proverbs advises the wise to seek a good name, not wealth, and to be generous (just) with those who have less. How do you follow this advice in a culture bent on accumulating wealth and goods and in a world in which the gap between rich and poor is growing rapidly? What guidelines do you follow for the responsible gaining, spending, saving, and giving of material resources?

Psalter: Psalm 125

Psalm 125 reminds pilgrims and other believers that their stability derives from trusting God who will always surround and protect them. It assures them that God's peace will win out over any foreign power that oppresses them. The "allotted land" was land they believed was promised by God in Moses' time, even though it was then already inhabited by Canaanites. This transfer of land is a troublesome event in the Old Testament for it seems to show that God is not concerned with the indigenous people.

More positively, this psalm reminded pilgrims that God's peace is always experienced amid worldly opposition. Though the wicked seem to rule, those who trust in God will proclaim God's rule and will try to embody God's peace in the face of all such hostility. We too experience (and participate in) the dynamics of hostile and cruel worldly power. In order to embody God's peace, we must diligently identify all such human cruelty, name it for what it is, and oppose it. Claiming that "God is on our side" and pleading with God to help "us" while removing "them" are two kinds of pious hostility that are so ingrained in the psalmist's mentality as to be very hard to counteract. The gospel requires a different standard!

Epistle: James 2:1-10, (11-13), 14-17

Even though Jesus is mentioned only twice in James (1:1 and 2:1), the Letter of James is unmistakably Christian in its moral instruction. Unlike other ancient wisdom literature, James is concerned with broad moral principles in the community of faith rather than with specific social manners, household relationships, or sexual behaviors. Two of these broad principles (impartiality and living faith) are found in Chapter 2.

Show No Partiality

First, James urges inclusivity. He addresses the people's worldly tendencies to play favorites by according special honor and favors to the wealthy and powerful (2:1-13) and argues that discrimination is incompatible with faith in Christ. He specifically notes that the wealthy oppress the poor, drag them into court, and dishonor them; but God chooses the poor. Therefore, instead of discriminating against the poor like the world does, believers are urged to obey God's royal law: love your neighbor as yourself (Leviticus 19:18).

Think About It: James urges believers not to engage in acts of partiality. How are you tempted to play favorites and discriminate against a person or group? On what basis do you justify your acts of discrimination?

Although he specifically mentions "the poor," James really speaks to all forms of discrimination, strongly forbidding favoritism within the Christian community. Practicing partiality is so serious that those who practice it stand under "judgment . . . without mercy," no matter how meticulously law-abiding they may otherwise be (2:10, 13).

Choose Living Faith

Second, by highlighting the inadequacy of faith without deeds (2:14-26), James urges faithful living. Merely having correct beliefs is dead faith. Believers cannot just tell needy persons that God will provide for them and be done with it; faith alone cannot save. True faith is living faith; it results in acts of mercy (2:19, 26).

Traditionally, scholars have argued that James's emphasis on works is a response to persons who misconstrued Paul's emphasis on justification by faith (see Romans 3:19-24; Galatians 2:15-16). James emphasizes works of charity that emerge out of faith. In contrast, Paul objected to works of obedience to the Jewish law as a means to gain faith. Paul would have agreed with James that true Christian faith results in ethical behavior (see Galatians 5:16-26 and Romans 12).

Gospel: Mark 7:24-37

The Syrophoenician woman in our story is a Gentile from the region of Tyre in Phoenicia (today's Lebanon), which in Jesus' day was part of the Roman province of Syria. According to Matthew 15:22, she was a Canaanite, a descendant of those who had inhabited the land at the time of the Israelite invasion. She was a non-Jewish outsider.

Insiders, Outsiders

This outsider woman sought out Jesus and begged him to heal her daughter who had an unclean spirit (mental illness?). Jesus responded in a way that sounds harsh: "Let the children be fed first, for it is not fair to take the children's food and throw it to the dogs" (7:27). The story appears in the text to explain why the church welcomed Gentiles. This story demonstrates that participation in the kingdom of God is based on faith. The faith of the woman is contrasted with the unbelief Jesus found in many co-religionists. The story reflects the pattern of Paul who first preached to the Jews and then to Gentiles when rejected by Jews.

To fully understand the barrier between Jews and Gentiles, we must look not only at Israel's strained history of coexisting in Gentile land but also at the socioeconomic fact that Jewish peasant farmers in Upper Galilee produced food for Gentile coastal cities such as Tyre. In periods of famine or crisis, Jewish farmers probably resented that food they produced was going to those wealthy Gentiles instead of to their own children. Galilee itself was a largely Gentile region with the Jewish population in the minority. Thus, hostility and prejudice existed on both sides.

These barriers made it very hard for the Gentile woman to approach a Jewish teacher for help. But she answered Jesus boldly and pointedly: "Sir, even the dogs under the table eat the children's crumbs." In Mark, Jesus replied that because of her excellent argument, the demon had left her child. Matthew, in contrast, has Jesus say that the woman's faith has healed her daughter. The real miracle, however, may go beyond the healing. By the time Mark told this story, the "dogs under the table" were part of the Christian family, and he was challenging Jewish Christians to reexamine how they treated Gentiles.

Mark summons us too to reexamine how we treat outsiders. Do we welcome persons of a different racial or ethnic background into the household of God? Are we able to recognize faith and accept any believer despite differences represented by ethnicity, religion, education, or status?

A Deaf Man's Confession

In Mark 7:31, Jesus left Tyre for the Sea of Galilee by way of Sidon. One look at a map reveals that this route was a circuitous one that started for a destination by going in the opposite direction. It is unclear, then, whether the deaf man in this story was Jewish or Gentile.

The format in this miracle story is similar to others: Friends brought the deaf man to Jesus who healed him privately; then Jesus instructed the man and his friends to tell no one. Yet to demonstrate that he was healed, the deaf man had to speak. He confessed: "He has done everything well!" Mark probably told this story to provide his readers with an initial way to understand Jesus. However, later stories reveal that Jesus is more than a miracle worker; healings are among signs of the arrival of the messianic age. Mark would finally reveal that Jesus was the Messiah.

Think About It: How does our normal way of life lead to automatic exclusion of others? Most persons join a church because of family or friends. How many friends do you have who are different ethnically, educationally, or economically?

Study Suggestions

A. Make Two Lists

Compile two lists of factors or perceptions that lead people to practice partiality: Favoritism Factors (example: deferring to or preferring persons with money) and Marginalizing Factors (example: looking down on welfare recipients). Why do we favor some and marginalize others?

B. Identify Two Ways of Living

Read Proverbs 22:1-2, 8-9, 22-23 and the commentary. What are wise and foolish ways in regard to wealth? power? personal conduct? Who are the persons to be admired here? Even though these proverbs were written for people who lived twenty-five hundred to three thousand years ago in a very different culture, what wisdom might they offer us in the twenty-first century?

C. Explore Reality and Hope

Read Psalm 125 and the commentary on pages 299–300. In whom do pilgrims trust? What is their reality? (Oppression by foreign powers.) In what do they hope? How do we acknowledge the reality of evil in the world but not demonize people who oppress us?

302

Biblical commentators say this psalm suggests that God's people always live amid circumstances where the wicked seem to be in control. Is this true? If so, how are the faithful supposed to respond? (Trust God; proclaim God's rule; embody peace.) How can we embody God's peace?

D. Examine a Faith Change

Read Mark 7:24-30, and review "Insiders, Outsiders" on pages 301–302. Who are the insiders in this story? Why are they favored? Who are the outsiders? Why are they outsiders? What can we learn from the outsider woman? (Possibilities: "acting" as an equal in an unequal situation, speaking the truth boldly.) What can we learn from Jesus' responses to the outsider woman? (Possibilities: how to recognize faith in others, how to change a key component of one's faith.) What major new insight was Mark trying to convey to his readers? (God welcomes everyone to the table of Christian fellowship.) How does this story call you to examine your acceptance of others?

E. Analyze Two Moral Values

Read James 2:1-10, (11-13), 14-17, and review the interpretation on pages 300–301. To whom is James speaking? (See 2:1.) Who is a believer's neighbor? (See 2:2, 8. The context is the Christian assembly (in Greek the word is *synagogue*), implying that a neighbor is anyone who enters Christian space, not just those who are attractive or wealthy. What are the two broad moral principles James discusses here? (Inclusivity and living faith.) What does James strongly forbid? (Acts of partiality in the Christian community.) What, for James, is living faith? (See 2:14-17.) How do Paul and James complement each other?

F. Put It Together

Discuss: All four lections explore two ways of living and being in the world. What words or images does each lection use? List them in two columns: foolish/wise (Proverbs); hostility/peace (Psalms); dogs/children (Mark); favoritism/inclusivity (James). Even the healing of the deaf man in Mark implies two meanings: Jesus as miracle worker/Jesus as Messiah. What key message do you take from today's passages?

G. In Closing

Read stanzas 1 and 2 of the hymn "Jesu, Jesu." Create a new stanza patterned after stanza 2, but name others who may be ignored or unacceptable in our congregations. (Possibilities: those on the far right and left of the religious spectrum, homeless, sick, Arab, Jew.) Sing the hymn as a closing prayer, placing your new stanza between stanzas 3 and 4.

Lections for Sunday Between September 11 and 17

Old Testament: Proverbs 1:20-33

CHAPTERS 1–9 are wisdom poems used to instruct young men entering adulthood. The poems present fundamental values metaphorically as Woman Wisdom and Woman Stranger, two images certain to catch young men's attention. Yet ultimately the poems invite everyone to choose wisdom (to fear God and pursue righteousness, justice, wisdom, and discipline).

Woman Wisdom

In the Bible, divine speech usually is reserved for God or an authorized male intermediary; but in Proverbs, God's wisdom is personified as a woman who speaks with divine authority. Some scholars view this woman figure as a remnant of ancient goddess worship. Others see her as an extension of the attributes of God that subsequently took on independent life. In other words, God has feminine as well as masculine qualities. Still others believe she represents real Israelite women, just as Woman Stranger represents real male fears of female temptation. Some simply label the woman "a prophet" or "the embodiment of the sages' teachings." The point is that Woman Wisdom (God) has such great power that to disregard her teaching is to court folly and death.

> **Think About It:** God's wisdom is personified as a woman who speaks with divine authority. Does it enhance your spiritual life to think of relating to God with male (Father) or female (Wisdom) attributes? What do you think wisdom represents in Proverbs?

Woman Stranger

In Chapters 1–9, young men are instructed to avoid Woman Stranger. Sometimes erroneously translated as "loose woman" or "adulteress," the

304

Hebrew word literally means "strange, foreign, or alien." Woman Stranger symbolizes folly—anything off-limits or out-of-bounds in Israel's life. She could be a foreign religion or a neighbor's wife. In relational terms, the counterpart to the strange or foreign woman in ancient Israel was the strange or foreign man. (see Deuteronomy 25:5).

Wisdom's Warning

In our verses, Woman Wisdom seeks young men where they live and asks: How long will you stay simple, scoffing, and foolish? *Simple* means "untutored but capable of learning." Wisdom warns the young men that because they did not respond when she called them, she will laugh at them and mock them. Because they hated knowledge and did not fear God, she will not answer their calls.

They choose Woman Stranger, and their choices have inevitable consequences. Woman Wisdom ends her first speech with a proverb: "Those who listen to [wisdom] will be secure / and will live at ease, without dread of disaster" (Proverbs 1:33).

Following Wisdom Today

It sounds simple enough: Follow Wisdom and avoid things that are outside God's boundaries. However, in an effort to ensure life and prevent evil, societies legalize many things and make many others off-limits. We then sometimes call these human laws and taboos "divine." We confuse God's boundaries with society's limits. Thus, we must diligently search for what is truly outside God's boundaries; only they can be labeled "Woman Stranger." Then those things that are truly divinely ordained can be labeled "Woman Wisdom."

> ***Think About It:*** We sometimes call human laws and taboos "divine." Conversely, society may approve conduct God condemns. How do we find the way of life? What guidelines exist?

Psalter: Psalm 19

This psalm proclaims that God's creation wordlessly instructs humanity about God's way (verses 1-6) and that God also offers a personal word of instruction (verses 7-10). God's personal word (Torah) is all-encompassing; it provides wisdom, joy, enlightenment, and righteousness. However, even God's creation and instruction cannot ensure that human behavior will always be in harmony with God (verses 11-14). People make mistakes and have hidden faults. Thus, the psalmist prays for forgiveness in order to be "blameless" (meaning, "dependent on God").

"Redeemer" refers to the ancient familial responsibility of the next-of-kin to "buy back" relatives who had fallen into slavery. Thus the psalmist claims that the God who created the sun and gave humanity Torah is our "next-of-kin." Both humanity and all creation are part of God's family. Such a claim has implications for how we treat the universe. It also challenges our modern secular culture's creed of autonomy based on our ability to earn, achieve, and acquire possessions.

Epistle: James 3:1-12

James warns teachers about misusing speech, a warning that can also be applied to those who shape the theological language of faith. He notes that all make mistakes; for if we were perfect, we could control our tongues like we rein a horse, guide a ship, or tame a wild animal (3:2-4).

James draws these three images from ancient wisdom literature but is more pessimistic than that literature was. He believes the tongue is a fire that cannot be tamed; it is poisonous; it causes evil (3:5-6). By referring to hell, he invokes an image of the forces of evil that oppose the good. Humans are free to choose good or evil. We can use our tongues to both bless and curse, but the righteous bless and do not curse.

A Perilous Power

> **Think About It:** James claims that the tongue can either serve God's way or the world's way. In what ways do you struggle to be truthful and helpful?

The Bible says the world was created by divine speech and that God's first gift to humans was the power to name, to create language and meaning (Genesis 2:20). This is a perilous power! And the real danger lies, not in our occasional angry words, incidental curses, or petty bits of slander, but in our tendency to create distorted worlds of meaning that suppress truth and destroy life.

We suppress truth in the seductive language of advertising with its illusions of power and status based on desire, avarice, and envy. We distort meanings in the slippery half-truths of politics cleverly crafted to sell a candidate or to destroy an opponent. We distort truth when we use the language of patriarchy that denies women's experiences, perceptions, and identities. We distort truth when we glorify the language of science and social science that reduces everything to categories and statistics.

> **Think About It:** We deaden the language of faith by isolating it from God's current revelations. What issues of religious language most concern you?

We distort truth if we offer rigid doctrine and biblical interpretations that isolate God's word from current revelations. As believers (and especially as religious teachers, preachers,

306

and theologians), we are called to pay attention to and nurture the language of faith. We are called to keep it open, fresh, and inviting in order to welcome all God's people into relationship with God.

Gospel: Mark 8:27-38

In the first half of Mark's Gospel, Jesus' actions evoke questions and comments about his identity. Mark builds suspense, with demons shouting out the truth about Jesus (1:23-26), while human beings incorrectly name him (6:2-3,14-16). Jesus' disciples seem especially dense (4:41; 6:51b-52; 8:14-21). Now, in Chapter 8, Mark narrates a dialogue between Jesus and his disciples: "Who do people say that I am?" "[They say you are] John the Baptist; others, Elijah; still others one of the prophets." "But who do you say I am?" "You are the Messiah" (Mark 8:27-29).

Who Is This Messiah?

The Hebrew word *mashiah* (messiah) is the same as the Greek word *christos* (Christ). Both literally mean "anointed one." In Jesus' time, various persons (kings, prophets, priests) were called "messiah," which indicated that they were anointed by God to accomplish a task for God's people.

After the Exile, the Jews (who had been promised that David's dynasty would rule forever) looked for a messiah who would be their future king. Thus, Peter may have used the title "Messiah" to describe Jesus as an anointed agent of God without meaning to imply that Jesus alone offered God's saving power. The distinctive Christian claim that Jesus was God's ultimate saving power may have come only after the first Easter.

After Peter's confession that Jesus was the Messiah, Jesus immediately began to teach the disciples that the Son of Man would experience great suffering, be rejected by those in power, be killed, and rise again (8:31). Peter's view of messiah did not include suffering! He treated Jesus' prediction as the words of a possessed person who needed exorcising (8:32). Jesus swiftly responded that Peter was focused "not on divine things but on human things" (8:33). He was neither a powerful healer and miracle worker nor God's agent come to rule as Israel's earthly Davidic king; instead he redefined *messiah* as the suffering Son of Man.

How Do We Follow Him?

Finally, Jesus taught the crowd as well as his disciples what it meant to be his followers. They must deny themselves, take up their cross, and lose their lives for the gospel's sake (8:34-38).

This call to suffering must be understood in light of a common apocalyptic belief of early Christians that because those in authority had murdered

307

Jesus, God would soon destroy the present human world and install a new order. Mark was not telling his readers to endure suffering for years; rather, he and other early Christians were convinced that the period for such suffering would be short. In that brief time, persons who followed Jesus were to deny themselves and take up their cross. They were to risk everything (security, possessions, status, power) in return for release from illness and demons in the present and for hope of eternal life in the near future.

The Challenge

This passage is the heart of Mark's Gospel and a watershed event. From here on, Jesus headed toward Jerusalem and the cross. On the way, he spent much time teaching his disciples about what kind of messiah he really was. For Mark's readers (and for every subsequent generation), the challenge is twofold: First, we must determine what we mean (among conflicting claims) when we say Jesus is Messiah. Second, we must determine what it means to be his disciple.

Think About It: Mark's Jesus calls people to take up their "cross" of suffering and to follow him. How is suffering different from unavoidable pain and discomfort? What suffering would you choose to endure for Jesus' sake?

Study Suggestions

A. Examine Wisdom's Warning

Read Proverbs 1:20-33, and review the commentary on pages 304–305. Ask: What are the two female metaphors? How do some Bibles translate "the strange or foreign"? What is Wisdom's warning? What happens when one chooses Woman Stranger instead of Woman Wisdom? (Folly/death instead of wisdom/life; losing direction, violating boundaries.) Discuss the "Think About It" questions.

B. Sketch Human Boundaries

List on a large sheet of paper possible human boundaries that we mislabel as divine. (Possibilities: promoting white privilege, interracial marriage, sacred right of property, deciding that God supports some causes because we label them "Christian.") Why do we sometimes confuse societal boundaries with God's limits? What steps might we take individually and as a church to avoid confusing these two kinds of boundaries?

C. Identify God's Instruction

Read Psalm 19 and the interpretation on pages 305–306. What two ways does God instruct humanity? Even though God instructs us, what happens? For what does the psalmist pray? What does "the insolent" in verse 13 mean? (This term implies the psalmist is pleading for protection from others who are presumptuous, impertinent, or controlling. It may also be translated as "proud thoughts," suggesting he is seeking protection from his own insolence.)

Explore what "redeemer" meant in ancient Israel. What do we believe is a third way that God instructs humanity? (Through Jesus' life, death, and resurrection.) What can we learn from this psalm about how we treat the environment? about our emphasis on self-reliance and personal autonomy?

D. Analyze Distorted Speech

Read James 3:1-12, and review the commentary on these verses on pages 306–308. What does James say about the tongue (speech)? How is the tongue "double-edged"? How does this relate to James's warning against being "double-minded"? (See 1:8, 26.) How do we misuse speech? (Possibilities: angry words, slander, libel, arrogant speech, flattery, dominant or controlling speech.) Why does James single out teachers and warn them specifically?

E. Identify Messiahs

Read Mark 8:27-38 and the comments on pages 307–308. Who did the crowds say Jesus was? Who did the disciples say he was? What meanings did "messiah" carry in Jesus' day? After Peter called Jesus "Messiah," how did Jesus define it? (As the suffering Son of Man.) What does it mean to call Jesus "Son of Man"?

F. Explore God's Way

What do our lections say about following God's way? (Seeking wisdom, having faith, telling the truth, following Christ, confessing our humanity, depending on God, controlling our speech, following Woman Wisdom and a suffering messiah.)

G. In Closing

Sing "Must Jesus Bear the Cross Alone"; then offer a general prayer that we will follow God's way of wisdom, faith, and truth.

Lections for Sunday Between September 18 and 24

T Old Testament: Proverbs 31:10-31

THIS is an ancient wisdom poem directed toward young Israelite men about the woman who is a capable, good, or perfect wife. However, the Hebrew literally means "a woman of worth." In ancient Israel "worth" was usually applied to capable men at the height of their power. This passage refers to the female counterpart, so "woman of worth" would have immediately caught the attention of young men hearing the poem. They are urged to seek a wise and worthy woman, the living embodiment of Woman Wisdom who has been recommended to them in previous poems. The prosperous family images here would remind them that choosing a woman of worth leads to Wisdom's gifts: wealth, honor, acclaim, preserving family assets, and long life.

> **Think About It:** Wisdom's gifts are wealth, honor, acclaim, and long life. What is the relative influence of our culture and our faith on the gifts and goals we most value?

Woman as Provider

The worthy woman in the poem is the capable wife who fulfills all the roles needed to support and empower the lives of the men and others in her household. She works diligently at spinning, weaving, sewing, and growing food to keep her household going. She purchases raw materials and food and sells linen garments. However, she also is compassionate and generous to the poor; she speaks wisely; she teaches. She purchases a field, an economic enterprise usually reserved for men.

It was not unusual for women of extremely high (or low) status in ancient Israel to enjoy more public freedom than the average woman. Still, the ultimate worth of her work is that it contributes to her husband's good name, gaining him respect in public places of power and influence.

The worthy woman does benefit from her male-identified arrangement. Her sons and husband praise her. She is judged by her fear of God rather than by common ancient standards of sex appeal and external beauty. She receives a share of the profits from her work (although the command to her husband to share suggests that she might not profit automatically from her work, without her husband's agreement).

Finally, she is praised in the same city gates (the place of business and legal proceedings) where the men gather and where Woman Wisdom issues her call (see 1:21). The husband's language extolling his wife (31:29) and the praise at the city gates (31:31) both use idioms that parallel the praise accorded to YHWH, which suggests the high status and recognition due a worthy woman.

An Adequate Image?

This unusual portrait of a woman of worth provides a needed corrective to common portrayals of women as "loose," "seductive," and "dangerous" beings who lead men astray, sap their strength, disrupt their lives, and ruin their fortunes (see 2:16; 7:10-20; 31:3). Today, we may ask: What are the qualities that give a woman her sense of worth? Do the values expressed in this passage represent what Jesus valued in women?

> ***Think About It:*** Proverbs instructs a young man to seek a worthy woman and, by implication, instructs young women to structure their lives around the needs of men. Do you personally find value in this old wisdom poem? If so, what? If not, why not? How would you describe a worthy woman today? How do the teachings of Jesus and his attitudes and relationships with women influence our view of the worth of persons of whatever gender?

Psalter: Psalm 1

Verse 1 begins with a beatitude announcing that the psalms will offer persons a choice between God's way and the way of the wicked (those who arrogantly resist God's instruction). God's way brings blessings; the wicked way brings downfall. The psalm speaks not of two classes of people but rather of two ways of living. And no one should feel self-righteous because anyone can leave God's way at any moment. We must intentionally walk God's way and delight in God's instruction.

The Hebrew word *torah* in verse 2 does not mean "law" in the rigid sense of a closed code; rather, the psalmist is recommending a devotion toward the whole sacred tradition of God's revelation. Those who are open to God's ongoing revelation are like deeply rooted trees planted by water. Those who are not open to God's ongoing revelation are like unstable chaff in the wind; they will not "stand" (1:5).

Some scholars believe this means the wicked will be punished during God's final judgment; however, most say it means they will lack influence in human interactions. Verse 6 summarizes the psalmist's thought: God watches over the righteous because they are God-centered and rooted to the source of life. But the wicked will die because they refuse God's influence, becoming self-centered, self-instructed, unrooted, and unstable.

Epistle: James 3:13–4:3, 7-8a

Our verses are part of the fourth essay in James, which offers a call to conversion in two parts: indictment (3:13–4:6) and response (4:7-10).

The Indictment

James begins with a rhetorical question meant to remind his readers that everyone continually has to choose whether to live by the wisdom of the world or the wisdom of God. The world's wisdom is earthly, unspiritual, and devilish (3:14-15). It shows itself as bitter envy, expressed as selfish ambition, boastfulness, and lying. Envy equates "having" with "being" (3:16-18), resulting in disorder. In contrast, God's wisdom is pure and peaceable, showing itself as gentleness and a willingness to yield. It is full of mercy and good fruits (3:17-18).

James concludes that these two ways of life are absolutely incompatible. One cannot be a "friend of the world" (living by envy) and at the same time "a friend of God" (living with humility). He summarizes his indictment with more rhetorical questions: Does Scripture speak in vain? Is our spirit meant for envy (4:1)?

He answers the question by quoting a proverb: "God opposes the proud, / but gives grace to the humble" (4:6; see Proverbs 3:34). Pride is the flip side of grace. Arrogance prompts the "haves" to boast about what they have taken from others; envy pushes the "have-nots" into competition and violence against people who have what they want.

> **Think About It**: James calls envy and arrogance actions of the world, while humility expresses God's way. How do you cultivate humility?

The Call

In his call to conversion, James speaks, not to the person who lives entirely by the wisdom of the world, but rather to the "double-minded" Christian who tries to live by both kinds of wisdom at once. James calls them to convert, to become single-minded. He offers them three assurances: If they resist the devil, the devil will flee from them (James 4:7); if they draw near to God, God will draw near to them (4:8); if they humble themselves before God, God will raise them up (4:10). How ironic! Exaltation is exactly what double-minded persons are trying to gain through their envious and arrogant actions!

Gospel: Mark 9:30-37

This is the second of three Passion predictions of Jesus. Like the first in the previous chapter, it is immediately followed by a teaching about what it means to be a disciple of Jesus.

A Second Prediction

Jesus' second prediction, like the first, is made privately to his disciples. He teaches that the Son of Man is to be betrayed and handed over to powerful human opponents who will kill him, but that in three days he will rise again. The disciples react with incomprehension and fear but do not question Jesus (9:30-32).

The Son of Man

Biblical scholars debate the origin and meaning of the phrase "Son of Man." Some believe it was simply Jesus' self-effacing way of referring to himself as a human being. Others believe Jesus took the image from Old Testament apocalyptic material where "one like a human being" appears as God's anointed end-time agent of judgment and salvation (Daniel 7:13-14). These scholars believe that Jesus used "Son of Man" to describe a future transcendent salvific figure, not himself. They also say it was only after the first Easter and the rise of a Christian faith in Jesus as "the Messiah"—God's Anointed One—that believers like Mark applied this apocalyptic title to Jesus.

No one really knows how early Christians would have heard the phrase "Son of Man," given its several connotations. What is obvious is that Mark was building up to the last chapters of his story of Jesus—to the Resurrection.

Greatness in God's Eye

While the disciples were afraid to question Jesus' prediction about the Son of Man, they immediately demonstrated a lack of understanding of its implications when they began to argue among themselves about who was the greatest. This story may reflect the disciples' actual struggles for position and power right after Jesus' death. And it may have had a strong impact on the fledgling Christian community of Mark's day where believers may have argued about their leaders.

Think About It: Mark's Jesus taught that to be first with God, one must be last and a servant. How do you feel about being "last of all," a servant? What would it take to make this shift?

Jesus told the disciples (and Mark's readers) that "whoever wants to be first must be last of all and servant of all." To be his followers persons must not think and act as the world did. Society was concerned about status, position, power, and greatness; but in God's world the greatest (the powerful, wealthy, those with the most status) would be last (9:33-35). Those who had no status, no power, no wealth—servants—would be first.

The image of a servant, though a strong example, did not seem to satisfy Jesus. He further developed his point by placing a child among the disciples. In the biblical world a child was not the symbol of innocence as we think today. Children in Jesus' day symbolized powerlessness and vulnerability; children were akin to "nonpersons." Jesus told the disciples that whoever welcomed a powerless person of low status, like a child, also welcomed him (9:36-37). This child, Jesus suggests, represents him. Any child, all children, anyone who is powerless—all are to be welcomed. To follow Jesus means affirming the powerless. By doing so we welcome not only Jesus but also the God of the Bible, the God of Jesus, who consistently stands beside and champions the powerless.

Study Suggestions

A. Demonstrate Two Ways

Form two groups and create group "statues" (fixed bodily poses) that reflect: (1) God's way—trust, wisdom, faithful works, a spirit of being inclusive, humility, and (2) the world's way—self-reliance, folly, faith without works, partiality, and pride. View the poses and discuss the contrasts and implications of the two ways.

B. Explore Worthiness

Read Proverbs 31:10-31 and the interpretation on pages 310–11. To whom is the poem addressed? Who is the woman? What positive female-identified images could be used to describe a woman of worth today? What attributes create a good marriage partner?

C. Discuss God's Instruction

Read aloud Psalm 1, and review the commentary on pages 311–12. What are the two ways? Who are the "happy" and the "wicked"? What are people supposed to "delight in"? What two interpretations can we give to this psalm? (Static: One class of people follows a code of laws, the other does not;

314

Dynamic: One way of living is open to God's instruction the other is tied only to ancient revelation.) What difference do these two interpretations make in the life of the church today? in your own sense of discipleship and Christian identity?

D. Examine Envy and Arrogance

Read James 3:13–4:3, 7-8a. Review the commentary on pages 312–13. What indictment does James make? What is envy? (Painful, sorrowful, resentful desire for what others have.) How does envy cause us to compete for our own worth and our very existence? (It leads to the stance that "I have more; I am better; I belong. You have less; you are unworthy; you do not belong; so I will destroy you." Envy ultimately leads to the removal of rivals—murder.) How is pride related to envy?

E. Analyze Greatness

Read Mark 9:30-37 aloud, and review the commentary on pages 313–14. How did the disciples respond to Jesus' second prediction of his death? What did he teach them about greatness? How is following Jesus like being a powerless child? How does Jesus' teaching about being last and a servant relate to James's view of God's wisdom? (Both teach that believers are to be humble before God rather than arrogant or envious.)

F. Draw Two Ways

Over four weeks, we have studied many Scriptures describing "two ways" of living. Create pictures of human autonomy and dependence on God. (Ideas: For autonomy, consider pride, self-centeredness, self-fulfillment. For dependence, consider selflessness, humility, self-sacrifice. Add images of whatever the autonomous or dependent person would "delight in.") Discuss: Which picture represents modern society? faith? How might the call to depend on God differ for the powerful and for the powerless? (The powerful may need to practice more compassion and humility; the powerless more autonomy and personal pride.)

G. Close With Song and Prayer

Sing "Lord, I Want to Be a Christian." Pray for humble, heartfelt devotion to God's way.

Lections for Sunday Between September 25 and October 1

Old Testament:
Esther 7:1-6, 9-10; 9:20-22

*E*STHER is unique among biblical books, being the only one not to mention God. Its secular nature has caused some (such as Martin Luther and first- and second-century Jews) to question its place in the canon. Its purpose was to demonstrate the resiliency of the Jews and the vengeance due those who oppose them (4:14; 6:13) and to explain the origin of the Feast of Purim and commend its dutiful celebration by subsequent generations (9:26-32). Esther tells a story (that cannot be independently verified) that is purported to have taken place in the Persian Empire, complete with kings, queens, villains, rescuers, hangings, secrets, and the triumph of good over evil.

Today's lection is set in the middle of Esther's second banquet. After disposing of Queen Vashti, who dared oppose him, King Ahasuerus (either Xerxes I, 486 to 465 B.C., or Artaxerxes II, 404 to 358) chose Esther as his queen. Unbeknownst to him, she was of Jewish descent.

An underlying plot develops as the story continues. It seems that Mordecai, cousin and guardian of the orphaned Esther, refused to bow to Haman, an honoree of the king. Enraged, Haman arranged the execution of Mordecai as well as the genocide of all other Jews, which would include Esther. Learning of the subversive plan, Esther designed a series of banquets in order to expose Haman and his scheme, thus saving the Jews from certain slaughter.

Esther's Plan

Esther showed remarkable ingenuity in her carefully laid groundwork. As they drank wine the second day of the banquet, Ahasuerus offered Esther anything she desired, even as much as one-half of his kingdom. Esther seized the opportunity to intercede on behalf of her people.

316

Rather than go against the traditions of her time—the very act that led to her predecessor Vashti's downfall—Esther used these traditions to secure her request. Asking if she found favor with the king, Esther petitioned Ahasuerus for her own life and requested that the lives of her people also be spared. Likely expecting a request for baubles or jewels, Ahasuerus was staggered by her appeal. What could it mean? Immediately irate, Ahasuerus demanded to know the name of the culprit who was set to destroy his wife and her people. It is "a foe and enemy, this wicked Haman!" came the startling revelation (7:6).

The Outcome

A eunuch serving at the banquet suggested to Ahasuerus a just punishment for the wicked Haman: Use the gallows already constructed by Haman's order to carry out the execution of Mordecai. Dismissing them with a terse "hang him on that," the king's anger diminished as the eunuchs took Haman away to his death.

Happily Ever After

Appropriately, Mordecai himself recorded the events of Esther's action to save her people. He communicated to all Jews "near and far" the exploits of his orphaned charge. A festival was to be kept, he instructed, to remember her courageous acts. To this day, in honor of Queen Esther, the Jews keep the Feast of Purim.

> *Think About It:* Let my life be given me—that is, my petition—and the lives of my people—that is, my request (Esther 7:3). When do you as an individual and we as a church need to intercede for "our" people? Who might these people be? Who are at risk of harm and in need of protection or support? (Consider the homeless, the imprisoned, refugees, the jobless, Palestinian Christian Arabs, racial profiling, or welfare reform.) What happens if we do not have Esther's courage?

Psalter: Psalm 124

In current vernacular, Psalm 124 could be titled, "If God be for us, who can be against us?" The first five verses, set in a pattern of "if/then" statements, profess that had YHWH not been aiding the Israelites, disaster would surely have rained down. Verses 6–8 offer splendid images of Israel's escapes to freedom from the hands of its enemies.

Set next to Psalm 123, which speaks of God's presence in the midst of troubles, this psalm's placement is not accidental. God is not only present in times of trials, but God delivers the people from them. Psalm 124 is a vivid example of "let go and let God." Under their own power, the people would surely meet defeat if not actual annihilation. But under God's power, they find deliverance and salvation.

Epistle: James 5:13-20

James is a remarkable book tucked into the last half of the New Testament. It is concise and unambiguous in speaking about living within a Christian community.

Sickness and Prayer

In an apparent reversal of the natural order of things, James urges the community to pay particular attention to those who are suffering and sick. Societies often view such persons as burdens, casting them out in order to have more resources for the strong and healthy. James counters this callous attitude by saying that we are to "pray for" the sick. Indeed, he urges persons who are sick to call on the church elders to minister to them. Healing would come through the "the prayers of faith."

Sickness and Community

Think About It: How do we treat those among us who are weak, sick, or just different? What healing ministry does your church provide to the ill?

In verse 14, James uses the word *ekklesia* (church) for the first time in his letter. He reminds readers that sickness affects not only the individual, but the entire community as well. How will the sick be treated? Will there be nurture or isolation? Will they be valued as part of the community or cast aside as encumbrances?

James suggests that healing needs to take place not only for individuals but also in the life of the community. As the elders come, anointing and praying for the sick, so the community is charged to "confess your sins to one another, and pray for one another, so that you may be healed" (5:16). The laying on of hands in the anointing of oil and the prayers of the faithful restore persons to health and the community to wholeness. Thus, physical, spiritual, and communal healing are intricately woven together. Moreover, all healing comes from God.

Should one doubt the healing power of prayer, James offers as an example the prophet Elijah. Elijah opened and closed the heavens with prayer, deciding when rain would stop and when it would begin again. If Elijah's faithful prayer could accomplish such a feat, the prayers of the church can do the same.

Character of the Healed

James concludes his letter by exhorting the community to faithfulness and accountability. In no way should the church use correction out of boastfulness or suspicion; rather, community members are to bring back those who wander from the fold because they are cherished and valued. Born of love, the restoration of another to the community at the same time brings healing and salvation to the one who put forth the hand of encouragement.

Gospel: Mark 9:38-50

The disciples give us hope that, despite numerous blunders, we can still become faithful followers of Christ. In the first few verses of this passage, the disciples made the same error of judgment that many contemporary Christians make. They attempted to possess Jesus and his ministry.

Outsiders Inside

With righteous anger, the disciples approached Jesus. We can almost hear the passion in their voices as they proclaimed, "We saw someone casting out demons in your name." Further, the disciples tried to stop this exorcist; but he would not listen to them (9:38).

Their error was in wanting the ministry to remain in their hands. They were the chosen Twelve, to whom Jesus had given power. They were the ones who went from town to town with no purse or spare clothes or staff. Confronted with a stranger exorcising in Jesus' name, they suddenly realized that the ministry was growing beyond them.

This event speaks loudly to us today. So often, the church wants to remain an exclusive coalition, an "invitation only" club. No outsiders will be tolerated. Everything must be as we prescribe, with no variation from the rules. John said, "We tried to stop him, because he was not following us." This man was an outsider.

Jesus patiently explained that they must not stop anyone who healed in his name. Indeed, such people would benefit his ministry, for if they did good in his name, they would not be able to speak against him, for "whoever is not against us is for us" (9:39-40). Jesus stretched the scope of his ministry to include as many people as possible.

Fire and Millstone

Jesus then moved to a series of sayings against those who cause others to sin, which are difficult for some Christians to hear. Amputations, drowning, and eternal fire are hardly good news. Jesus, however, created strong images to emphasize crucial points (9:42-50).

Jesus' audience would realize Jesus was speaking in hyperbole. Injuring, even losing, body parts was part of normal life for the agricultural community. The listeners undoubtedly knew someone who had lost a limb if they, themselves, had not. The forcefulness of Jesus' words made it clear that leading others astray was a serious offense against God.

Job 1–2 asks a similar question. (See next week's Old Testament commen-

Think About It: When have you allowed sin to take place rather than taking a stand for righteousness? Was the situation worth losing an eye or a foot for (Mark 9:45-47)? That is, are we wise to avoid challenging injustice now but risk judgment later?

tary on pages 322–23.) What is the believer willing to sacrifice to be faithful to God—life? limb? sight? eternal torment (worms and fire)? Jesus calls believers to exhibit the sort of faith that would willingly sacrifice anything that might cause them to fall away. (We do not see this passage as advocating self-mutilation, but rather single-minded dedication.) Christians are challenged to examine their faith to see if it, indeed, stands up to the test of fire.

Salt and Peace

Ending these exhortations, Jesus reminded hearers that the strength to embrace total faith comes from within community. Believers are to "have salt" and "be at peace with one another" (9:50). Salt was used as part of the sacrificial offerings required by law (Exodus 30:34-36; Leviticus 2:13) as well as to season and preserve. It was not enough to look like salt; salt was useful when it possessed its proper chemical properties. Jesus instructed people to be salt for one another, to edify one another, to be in union with the community, and to keep loyalty to him as the central purpose of their lives.

Study Suggestions

A. Open With Prayer and Singing

Ask each group member to offer a sentence prayer for his or her "people." Allow a moment for everyone to reflect upon who their "people" are. After the prayer, list the peoples for whom the prayers were offered. Then sing "Here I Am, Lord" or another hymn about the people of God.

B. Who Cares for Us?

Read Psalm 124 and the commentary on page 317, emphasizing verse 8. Explain the background of the psalm in the early belief that "God is on our side," as contrasted with God causes the sun and rain to bless both just and unjust (Matthew 5:45). Ask: What do the "enemies," the "torrent," and the "escape" represent in our lives? When have we experienced the "help" of the Almighty?

C. Who Are We?

On poster paper prepare a collage (with either drawings or magazine pictures) of all kinds of people. Be inclusive as to race, ethnic group, physical ability, economic status, age, and lifestyle. Ask each person to point out one or two pictures that reflect his or her "people."

D. Who We Are

Read Esther 7:3-4, James 5:13, 16, Mark 9:38-41, and the commentaries on pages 316–20 about these passages. All these texts discuss the people of God in varied ways. Discuss the growth in numbers (or in perception) of those who are included as God's people, from the Jews in Esther, to the church community in James, to "whoever is for us" in Mark. Ask: Whom do we, as the church, consider our people? How inclusive is our church as regards race, ethnic group, physical condition and appearance, mental ability, economic status, and lifestyle? How much comfort (or discomfort) does our church's constituency and image bring you?

E. What We Do

Review James 5:13-20 and the commentary on pages 318–19. Discuss the responsibilities of the members of the Christian community. Write the answers on chalkboard or poster paper. Ask: How well do we (in this group and in our church) fulfill these responsibilities? Has your church ever conducted a healing service? How does anointing the sick provide healing?

F. How We Treat "Them"

Review Mark 9:38-50 and the interpretive comments on pages 319–320. Discuss the metaphorical consequences of causing another to sin. Ask: What are ways in which someone might cause another person to sin? What sacrifice do you make in order to be faithful?

Ask: How can we as a community gently lead others into righteousness and away from sin without using shame or judgment? How are we as Christians accountable to one another?

G. Closing Worship

Look over your lists of "our people" and of our responsibilities for one another. Invite participants to spend a few moments in silent prayer, thanking God for those people and confessing the ways we have neglected our responsibility to them and to one another. Ask one member to offer, on behalf of the whole group, a sentence or two assuring pardon for the sins confessed. Have participants look one another in the eye and say, "Your sins are forgiven" as one voice. End with the chorus of "Here I Am, Lord," or another suitable hymn.

Lections for Sunday Between October 2 and 8

*T*HE Old Testament: Job 1:1; 2:1-10

*T*HE Book of Job is the work of several authors, brought together in the fifth or fourth century B.C. The prose prologue (Chapters 1 and 2) and epilogue (42:7-17) probably were written before the poetic discourses (3:1–42:6), which may be an Israelite revision of an older Canaanite or Edomite epic poem. Differences in style, theology, and tone suggest that the speeches of Elihu (Chapters 32–37), the wisdom poem (Chapter 28), the discourses of God (Chapters 38–41), and Job's responses (40:3-5; 42:1-6) all come from different writers than the main poem (Chapters 3–31).

This lection, taken from the prologue, introduces an intriguing story about faith and suffering and our human response to the inexplicable. It describes Job as a man who was "blameless and upright, one who feared God and turned away from evil" (1:1). A man both pious and prosperous, Job had many children, lands, livestock, and servants. Wealthy, respected, and faithful, he was well known in his region.

Tribulation and Woe

The remainder of Job 1 tells the reader that God and Satan (here seen as an "adversary," rather than "the evil one") considered the character of Job. Satan taunted God by saying that Job was only faithful because so many blessings were bestowed upon him. God thought otherwise and gave Satan the power to take away all that Job had. In one day, everything Job possessed was gone, including his beloved children. Job tore his clothing in anguish, yet continued to praise God. The contest continues in Job 2. Not satisfied, Satan wanted "skin for skin" (2:4). God, still believing in Job's uprightness, granted that Satan might touch Job's body but had to spare his life.

Grace Versus Works

In the time of Job, material blessings were believed to come directly from God as rewards for good behavior. Curses or hardships, therefore, indicated sin. Into this belief system came Job, a man magnificently blessed, yet tormented with the loss of all he had, including his health. There he was, an upright and blameless man, exhibiting the classical Eastern signs of grief (1:20-21; 2:8), yet he continued to praise God. How could this be? Even Job's wife urged him to "curse God, and die" (2:9). Yet he remained faithful to God.

Job took the perplexing position that all things come from God. Understanding that humanity's gifts of love and devotion come with the risk of heartache and violence, Job managed to recall that God is always present, even in the most forsaken wilderness and the direst of circumstances.

Job's wife felt differently, and her voice is often unheard. She alone, perhaps, represents what most of society believes. With righteous indignation, she compelled Job, as popular phrasing suggests, to "get in touch with his anger" and lash out at God. After all, she too had lost her children and her way of life. Affected by the God-Satan struggle, she stood by, urging her husband to do something, to take charge, to at least share her rage.

Calling her foolish, Job dismissed his one remaining family member but preserved his integrity. Aching, suffering, grieving, scraping at his sores, Job remained faithful to the God, who, in his life "gave . . . and has taken away" (1:21).

> ***Think About It:*** How is living righteously related to blessings in life? Do bad things happen to bad people as a consequence of their badness? Why does evil come to all persons, good and bad?

Psalter: Psalm 25

Psalm 25 is a plea for help, for deliverance, for forgiveness, for relief. It draws a picture of the relationship between God and humanity. It may sound foreign to today's readers, products of the "me generation," which promotes self-reliance as opposed to trust in God. Upheld by "integrity and uprightness" the psalmist "waits for God," a concept almost lost amid the instant gratification of the twenty-first century.

This psalm gives the Christian community permission to admit faults; to turn over guilt; to offer our troubles to God; to trust in God as protector, healer, deliverer, and redeemer; and to wait upon God's answers to our prayers. The psalmist abides so closely in God's love, that he or she freely admits sin and guilt. Trusting God to be faithful, he offers his soul to God for protection, guidance, and forgiveness. Penitence and patience are timeless virtues, taught to generations through the words of Psalm 25.

Epistle: Hebrews 1:1-4; 2:5-12

The Book of Hebrews could be aptly subtitled "God speaks," for from the beginning the writer lifts up the imagery of the Word of God. God "spoke to our ancestors" and "in these last days has spoken to us by a Son" (1:1-2).

Word of God

God spoke and all of creation came into being (Genesis 1–2). In fact, the Word, using the language in the Gospel of John, was "in the beginning . . . and the Word was with God and the Word was God. . . . All things came into being through him. . . . What has come into being . . . was life" (John 1:1, 3-4). Furthermore, the Son, who was with God from the beginning, is painted as a priest sacrificing his own life at the altar of the cross. The Word of God, Jesus, according to Hebrews, is higher than the angels in heaven.

Word From God

Think About It: What are the responsibilities of a priest? Study Leviticus 20 and Numbers 18. How do these passages speak to Jesus as high priest?

Think About It: Hebrews speaks of Christ as pioneer, advocate, sanctifier, mediator, and sacrificial lamb. Which of these (or other) images of Christ are most meaningful to you?

The writer of Hebrews stresses that Jesus is the Word, but that he came from God, a truth believers should constantly bear in mind. Moving from a consideration of God to a consideration of Jesus Christ, the community is reminded to reflect upon Jesus in union with God. Christ was with God, came to earth to take on human form, and returned to God to be seated on God's right hand.

Described as a pioneer of their salvation, Christ is made perfect through sufferings (Hebrews 2:10). Christ is trumpeted as sacrificial high priest. Such images give encouragement to the community. In him the people find an advocate, a sanctifier, a mediator, and a lamb who is willing to sacrifice his life for the sins of the world.

The Suffering High Priest

In Chapter 2, the reader finds it heartening that Jesus, though a high priest in glory, exhibited his full humanity (2:17-18) and suffered with all humanity. All trials and sorrows were his to bear. Jesus, who came to save the lost, felt no shame in calling them his "brothers and sisters," promising to call them by name and to praise them "in the midst of the congregation" (2:11-12). Through the high priest's sacrificial suffering, "many children" shall be brought to glory. Through his sacrifice, Christ gained honor and glory, not just for himself, but for humanity as well.

Gospel: Mark 10:2-16

Pharisaic challenges were not uncommon for Jesus. Throughout his ministry, the Pharisees taunted him with trick questions and seemingly impossible dilemmas. But each time, Jesus refuted their trickery and revealed a bit more of God's realm.

Marriage Under God

Part of the historical context of Mark 10 was the perfidy of Herod Antipas, who had divorced his wife to marry his brother's ex-wife. Sensing a political trap, Jesus formulated his reply to reflect God's will, not to create new legislation.

Asked whether divorce was lawful, Jesus referred the Pharisees to the Mosaic code, which they already knew and really did not need to ask about. But Jesus reeducated them about God's will for marriage, which was something greater than the law. In marriage, he said, God intended for a man to "leave his father and mother and be joined to his wife, and the two shall become one flesh" (10:7-8a; see Genesis 2:24).

The problem faced by humanity, however, is caused by "hardness of heart" (Mark 10:5). Human sin puts custom before the will of God. So many marriages have been based on motives other than love of God, or even love of each other: to leave home, gain wealth or status, produce an heir, fill an unmet need, fulfill expectations. None of these represents a marriage that is necessarily of God. If God joins a couple together, what can possibly break them apart?

The Struggle With Divorce

The church has long struggled with divorce. The ending of a marriage is tragic for all involved. Frequently, by the time many couples come to seek healing for their marriage, their estrangement is too vast to overcome. Pastors sometimes perform weddings in which marital success is already in doubt. The church seeks to address the crisis of divorce by offering in-depth premarital counseling, marriage enrichment and divorce recovery classes.

Jesus' response to the Pharisees placed marriage under the grace of God instead of the legal system. In the first century, and often today, marriage was viewed as a contractual agreement between families or individuals. Jesus reminded his hearers that marriage is more than a legal contract; it is a covenant between two people and God. Those whom "God has joined together, let no one separate" (10:9).

Jesus Loves the Little Children

Interestingly, the Gospel writer places Jesus' comments on divorce in the context of the needs of children. Both women and children possessed low social status and thus were vulnerable. Jesus' teaching requires the protection of women and children. In this passage, women are discarded by divorce and children are ignored. Jesus rebukes the hard-heartedness of men who divorce their wives and men who ignore children.

Perhaps after the heated discussion about adults with hard hearts and the trauma they produced, Jesus was relieved to be in the presence of persons with such little status and clout. Unless his followers became as nothing and accepted this utter relinquishment as the way to God, they would never enter God's realm (10:16).

Think About It: "Whoever does not receive the kingdom of God as a little child will never enter it" (10:16). How do we experience solidarity with the oppressed in our world?

Study Suggestions

A. Open With Prayer and Singing

Invite participants to name persons they know who are hurting in some way. Using only first names or the word *unspoken*, list these on chalkboard or poster paper. Offer bidding prayers for each, with the group responding, "Lord, hear our prayer."

Sing the first stanza of "Precious Lord, Take My Hand," or another prayer hymn.

B. What About Me?

Read Job 1:1, 2:1-10, and the commentary on this lection. Ask: How did the actions of God and Satan affect Job and his wife? How do you reconcile innocents caught up in evil (such as children dying of cancer, victims of natural disasters, innocent bystanders hit by stray bullets) with the notion of a loving, graceful God?

C. Why Me?

Read Psalm 25 and the commentary on page 323. Ask: Have you ever prayed but felt God did not answer? Why does God seem to grant healing to some and not to others?

It is said that God responds to prayer with either yes, no, or wait. Invite members to share their experience with each of these responses.

D. Why Not Me?

Ask: Does anyone deserve suffering? Discuss the differences between the questions, "Why me?" and "Why not me?" as they pertain to one's spiritual life.

E. For Me?

Read Hebrews 1:1-4, 2:5-12 aloud; and review the commentary on page 324. Have the group imagine themselves in the church's worship space; if possible, take the group there. Ask: How would the altar be different if it were covered with the blood of an animal sacrifice? Remaining in the worship space, discuss the duties of the pastor. Ask: Is offering a sacrifice to God among those tasks? How does the pastor act as priest, in addition to his sacramental ministry? (The roles of pastoral counseling, intercessory prayer, hospital visitation, and representing God on occasions of death, transition, community trauma, and life crisis might be mentioned.)

Discuss the "suffering savior." Distribute a handout listing the words *priest, atonement, redemption, suffering, mediator, intercession, sacrifice,* and *Christology*. Ask members to write a word or phrase opposite each word representing their understandings. Use a Bible dictionary in explaining and discussing the words' meanings.

F. He or She and Me

Read Mark 10:1-12 and the commentary on page 325. Ask class members to imagine someone who is in a "bad" marriage, one in which the vows "love, honor, and cherish" have been broken. Ask: How do we reconcile the necessity of divorce, on occasion, with the words of Jesus? How is God's forgiveness at work in the lives of those surviving divorce?

G. Become as a Child

Read Mark 10:13-16 and the commentary on pages 325–26. Ask: What characteristics of children do we need to emulate to enter God's realm? Note that in Jesus' time our modern notion of children's innocence was unknown; children then were nonpersons. How does this affect your understanding of Jesus' words about entering the Kingdom?

H. In Closing

Pray for God's blessing on victims of suffering, persons facing marital difficulties, children, and others going through troubled times. Then read together Psalm 25:4-5 as a benediction.

Lections for Sunday Between October 9 and 15

Old Testament: Job 23:1-9, 16-17

*C*HAPTER 23 finds Job still struggling with loss and grief and the question of why misfortune has befallen him, a righteous man. His friends have advised him in different ways, but he has rejected their counsel. He is confident that the traditional Hebrew wisdom that calamity is the result of sin does not apply to him because he is innocent of any offense against God or humanity.

In today's lection, Job answers Eliphaz's admonition to repent of some unnamed wickedness with the words, "Today also my complaint is bitter" (verse 2). But he refuses to repent of sins he knows he has not committed. He will not betray his integrity nor succumb to pressure. He knows his heart is pure.

Lost in All Directions

Despite his great loss and his oozing sores, Job believes that if God would only grant him a trial, he could prove his innocence. Vindication would come if only God would listen. God is a God of justice and compassion, Job believes. If he could only sit down and logically explain his situation, surely God would issue a fair and just verdict of his innocence (verses 3-7).

As fanciful as the imagined trial appears, Job experiences a problem that brings him back to reality. Where is God? One cannot have a trial without all parties present, all sides represented. Job looks forward. He turns backward. He faces right. He gazes left. But Job cannot find God. Somehow, God is completely absent (verses 8-9).

328

To Job, God's obscurity was as unimaginable as the fact that all he possessed was gone. God's presence was something he took for granted. As trustworthy as the rise of the morning sun, God was immanent in Job's life. God walked with the people throughout their history, rescuing them

> **Think About It:** God is completely absent. When have you asked, sought, and knocked, but could hear no answer? Why do we want to put God on trial?

from trouble time after time. God was faithful even when they committed blatant sin. It was only in God's apparent absence that Job realized he had presumed that God would always be there.

Justice Calls

Job struggled here, and other places in his story, with belief in a God of justice while faced with incomprehensible injustice. Could a just God allow suffering? Could God be on the side of the righteous when terrible, undeserved suffering was plaguing God's children?

The tension found in this conundrum—why do the innocent suffer?—spans the ages. Through the story of Job we see the timeless dilemma of how a just God could permit an unjust world. With no ready answer available, Job retreated into the dread and trepidation that were his constant companions during his plight (verse 17). Indeed, he moaned, "God has made my heart faint; / the Almighty has terrified me" (verse 16).

Verse 17 is more difficult exegetically. Was Job surrendering to fear as he had previously, wishing that he were dead (3:11-26)? Or did he manage to find the spunk with which this lection opens? Sometimes it seems easier to disappear into the darkness than to continue struggling in the midst of torment.

> **Think About It:** When have you felt that if God would just listen, you could make God understand the undeserved pain in your life? How adequate is our understanding of what is just and unjust?

Psalter: Psalm 22:1-15

Although not as beloved as its neighbor, Psalm 23, Psalm 22 is nonetheless familiar. A genuine cry for help, it opens with the words so familiar during Lent. In his final hours on the cross, Jesus cried out, "My God, my God why have you forsaken me?"—the opening line of Psalm 22.

Psalm 22 juxtapositions opposing philosophies. On the one hand, the psalmist laments the perceived absence of God, but cries for vindication. On the other, the psalmist rejoices in the presence of God. Such struggle encapsulates the human condition. Even in the midst of affliction, God is at hand

and yearns to restore and renew the life of the community. Here is a God who shares in suffering, opening the way for future generations to come to understand Jesus as suffering savior.

Jesus' story is told in the Gospels using images from Psalm 22. He ministered among the poor, the sick, the guilty, and the stranger—those to whom the words of the psalm would bring relief and hope. He invited to the table those considered "a worm, and not human; / scorned by others, and despised by the people" (verse 6). To them he gave the gift of eternal life.

Epistle: Hebrews 4:12-16

This lection confronts us with a dilemma. How do we understand the term *word*? Is it to be understood as Jesus, the Word of God? the proclamation found in Scripture? the continuing revelation of God throughout the ages? The answer is, "Yes"—all three.

Living Word

"The word of God is living and active, sharper than any two-edged sword" (verse 12). To fully comprehend the reading, the community must understand that, in this passage, the writer's intent is not to define the term *word*. Rather than dwell on what the word is, the writer proclaims what the word does. The word of God lives, acts, pierces, and judges (verses 12-13).

In order to receive the word of God, the community must be open to hear. Upon hearing, there is indeed revelation, for, "nothing in all creation is hidden from God's sight. Everything is uncovered and laid bare before the eyes of him to whom we must give account" (verse 13, NIV).

Passing Through the Veil

On the Day of Atonement only the high priest entered through the curtain into the "holy place" where the ark of the covenant rested. He was to come in a specified manner at a precise time. He was to perform many rituals for the atonement of Israel's sin (Leviticus 16). The writer of Hebrews brings this image forward to the time of Jesus. Jesus has "passed through the heavens" (verse 14) and was now the high priest who, though he reigned in glory and was without sin, has become human and thus able to understand our weaknesses.

Boldly Go

That the word was living and active, sharp and strong, and that Christ had become human, had passed through the heavens, and now reigned as high priest in the heavens, provides us the privilege to "approach the throne of grace" (verse 16). Believers could rest in the assurance that the one seated on the throne would receive them with mercy. Moreover, believers were to approach the throne not in sackcloth and ashes with heads bowed in shame, but boldly and with confidence, expecting to "receive mercy and find grace to help in time of need" (verse 16). Through Jesus, the gate to God was open for all with Jesus ready to act as mediator for all of humankind.

> **Think About It:** "Let us therefore approach the throne of grace with boldness" (verse 16). How do you approach God? What makes you hesitant? What gives you confidence?

Gospel: Mark 10:17-31

Our response to this lection may well depend on our economic status. Persons who are poor will find hope and justification in this story of the rich man, while those with wealth and status may face the dilemma of justifying their financial situation in light of Jesus' call to "sell everything you have and give to the poor" (verse 21, NIV).

Young, Upstanding Person

As Jesus journeyed from across the Jordan, a man came and knelt at his feet. The text does not mention his economic status until the end of the encounter. Through either intuition or the man's dress and demeanor, Jesus determined that he was well-to-do. Apparently familiar with Jesus' ministry, the rich man had but one question for him, "Good Teacher, what must I do to inherit eternal life?" (verse 17).

Not only did this man enjoy great affluence but he also observed all the commandments and tenets of the Jewish faith. After Jesus recited these—the prohibitions against murder, theft, false witness, and adultery—we learn that the rich man was already familiar with them, and had "kept all these since [his] youth" (verse 20).

His life seemed to be in perfect order. To have wealth, in the tradition of the day, was proof of one's uprightness. He claimed to be faithful in keeping the commandments of God. Yet Jesus sensed that something was missing. The man had everything the world had to offer, yet he came seeking spiritual well-being as well.

The Look of Love

In the hymn, "What a Friend We Have in Jesus," the line, "Jesus knows our every weakness" describes Jesus' insight into this man's need. Yes, he kept the commandments; he had done so all his life. But Jesus looked at him with what we can imagine was a sad smile. For he knew his weakness. Tenderly Jesus told him, "Go, sell what you own, and give the money to the poor, . . . then come, follow me" (verse 21). Taken aback by this request, the rich man went home brokenhearted, apparently unwilling to give up his earthly fortune for the glory that was eternal.

Can One Enter Heaven in a Mercedes (Camel)?

Observing the exchange, the disciples were as troubled as the rich man. If the rich, considered to be the most blessed, could not enter heaven, who could? Would salvation be offered to anyone if not to the rich? Jesus answered them with words of hope: "For mortals it is impossible, but not for God; for God all things are possible" (verse 27). Typically, Peter then protested, citing the sacrifice the disciples had made (verse 28).

The rich man thought that with all his wealth he could afford to do some good thing that would entitle him to eternal life. Jesus demanded that he give away all that he had so that he would become a disciple who possessed nothing. In that condition, he would become totally dependent on God. In being dependent on God he would realize that God alone could save him—he could do nothing to save himself.

Think About It: The rich man went away grieving. What must you give up so that you become totally dependent on God for salvation? How is the gospel of prosperity preached in some churches and on television to be understood in light of this passage?

We are called to be radical disciples of Jesus Christ and to shun preoccupation with the things of this world. But what is given up on earth, Jesus says, will be received a hundred times over in heaven (verse 30). Those "many who are first [sitting in the box seats here] will be last [left outside the gate of heaven], and the last will be first" (verse 31). This is the good news!

Study Suggestions

A. Confessing Weaknesses

Ask each member to write on a slip of paper one of their weaknesses. During a time of silent prayer, invite them to come forward and drop their papers in a basket on the worship table, then offer brief prayers asking God for strength to move beyond these weaknesses. Then sing "What a Friend We Have in Jesus," noting the line, "Jesus knows our every weakness."

B. A Divided Table

Beforehand place on one side of a table symbols of affluence (money, pictures of fancy appliances, clothes, cars, homes). Make this side very crowded with no room for one more thing. On the other side place symbols of the life of discipleship (candles, Bible, Communion set, towel and basin, wooden cross, crown of thorns).

Read aloud Job 23:1-9, 16-17, and Psalm 22:1-15; review the commentaries on both (pages 328–30); and discuss the questions in the "Think About It" boxes. In sharing times when God seemed absent, list on a chalkboard or poster paper feeling words that describe such experiences. Then say together, "My God, my God why have you forsaken me?" Discuss: Think about a forsaken place. What sounds are heard? What sights are seen? What is the temperature? Is there light or darkness? Who is there? Record responses alongside the feeling words.

Ask a volunteer to take the cross or crown from one side of the table and, without moving anything, attempt to find a space for it on the other side. Name the ways in which we crowd God out of our lives, then wonder why we cannot find God when we need spiritual help.

C. Not a Care (in Heaven)

Read Hebrews 4:12-16 and the commentary on pages 330–31. Note the three meanings of God's word. Place a sword (either a real one or one made of cardboard and covered with foil) on the table. Ask: How is God's word sharper than a sword? What other metaphors does the Hebrews passage use for God's word? When has a Scripture cut into your heart and revealed a truth to you?

Consider the image of a living and active God. Ask: Where do you see evidences of God's active word? God speaks through Scripture. How does God continue to speak to you?

Call attention to the world side of the table. Ask: Why do things like this attract us? Which are necessities and which could we get along without? Which can be used in Christ's service?

D. Saying "Yes"

Read Mark 10:17-31 and the interpretation on pages 331–32. Create a modern rich person. What might be his or her job, social status, living quarters, lifestyle, community involvement, "toys" (car, electronic gadgets)? Ask: What might be this person's response to the gospel? If you had everything you could imagine, as Job and the rich man did, and felt Jesus calling you to give it all up as a condition of following him, what would be your response? What would be the pros and cons of saying "yes"? Is an affluent lifestyle compatible with commitment to Christ? Why or why not?

E. In Closing

Have participants each take from the possessions table one thing they might give up for Jesus. When all have done so, ask the original volunteer to place the crown or cross on the world side, where there will now be room. After a moment of silent contemplation, sing the chorus, "Seek Ye First"; then close with a prayer of commitment.

Lections for Sunday Between October 16 and 22

T Old Testament: Job 38:1-7 (34-41)

HE long-awaited trial before God for which Job had yearned was now at hand. Satan, sure that Job would curse God in the face of his heartbreak and misery, must have been waiting in the wings in breathless anticipation. Undoubtedly, Job would break, giving up his ridiculous piety for a chance to rail at God. Even if Job remained faithful to God, the question persisted as to why he, an innocent man, had had to suffer. How could he restrain himself from cursing God, now that he finally had his hearing?

A Challenge From the Whirlwind

Out of the whirlwind, God began to speak to Job. But God's utterances were not full of compassion and solace. In 13:23, Job had asked: "How many are my iniquities and my sins? / Make me know my transgression and my sin." Now, instead of giving a direct answer, God showered Job with a series of questions. "Who is this . . . ? Where were you . . . ? Who determined . . . ? Do you know . . . ? Can you . . . ?" (38:2, 4, 5, 33, 34). God was challenging Job's pride and impudence in asserting his innocence before the Almighty.

Job, God was contending, was indeed ill-prepared to take on a trial with God. As a mere human being, Job's intellect and capacity for understanding the mystery of the universe were exceedingly limited. God's wisdom, creative power, and greatness, on the other hand, were boundless. God had "laid the foundation, . . . loose[d] the cords of Orion, . . . sent forth lightnings, . . . put wisdom in the inward parts, . . . number[ed] the clouds, . . . [and] provide[d] for the raven" (38:4, 31, 35-37, 41). God was the Almighty Creator. Whatever comes into being does so at God's command and no one else's.

Lions and Ravens and Storms!

Job 38:34-41 records feats that Job, as a mere human being, could never accomplish. Could Job provide rain and lightning when needed? Could Job scatter the stars in the heavens? Could Job give understanding to the mind? Could Job go out and hunt for the lion known throughout the Hebrew Bible as the great hunter? Could Job provide the raven with its prey so its young would not hunger? Job could not. God could. Job was being brought down to size—humbled before the awesome majesty of the Creator.

In this series of rhetorical questions, God was reminding Job of what he seemed to have forgotten—that after all it was God, not he, who was in charge. God was the master of the universe. God was the creator and Job the creature. To question and rail against such truths would shroud the grandeur and mystery of God and God's design of the universe.

Think About It: God's questions reminded Job of the order of creation and his place in it. How does the illusion that we are in control of the universe and our place and destiny in it undermine our trust in God? What signs of this human arrogance do you see in our society? (Consider the worlds of science, economics, politics, the military, international relations, and human relationships.) How would our lives be different if we acknowledged God's sovereignty and surrendered our lives to God's purpose?

Order and Chaos

Job had lost all he had, including his faith. God now had the task of rebuilding Job's trust and reordering his perspective on the world. Not only did God's questions remind Job of the order of creation and his place in it, they also recalled the reality that amid the order there was also chaos. God inquired, "Who shut in the sea with doors / when it burst out from the womb?" (38:8). Still wallowing in his misery and self-pity, however, Job as yet seemed unable to grasp God's line of reasoning or acknowledge his sin of pride.

Psalter: Psalm 104:1-9, 24, 35c

The opening words of the psalm remind us of the familiar table grace: "God is great, God is good, let us thank God for our food."

This psalm draws a portrait of a wondrous God dressed in robes of honor and majesty. So great is God that God's clothing is the very light itself. This extraordinary God, who rides in a chariot of clouds on the streams of the wind, has created for humanity a magnificent world.

The God who ordered the watery chaos to recede to "the place [God] appointed" (104:8) also laid the foundations of the earth. All creatures were created by God's wisdom (104:24). In today's terms, the psalmist was an environmentalist. Rather than save the earth so that it will support human consumption, however, the psalmist says that preserving the world begins with praising its Creator. Realizing the wonders of creation and the holiness of the Creator is the only way humans can preserve their place in the world. The psalmist sings, "O LORD, how manifold are your works! / In wisdom you have made them all" (104:24).

Epistle: Hebrews 5:1-10

Hebrews 5 continues the theme in earlier chapters of the image of Christ as both of the people and of the priesthood—a mediator between God and humanity. Because God became human in Jesus, Christ can serve as high priest with sympathy, patience, and grace. He intimately understands human suffering because he has experienced it in its depths.

Qualities of a Priest

The author begins with a "job description." A priest is responsible for the link between humanity and God, offers sacrifices for the atonement of himself and the community, understands human weakness in himself and others, and is patient with those who have received no education in the law and therefore tend to stray from it.

A Priest Called by God

The writer refers to Aaron as a priest, one who did not choose to be a priest but was called by God (Exodus 28:1; Leviticus 8:1-36). Likewise, Jesus, who "did not glorify himself in becoming a high priest," was appointed by God, who declared him to be "a priest forever according to the order of Melchizedek" [an ideal priest-king, a heavenly judge, a mysterious, supernatural, eternal figure who was the precursor of Christ Jesus, God's Son] (Hebrews 5:5-6; see Genesis 14:17-20; Psalm 110:4; Hebrews 6:20–7:22). Priesthood is not an occupation one chooses; rather, it is a work to which one is called.

Jesus Our Model

Thus called, Jesus lived an ideal life to which we are to aspire. But Jesus was more than just an example. He did not pray just to model prayer. He made devout prayer a way of life. His prayer kept him in relationship to God and modeled for us how to do the same. "Jesus offered up prayers and supplications, with loud cries and tears, . . . and he was heard because of his reverent submission" (5:7). Although he cried out and was heard, he was not rescued from suffering just because he was the Son. As Jesus endured suffering, so must we. As he cried out with shrieks and moans in pain and suppli-

336

cation, so will we. As Jesus learned obedience through suffering, so do we. It was not through the sinning, but through the testing, that he learned obedience and deepened his commitment. And so must we.

> **Think About It:** How does suffering (choosing a difficult path to serve a redemptive purpose for others) lead us to become perfect? Apart from testing, how can the validity of our faith be demonstrated?

Gospel: Mark 10:35-45

As impossible as it sounds, the disciples were on the verge of entering Jerusalem without much, if any, understanding of the purpose and Passion of Christ. On the heels of the encounter with the rich man who was challenged to sacrifice his riches to enter the realm of heaven, the request of James and John for positions of honor in the Kingdom seems absurd.

At the Left and Right

The sons of Zebedee, James and John, came to Jesus requesting that he "do for us whatever we ask" (10:35). Moments before, Jesus had told them he would suffer being spat upon, mocked, flogged, and killed (10:34). As though they had not even heard him, their immediate response was to ask for the seats of honor next to him in the next life. Were they listening?

Cup of Sorrows

Jesus warned them to be sure they understood the implications of their request. Were they willing to drink from the cup of sorrows? Were they willing to be baptized with waters that would overwhelm? Were they ready to suffer and die?

Still misunderstanding his metaphoric language, James and John declared that they could drink from the cup and stand fast under the baptizing water. Given all that had recently transpired, their response seems naïve at best and arrogant at worst. Could they possibly stand the persecution and execution that was soon to come? Would they pass this test?

> **Think About It:** What might it mean for you to drink Jesus' cup and receive his baptism? Where in your life do you feel called to follow the example of the suffering servant?

Jesus told them they would, indeed, drink from his cup of suffering. James was executed by Herod Agrippa in Jerusalem (see Acts 12:2). Tradition holds that John was boiled in oil. Yes, they would be baptized into his baptism. But Jesus went on to say that he could not grant their request for seats of honor, for it was God alone who would make that determination (10:40).

Trouble Among the Twelve

When the other disciples heard about James and John's appeal, they got angry. No doubt each hoped for a place of honor for himself, so they were filled with jealousy when they found out that James and John had beaten them to it. Sensing strife, Jesus called them together. Time was running short. They were hours from Jerusalem. Jesus knew they would betray, deny, and abandon him in his final hours. Trying once again to make them understand what they must endure, he gave some advice about discipleship.

To be honored, a follower of Jesus must be as a servant (10:43). Those who desire first place "must be slave of all" (10:44). Disciples are not to be like the world in which leaders "lord it over" underlings. They are not to torment or despise the least, nor can they debase the broken. They are not to expect to be served as great and mighty leaders, but instead must humbly serve.

These images conflict with common perceptions of greatness. Military leader, conqueror, warrior, king, yes, but a servant? How could one be great and stoop to such a level? He came "not to be served but to serve, and to *give his life* a ransom for many" (10:45, italics added).

Study Suggestions

A. Open With Prayer and Song

Invite members to recall memorable times when they either took a servant role or were served by others. Have these shared in the form of a litany, with the group responding after hearing each instance of servanthood with the refrain, "Thank you God, for this servant experience." Then sing the first two stanzas of "Are Ye Able."

B. God Is Great

Read Psalm 104 in unison. Then read Job 38:1-7, 34-41 in turn around the group, question by question. Review the commentaries on both passages (pages 334–36). Ask: Where do we see evidences of human attempts to control creation—locally, nationally, and globally?

Explore the difference between caring for the earth in order to support a consumerist lifestyle as opposed to preserving the planet to show our love for God the Creator. Give examples of each. (Possibilities: tree farms to replace old growth, genetic engineering of corn and fish, emissions controls to foster tourism versus closing national forests to vehicular traffic to reserve the experience of awe and wonder to hikers and campers, barring commercial fishing from some coral reefs to allow for snorkeling and scuba diving, and developing alternative sources of energy and building materials to preserve the rainforest for indigenous peoples).

C. Qualities of a Priest

Read Hebrews 5:1-10, then review Exodus 28:1, Leviticus 8, and the commentary on pages 336–37. List on chalkboard or poster paper the duties and qualities of a priest as described in these sources. Ask: How do you understand Jesus as high priest? your minister as priest? What is the difference between being chosen by God for the role of priest and choosing the priesthood as an occupation?

D. Jesus: Human and Divine

Read Mark 10:35-45 and the commentary on pages 337–38. Reread Hebrews 5:7. Ask: In what instances did Jesus exhibit his humanity? What does it mean in your life for Jesus to have suffered?

E. Seeking Honor or Servanthood?

Display on a table materials that represent servant ministry, such as an apron, a towel and basin, a crown of thorns, a rustic cross. On another table, place symbols of royalty or status, such as a foil-covered crown, a ring, precious stones, purple cloth, candles in ornate holders, and a gold cross. Ask: In what ways do each set of items appeal to you? Can you empathize with those in Jesus' time who expected "gold" but received "wood"? When have we been like James and John, seeking honor instead of servanthood? What does this teach us about our relationship with God and our sense of ministry? about our ego needs and level of commitment?

F. In Closing

Sing the third stanza of "Are Ye Able." Ask members to write how they understand their commitment to Jesus Christ, then fold the paper and place it at the foot of the cross of their choice. Lead the group in a prayer of confession, pardon, and reaffirmation of faith. After singing the last stanza of "Are Ye Able," ask the group to leave in silence, contemplating their renewed commitment to Christ.

Lections for Sunday Between October 23 and 29

Old Testament: Job 42:1-6, 10-17

*A*FTER a long period of unremitting suffering, Job finally gained the opportunity to speak with God. The tension in the story, thus far, had been whether good would triumph over evil. Who would win the contest for Job's soul—God or Satan? Would Job break under the weight of his misfortunes and curse God, or would his faith continue to sustain him?

Culmination

Job's answer to God began with confession. About God he said, "I know that you can do all things," thus confessing his belief in God's omnipotent power. In response to God's speech from the whirlwind, Job acknowledged his limitations by conceding that he had spoken of things about which he had no understanding.

From confession, Job moved to declaration. He admitted to God that he "had heard of you by the hearing of the ear, / but now my eye sees you; / therefore I despise myself"—words used also by Isaiah in a similar fashion (42:5-6; see Isaiah 6:1-13). To be in the presence of God's goodness requires that one humbly recognize one's own sinfulness and finitude. Job ended his soliloquy in an attitude of penitence for misspeaking and arrogantly demanding God's response.

The End . . . Or Was It?

Thus, in the end, Job lived up to his reputation as "blameless and upright, one who feared God and turned away from evil" (1:1). The epilogue describes how his faithfulness was subsequently rewarded with the restoration of his fortunes and family. Still, there remained the lingering question of "why?" Why was this innocent, upright man subjected to so much suffering? Job was stripped of everything but his life. He lost his family, his livelihood, his health, and his possessions. Such losses affected not only Job, but also his wife, about whom we have no information other than her plea for Job to "curse God and die" (2:9). Who listened to her and soothed her grief? Does God hand out suffering just to prove God's strength in a contest?

Questions surrounding suffering are rarely simple; answers, too, are often complex. The wisdom comes, not from living a neat story with a discernible beginning, intriguing middle, and happy ending. The theology of Deuteronomy—the righteous are rewarded with material blessings, the wicked are punished with pain and trouble—was simply not adequate to explain what happened to Job. Instead, true wisdom and humble faith come from undergoing the affliction and ambiguity and meeting God in the midst of the struggle. It is not that there are no answers to human misfortune. It is that humanity grows and learns in faith, hope, and love from experiencing God in the midst of the fray.

> **Think About It:** "Wisdom and faith come from meeting God in the midst of the struggle." Does this central message of Job help you deal with the ambiguities of your life? What nagging questions remain?

A Restoration of Fortune

Job's story came to an end in the epilogue with the restoration of his fortunes and family twofold. (See the code for restitution in Exodus 22:4, 7, 9.) He received twice as many sheep, camels, oxen, and donkeys as had been destroyed. He and his wife conceived seven more sons and three more daughters. His daughters were famed for their loveliness and were guaranteed an inheritance. Job's life was long and full, spanning 140 years. In his latter days he saw four new generations come into being. Finally, Job, presumably spirited and strong, came to the end of his life "old and full of years" (42:17, NIV).

Psalter: Psalm 34:1-8 (19-22)

The running theme in the psalms for the October lections has been dependence on God even in the midst of strife. Hence it is no surprise that Psalm 34 embraces this theme. The writer not only praises God but also invites those listening to join in. The psalmist praises God both for his or her own deliverance and for God's grace shown to all who are meek, broken, and downtrodden. They are called to "hear and be glad" and to "exalt [God's] name together" (34:2-3).

This indicates that the psalmist lives in brokenness, affliction, fear, and destitution. But he did not wait for the good times to offer God praise. Life is the way it is, says Psalm 34. God's faithfulness, no matter what the circumstances, remains constant. God rescues. God delivers. God redeems. God saves. Trusting God's goodness, we can, "taste and see that the LORD is good" and count themselves "happy [as] are those who take refuge in [God]" (34:8).

Epistle: Hebrews 7:23-28

The previous lections from Hebrews have presented Christ as high priest and mediator. Chapter 5 highlights the historic lineage of Christ's priesthood, with Aaron, the brother of Moses and the first high priest, lifted up as the prime example.

Permanent Priest

The instructions in Exodus 28 provided for Aaron and his sons to act as priests (28:1, 4, 41). They established a hereditary priesthood (28:43). The author contrasts the earthly, limited service of these mortal priests with the constancy of Jesus Christ by saying: "Former priests . . . were prevented by death from continuing in office; but he holds his priesthood permanently, because he continues forever" (Hebrews 7:23-24).

Offering the definitive sacrifice and atonement, Christ, the eternal word of God, conquered death through his Passion and Resurrection. Therefore, he is high priest for time and all eternity, for in him there would be everlasting life.

Intercessor

Bridging the gap between the first and second comings of Christ, his role as one who intercedes on behalf of humanity presents a dynamic image of Christ as active in the life of the community. No limitation of time or place could be put on him. He is as freshly present with the church today as he was when Hebrews was written, and he will be thus for evermore.

The role of Christ as intercessor is an aspect that we sometimes overlook. It is seen most clearly, for example, throughout the Gospel of John. In John 17, a passage known as Jesus' high priestly prayer, he intercedes for himself (17:1-5), for his disciples (17:6-19), and for the whole world (17:20-26). Earlier in that discourse, Jesus had asserted that, "No one comes to the Father except through me" and "If in my name you ask me for anything, I will do it" (14:6, 14). Jesus prays to God on behalf of those who love and follow him.

> **Think About It:** Jesus prays for those who love and follow him. Do we as a church intercede for others as Christ intercedes for us?

The Promise of the Priesthood

Because there is an oath, indeed, a promise, from God, Christ's priesthood supersedes the priesthood that existed under the rules of the Torah. The law framed an order in which Israel could live as a holy people, united by God's blessing. But human frailty makes complete fulfillment of the law impossible. Previous high priests, who interceded on behalf of the community, were themselves "subject to weakness." Not so for Jesus, "who has been made perfect forever" (Hebrews 7:28).

Gospel: Mark 10:46-52

These few verses provide a transition to the events about to take place in Jesus' passion. His final act before entering Jerusalem, the healing of Bartimaeus, brought to an end the series of miracles described in the preceding chapters.

A Shout of Faith and Expectation

As usual, a crowd was following Jesus on this journey. Presumably, beneficiaries of his miracles, recipients of his teaching, witnesses to his compassion, and general hangers-on all helped to make up the swelling crowd. Whoever they were, their reverence for Jesus and gratitude for what he had done for them were apparent.

Sitting at the side of the hot, dusty road, blind Bartimaeus must have sensed excitement in the air. Perhaps he felt the shuffle and pounding of many footsteps. Perhaps he heard the raised voices of enthusiastic believers. Perhaps others came to tell him who was coming. Whatever the case, Bartimaeus soon realized that in the center of the crowd was none other than Jesus of Nazareth. Clearly aware of who Jesus was, his shout of faith and expectation—"Jesus, Son of David, have mercy on me!"—was heard over the din of the crowd (10:47).

The multitude, reacting like many contemporary Christians, immediately tried to silence this noisy, blind beggar. This outcast must not disturb the Lord with his raucous outbursts. So they hushed him, roughly ordering his silence.

Bartimaeus had nothing to lose, however. He lived on the fringes of society. Whatever income he received came from begging in the streets. His options were limited, his alternatives few. Then along came Jesus. Jesus of Nazareth. This was his chance. Maybe his miserable life was about to take a turn for the better.

A second time Bartimaeus shouted, "Son of David, have mercy on me!" Jesus, hearing his name, stopped still in the roadway. Compassionate even in the last days of his life, Jesus asked the people to call Bartimaeus into his presence. Urging him to "take heart," the crowd conveyed to him Jesus' request. Excited by Jesus' attention, Bartimaeus threw aside his cloak, leaped to his feet, and hurriedly, hopefully made his way to Jesus.

What Do You Want Me to Do?

When he finally reached Jesus, Bartimaeus was greeted with a question—"What do you want me to do for you?" (10:51a). Referring to Jesus as his teacher and getting straight to the point, Bartimaeus answered that he wanted Jesus to heal his eyes: "Let me see again" (10:51b). Without the drama involving spittle and the laying on of Jesus' hand found in the earlier healing of the blind man in Mark 8:22-26, Jesus said without fanfare, "Go; your faith has made you well" (10:52). Instantly, Bartimaeus regained his sight. In response, Bartimaeus joined the band of followers as they prepared to enter Jerusalem.

> **Think About It:** Jesus asked Bartimaeus, "What do you want me to do for you?" How would you answer that question if Jesus were to direct it to you? What need do you most want Jesus to meet?

A Sign of Things to Come

This healing story not only recounts a miracle, it also provides a glimpse of things to come. Bartimaeus shouted out the gospel truth: Jesus is the Son of David, merciful and able to work miracles. In vain the crowd tried to squelch his cries, but they could not—just as the cross could not silence the Word of God.

Bartimaeus's enthusiasm was in direct contrast to the frightened, confused disciples. Did he somehow know that this Jesus would overcome not only his darkness but the darkness of the world? He at least did have faith enough to ask, and expect, to be made well.

Study Suggestions

A. Wisdom Comes Through the Struggle

Begin by having one person read aloud Job 42:1-6, and another verses 10-17. Ask: How do these passages differ in style and emphasis? Note that the first passage is poetry, the second prose. The first recounts Job's penitent acknowledgment of his arrogance and finitude, the second describes his restoration to abundance and contentment. Is it possible these passages come from different hands? Ask: Which was the greater blessing: the wisdom or the wealth? Invite members to share misfortunes they have encountered and what they learned from them. Ask: How was God present with you?

B. God's Faithfulness Remains Constant

Read aloud Psalm 34:1-9, 19-22, and review the interpretation on pages 341–42. Comment that the theme of dependence on God is present in all the psalter lections this month. Ask: What is the central message of this psalm? How does your experience of God compare with that of this psalmist?

C. Jesus as Intercessor

Read Hebrews 7:23-28 and the commentary on pages 342–43. Also read John 17, noting the three objects of Jesus' intercession in verses 1-5, 6-19, and 20-26. Explain that John 17 is an illustration of Jesus' role as intercessor that is emphasized in the Hebrews passage. In the text, are prayers offered to Christ, or does he pray for us? What does the priesthood of all believers imply about our responsibility as intercessors? How regularly do you practice intercessory prayer?

D. A Look at Healing

Invite members to talk about healing services they have seen or attended. Read over the liturgy of the healing service in your book of worship. Ask: What place does healing have in the life of our church? When have you experienced anointing with oil and the laying on of hands? How is God present in medical healing and spiritual healing?

E. A Blind Man Is Healed

Read aloud Mark 10:46-52 and the commentary on pages 343–44. List on the chalkboard or poster paper the similarities and differences between the healings of Job, Bartimaeus, and those you have just discussed.

Blindfold half the members, and ask both them and the rest of the group to perform simple tasks like signing their names, finding the Psalms in the Bible, going out the door, or tying a bow. Discuss: What impact would visual impairment have on your life? What must it have been like for Bartimaeus to be blind? to gain his sight?

Discuss the crowd in the story of Bartimaeus. Ask: What would happen in your church if someone acted like Bartimaeus during the service? When does the church become like the silencing crowd?

E. In Closing

Review the major themes of these lections—wisdom through suffering, dependence on God, intercession, healing. Sing a hymn of healing like "Have Thine Own Way, Lord" or "Jesus' Hands Were Kind Hands." Pray for the things members said in response to the question of Jesus, "What do you want me to do for you?"

Lections for Sunday Between October 30 and November 5

Old Testament: Ruth 1:1-18

*T*HE Book of Ruth is a story of love and loyalty first passed down by word of mouth, then finally recorded in the fifth or fourth century B.C. It is set in the earlier period of the Judges, when a loose confederacy of Hebrew tribes lived among a number of Canaanite peoples still occupying much of the land. The Hebrews were led by a series of charismatic warlords.

A Subversive Parable

The story, presenting a Moabite woman as an admirable character, was used as a "subversive parable" against an obsession with ethnic purity and exclusivism that emerged during the time of Ezra and Nehemiah after the return from exile. Other probable purposes were to stress the duty of a man to marry his dead brother's childless widow so as to produce an heir, to legitimize the ancestry of David, and to demonstrate God's blessing on persons who showed love for God and neighbor, including the alien and stranger.

"Where you go, I will go; / where you lodge, I will lodge; / your people shall be my people, / and your God my God" (Ruth 1:16). These beautiful words of fidelity spoken by the Moabite, Ruth, to her bereaved Israelite mother-in-law, Naomi, are read at weddings and cherished as expressions of friendship. A key theme in Ruth is *hesed,* translated as "deal kindly" in the NRSV, "show kindness" in the NIV, and "steadfast love" elsewhere. It refers to devoted acts of love and loyalty far exceeding expectation.

How Would God Deliver?

The story begins in Moab, a country east of the Dead Sea despised by the Israelites ever since the wilderness wanderings. Moabites and other aliens

346

were not allowed in "the assembly of YHWH" (Deuteronomy 23:3). Famine in Judah had driven Elimelech to Moab, an irony in that he was from Bethlehem ("house of bread"), one of the few grain-producing regions in Judah. Elimelech's migration echoed the journeys of Abraham (Genesis 12) and Jacob (Genesis 42) to Egypt, begging the question of how YHWH would deliver the people from calamity this time.

From Sweet to Bitter

Elimelech and his two sons had died in Moab, their names symbolic of their fates, Mahlon meaning "disease" and Chilion "weakness." Naomi, whose name means "sweet," became bitter, believing God had turned against her. After a time, the famine was over in Judah and she decided to return home. She urged Ruth and Orpah, her Moabite daughters-in-law, to return to their mothers' houses and seek new husbands. Perhaps God would "deal kindly" (show *hesed*) with them, Naomi said. Her bitterness came out as biting sarcasm: "Do I still have sons in my womb that they may become your husbands?" (Ruth 1:11).

Steadfast Love

Yet Ruth insisted on returning with Naomi, declaring that she would thenceforth adopt Naomi's home, people, and God as her own. As the story later unfolded, Ruth would help secure Naomi's future and continue the family line, giving birth to a son who would become the grandfather of King David. A foreigner's faithfulness would help preserve the people of Israel. The writer of the Book of Ruth is suggesting that Ruth's steadfast love for Naomi parallels God's steadfast love for Israel.

Think About It: "Ruth's steadfast love for Naomi parallels God's steadfast love for Israel." When have you seen the love of God demonstrated in faithful love between human beings? Do you feel God's love in the love you experience with family, friends, and fellow members of the household of God? How do you express God's love to aliens and strangers?

Psalter: Psalm 146

Unlike most psalms, which call upon the congregation to praise God, this hymn begins with self-exhortation: "Praise the LORD, O my soul!" (146:1). In Hebrew, the soul was understood as the whole living self that has desire and will (not the immortal spirit of Greek philosophy). Thus, the psalmist enjoins his or her whole self to "sing praise to my God as long as I live" (146:2, NIV). Doxology is one's true, lifelong vocation.

The beatitude at the center of the psalm tells who God is by what God has done: created the cosmos (146:6a), kept faith with the people (146:b), and

347

cared for those who cannot care for themselves (146:7-9). God is trustworthy, unlike mortal rulers, who oppress the poor and die before their plans can be realized (146:3-4).

Psalm 146 echoes repeated commandments in the Torah to provide food for foreigners, orphans, and widows (Leviticus 19:9-10; Deuteronomy 14:28-29) and anticipates the ministry of Jesus, who saw his purpose to be preaching good news to the poor (Luke 4:16-21). God's reign of justice reverses the present order, bringing down the wicked who trust in themselves rather than God (Psalm 146:9b). This psalm foreshadows Mary's song of praise, the Magnificat, in which she calls on her soul to magnify God for saving the poor and oppressed (Luke 1:46-55).

Epistle: Hebrews 9:11-14

The Hebrews lections we are currently considering are indeed difficult. Intense and closely reasoned, full of strange customs and terms, these passages assume the sacrificial practices associated with the desert tabernacle of Moses (Leviticus 16). On the annual Day of Atonement, the high priest went alone to the innermost sanctuary (the Holy of Holies) of the tabernacle to offer sacrifices to expiate the sins of the people. He sprinkled the blood of a goat and a bull on the mercy seat (a slab of gold on top of the ark of the covenant) to effect forgiveness of sin.

A Superior Sacrifice

Think About It: "Those who believe in Christ are purified from sinful behavior and their consciences cleared." How do you gain assurance that your sins are forgiven—by confession during worship or in another setting? by baptism? during Holy Communion? in your private prayer time?

In Hebrews 9:11-14, the author compares Christ to this Jewish high priest, arguing that Jesus' self-sacrifice on the cross was far superior to the action of the high priest for three reasons: (1) Christ's own blood effected the purification; (2) Christ's sacrifice only had to occur once; and (3) the expiation took place before the throne of God rather than before an ark in a tent made by humans (9:11-12). Therefore, those who believe in Christ would be purified from sinful behavior ("dead works") and their consciences cleared (9:14). God's new covenant, replacing the Jewish sacrificial cult, is ratified by the blood of Christ.

The theme of the superiority of Christ pervades the Letter to the Hebrews. Christ is presented as superior to the angels (1:5-14), to Moses (3:1-6), to Aaron (5:1-10), and to all the Levitical priests (7:1-28). The letter draws heavily on the Greek Old Testament, the Septuagint, as well as on first-

348

century Jewish speculation about the priest Melchizedek (Genesis 14; Psalm 110) to whom Christ is compared in Hebrews 7.

Polarization

Some scholars believe that this letter, with its sophisticated Greek and highly developed imagery, was written several decades after Jesus lived (A.D. 60–95) and reflects a growing awareness among the followers of Jesus of the distinctions between themselves and other Jewish sects.

Gospel: Mark 12:28-34

Mark consistently depicts the scribes and Pharisees as hostile to Jesus. They challenged his authority (Mark 11:27-28), sent questioners to entrap him (12:13-37), and sought a way to kill him (11:18).

A Friendly Scribe

Scribes were professional interpreters of the law, often from priestly families, who with the chief priests and the elders comprised the Sanhedrin, the highest Jewish council that would finally sentence Jesus to death. Yet here in this passage, one scribe, seeing how well Jesus answered his opponents, asked Jesus a genuine and respectful question: "Which commandment is the first of all?" Apparently alone among his peers, this scribe recognized Jesus' teaching authority.

A Fundamental Question

The scribe's question to Jesus was much debated by rabbis of the time, who attempted to boil down the whole law to a few fundamental principles. A famous rabbi, Hillel (35 B.C.), said, "What you yourself hate, do not do to your fellow; this is the whole law; the rest is commentary."

> **Think About It:** The rabbis tried to state the whole law in a few basic principles. What would you say is the essence of the biblical message? How would you summarize God's commands?

Jesus offered no new answer to the scribe's question. He spoke what every Jew already knew, the *Shema*: "Hear, O Israel, YHWH is our God, YHWH alone"—the first words of the instruction given by Moses to the people of Israel at Mount Horeb after the Ten Commandments (Deuteronomy 5:1; 6:4-5). Pious Jews recited the *Shema* twice daily and taught it to their children. Jesus' response also echoed the first commandment, which begins, "I am the LORD your God." On this commandment Jesus and his orthodox opponents would have been in complete agreement: God alone could command human love and obedience.

Love of God and Neighbor

Jesus then quoted Leviticus 19:18, also familiar to his hearers. These two quotations yoked love of God and neighbor. This was the essence of the law, Jesus said: Humans show their love for God by concrete acts of goodwill toward their neighbors. In the Hebrew Scriptures, neighbor was understood to mean a fellow Israelite. But Jesus' ministry to outcasts and foreigners expanded the boundaries of what *neighbor* meant.

More Than Burnt Offerings

But the scribe pushed Jesus' point even further. Applauding Jesus' answer, he added that this was "more important than all burnt offerings and sacrifices" (Mark 12:33, NIV). He saw that Jesus stood in the prophetic tradition that put justice above the cult. Jesus' answer put him at risk with his peers, especially since he had just routed the moneychangers from the Temple. Jesus seemingly had won a convert. "You are not far from the kingdom of God," he said. His enemies, though incensed, dared say no more (12:34).

This story shows that not all scribes were antagonistic to Jesus, further reinforcing his credibility. It lodges his teaching firmly in the basic credos of the Jewish faith. (Jesus quoted Deuteronomy more than any other book in the Hebrew Scriptures.) By placing this triumphal story second-to-last in the testing scenes before the Passion, Mark foreshadows Jesus' ultimate victory over his enemies in the Resurrection.

Study Suggestions

A. Sing Praise

Open by singing the first two stanzas of the hymn setting of Psalm 146, "I'll Praise My Maker While I've Breath."

B. Explore the Meaning of *Hesed as Used in the Ruth Story*

Read Ruth 1:1-18, and summarize the story of Ruth and its background and purposes. Review the meaning of the Hebrew word *hesed* from the commentary on page 346. Ask: How does Ruth show *hesed* to Naomi? What does the emphasis on the inclusion of foreigners imply for our relationships with immigrants and other outsiders today?

C. Clarify, Define, Discuss

Read Hebrews 9:11-14 in several versions and translations to uncover different nuances of meaning. Have participants highlight unfamiliar phrases or customs in the passage. Using the commentary on pages 348–49, a Bible dictionary, and/or a study Bible, clarify terms. Define *high priest, tent, holy place, sanctify*, and *redemption*.

Discuss: If the "polemics [of the Letter to the Hebrews] reflect a situation of increasing polarization between Christians and Jews," how does our contemporary situation compare with that of Hebrews? Ask: What is the relationship between Christians and Jews (and persons of other faiths)?

D. Consider the Poor
Read Psalm 146 in unison. List the categories of persons for whom God cares in verses 6-9. Ask: Who is needy in our community? What policies or laws protect them? If you are among the needy, what do you most need from the church?

E. Write a Psalm
Have each member write a psalm in the form of Psalm 146. Insert his or her name; what God has done for humankind, for him or her, for the needy; and a way that each sees God opposing the wicked. Open and close with praise. Invite volunteers to share their psalms with the whole group. Post them for viewing after class.

F. Create a Drama
Read Mark 12:28-34, and review the commentary on pages 349–50 about the relationship between Jesus and the scribes and the apparent conversion of this one in defiance of his colleagues. On what did they agree? disagree? Imagine a scenario in which the scribe friendly to Jesus is at a dinner party later that night with a scribe hostile to Jesus. Invite two persons to roleplay their dialogue. Ask other members what they have learned from the drama.

G. Pantomime Holistic Love
Read Mark 12:30 aloud. Ask a member to use motions to demonstrate the text, such as tapping the chest for "heart," cupping the hands to signify "soul," pointing to the head for "mind," and flexing the biceps for "strength." Repeat the pantomime several times, inviting others to follow along. As people become comfortable with the motions, discuss: How did the pantomime help you experience a holistic love of God? What does it mean to love God completely? Ask someone who signs to teach the group to sign this passage in sign language.

H. In Closing
Invite intercessions for the needy named in Activity E. Ask someone to read aloud her or his version of Psalm 146. Sing stanzas 3 and 4 of "I'll Praise My Maker While I've Breath."

Lections for All Saints (November 1, or may be used on first Sunday in November)

Old Testament: Isaiah 25:6-9

*A*LL Saints Day is a festival of the church honoring the departed faithful. It was originally based on the belief that souls not pure enough at death to enter heaven could be helped along by the prayers of believers on earth. Through the centuries people have decorated the graves of the departed, poured milk or holy water on their tombstones, and left food on the table in the belief that the souls of the dead would revisit their homes during the night.

These old customs have given rise to today's celebration of All Hallows Eve or Halloween, on the eve of All Saints Day, an observance that began with the pre-Christian Druids. It included the lighting of bonfires and the belief that ghosts and witches were abroad during this one night of the year. Today's customs—trick or treating in the costumes of ghosts and goblins, apple bobbing, bonfires, jack-o-lanterns, and harvest decorations—can be traced to these pagan practices and beliefs.

Think About It: The church has transformed the pagan origins of All Saints Day into an affirmation of the triumph of life over death. How can we keep the fun and mystery of Halloween in balance with the commemoration of departed saints and loved ones?

A Revival of All Saints Day

In the church the observance of All Saints Day has seen a recent revival. Worship services honor members and family who have died during the year, with bulletins listing their names and prayers of tribute and gratitude said in their memory. Faith in life after

352

death is avowed, the community of saints here and beyond is affirmed, and continuity with church tradition is strengthened. The lections selected for the day undergird this commemoration.

An Eschatological Feast

This passage from First Isaiah in the eighth century B.C. depicts the eschatological (end-time) feast of the faithful on God's holy mountain. Like a monarch celebrating his coronation, YHWH invites all peoples to Mount Zion for a grand banquet (representing peace, fulfillment, and joy), featuring the best of food and drink (verse 6). The veil of death and mourning is wiped away (verse 7), weeping is banished (verse 8a), and the misfortune and antagonism experienced by God's people are abolished (verse 8b).

The long period of waiting for the vindication and blessing of the Almighty is over at last, and God's deliverance and victory are at hand (verse 9). The people may now express their faith and joy, for God's promises are being fulfilled. This is a vision of the gladness and consummation experienced by the saints in their heavenly home.

The best-known verses in this passage are 7 and 8, which are behind Paul's words in 1 Corinthians 15:26, 54-55. In powerful metaphors and poetic rhythm, they voice the profound hope of an end to death and grief. The images of the shroud and the tears wiped away come from a Canaanite myth, in which the high god Baal conquers the lesser gods Yam (Sea) and Mot (Death). In its historical context, this passage refers to the yearning of Israel for the end of their exile and of wars and military losses; but more generally it voices a universal affirmation of life and of God's ultimate victory over death and sorrow.

Think About It: This passage affirms God's victory over death and sorrow. What sustains your faith in the eternal destiny of your departed loved ones—and your own?

Psalter: Psalm 24

This psalm, first used in an Israelite festival for the enthronement of YHWH, has three parts—a hymn of creation (verses 1-2), a liturgy for the people's entrance into the Temple (verses 3-6), and a liturgy celebrating YHWH's arrival (7-10).

A procession of priests carrying the ark of the covenant, YHWH's throne (see Exodus 25:10-22; 1 Samuel 4:1-9; 2 Samuel 6:12-15), is ascending the Temple mount (verse 3) toward the gates, praising the stability of God's creative wonders, which rest on the waters of chaos (verses 1-2; see Psalms 18:7-18 and 19:1-6).

Integrity and Purity Required

To enter the Temple, worshipers must be ritually and morally pure (verses 3-4; see Psalms 15; 25:1; 31:6). Only those who meet these conditions will be blessed and justified (verse 5) and admitted into the select fellowship of those allowed into God's holy presence (verse 6).

<table>
<tr><td>

Think About It: The psalm celebrates the coronation of God as king, creator, and warrior. How do you relate to these images of God? What images of God best invite you into worship?

</td></tr>
</table>

The gala procession twice requests the gates to open so YHWH can enter (verse 7). The One they have come to worship is a stalwart warrior, head of Israel's armies, possessing vast grandeur and power (verses 8-10; see Psalm 20:6-9).

Like the Isaiah lection, this psalm is often interpreted as an eschatological vision of the procession of the faithful into the heavenly realm and the awesome presence of almighty God.

Third Reading: Revelation 21:1-6a

A third vision of heaven and a majestic God on the throne is this well-known passage from the Apocalypse of John the Seer. It appears in a book that can be puzzling and hard to understand. Revelation was written during the reign of the Emperor Domitian (A.D. 81–96) to Christians facing both severe persecution from without and internal divisions over false teachings. John had been exiled to a penal colony on the isle of Patmos. During his exile he saw visions. He later recorded these visions and communicated them to the church in enigmatic, symbolic metaphors and allusions to give them comfort and hope.

A New Heaven and Earth

The book culminates in a final vision, introduced by the reference in today's lection to a new heaven and earth. The first creation—the universe we inhabit—has been replaced by an entirely new existence. Both the stability and sustenance provided by earth and the mystery and threat of the deep have been removed, and God has provided something much more awesome and wondrous in their place (verse 1). The first expression of this new creation is a heavenly city, approaching like a bride coming down the aisle to meet her groom (verse 2). Next comes a voice from the throne proclaiming that this city is to be the new home of the faithful who will live in intimate relationship with the Almighty (verse 3). As in Isaiah's vision, death, pain, and grief will be eliminated, since they are part of the first order of creation that is no more (verse 4; see 7:17).

The voice from the throne reiterates that all the old is to be replaced by the new, and commands John to record this true and reliable promise (verse 5). This comes with surety and finality ("It is done!") from the God who begins and ends all things (verse 6a; see 22:13). The saints are to be ushered into the very presence of God, to receive comfort and healing, and to inherit life eternal.

> **Think About It:** The saints are to be in God's comforting, healing presence and to receive everlasting life. How do you respond to this vision? What is your view of life after death?

Gospel: John 11:32-44

Our fourth All Saints lection is the story of the raising of Lazarus. The promise to the saints of life after death, which has been expressed in vision and song, is now confirmed in a miraculous (God-revealing, truth-disclosing, life-giving) event.

This is the second reference to the household of Mary, Martha, and Lazarus in the Gospel story (see Luke 10:38-42). These were Jesus' very good friends, and he seems to have felt very much at home with them. Hearing from the sisters of the illness of his friend Lazarus, Jesus risked the dangers posed by enemies in Judea and came to Bethany from across the Jordan—against the advice of his disciples. Even though bringing a dead man back to life in the outskirts of Jerusalem would surely draw the attention and anger of the authorities, Jesus determined to return. He was supported in this decision by Thomas, who in this instance showed real courage instead of the doubt usually associated with him (11:1-16). Jesus seemed to realize that the raising of Lazarus would inevitably bring about his own death (11:4), yet deliberately made the miracle prominently visible (11:6, 15, 39).

The Resurrection and the Life

John presents the raising of Lazarus so as to provide a deep theological interpretation of the event. Restoring Lazarus was symbolic of the promise that all who would find salvation in Christ were to inherit eternal life (11:25-26). This was recognized by Martha in a confession of faith equaling Peter's more famous one (11:24, 27; see Mark 8:27-29). Jesus had earlier chided her for her lack of spiritual insight (Luke 10:41-42), but now she redeemed herself (though this is often overlooked by those who stereotype her as a mere busybody) by recognizing him for who he truly was.

> **Think About It:** Martha made a confession of faith equaling that of Peter. Why do you think Martha is remembered more for being preoccupied with mundane tasks than for her spiritual insight and affirmation of faith? What parallel do you see between this stereotype and our tendency to confine women to serving roles? How can we recognize and affirm the spiritual gifts of all God's people, regardless of gender, reputation, class, or origin?

Think About It: Jesus said, "Unbind him and let him go" (11:44b). Even after he was restored to life, Lazarus was still tied up in his graveclothes and needed the help of others to be released from them. What are the graveclothes that keep you tied up and prevent you from real living? What help do you need to be freed from them? How can we assist one another become "unbound"?

Lazarus would eventually die again, said Jesus, but he would be raised from the dead by the One who is the resurrection and the life. This same promise and hope were available to all the saints who from then onward would accept the grace of Christ to free them from sin (11:25-26).

Jesus' distress during this happening (11:33, 35, 38) grew out of his concern for his friend (11:35a), the drain on his energy by the effort to heal, the skepticism of the onlookers (11:37), and the dread of what was to come. Summoning his inner resources, he commanded that the stone be removed (1:39), called on the power of God (11:41-42), and shouted with divine authority, "Lazarus, come out!" (11:43). Then he who was dead emerged, had his graveclothes removed, and returned to normal life.

Such is the offer of new life that comes from him who is the author of resurrection and of life! All saints (believers) inherit this promise.

Study Suggestions

A. Halloween and All Saints

Begin with a sharing of Halloween practices. Note the pagan origins of these customs and their ties to the Christian festival of All Saints. Discuss the "Think About It" questions about keeping the emphases of these two observances in balance.

B. Remember the Saints

Sing the first three stanzas of "For All the Saints." List the names of friends, family, church members, and public figures who have died during the past year. In a spirit of prayer, read the names one-by-one, with the group responding after each: "For the life of *(name)* _____ we praise your name, O God." During a time of silence, invite members to offer brief prayers.

C. A Coronation Banquet

Read aloud Isaiah 25:6-9, and review the commentary on pages 352–53. Explain the setting as a coronation feast, with imagery anticipating an end-time banquet in which God's promise to banish death and grief and bring joy and fulfillment is realized. Read 1 Corinthians 15, especially verses 26 and 54-55, and recount the Resurrection faith. Discuss the "Think About It" questions regarding what members believe about life after death.

D. A Festival of Enthronement

Read Psalm 24. Draw on the commentary (pages 353–54) to explain the setting and identify the three sections. Note the admission requirements—moral and ritual purity. Ask: What do you think are the standards for entrance to heaven? Explore the tension between faith and works in this regard.

Read verses 7-10 again, with a leader reading the first line of each verse, half the group reading the second, and the rest the third. Ask: What feelings does this reading evoke? How is God portrayed? What images of God are most meaningful to you?

E. A New Heaven and Earth

Read Revelation 21:1-6a. Explain the period and purpose of Revelation from the background material (pages 354–55). Play a recording of "The Heavenly City." Ask: How do you respond to this depiction of heaven? Why would this description of heaven have given hope to first-century Christians enduring persecution? What gives you encouragement in the midst of trouble? What is your expectation of heaven?

F. A Miraculous Restoration

Before reading the Gospel lection, ask: How do you define *miracle*? Is it a supernatural event or a sign of God's presence and power? By either definition, what miracles have taken place in your life? Tell the story of the raising of Lazarus, highlighting the exchange with Martha in John 11:21-27 and the climax in verses 43-44. Discuss the "Think About It" questions related to Martha's confession of faith.

Explore the "Think About It" questions related to becoming unbound from our "graveclothes." Ask: Does resurrection only take place after death or in the last days, or is God's liberating power also at work in everyday transformations? Invite members to tell of times when they have been freed from binding habits, circumstances, or unhealthy relationships? Ask: How was God present? Who helped unbind you? How can we assist God's liberating work in lives and situations around us?

G. Finding Common Themes

Identify the threads running through the four lections—eschatological visions; promises of joy and fulfillment; hope of eternal life; use of imagery to convey truths, renewal, and transformation. Ask: How do these Scriptures help you face trials and death? What comfort do they provide as we grieve the loss of loved ones? How do we best honor the memory of the saints?

H. In Closing

Sing the last three stanzas of "For All the Saints." Pass the peace with a hug or handshake and the words, "Keep the faith sister (or brother)."

Lections for Sunday Between November 6 and 12

Old Testament: Ruth 3:1-5; 4:13-17

As we saw last Sunday, Naomi came back to Bethlehem after more than ten years in Moab, a sojourn that had robbed her of her husband and two sons. She told the women of Bethlehem that she "went away full, / but the LORD has brought me back empty" (1:21). As widows, she and her daughter-in-law Ruth, a Moabite, had no means of support except begging or gleaning.

> **Think About It:** Naomi told the women of Bethlehem that she "went away full, / but the LORD has brought me back empty." Have you ever heard someone blame his or her misfortunes on God? Do you believe that "the Lord giveth and the Lord taketh away"? How do you explain undeserved suffering? (Reflect on the earlier lections from Job.)

There were kinsmen who should have assumed responsibility for Naomi and Ruth's care according to inheritance laws of the time (Deuteronomy 25:5-10). In a custom called levirate marriage, the brother of a dead man was supposed to marry the widow who would conceive a son to carry on the family name and hold the family property. Naomi seemed to have some version of this law in mind when she sent Ruth to the threshing floor at night to gain the attention of Boaz, a kinsman and a "prominent rich man" (2:1).

Ruth Took the Initiative

The storyteller does not spell out what happened on the threshing floor that night. In Hebrew, Naomi's instructions to Ruth contain sexually suggestive language: "lie down" (3:4) was frequently used to imply sexual intercourse; the "feet" she was told to "uncover" is a common euphemism for

358

"private parts." Even the verb meaning "to know" (3:3) has a dual meaning in Hebrew—either mental knowledge or sexual relations. What did Naomi have in mind for Ruth? What took place? The storyteller leaves the language ambiguous. The reader must decide.

Boaz Took a Wife

It is clear by the ensuing narrative, however, that Boaz understood Ruth's request to "spread your cloak over your servant" as a proposal for marriage (3:9). "Spread your cloak" provides a clue to the storyteller's theological purpose, too. In Chapter 2, Boaz had given this blessing to Ruth: "May you have a full reward from the LORD, the God of Israel, under whose wings you have come for refuge!" (2:12). "Cloak" and "wings" are the same word in Hebrew. Human love and divine protection are closely related.

> **Think About It:** "Cloak" and "wings" are the same word in Hebrew. Was the writer suggesting a parallel between marital love and the divine-human relationship of intimacy and care? Do you think Ruth's bold initiative was in keeping with or in violation of the customs of the time?

If God was going to provide shelter to Ruth and Naomi, it had to happen through the care of someone like Boaz, who was well situated to give aid. Boaz acted as "next-of-kin" (4:14). (The Hebrew word can also mean "redeemer.") The only place in the Book of Ruth where the storyteller directly attributes action to God was in causing Ruth to conceive (4:13). Their child Obed was grandfather of King David and ancestor of Jesus (see Matthew 1:5, 16 and Luke 3:23, 32).

Naomi Was Provided For

What of Naomi? Her empty arms became full. The women of Bethlehem who first heard Naomi's lament upon her return narrated her reversal of fortune, saying that Ruth's love and loyalty were worth "more . . . than seven sons" (4:15). Naomi's laments and scheming had been answered by acts of kindness (*hesed*) from Ruth, from Boaz, and ultimately from God.

Psalter: Psalm 42

Psalms 42 and 43 are one unit, sharing common themes and a threefold refrain (42:5; 42:11; 43:5). Oscillating between hope and despair, the psalmist longs for a renewed assurance of God's help against scornful enemies. Recalling former pilgrimages to the Temple, the speaker wishes he could gather again with other worshipers (42:4) to play the harp at the altar (43:4). The Korahites, to whom this psalm is attributed, were a group of

Temple singers who collected and preserved a repertoire of psalms (2 Chronicles 20:19).

The poet's current distress is heightened by the taunts of enemies who assume that he has been forsaken by God (42:10). The exact nature of the speaker's situation is not specified, allowing the psalm to speak to a variety of personal and national troubles. Exiles would resonate with its fierce longing to worship again in the Temple.

Scholars debate whether the psalm's composer actually lived near Mount Hermon at the headwaters of the Jordan, or was only remembering that setting as a place of blessing (42:6). The whitewater cataracts of the upper Jordan suggest relief for the psalmist's "thirsty" soul (42:6b-7a), although he turns again to feeling overwhelmed: "All your waves and your billows have gone over me" (42:7b). The repeated refrain steadies the psalmist and ends on a note of hope.

Epistle: Hebrews 9:24-28

In this passage, the author of the Letter to the Hebrews repeats and reinforces earlier arguments that the self-sacrifice of Christ is superior to the sacrifices made by the Jewish high priests on the Day of Atonement. Made by his own blood, once and for all, accomplished in heaven, Christ's sacrifice effects full and final forgiveness of sin. Moreover, Christ intercedes for sinners in the very presence of God (9:24), his role as intercessor having already been described in 7:25.

No Fear

In the Old Testament, an offering of blood was used to inaugurate covenants and provide cleansing from sin. The author of Hebrews says that "without the shedding of blood there is no forgiveness of sins" (9:22). Though strange to modern readers, ancient peoples saw blood as equivalent to life. A blood offering was a substitute for one's whole life, which God, being God, had a right to demand. People dared not approach God without the blood substitute. In the view of Hebrews, Christ's offering of himself provided that blood sacrifice, making it possible for Christians to approach God without fear.

> **Think About It:** "A blood offering was a substitute for one's whole life, which God, being God, had a right to demand." What does God have right to demand from you? If we do not make blood sacrifices, how do we offer our whole lives to God?

The Shadow of the Real

Jews believed that the desert tabernacle (the "sanctuary made by human hands" in 9:24) was an earthly representation of the real heavenly sanctuary.

360

The Greek philosopher Plato believed that the earthly, material world was but a shadow of the real world of ideas and invisible substances. The author of Hebrews may have been trying to appeal to educated, Greek-speaking believers with this allusion to the Platonic understanding of reality.

Ransom for Many

Verses 27 and 28 may have been part of an early catechism associated with baptism. They use parallel reasoning: just as mortals die once and face judgment, Christ died once but will come again for the faithful. The phrase, "to bear the sins of many," echoes the suffering servant motif of Isaiah 53:12, as well as Jesus' own words in Mark 10:45, "The Son of Man came . . . to give his life [as] a ransom for many."

Gospel: Mark 12:38-44

This lection joins a warning and a commendation. Jesus warned the crowd to beware of scribes who parade their piety but "devour widows' houses" (12:40). He commended a poor widow whose tiny offering to the Temple outshone the lavish gifts of the wealthy (12:41-44).

> **Think About It:** The disciples could not see that wealth was a barrier to entering God's realm. How do material concerns hinder our faith? When do we rely on our own resources instead of God?

Scribal Practice and Privilege

Widows, orphans, aliens, and the poor were the most vulnerable members of ancient society, prey to unscrupulous leaders whose business practices legitimated eviction and debt slavery. The privileges the wealthy assumed as normal were ornate robes, seats of honor, and titles of respect (12:38-39). The special robes of the scribes, usually worn for prayer and scribal duties, were a trademark of their profession when seen in the marketplace and a visual reminder of their piety.

An Echo of the Prophets

Jesus' barbed words echoed Old Testament prophets such as Amos, Isaiah, and Micah, who condemned the wealthy who took advantage of the poor (see Amos 4:1-5; Isaiah 10:1-2). Such prophets predicted the wrath of God upon corrupt leaders, even as Jesus predicted the coming of the Son of Man in judgment and glory (Mark 13). The scribes could expect "greater condemnation," Jesus said, because they used the name of God to mask what they were doing (12:40).

This teaching, which took place in the Temple where Jesus had been disputing with various religious leaders since arriving in Jerusalem, was scathing. Jesus impugned their character and motives, implying that all scribes were alike. Having issued similar warnings about the Pharisees and Herodians (8:15), Jesus seems to have burned all his bridges in relation to these leaders. Yet the "large crowd was listening to him with delight" (12:37b). These words of Jesus were recalled by Mark when he wrote his Gospel during the time Christians found it necessary to separate themselves from Jewish traditions and practices.

An Exemplary Widow

Widow seems to be the catchword that joins the two incidents. Moving to another area of the Temple, the treasury (perhaps near the women's court), Jesus praised a poor widow's offering. How did he know she had given "all she had to live on"? Perhaps he inferred it by knowing the destitution in which most widows lived. How did he know how much the rich were giving? Perhaps it was obvious by their large money pouches.

At any rate, Jesus told his disciples that, with her two coins of the smallest denomination (worth about 1/64 of a daily wage), the widow had put in more than all the rest. This was a shocking statement, given the bulging pouches they had just seen emptied. Her gift exceeded all the others because, while they had given out of their surplus, she had given "all she had to live on," which means literally "her whole life" (12:43-44). Perhaps Jesus was implying that the Pharisees gave gifts they had improperly taken from others, but the widow gave of her own meager means.

Think About It: They gave out of their surplus; she gave her all. Reflect on your giving practices in light of this comparison.

With this teaching, Jesus countered the usual practice of religious institutions—to court the rich and disregard the poor. The story of the widow also anticipates the Passion, in which Jesus would give up "his whole life."

Study Suggestions

A. Open With Praise

Form two groups and recite Psalm 42:1-5 aloud, responsively, alternating each half-verse.

B. Ruth and Boaz

Read Ruth 3:1-5; 4:13-17, recalling the beginning of the story. Review the commentary on pages 358–59. Ask: Where is God at work in this story—according to Naomi? the narrator? your own view? What is the relationship between human planning and God's action? How do you see that relationship in your own life?

As their kinsman, Boaz was well situated to provide help to Ruth and Naomi. Invite members to think of their extended families. Ask: How do our inheritance laws and practices differ from those in this story? In what ways do persons care for one another in your family? To whom are you well situated to provide help?

C. A Thirst for God

Bring in a pitcher of water, a bowl, and some paper cups. Pour water from pitcher to bowl several times. Take a noisy drink without offering water to others. Ask participants to remember times when they were really thirsty—hiking in a desert, taking medication that dried their mouths, waiting in a line in the hot sun. Then read Psalm 42:1-2. Reflect: How does the image of thirst express our longing for God? Now give water to all.

D. Mood Swings

Read all of Psalm 42 and the commentary on pages 359–60. Invite members to recall times when their moods oscillated between hope and despair. Ask: What caused your distress? Did worship help? What did you say to God? Read verse 11 several times to memorize it for comfort in difficult times.

E. Blood Sacrifice

Read Hebrews 9:24-28 and study the commentary on pages 360–61. Hebrews assumes the legitimacy of a sacrificial system, arguing that Jesus' self-sacrifice supersedes the animal sacrifice associated with the Temple. Ask: How do you describe what Christ has done for us? Also discuss the "Think About It" questions.

F. Present-Day Scribes

Read Mark 12:38-40 and the related commentary on pages 361–62. Explain the position of scribes in the society of Jesus' time. Brainstorm: Who is the modern equivalent of the scribes—television evangelists who get rich by soliciting money from elderly viewers? churchgoers who lead in worship but engage in unfair labor practices? clergy absorbed with their own egos? What would Jesus say to them? What is the word of grace for them?

G. A Widow's Giving—and Ours

Read Mark 12:41-44 and the commentary on page 362. Ask: What does the story of the poor widow imply about how our church conducts its financial campaigns? What does it say to our personal financial situation and giving habits? How might our stewardship practices change if Jesus were to confront us about them?

H. Close With Consecration

Invite members to reflect on their lives in light of this week's themes of family responsibility, spiritual thirst, Christ's redemption, and sacrificial giving. Then sing a hymn of consecration such as "Take My Life, and Let It Be" or "When I Survey the Wondrous Cross."

Lections for Sunday Between
November 13 and 19

F Old Testament: 1 Samuel 1:4-20

IRST Samuel 1:4-20 tells of how God hears the prayer of a stubborn woman. It returns to pick up a part of the Samuel narrative that preceded the lection for the second Sunday after the Epiphany. The Samuel narrative was also studied the Sunday between May 29 and June 4 and the following weeks. Hannah, the favored wife of a hill-country man named Elkanah, could endure the taunts of Penninah, the fruitful wife, no longer. Hannah was unable to conceive. She left the celebratory meal following the family's yearly offering at Shiloh and went to the sanctuary to pour out her bitterness before God. She vowed that if God would give her a son she would dedicate him to God.

A Poured-Out Soul

Hannah prayed so intensely that Eli, the priest on duty, thought she was drunk (the same charge made against the spirit-filled disciples at Pentecost in Acts 2:13). She defended herself as a "troubled" woman (1 Samuel 1:15), which could also be translated as "obstinate" or "stubborn." Instead of pouring out wine, however, she had been pouring out her soul. Eli blessed her and, though not knowing her vow, asked God to grant it.

The Nazirite Vow

Hannah vowed that, should she be granted a child, he would become a Nazirite, that is, "one separated" or "one consecrated" to God. Nazirites abstained from alcohol and did not cut their hair (Numbers 6). Samson, a well-known Nazirite, was set apart to deliver Israel from the Philistines (Judges 13:1-24). John the Baptist, who was told to abstain from "wine or strong drink" like a Nazirite (Luke 1:15), was set apart for the work of preparing for the Messiah.

Perseverance in Prayer

Hannah's story echoes that of Sarah (Genesis 16) and Rachel (Genesis 30), as well as foreshadowing the story of Elizabeth (Luke 1:5-24). In contrast to the others, however, Hannah took the initiative and went directly to God with her prayer, trusting in God to provide. Jesus commended that same kind of *chutzpah* in the parable of the persistent widow, urging his followers to persevere in prayer (Luke 18:1-8).

> ***Think About It:*** Jesus commended Hannah's *chutzpah,* urging perseverance in prayer. How do you relate this emphasis on perseverance to Jesus' statement that "[God] knows what you need before you ask" (Matthew 6:8)? How persistently do you ask God for your needs? Are you too polite with God? What is the difference between being polite and just trusting?

Given and Given Back

When Hannah and Elkanah returned home and resumed marital relations, God "remembered" Hannah, and she conceived a son (1 Samuel 1:19-20). She named him Samuel (which means "name of God" or "God hears"), declaring that she had asked him of the Lord. But what she had asked of God she would give back by dedicating him to God's service. Samuel became a great prophet, anointing the first king of Israel, Saul, and overseeing the transition from a tribal confederacy to a monarchy.

> ***Think About It:*** What Hannah had asked of God she would give back. The prayer and dedication of a godly mother formed Samuel for future service. How have your family relationships formed the lives of your children? How do you pray with and for your children?

Psalter: Psalm 113

This hymn of praise, traditionally used at the Passover meal, may well have been sung by Jesus and the disciples (Mark 14:26). Psalm 113:1-3 calls upon the congregation to praise God all day long. Verses 4-6 describe God seated in glory above the earth. Verses 7-9 exhort praise because God has exalted the humble, a theme also preached by Jesus (Luke 18:14).

The psalm expresses God's desire for economic justice and compassion, as conveyed by repeated commands in the Law and the Prophets to care for the widow, the orphan, and the poor—as well as by the Year of Jubilee, which mandated the release of slaves and the forgiveness of debts (Leviticus 25; Deuteronomy 15).

Psalm 133:7-8 has a direct parallel in 1 Samuel 2:8, a very old poem of thanksgiving. The psalm's joyous themes are voiced by women throughout the Scriptures: Sarah, who called her long-awaited son Isaac, meaning "laughter" (Genesis 21:6-7); Hannah, who dedicated her prayed-for son to the priesthood (1 Samuel 1:1–2:10); and Mary, who sang for herself and her once-childless cousin, Elizabeth (Luke 1:46-55).

Epistle: Hebrews 10:11-25

The author of the Letter to the Hebrews brings his arguments about the superiority of Christ over the sacrifices of the Temple cult to a close here in Chapter 10. Summarizing previous points, the author stresses the repeated, ineffective, even tedious nature of priestly sacrificial rites as contrasted with the one-time, fully sufficient sacrifice of Christ.

Going on to Perfection

By this single offering Christ has "perfected" those "who are sanctified" (10:14). The Greek *hagiazo* is present tense, suggesting that this perfection is in process. By *perfection,* the author of Hebrews does not mean moral flawlessness but rather being wholly dedicated to God, completing what God has given one to do (5:8-9; 7:19). "Going on to perfection" became a key element in the theology of John Wesley, who believed that persons, though they still made mistakes, could become "perfected" in love.

> **Think About It:** Perfection refers to being wholly dedicated to God. Are you "going on to perfection"? Do you expect to be made perfect in this life?

A New Covenant

The author triumphantly cites Psalm 110:1, a favorite of Greek-speaking Christian writers, who understood it as David's prediction of the exaltation of Jesus (Hebrews 10:12-13; Mark 12:35-37). The "enemies" that will become a "footstool for his feet" (Hebrews 10:13) are not specified, but could point to "the one who has the power of death, that is, the devil" (2:14). The author also refers to Jeremiah 31:31-34, which describes a new covenant God will write on people's hearts (Hebrews 10:16). All of Hebrews 8:1–10:18 is a commentary on Jeremiah 31, claiming the promises of the prophet by the power of the Holy Spirit (10:15).

Verses 19 through 25 spell out the implications of Christ's sacrifice for human behavior, using the formula, "therefore, . . . let us. . . ." The author, sounding like a preacher, gives his congregation a threefold admonition: have faith, hold fast to hope, and care for one another with love. (The triad of faith, hope, and love is familiar to many Christians from 1 Corinthians 13:13.) The second verb in the intriguing invitation, "let us consider how to provoke one another to love and good deeds" (Hebrews 10:24), can also be translated "to pester." They should pester each other to meet together in worship and encourage those dismayed by the delay of Christ's coming (10:25).

Gospel: Mark 13:1-8

Jesus prepared the disciples for what would happen after his crucifixion: years of persecution and turmoil. The community for which Mark prepared his Gospel was struggling with confusion, false teachers, and discouragement. Chapter 13 combines apocalyptic elements (revelation about the end times, including cosmic signs, such as in Daniel and Revelation) and a farewell discourse (a special address in which a great leader teaches his followers just before his death, such as those given by Jacob and Moses).

A Private Lesson

After leaving the Temple, Jesus took Peter, James, John, and Andrew aside—not the first time he had instructed his disciples privately (see 4:10; 7:17; 9:28; 10:10). The setting on the Mount of Olives was significant. From this high hill east of Jerusalem, one could see the whole Temple complex. King Herod built a series of public buildings on the Temple mount as a major public works program to provide employment in job-scarce Judea. The Temple was a magnificent architectural achievement. Massive stones, 37 by 12 by 18 feet, undergirded the courtyard. When the Romans razed Jerusalem in A.D. 70, they burned the Temple, then dismantled the entire complex of buildings. Only part of the supporting wall remained, still visible today.

What About the End?

Though Chapter 13 contains apocalyptic themes, it lacks the complex timetables and bizarre images found in other apocalypses. This restraint suggests that Jesus wanted to discourage end-time speculation. When the disciples asked Jesus when the Temple would be destroyed, he sidestepped their question, urging them to beware of deception, rumors, and conflict (13:5-8). This was the same advice Jesus gave to Peter, James, and John in Gethsemane when he went off to pray (14:34). He wanted to strengthen them for difficult times. They must persevere through suffering as he did (13:13).

> **Think About It:** Jesus wanted to strengthen the disciples for difficult times. Recall times when things were bad. How were you tempted to lose faith? What choices did you have? What strengthened you?

Since Mark was written after A.D. 70, the prophecy of Jesus about the destruction of the Temple had come true.

Beware False Teachers

False teachers, products of the fanatical times, troubled the early church. Some were revolutionaries (Acts 21:38), claiming to be the messiah—"I am he!" (Mark 13:6). Others said they were a reincarnation of Christ—"in my name" (13:6). In Acts 20:29-30, Paul warned the Ephesian elders that "savage wolves will come in among you, not sparing the flock, . . . distorting the truth." These impostors taught that the end was near—against 2 Thessalonians 2:2-3. "Do not be alarmed" (Mark 13:7) is the consistent advice.

Some Christians believe that Chapter 13 is about the end of the world rather than Jesus' specific prediction that the Temple would be destroyed. Jesus' prediction was taken seriously. Jesus was arrested and tried on the charge that he predicted the Temple would be destroyed (14:58). Jesus refused to give a precise date, but many who heard his prophecy were alive when the Temple was destroyed.

Jesus was not the only prophet to predict the destruction of the Temple. Jeremiah (26:6) and Micah (3:12) had warned that the first Temple, Solomon's Temple, would come down. Another man, Rabbi ben Zakkai, a contemporary of Jesus, foretold the fall of the second Temple. Jesus' enemies thought he threatened to destroy the Temple himself (John 2:19-22; Mark 14:58; 15:29), not understanding he was referring symbolically to his own body.

Study Suggestions

A. Open With Praise

Recite Psalm 113 aloud together. Point out its emphasis on God's concern for economic justice.

B. Tell the Story

Review 1 Samuel 1:4-20 and the commentary on pages 364–65. Form four groups. Assign each group one character—Hannah, Penninah, Elkanah, or Eli. Have them tell the story from the perspective of their character. Ask: According to this character, how was God at work in these events?

C. Reflect on Vows

Review the paragraph, "The Nazirite Vow." Read Numbers 6. Compare the vows taken by ancient Nazirites to contemporary vows such as those made in marriage, at baptism, or for religious orders (such as "poverty, chastity, and obedience"). Discuss: What do vows accomplish? Why are they important? What vows have you made? What holds you faithful to them?

D. Draft a New Covenant

Read aloud Hebrews 10:11-18 and the related commentary on page 366. Compare the Hebrews passage to Jeremiah 31:31-34. How does the author of the Letter to the Hebrews use the passage from Jeremiah in his argument? How has Christ accomplished what was promised by Jeremiah? Write Jeremiah's new covenant in your own words.

E. Desire Good Deeds

Review Hebrews 10:19-25 and the final paragraph of the Hebrews commentary on pages 366–67. List the things the author wants the hearers to do. Read Hebrews 13:1-6 to expand the list. Put an * by those "good deeds" that occur regularly in your congregation. Put a + by those you need to work on.

F. Interweave Songs of Praise

Make large-print copies of Psalm 113 and Luke 1:46-55. Have group members cut the copies into separate verses and group similar ideas together. Note how the two songs of praise contrast or complement each other. Fit the various verses into one long song of praise. Recite in unison or divide into two parts according to source.

G. Sit With the Disciples

Read Mark 13:1-5 and the commentary through "A Private Lesson" (page 367). Review the other passages in Mark in which Jesus instructed his disciples privately (4:10; 7:17; 9:28; 10:10). Imagine what it must have been like to be in Jesus' inner circle. What were the joys? the responsibilities? How well did the inner circle understand and follow Jesus' teaching? How would you have done?

H. Explore "Apocalypse"

Read Mark 13:1-8 and the commentary on pages 367–68. Using a study Bible or theological dictionary, define *apocalypse*. Review Mark 13 for some of the elements of apocalyptic literature, such as predictions of wars, famines, political turmoil, earthquakes, cosmic disturbances, battles between angelic and demonic powers, and symbolic numbers. Ask: Why did apocalyptic literature speak so strongly to people in Jesus' time? How are our times like those times? different? How is apocalyptic thinking expressed in our day? How do you respond to it?

Ask participants to discuss in pairs: How are all of us confronted by our end? Does the knowledge you will die one day determine how you live your life?

I. Close With Song and Prayer

Sing a hymn of expectation in times of turmoil, such as "It Is Well With My Soul" or "Lo, He Comes with Clouds Descending." Close in silent prayer, inviting members to make vows to God about the changes in behavior considered in Activity H.

Lections for Reign of Christ, Sunday Between November 20 and 26

Old Testament: 2 Samuel 23:1-7

*T*HIS Sunday celebrates Christ the King. The Scriptures show Jesus as the one who fulfills the Old Testament messianic promises about the dynasty of David and yet changes the understanding of what God's king will be like and what he will do. This observance on the last Sunday of the church year acknowledges both Christ's sovereignty over all of creation and his lordship over our individual hearts and lives.

Last Will and Testament

The poem in 2 Samuel 23:1-7 is presented as David's last words and is appended to the narratives about King David and his family. Because most cultures believe dying persons are given special insight through their maturity and their proximity to death, these words carry extra weight. The poem is also understood as an oracle, an inspired prophetic utterance given to the speaker by God, who raised him up for a special purpose (23:1-2).

> **Think About It:** David is identified as someone who was lifted up by God's power for a special purpose. Was this unique to David or does God have a special purpose for each of us? What is God's purpose for you? What will never happen in this world unless you do it?

Reliance on God

David is identified by his full name, "son of Jesse," and as "the man whom God exalted," a phrase that suggests someone with no hereditary claim to kingship who was lifted up only by God's power. Some scholars believe the poem dates to the time of the early monarchy and could have come from David himself. The poem's artistry, the theme of reliance on God (see 1 Samuel 18:14), and the awareness of the distance between God's expectations and human sinfulness (see 2 Samuel 12:13) all fit with David's life.

The final phrase of verse 1 is translated in some manuscripts as "the favorite of the songs of Israel" or "the sweet singer of Israel," referring to David as the subject (1 Samuel 18:7) or creator (1 Samuel 16:23; 2 Samuel 1:17-18) of songs.

An Eternal Covenant

The oracle, comprising verses 3-4 and 6-8, compares a righteous king to the rising sun on a bright morning, contrasting him with "godless" or "evil" (NIV) people, who are thorns that cause pain and choke off life. David interrupts the oracle with the assertion that his "house" (his rule and descendants) is right with God, and that God has promised to secure his dynasty forever. This Davidic covenant, which sustained Judah after the Exile and fanned later messianic hopes, was first spoken by the prophet Nathan in 2 Samuel 7:8-17 (see also 2 Chronicles 13:5; Psalm 89:3, 28-29; Isaiah 55:3; and Jeremiah 33:15-17).

An Ideal King

The Davidic covenant represents an idealized picture of kingship. The king must rule over people "justly" and "in the fear of God" (23:3). The actual story of David's life shows many times when he failed to live up to this ideal, such as his sin against Bathsheba and Uriah (2 Samuel 11–12; see lections for Sundays between July 24 and August 6). Yet he repented and maintained the image of a king who knew and obeyed God's law and thus deserved the adulation of his people and became the model and forebear of the Messiah and of "Christ the King."

The placement of this poem at the end of Second Samuel shows that David's abuses of power and family tragedies were not the last word. God would continue to work through David's heirs to secure justice in the land.

Psalm 132:1-12 (13-18)

This royal psalm was sung by worshipers as they climbed the slopes toward Jerusalem on pilgrimage to the Temple. It reenacts the procession of David bringing the ark to Jerusalem after making it his new capital (2 Samuel 6:1-19). It then asks God to remember David and his dynasty, securing their future reign. The psalm accents God's choice of David as king and of Zion (Jerusalem) as dwelling place.

Psalm 132 points backward and forward in the story of the Jews. Verses 8 and 9 call upon God to march forth in victory to protect the people, recalling the words of Moses whenever the ark moved: "Arise, O LORD, let your enemies be scattered" (Numbers 10:35). According to 2 Chronicles 6:41, Solomon spoke verses 8-9 of the psalm at the Temple dedication. For the community in exile, bereft of both Temple and king, these verses would express hope for the future in the form of a Davidic messiah to come.

Verse 1 calls on God to remember "all the hardships" that David endured, perhaps referring to his effort in bringing the ark to Jerusalem or to his trials as a fugitive before becoming king. *Hardships* can also be interpreted broadly to refer to the trials of the nation of Israel whom David represents. *The Tanakh*, an English translation of the Hebrew Scriptures, renders verse 1 as "remember in David's favor / his extreme self-denial," suggesting all David did to insure the welfare of his people. That self-denial presages the life and death of Jesus, hailed as a "Son of David" by a festal crowd, who humbled himself and was exalted (Philippians 2:8-9).

Third Reading: Revelation 1:4-8

After a brief introduction (1:1-3), the Revelation to John opens with a greeting (1:4-5a) which is interrupted by a doxology (1:5b-6) that is interrupted again by an ecstatic vision (1:7-8). It is as if John could not get the words out fast enough to convey his sense of the unutterable glory of God accompanied by the triumphant presence of the resurrected Christ.

Apocalypse

The Revelation to John is an apocalypse containing letters to seven churches in Asia Minor that were experiencing severe persecution. Threatened with imprisonment (2:10) and death (6:9-11), these Christians in crisis needed reassurance that God controlled history and that Christ, who also had suffered, was victorious. The strong imagery and symbolic language of apocalyptic writing stirred the hearers' emotions and gave them comfort.

> **Think About It:** These Christians in crisis needed reassurance that God controlled history. Recall a time of crisis or chaos in your life. How was God present? What gave you reassurance?

Greetings From God

The traditional greeting (1:4-5), like those in Paul's letters, conveys good will and blessing from God through John. God is named as "him who is and who was and who is to come," a phrase that echoes Exodus 3:14. "Who is to come" stresses God's future action of vanquishing evil and redeeming the faithful. The "seven spirits" around the throne were viewed as "guardian angels" for the seven churches.

The Witness of Christ

The portrait of Jesus in 1:5a encompasses his death, resurrection, and sovereignty. Our English word *martyr* is derived from the Greek word meaning "witness." The doxology (1:5b-6) that praises Christ's atoning death again echoes Exodus 19:6, describing the "priestly kingdom" of disciples. John envisions Christ's return to rule as king over all the earth (Daniel 7:13-14; Mark 8:38).

Gospel: John 18:33-37

"Are you the king of the Jews?" This question drives the dialogue between Jesus and Pilate in John 18:33-37. The question was a political charge (treason) with religious overtones. For centuries, devout Jews had been hoping for a king like David, anointed by God, who would expel foreign rulers and restore the nation to Jewish rule. Hatred of the corrupt and barbaric Roman Empire had further inflamed this messianic hope. Different leaders had risen up, claimed to be the Messiah, amassed followers, led armed revolts, and been ruthlessly put down. During the great pilgrimage festivals such as Passover, when Jerusalem swelled to several times its normal population, the city seethed with anti-Roman sentiment.

What Kind of King?

Into this highly charged atmosphere Jesus rode on a donkey, an action expected of the Messiah (Zechariah 9:9). The crowds met Jesus waving palm branches, a symbol of Jewish nationalism, and shouting "Blessed is the one who comes in the name of the Lord—/ the King of Israel!" (John 12:13). Hearing Jesus say he would be "seated at the right hand of the Power" (Mark 14:62), the Jewish authorities charged him with blasphemy (claiming power held only by God). In a gesture to Rome, they brought Jesus to Pilate.

Pilate in the Middle

The interrogation of Jesus took place inside the praetorium, which included the governor's palace. The Jewish leaders waited outside so they would not be defiled by contact with Gentiles before the Passover feast (18:28). Pilate moved back and forth between the Jewish leaders and Jesus (18:33). The choreography illustrates the complex political situation—Pilate was caught between the demands of the Jewish leaders and the innocence of the accused (18:38 and 19:6). The high priest Caiaphas owed his job to Rome, and Pilate relied on the Jewish leaders to help keep order. Yet the Jews hated the Romans, and Pilate despised them.

A Strange Dialogue

Jesus answered Pilate's question with a question of his own, amazing behavior for a man facing a capital charge. Jesus put Pilate on the spot, challenging him to take responsibility for his own judgment (18:34). Pilate sidestepped Jesus' question by reminding him that his own people, not the Roman soldiers, had brought him in. Jesus replied that were he interested in political kingship, his followers would have fought his capture. Though a king, his kingdom was not "from this world" (18:36).

Power From Above

The preposition *from* can also mean "of," as in "belonging to" or "originating from." Jesus meant that his authority came not from the coercive power of earthly rulers but from his relationship with God. "I am from above," Jesus had told them (8:23), but they had not understood (8:27). Neither did Pilate. However, Jesus said (18:37), those who "belong to the truth," who "listen to my voice," do understand.

> **Think About It:** "Jesus would guard and guide his sheep in time of trouble." Though US Christians rarely face situations of outright religious persecution, they may face resistance when taking a moral stand. What risks have you taken because of your faith? How has Christ strengthened you?

Jesus Unafraid

By showing this picture of Jesus unafraid in his witness before Pilate, the Gospel writer strengthened the members of his community who were facing persecution for their testimony. The phrase about listening to Jesus' voice recalls the image of the good shepherd (10:3-5). Jesus would guard and guide his sheep in time of trouble.

Study Suggestions

A. Open With Praise

Sing a hymn celebrating the kingship of Christ such as "O Worship the King" or "At the Name of Jesus."

B. Consider Kingship

Comment that this is Christ the King or Reign of Christ Sunday, and draw on the commentary (page 370) to explain its significance. Invite participants to free-associate on the word *king*. What images or ideas come up? Then ask them to free-associate on *Christ the King* and note any new images or concepts. Discuss what it means for citizens of a democracy to use the word *king* to describe Jesus. Does the image have power for us? What other images might be used to express Christ's claim on our allegiance?

C. Write a Job Description

Read aloud 2 Samuel 23:1-7, and review the commentary on pages 370–71. Make a job description for a perfect king. What qualities does a good ruler have? What are the sources of his power?

D. Last Words
Compare 2 Samuel 23:1-7 with 1 Kings 2:1-9, other final words attributed to David. What does each source say about David? What words of wisdom might you pass on to others near the close of your life?

E. Titles for Christ
List the different titles for Jesus in Revelation 1:4-8. Ask: What does each suggest about him? What are your favorite names for Jesus? Why?

F. Experience Revelation
Ask three persons to read Revelation 1:4-5a, 5b-6, and 7-8 with dramatic emphasis. Ask other group members to listen and report: What phrases or images struck you? How did you feel? What did hearing this Scripture make you want to do? Distribute paper and markers and ask members to express these responses in an art form.

G. Make a Pilgrimage
Review the commentary on Psalm 132:1-12 (pages 371–72). Imagine worshipers climbing the hill toward the Temple singing this psalm. Imagine their pride and their hope. Lead the group in reciting the psalm aloud, picturing themselves among the pilgrims.

H. Dramatize a Dialogue
Ask two persons to stand facing each other and read aloud the dialogue between Jesus and Pilate in John 18:33-37, omitting narration and speaker attribution. Then discuss: What was at stake in this dialogue for Pilate? for Jesus? What did Pilate want? What did Jesus want?

I. Clarify "Kingdom"
Review the Scripture reference and commentary (pages 373–74) on John 18:33-37. Clarify: What did Jesus mean by "my kingdom is not from this world"? What are the hallmarks of Jesus' kingdom? From where does Jesus' authority to rule come?

J. Play the "Hallelujah Chorus"
Play a recording of the "Hallelujah Chorus" from Handel's *Messiah*, noting the triumphal declaration, "The kingdom of this world is become the Kingdom of our Lord and of his Christ." Ask: How is this true? What are the signs of Christ's kingdom among us?

K. Close With Prayer
Review the Lord's Prayer, phrase by phrase (Matthew 6:9-13). What does this prayer tell us about "Christ the King" and the "Reign of Christ." Close by reciting this prayer in unison.

List of Scriptures

Revised Common Lectionary, Year B

SEASON OF ADVENT
First Sunday of Advent
Isaiah 64:1-9
Psalm 80:1-7, 17-19
1 Corinthians 1:3-9
Mark 13:24-37
Second Sunday of Advent
Isaiah 40:1-11
Psalm 85:1-2, 8-13
2 Peter 3:8-15a
Mark 1:1-8
Third Sunday of Advent
Isaiah 61:1-4, 8-11
Psalm 126
1 Thessalonians 5:16-24
John 1:6-8, 19-28
Fourth Sunday of Advent
2 Samuel 7:1-11, 16
Luke 1:46-55
Romans 16:25-27
Luke 1:26-38

SEASON OF CHRISTMAS
Christmas Day
Isaiah 52:7-10
Psalm 98
Hebrews 1:1-4 (5-12)

John 1:1-14
First Sunday After Christmas Day
Isaiah 61:10–62:3
Psalm 148
Galatians 4:4-7
Luke 2:22-40

SEASON OF EPIPHANY
Epiphany of the Lord
Isaiah 60:1-6
Psalm 72:1-7, 10-14
Ephesians 3:1-12
Matthew 2:1-12
Baptism of the Lord, First Sunday After the Epiphany
Genesis 1:1-5
Psalm 29
Acts 19:1-7
Mark 1:4-11
Second Sunday After the Epiphany
1 Samuel 3:1-10
Psalm 139:1-6, 13-18
1 Corinthians 6:12-20
John 1:43-51
Third Sunday After the Epiphany
Jonah 3:1-5, 10
Psalm 62:5-12

1 Corinthians 7:29-31
Mark 1:14-20
Fourth Sunday After the Epiphany
Deuteronomy 18:15-20
Psalm 111
1 Corinthians 8:1-13
Mark 1:21-28
Fifth Sunday After the Epiphany
Isaiah 40:21-31
Psalm 147:1-11, 20c
1 Corinthians 9:16-23
Mark 1:29-39
Sixth Sunday After the Epiphany
2 Kings 5:1-14
Psalm 30
1 Corinthians 9:24-27
Mark 1:40-45
Seventh Sunday After the Epiphany
Isaiah 43:18-25
Psalm 41
2 Corinthians 1:18-22
Mark 2:1-12
Eighth Sunday After the Epiphany
Hosea 2:14-20
Psalm 103:1-13, 22
2 Corinthians 3:1-6
Mark 2:13-22
Transfiguration Sunday
2 Kings 2:1-12
Psalm 50:1-6
2 Corinthians 4:3-6
Mark 9:2-9

SEASON OF LENT
First Sunday in Lent
Genesis 9:8-17
Psalm 25:1-10
1 Peter 3:18-22
Mark 1:9-15
Second Sunday in Lent
Genesis 17:1-7, 15-16
Psalm 22:23-31
Romans 4:13-25
Mark 8:31-38

Third Sunday in Lent
Exodus 20:1-17
Psalm 19
1 Corinthians 1:18-25
John 2:13-22
Fourth Sunday in Lent
Numbers 21:4-9
Psalm 107:1-3, 17-22
Ephesians 2:1-10
John 3:14-21
Fifth Sunday in Lent
Jeremiah 31:31-34
Psalm 51:1-12
Hebrews 5:5-10
John 12:20-33
Passion/Palm Sunday
Isaiah 50:4-9a
Psalm 31:9-16
Philippians 2:5-11
Mark 15:1-47

SEASON OF EASTER
Easter Day
Acts 10:34-43
Psalm 118:1-2, 14-24
1 Corinthians 15:1-11
John 20:1-18
Second Sunday of Easter
Acts 4:32-35
Psalm 133
1 John 1:1–2:2
John 20:19-31
Third Sunday of Easter
Acts 3:12-19
Psalm 4
1 John 3:1-7
Luke 24:36b-48
Fourth Sunday of Easter
Acts 4:5-12
Psalm 23
1 John 3:16-24
John 10:11-18
Fifth Sunday of Easter
Acts 8:26-40

378

Psalm 22:25-31
1 John 4:7-21
John 15:1-8
Sixth Sunday of Easter
Acts 10:44-48
Psalm 98
1 John 5:1-6
John 15:9-17
The Ascension of the Lord
Acts 1:1-11
Psalm 47
Ephesians 1:15-23
Luke 24:44-53
Seventh Sunday of Easter
Acts 1:15-17, 21-26
Psalm 1
1 John 5:9-13
John 17:6-19
Day of Pentecost
Acts 2:1-21
Psalm 104:24-34, 35b
Romans 8:22-27
John 15:26-27; 16:4b-15

SUNDAYS AFTER PENTECOST
Trinity Sunday
Isaiah 6:1-8
Psalm 29
Romans 8:12-17
John 3:1-17
Sunday Between May 29 and June 4
1 Samuel 3:1-20
Psalm 139:1-6, 13-18
2 Corinthians 4-5-12
Mark 2:23–3:6
Sunday Between June 5 and 11
1 Samuel 8:4-20 (11:14-15)
Psalm 138
2 Corinthians 4:13–5:1
Mark 3:20-35
Sunday Between June 12 and 18
1 Samuel 15:34–16:13
Psalm 20 or Psalm 72
2 Corinthians 5:6-10 (11-13), 14-17

Mark 4:26-34
Sunday Between June 19 and 25
1 Samuel 17:(1a, 4-11, 19-23) 32-49
Psalm 9:9-20
2 Corinthians 6:1-13
Mark 4:35-41
Sunday Between June 26 and July 2
2 Samuel 1:1, 17-27
Psalm 130
2 Corinthians 8:7-15
Mark 5:21-43
Sunday Between July 3 and 9
2 Samuel 5:1-5, 9-10
Psalm 48
2 Corinthians 12:2-10
Mark 6:1-13
Sunday Between July 10 and 16
2 Samuel 6:1-5, 12b-19
Psalm 24
Ephesians 1:3-14
Mark 6:14-29
Sunday Between July 17 and 23
2 Samuel 7:1-14a
Psalm 89:20-37
Ephesians 2:11-22
Mark 6:30-34, 53-56
Sunday Between July 24 and 30
2 Samuel 11:1-15
Psalm 14
Ephesians 3:14-21
John 6:1-21
Sunday Between July 31 and August 6
2 Samuel 11:26–12:13a
Psalm 51:1-12
Ephesians 4:1-16
John 6:24-35
Sunday Between August 7 and 13
2 Samuel 18:5-9, 15, 31-33
Psalm 130
Ephesians 4:25–5:2
John 6:35, 41-51
Sunday Between August 14 and 20
1 Kings 2:10-12; 3:3-14
Psalm 111

Ephesians 5:15-20
John 6:51-58
Sunday Between August 21 and 27
1 Kings 8:(1, 6, 10-11) 22-30, 41-43
Psalm 84
Ephesians 6:10-20
John 6:56-69
*Sunday Between August 28 and
    September 3*
Song of Solomon 2:8-13
Psalm 45
James 1:17-27
Mark 7:1-8, 14-15, 21-23
Sunday Between September 4 and 10
Proverbs 22:1-2, 8-9, 22-23
Psalm 125
James 2:1-10, (11-13), 14-17
Mark 7:24-37
Sunday Between September 11 and 17
Proverbs 1:20-33
Psalm 19
James 3:1-12
Mark 8:27-38
Sunday Between September 18 and 24
Proverbs 31:10-31
Psalm 1
James 3:13–4:3, 7-8a
Mark 9:30-37
*Sunday Between September 25 and
    October 1*
Esther 7:1-6, 9-10; 9:20-22
Psalm 124
James 5:13-20
Mark 9:38-50
Sunday Between October 2 and 8
Job 1:1; 2:1-10
Psalm 25
Hebrews 1:1-4; 2:5-12
Mark 10:2-16
Sunday Between October 9 and 15
Job 23:1-9, 16-17

Psalm 22:1-15
Hebrews 4:12-16
Mark 10:17-31
Sunday Between October 16 and 22
Job 38:1-7 (34-41)
Psalm 104:1-9, 24, 35c
Hebrews 5:1-10
Mark 10:35-45
Sunday Between October 23 and 29
Job 42:1-6, 10-17
Psalm 34:1-8 (19-22)
Hebrews 7:23-28
Mark 10:46-52
*Sunday Between October 30 and
    November 5*
Ruth 1:1-18
Psalm 146
Hebrews 9:11-14
Mark 12:28-34
*All Saints (November 1, or may be
    used on first Sunday in November)*
Isaiah 25:6-9
Psalm 24
Revelation 21:1-6a
John 11:32-44
Sunday Between November 6 and 12
Ruth 3:1-5; 4:13-17
Psalm 42
Hebrews 9:24-28
Mark 12:38-44
Sunday Between November 13 and 19
1 Samuel 1:4-20
Psalm 113
Hebrews 10:11-25
Mark 13:1-8
*Reign of Christ, Sunday Between
    November 20 and 26*
2 Samuel 23:1-7
Psalm 132:1-12 (13-18)
Revelation 1:4-8
John 18:33-37